P9-DFI-398

Redeeming Culture

UNITED STATES
SCIENCE EXHIBIT

JAMES
GILBERT

REDEEMING CULTURE

American Religion
in an Age of Science

CULTURE

The University of Chicago Press

Chicago and London

James Gilbert is a professor of history at the University of Maryland. He has published several books, including *Writers and Partisans: A History of Literary Radicalism in America* (Wiley, 1968), *Designing the Industrial State: The Intellectual Pursuit of Collectivism in America* (Quadrangle, 1972), and *Perfect Cities: Chicago's Utopias of 1893* (University of Chicago Press, 1991).

The University of Chicago Press, Chicago 60637
The University of Chicago Press, Ltd., London
© 1997 by The University of Chicago
All rights reserved. Published 1997
Printed in the United States of America

06 05 04 03 02 01 00 99 98 97   1 2 3 4 5

ISBN: 0-226-29320-3 (cloth)

Library of Congress Cataloging-in-Publication Data

Gilbert, James Burkhart.
    Redeeming culture : American religion in an age of science / James
Gilbert.
        p.   cm.
    Includes bibliographical references and index.
    ISBN 0-226-29320-3 (alk. paper).
    1. Religion and science—United States—History—20th century.
2. Religion and culture—United States—History—20th century.
3. United States—Religion—20th century.   4. United States—
Intellectual life—20th century.   I. Title.
BL245.G55   1997
306.4′5′09730904—DC21   96-47973
                                                                   CIP

⊛The paper used in this publication meets the minimum requirements of the American National Standard for Information Sciences—Permanence of Paper for Printed Library Materials, ANSI Z39.48-1984.

CONTENTS

v

99758

Acknowledgments

In the preparation of this book I owe a great debt to friends and to institutions. As always, the good fortune of historians rests on archives and archivists. I have been particularly favored by wonderful manuscript collections at Marquette University, the Jewish Theological Seminary and Yivo Institute in New York, N. W. Ayer and Company, the Hebrew Union College in Cincinnati, Wheaton College in Wheaton, Illinois, and the Lutheran Theological Seminary and the Moody Bible Institute in Chicago. Particularly rewarding were trips to Middletown, Connecticut, for the Frank Capra Papers, to Harvard for the Donald Menzel and Harlow Shapley Papers, to Philadelphia for the UFO Papers, to the University of Washington in Seattle, and to the Truman library at Independence, Missouri. The Library of Congress Manuscripts Division and the National Archives in Washington, D.C., and Washington State were indispensable.

Financing for all these trips was based largely on generous grants from the University of Maryland. I especially indebted to Rutgers University for a year's appointment to the Center for Historical Analysis, where I could work uninterrupted on the manuscript. A month at the Rockefeller Center in Bellagio provided an opportunity to try out some of my ideas in a wonderfully congenial atmosphere. Susan and Bob Silbey treated me with the skepticism and good humor I needed. I also appreciate the encouragement and friendship of Christa and Klaus Beyenback and Ed Fraga.

I owe large debts to a great many other people, among them my colleagues at the University of Maryland: Miles Bradbury, Ron Doel, Robert Friedel, Douglas Gomery, Gay Gullickson, and Robyn Muncy. Other friends and colleagues in Washington, D.C., were helpful and encouraging, including Peter Kuznick and the members of the Washington Seminar in Cultural and Political History. At Rutgers, Phyllis Mack, Jacob Meskin, Cleo Kearns, Caroline Goeser, Harriet Lutsky, and especially John Gillis, Bonnie Smith, and Don Kelly offered me friendship and good advice. Paul Boyer was particularly astute in criticizing the manuscript. John Findlay at the University of Washington helped me find several important photographic sources.

Those who helped particularly with locating primary material include Walter Osborn of the Moody Bible Institute, Leith Johnson of the Cinema Archives at Weslyan University, Kevin Profitt at Hebrew Union College, and David Malone and Larry Thompson at Wheaton College. Armand Mauss provided crucial material about the Society for the Scientific Study of Religion. I also deeply appreciate the help and encouragement of Philip Hefner of the Chicago Center for Religion and Science. I thank Ralph Burhoe, Charles I. Carpenter, and Don Jones for helpful interviews.

Finally, I thank my wife Susan for living with my paradoxes of religion and science for so long, and Douglas Mitchell for encouraging me to pursue them. Working with him and Matthew Howard at the University of Chicago Press is one of the great rewards of scholarship.

REDEEMING CULTURE

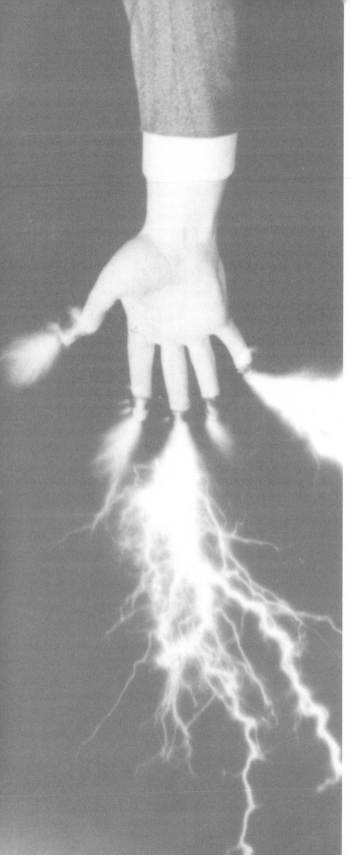

And God said, Let us make man in our image, after our likeness: and let them have dominion over the fish of the sea, and over the fowl of the air, and over the cattle, and over all the earth, and over every creeping thing that creepeth upon the earth.

Gen. 1:26

Chapter 1

The Promise of Genesis

Several years ago while doing photo research at the Moody Bible Institute in Chicago, I chanced upon an unusual print. It had nothing to do with my subject, Dwight Moody's evangelical crusade during the World's Columbian Exposition of 1893. This was a modern picture and very curious. It showed a man standing on a darkened platform before a table laden with scientific apparatus. The stage was poorly lit, but the man's figure was brightly outlined. His eyes and arms were directed upward, and from his fingertips bolts of electricity shot into the dark.

I took the photograph to the curator, who told me, "That's Rev. Irwin Moon of the Moody Institute of Science performing one of his Sermons from Science." "Do you have any papers?" I inquired. "Yes," he said, point-

Figure 1.1   Rev. Irwin Moon, during the finale of Sermons from Science, demonstrates the power of nature, science, and God as he (safely) transmits electricity through his fingertips from his million-volt machine. Courtesy of the Historical Collection, Moody Bible Institute Library.

ing to a large file drawer. I pulled it open and thumbed back the tab on the first folder; "U.S. Air Force," it said. What I discovered at that moment—that the Moody Institute of Science provided hundreds of copies of evangelical science films to the United States Air Force in the 1940s—is the genesis of this book. What I initially believed was an extraordinary mixing of science and religion spread under government auspices became the catalyst for the larger inquiry I have undertaken. Why had the Moody–Air Force connection gone unnoticed for so long? I wondered if the historical invisibility of this and similar events was silent testimony to their ordinariness. The further I pressed, the more such encounters I discovered—odd admixtures of religion and science in cultural artifacts at all levels of society. So I determined to open the subject into a larger examination of the remarkable but troubled relationship between science and religion after World War II.

This is not, of course, an exhaustive exploration of contemporary writings on religion and science. Nor is it a book about how religion and science should relate to each other. Prescriptive advice remains for theologians and scientists or for ordinary citizens who worry about such matters. My interest is in questions of culture and history. How, in a practical and real sense, have the domains of science and religion interacted? What have been the implications for each side in this engagement? How has this process helped shape American culture, particularly in the period since the Second World War when science rode the flashing steed of modern physics to the heights of prestige, only to plunge, toward the end of the 1950s, over the top and down again? All these queries constitute an even larger problem that intrigues me and a great many other students of American culture: the persistence of religion in modern society. How has religion managed to retain its place at the center of American culture when it might be expected to decline? How does it renew its force and energy inside a dynamic, pluralistic, and largely secular society? Part of the answer, I believe, is implicit in the dialectical interaction between science and religion throughout the twentieth century.[1]

To explore how is perhaps in the end to suggest some of the reasons why. Observers have speculated endlessly about why American religion is both persistent and culturally authoritative. They have displayed their numerous explanations in the bazaar of historical speculation. Most tend to be sweeping generalizations based on a description of American religion (primarily Protestantism) and its anomalies. These attempts restate the peculiarities of our culture: the multitude of religious sects, the deep dissenting Protestant tradition, the English background, the wall of separation between church and state, the impetus to Americanize and convert immigrants, the importance of democratic culture, and so on. These are all very useful notions, but I plan a different attack on the problem. I hope to show

how religion and science engaged each other as elements of American culture—not just as theories and theologies but also as everyday ideas. How did religion contend with the immense prestige of science after World War II, and how did this encounter affect its efforts to maintain its visionary authority? How did scientists respond?

A word about focus and scope: I have no intention of exploring this whole vast topic, which some might say engages everything in American culture. My subjects are very special and were selected with the purpose of being suggestive, not comprehensive. This book is episodic rather than encyclopedic; it chooses examples from a large array of possibilities, partly because I have a second objective in mind. I hope to demonstrate, through this selection, the process whereby American culture is assembled and integrated, how it assumes a shape that sometimes allows and even encourages a unity of discourse across class, professional, regional, and religious boundaries. To my surprise—a surprise that might be shared by the men and women who are the subjects of this study—Americans from many walks of life were, in their peculiar and distinct ways, engaged in a very broad joint intellectual venture. This venture was the attempt to discover a new religious-scientific dispensation, a way of holding the mirror of science up to religion or vice versa, to discover how the one might best be reflected on the other. This emphasis on the continuities of culture may seem an unusual approach for a historian to take in this day of divisions, diversities, and separate identities, in a period when American culture cannot even be imagined as the sum of its parts and the idea of American culture itself is sometimes dismissed as an ideological power grab by some interest group. That is not my debate. I intend to explore deep-seated assumptions that find expression at various points and on several levels of society, ideas that erupt through the crust of custom, forced up by the tectonic movements deep under the foundations of American life.

Consequently in this book I will be discussing scientists, intellectuals, and theologians, elite organizations and institutions, and also Hollywood films and television programs. The men and women engaged in producing culture in the shape of books, conferences, exhibitions, journals, and general popular culture were, I have found, engaged with each other across boundaries and broad gaps. Intuition tells us this is true, for few if any cultural productions are singular and solitary in origin. But more important, in this period there was a general recognition that relating religion to science and science to religion was a major problem that had to be confronted. If theologians rubbed shoulders with moviemakers, if scientists were consultants for Hollywood films, if evangelical Protestants donned white coats and imbibed the language and arguments of science to discover a new argument from the "design" of nature, it is because of the force of this concern and the plasticity of our culture. These intellectual links tied an extraordinary variety of men and women together in a quest to understand the relation between science and religion, to try to settle again questions that have, in times of crisis as well of creativity and change, seized the heart of American culture.

To claim this subject demands an explanation of the cultural and intellectual definitions of science and religion as I shall employ them in this book. The period I am describing comes toward the end of a larger age of scientific achievement and burns with the brightness of a flaring star. The years from the end of World War II into the early 1960s marked a high point in the prestige of science considered as a social model and a delivery system of social betterment. Not only did science and technology provide the material of progress, but in their intellectual processes, standards, and professions, they offered enticing and convincing ways to discover and organize knowledge. Even for those who denounced the malignant power of atomic energy, the very stridency of their words measured the prestige of science.[2]

This epoch of "big science" was sustained not merely by awe and accomplishment, but by large and growing public subvention of laboratories and experimental and technological applications, particularly in defense industries. While most forms of science—even social science—benefited from public generosity, physics in particular enjoyed a reputation as the epitome of science itself. Through the mid-1960s, the scientific community in America was invigorated by this public support and by its power to enforce standards and membership through professionalism and professional organizations. Unchallenged from the inside, it remained overwhelmingly white, male, and concentrated at elite institutions such as Harvard, Princeton, Columbia, and Berkeley. It was even granted moral superiority by C. P. Snow in his famous essay on two cultures: one progressive and scientific, the other literary, conservative, and retrograde.[3]

The erosion of this stature beginning in the early 1960s revealed stress in the metal sustaining this brilliant enterprise. Publication of Thomas Kuhn's *Structure of Scientific Revolutions* in 1962 corroded the internalist assumptions of scientific progress on which exclusivity had been partly based. The growth of the sociology of science flowered, among other things, into a broad attack from excluded women and racial minorities. In the public eye there developed a large and discouraged appraisal of the results of science typified in such works as Rachel Carson's *Silent Spring* and Theodore Roszak's *Making of a Counter Culture.* Intensified attacks on military research accompanied these hesitations about the endeavors of big science. In effect, such critiques demanded an expanded professionalism to include ecological considerations and affirmative action or political activism. From a completely different position, mainline science was challenged by the growing popularity of creation science, based on such works as the widely read *Genesis Flood* written by John C. Whitcomb and Henry M. Morris.[4] Even if the importance of science and technology did not diminish in American society after this time, public attitudes did change.

My exploration of the encounter between science and religion from the late 1930s into the 1960s reinforces the scholarship that has discovered exclusivity and a narrow perspective on the issues during this period. From the position of both big science and mainline or Fundamentalist religion, the participants in this discussion believed themselves to be strikingly different in origin, social position, and belief. Yet from the standpoint of those excluded from the conversation, they could appear very similar.[5]

The age of scientific dominion began in the late nineteenth century, during the Progressive Era. In the developing revolution of organization and order during the next twenty years, science in its various guises seemed a potent social model for reforming society. Scientific method, the ethics and practices of the scientific community, the organization of laboratories and scientific societies, the scientific version of truth telling, all appeared to offer the best chance, as many Americans believed, for governing the racing engine of technology and braking the excessive speed of industrial change. One scheme or another of scientific reorganization would surely reform society for the better, whether it concentrated on the school, the factory, the farm, or politics.

To religionists, such applications of science cast down a daunting challenge. How could religion retrieve the soul of America if its mind was enthralled by science? If science offered a model of organization and procedures that produced real results and visible change, then religion either had to accept this secular movement, offering an editorial suggestion here and there, or dig in its heels and resist. The period after World War II only intensified such reactions. But if one paid any attention at all, this whole era was also a time when many scientists too came to ponder the fate of society if the wish for secular hegemony came true. What would happen to the United States if religion shrank into a corner or passed behind a shadow of irrelevance? Even in moments of high achievement and prestige, the voices of doubt remained audible.

In 1945 science reconfirmed its high power and prestige by the devastating effectiveness of the atomic bomb. In a conspiracy of esoteric theory and secret technology, an international group of scientists created a monstrous achievement whose meaning seemed apparent to everyone but whose explanation could be known only to a few. Scientists with strange accents and foreign names became the heroes, the celebrities, and sometimes the villains of the postwar era. They had presented America with a quicksilver secret that to everyone's surprise brought extraordinary insecurity for fear others, especially the Soviet Union, would eventually grasp its principles and design. This was a bitter fruit of atomic knowledge. Its possibilities had come about through ideas about physics that were beyond the comprehension (and interest) of most Americans. Even the names of modern scientific theories could conjure an aura of misunderstanding and insecurity: the theory of relativity, the uncertainty principle, quantum physics, the principle of complementarity. What made these titles into potent metaphors was the implication that they described counterintuitive ideas. They contradicted common sense, which for most Americans was the basis of everyday scientific and technological thinking. The quality of uncertainty is exactly what the public identified with the new science. Consequently a certain portion of science—especially physics—was open only to a special few who could understand its opaque language and obscure theories. If this conferred enormous power and prestige on scientists, it also rendered them susceptible to suspicion, mistrust, and misunderstanding, especially in a democratic society.

The complexity of modern science also drove a larger wedge between theoretical science and practical technology, which was both more understandable and more democratic in its appeal. If scientific theory, particularly in physics, was markedly counterintuitive, technology in many respects remained accessible. Depending on which science or what theory, descriptions of the natural world lent themselves better or worse to the historic American tradition that science and religion were compatible.

In the late eighteenth and early nineteenth centuries this compatibility had been established by commonsense philosophy, Baconian induction, and revived arguments about the divine design of nature. Science appeared largely consistent with biblical creation and with historical accounts of civilization in the Old Testament, because scientists found no need to challenge religion. Most scientists accepted a division of labor and a parallelism between their efforts and those of theologians. This could represent either active pursuit of affinities or—as in the case of many geologists, for example—a general theory of catastrophism divorced from religious implications.[6]

For the most part, twentieth-century scientists relinquished the search for concordance, despite valiant efforts of religious modernists to modify biblical literalism and update theology by systematic investigation—by adopting, in other words, what looked like the scientific method. But even if the story of Genesis was taken as metaphor, or if Old Testament accounts were admitted to be corrupted by primitive scientific speculations, finding agreement between spiritual texts and natural theory was not an imperative for scientists.

The Darwinian revolution of the late nineteenth century best exemplified how this predicament developed. Darwin's story of evolution and the descent of man directly contradicted the biblical story of creation. It demanded a recalculation of the age of the world, transforming the emergence of life and humanity into functions of time, process, and geology, not history. The slow, almost imperceptible changes in environment, the great, empty eons, were as unimaginable as atomic particles. In this way Darwin's theory of natural selection resembled modern scientific theories. Darwin also challenged the compatibility of science and religion by connecting human beings and animals. Although he often stressed the development of "higher" life forms, implicit in Darwin's construction was a devastating implication that denied the first principle of Victorian religion. For Christianity, human beings are the special wards of creation, the centerpiece of the universe, and the objects of God's perfect attention. This assumption gives meaning to sin and salvation. To suggest otherwise would open the door to a flood of doubts and a tide of misgivings. If mankind was not the purpose of creation, then what was? What was creation? What was humankind? Implicitly, the Darwinian struggle for survival contradicted any generous interpretation of the existence of life. The objective of existence would be mere survival and reproduction. A theory that depended on a huge and confusing physical record of traces but with no acceptable laboratory proofs, Darwinism denied the intuitive instincts and the practical assumptions about design that seemed to confirm the Bible and that many scientists and religionists once accepted. If humans were not the center of the universe, then they had, in their hubris, constructed a complex mythology to justify the ransom of nature and ward off the night of self-doubt.[7]

This anxiety of the anti-Darwinists in the nineteenth century carried over into the twentieth. Although the Scopes trial in Tennessee in 1925 exposed the gulf between Darwinists and anti-Darwinists as a deep fissure of cultures—between rural and urban America, between ethnic groups, and between the differing impacts of educational institutions—transformation of these social divisions after the 1920s did not end doubt or diminish the disruptive impact of Darwinism on American culture. Perhaps the most surprising discovery of my research is how insidiously this devastation has continued. Theology and practical religion continued to confront Darwinism after World War II both in the development of creation science, which claimed the prestige of science for itself, and in the occasional but heartfelt outbursts against the insufficiency of a material world and the inevitable bleakness of Darwinian natural selection.

As this brief account suggests, neither science nor religion has had a stable and permanent definition in American culture. They continually shift in meaning and in their relation to each other. In the period following World War II, the two interacted in ways that both revived familiar arguments and introduced new thoughts and demands. The flux itself was a sign of crisis.

There are many ways to illustrate this momentous change, and I suggest the metaphor of the clock. In the late medieval world the cathedral clock was a precision instrument of interlocking gears capable of moving attached symbols in prescribed patterns, representing a scale model of God's world. Its measure of time was both circular (around the zodiac, phases of the moon and position of the planets, and the ages of man) and longitudinal, recording minutes, hours, weeks, months, and years. With human figures as the centerpiece, the clock transformed time into a narrative in which science and religion cooperated to demonstrate the basic meanings and patterns of life. A very different clock appeared on the cover of the *Bulletin of the Atomic Scientists,* published in Chicago after World War II. Founded to discuss the momentous dangers of atomic energy and nuclear warfare, the journal adopted the doomsday clock as a gauge of the approach of nuclear war. As its hands inched forward toward midnight, pushed by each successive international crisis, the editors conveyed a clear warning of ruin. This countdown was driven entirely by human folly: we had discovered nuclear energy and built the atomic and hydrogen bombs. We would be responsible for their use and the end of civilization. Humans, not God, had corrupted the meaning of time itself and detached mankind from the natural order.

Determining the meaning of science in postwar culture depends in part on identifying what sort of science is under review and who the discussants are. The older commonsense notions of observation and intuitive theory remained and perhaps even predominated in public dialogue about science. Yet scientists themselves as well as historians of science constructed a radically different vision of scientific thinking in the twentieth century. Probably the most distinctive element here was a recognition of the difficulty of doing science and the inevitable elitism of its practitioners. The assumption that science was open to amateurs and verifiable in the democratic community necessarily faded before the overwhelming complexity and difficulty of modern theories. Democratic aspirations for the application of science might remain, but universal comprehension was hardly a realistic expectation.[8]

As a model for social reform and reorganization, science had once promised the verification of experiment and hypothesis through the approval of the democratic community. But this pragmatic ideal, on which philosophers like John Dewey erected a host of reforms, faced the reality of a new science that could be understood only by a narrow circle of other scientists, who constituted its community of verification. As this circle of knowledge tightened, a belief emerged, articulated by historians and sociologists of science like Robert K. Merton and Thomas Kuhn, that science itself did not simply investigate natural phenomena and develop descriptive hypotheses. Like other forms of human knowledge, it too depended on paradigms of theory and on changing historical circumstances. Science was, it seemed, a human construction, a projection of ideas and language upon the universe. Quite obviously what it discovered could be understood only in terms of the limits of its assumptions and structures.[9]

Other serious complications crowded in on science during its optimistic moments after World War II. Principal among these was an edgy public fear of subversion and betrayal. The greater the specialization of scientists, and the more they argued for the unique and universal ethic of the scientific endeavor and the sacred community of research, the more they seemed prone to fall. In fact some American scientists, among them the developers of the atomic bomb, eventually came to reject the assumption that science was superior to other realms of knowledge.

Some of the deepest shocks came from abroad. The perversion of German science in the Nazi Holocaust and the weapon wizardry at Peenemünde that produced the V-1 and V-2 rockets deeply challenged the notion that scientists carried any special gene for ethical conduct. Observations of Russian science appeared to confirm this doubt. Beginning in the 1930s, pogroms of scientists in the Soviet Union corrupted the scientific establishment of that nation, making possible the emergence of Trofim Lysenko in the field of biology, evolution, and genetics during the early 1950s. Pronouncing his theories of scientific fundamentalism, Lysenko revived the pre-Darwinian theory of Lamarckian evolution: the idea that acquired characteristics could be passed on to offspring, that the social and cultural environment could break into and alter the somatic continuity of genetic reproduction. The political power of this astounding fantasy discouraged those who had hoped that the vaunted Soviet liberation of science from religious and ideological restraints would lead to a golden age of discovery. Even when these examples were dismissed as debauched science, they still raised questions about the discipline.

A further dilemma faced some scientists. As holders of secret knowledge, they became suspect as potential traitors. Perhaps this was inevitable in an age of Cold War, but the assumption that scientists would and did betray the United States resulted in sweeping loyalty oaths and damaging investigations, most of them quiet but some, like that of J. Robert Oppenheimer, public and contentious. The most disheartening aspect of my research for this book was the discovery of one of these cases: that of Donald H. Menzel, head of the Harvard College Observatory in the 1950s. An active and important participant in the war effort against Germany and Japan, Menzel applied for security clearance in 1950 to work on defense projects. A long and detailed investigation and hearing stirred up the sediment of his professional life but finally cleared him of charges that proved preposterous. Yet the case was not atypical, for it symbolized the precarious eminence and evanescent power of scientists after 1945. The World War and the Cold War made a group of scientists a privileged international class with loyalties to universal principles and behaviors. But these very principles and behaviors exposed many of them to the indignity of suspicion and investigation.[10]

Related to this growing uncertain reputation of scientists was the general decline of the public intellectual. Many of the scientists, theologians, and intellectuals who appear in this book commanded an attention and a public solicitude—a form of celebrity—that are increasingly rare in our own day. Whether this is to be regretted may be debated, but it marks off the new era we now live in.

During the years of its great importance and subsequent loss of luster, science in effect rediscovered that it was also a human science. This reaffirmed the older notion that science was a way of organizing the same material and answering some of the same questions that concerned religion. Scientists claimed to limit themselves to explaining the material world, depending of course on what was meant by *material*. Religion had somewhat different universal aspirations. Science appealed to experience and generated hypotheses rooted in the natural world, but it postponed truth with a series of proximate descriptions. Religion also evoked experience, but as illustrating what was already known through faith or experience that led to faith. Science moved and evolved, whereas religion changed primarily in order to restore and revive ancient truths. Sometimes the two coexisted comfortably, roaming over the same range of experience and speaking to the same sorts of human problems. Despite considerable effort, they could not really be kept apart; no artificial borders, distinctions, and traditions could prevent one from straying across to the other's territory.

Science and religion, then, are words suggesting two great and opposing philosophic systems—materialism and idealism—that, in a variety of forms, operate as polarities in American culture. They describe competing orientations toward the same insistent question: What can human beings really know about themselves? In what smaller or larger purposes should humans find comfort? Their answers suggest even deeper divisions. Science proposes technology, physical and human engineering, and paradoxically, a universe that is open to human wonder and understanding but skeptical about any privileged place for humans. The universe is abstract, not intimate, knowable but cold and elusive. On the contrary, religion affirms a realm of sublime otherness, accessible by faith or reason but preexisting and beyond nature. Religion is a system of knowing and responding to what it defines as unknowable and unapproachable. Upon the vastness of the universe and the timelessness of cosmic ages, it constructs a historical narrative in which human beings are the central and principal purpose. They people this narrative world, and their struggles articulate the design of an otherwise incomprehensible universe. Life would be bewildering if confined to and defined by the physical world. Put simply, religion is anthropocentric, science is naturalistic. Religion is a government of humans, science is a government of natural law. Religion is the imposition of narrative structure on an unstoried universe. It requires that nature accommodate the aspirations of human culture. It insists that human beings occupy the center of whatever physical world is discovered by science. Yet both science and religion respond to the ambition expressed in Genesis that is the essence of human culture—to understand and master nature.

Several special characteristics of culture and society make more precise definitions of religion and science in the American context a difficult but necessary task. Secularization has proceeded rapidly in the twentieth century. The logic of the mechanical now pervades the economic world, and the hand of the market mechanism has visibly penetrated and transformed social and cultural institutions. Science, along with its technological applications, defines the future. Yet in tandem with this transformation has come the continued expression of a particularly inventive religious genius, an American talent for defining new religions and revising old ones. The development of Mormonism and Christian Science in the nineteenth century and the distillation of Fundamentalism and Pentecostalism in the twentieth have been major achievements. Partly because of the creative energy of American Protestantism, religion has infused and saturated culture at all levels. In fact the period from World War II to the present has seen one of the longest sustained religious revivals in American history.[11]

Religion, of course, can refer to different forms of experience and expression depending on the purposes of the definition, and to some degree I will draw on several in the course of this work. In the broadest sense, religion is an anthropomorphic projection. It generates belief in a deity or force that is a reflection of the spiritual concerns of humans, a deity that, being described by human measure, is also immanent in human existence. Consequently the universe is agitated by human drama.

Another sort of definition can be described as anthropological-evolutionary (or sociobiological) and is attributed primarily to such thinkers as T. H. Huxley. Religion in his words is a social organ developed to manage questions about human destiny. A more descriptive (ideal type) definition can be extracted by compiling the characteristics of the world's major historical religions. The list might include belief in supernatural beings; a distinction between sacred and profane; ritual acts; a feeling of awe and mystery in the presence of sacred objects and rituals; a moral code believed to be sanctioned by the gods; prayer or propitiation of gods, or both; a holistic view of the creation, uniting its purpose and that of the individual; a total organization of life based on this view; and a social group bound together by the beliefs above.[12] Certainly not all religions exhibit all of these characteristics; indeed, Christianity appears to contain most and Eastern religions only a few. Thus constructing an ideal typology raises serious and important problems of deciding at what point to divide secular from religious groups.

A fourth possibility for defining religion simply accepts the testimony of religious persons: religion is what religious people claim it to be. To refuse the designation religious to a group or an individual that claims it reflects the temptation to secularize. To deny a sect or belief the privilege of "real religion" is certainly a reaction to rapid social and cultural change, and it very probably reveals a moral and aesthetic judgment based on the perspective of tradition. But the difficulty of defining what is religious may simply reflect an academic reaction to the creativity and change around the margins of established religions and identifiable creeds. In examining new ideas, historians, sociologists, and social commentators need to suspend judgment, leaving a place at the table for those who invite themselves and a chance for religion to grow and shape itself.

Like religion, the meaning of natural science and scientific endeavor in modern America has also undergone rapid evolution, particularly with the development of sweeping new theories in physics and astronomy and remarkable discoveries in biology and chemistry. Its principles can be derived from analyzing successful scientific endeavors: science is what science does best. It offers explanations of natural phenomena capable of verification within a materialistic framework. By definition, it denies the intervention of deity in any explanation. Since this was not always the case (and in some contemporary cosmological speculations still is not), most modern science is careful to stress the limits to the questions it asks and the answers it proposes.[13]

Social science (or the scientific study of human behavior and institutions), on the other hand, ventures into almost every place where religion once held sway: into politics, psychology, and sociology, for example. In fact social science has secularized much of the sort of learning and common wisdom that earlier American society reserved for religious explanation. And social science generally, though not always, aspires to a scientific, not a religious, model of explanation.

To compare religion and science, to place them side by side in American culture, affirms the similarities that provoke competition and cooperation between them. Both are human projections onto the human and natural worlds; each can be construed as a body of knowledge with a community of practitioners. Within a democratic culture that empowers individual citizens or groups to decide the truth by common consent, both are beholden to the assent of outsiders. American religion, so deeply embedded in democratic culture, is open to dramatic revision. Change votes with its feet when millions of believers are willing to shift from one sect to another. Science, on the other hand, while increasingly the province of the expert, still must live and justify itself within a democratic culture. In a very practical sense, it requires public approval to continue.[14]

The democratic, public face of religion is but one of three levels of religious expression in American life. These include the individual, the confessional or religious community, and diffusion in culture. Certainly these levels overlap and enable and empower each other: each depends on all. This same tripartite division appears helpful in discussing American science. There is the individual or actual practice of scientific investigation; the level of institutions; and finally public science expressed through popularization and other forms of cultural activity to maintain public understanding, sympathy, and support for funding and other continuing projects and institutions. With science too, each level interacts and supports the other two even if cultural, institutional, and private practices are very different from each other.[15]

This book is concerned primarily with religion and science as they interact in public culture. In particular, it examines the opening of cultural space for religious ideas in an otherwise scientific world. It explores how this space is preserved and expanded in competition with scientific models of explanation and order. It speculates about how American culture dwells in paradox, tolerating and even encouraging the coexistence of two very different and potentially hostile systems of explanation. It concludes that without the persistent religious expression in culture, where a hospitable climate for belief and practice is maintained, the religious intensity of American civilization would surely diminish. So too, the compromises between religion and science might collapse.

The dynamics that create the renewal of religious ideas in culture as I shall describe them saturate every aspect of America civilization, from elite expressions of theology and science to Hollywood films, world's fairs, and television programs. This is significant not simply because it appears to signal a difference from other cultures (particularly those of Western Europe), but because the cultural energy invested in religion at this level invigorates the other two levels of religious expression as well. A culture that welcomes religion into its common places as well as in its most elite universities and intellectual circles empowers both religious institutions and individuals. It makes available a cultural software of religious icons and text that reinforces individual and communal religious experiences. To provide cultural space for religious expression is to normalize religious belief. It thus constitutes a part—and I stress only a part—of the explanation for the persistence of religion in America.[16]

This is not, however, merely to reaffirm Robert Bellah's famous argument about "civil religion." This interesting and useful concept identifies a religious dimension in the political realm, a sense of America's mission and a notion of sovereignty rooted in God.[17] It also suggests the Protestant overtones of American nationalism. Although this idea certainly describes a part of what I have identified as the cultural space occupied by religion, it is only a small part of a much larger ongoing relationship. Bellah explains why Americans might wish to unite religious and secular proposes, but he does not explore what is at stake in trying to maintain the opposite: what is at issue in defining science and religion as opposites of thought and culture.[18]

For reasons of self-preservation and expansion, American religions have been deeply concerned about the impact of scientific law and discovery. Consequently every advance in science invites the watchful comment of religious men and women. This behavior exhibits the essential cultural strategy of religious people: their refusal to accept marginalization.[19] Their restless attention and cultural vigilance is characteristic not just of Protestantism, but also of other faiths shaped and tempered in American culture. The refusal to accept a peripheral orbit helps account for the aggressive resilience of American religion. In the postwar period, when science offered an alluring model for social emulation and reorganization, religion was never more engaged in criticizing and refashioning itself to meet this challenge. To reveal how the considerable agitation about science and religion after World War II reshaped American culture is to examine the persistence of religion in American culture. To explore the consequences of this interaction for religion and science is my purpose. How this interaction occurs in the production of culture defines the scope of this book.

I begin my story with a retelling of the Scopes antievolution trial of 1925. This momentous court case set the stage for future encounters between religion and science, but not quite in the way historians have argued. In the name of the older commonsense compromise of science and religion, William Jennings Bryan pronounced Darwinism to be unscientific and its teaching counter to American democracy. In doing so he revealed a deep fissure in the definition of science that would reopen after World War II. Seen in this light, this historic encounter suggests significant popular hesitations about modern science and its counterintuitive theories.

The next chapter explores the heyday of science prestige from the end of the 1930s into the early 1950s by considering the growing authority and controversy surrounding the role of atomic scientists, seen as stewards of modern scientific theories and, by their own definition, as special citizens of the world. Together these two chapters suggest some of the complexities and controversies involved in defining the meaning of science within American culture.

There are several possible ways to consider the chapters that follow this opening, partly because of the genetic links among them. The broadest connections, however, are chronological. World War II and its aftermath define the first large division. Part of the response to that terrible catastrophe was a reaction (primarily) by nuclear scientists, who immediately after the war offered science as a model for the social and moral reconstruction of Western society. Such thinking was challenged by an organization founded in 1939, the Conference on Science, Philosophy, and Religion, which persisted well into the postwar period. Its annual meetings explored important contemporary social and intellectual problems, but always with a prevailing fear that science without religion was an invitation to human irresponsibility. Another outcome of the war was the federal experiment in universal military training, a concept of modern technological recruitment for the American armed services that included a heavy dose of religious instruction. This program in turn became the structure on which the Moody Bible Institute built its relationship to the air force, eventually resulting in the exposure of hundreds of thousands of military recruits and civilians to the creationist films called Sermons from Science. A final direct outgrowth of the war was the American Scientific Affiliation, a Fundamentalist scientific association that succumbed to the temptation of scientific professionalization and accepted some of the tenets of evolutionary theory. Also, from its diverse and contentious membership modern creation science was born.

A second major chronological division explores the 1950s and the clamor of cultural expressions that increased the audibility of the science-religion dialogue. The first chapter in this section will trace the reaction of two eminent men of science—Horace Kallen, the philosopher of democratic pluralism and student of William James, and the Harvard astronomer Harlow Shapley—to the scientific fabrications of Immanuel Velikovsky. In the 1950s Velikovsky's best-selling books created a bitter controversy between the two men about the nature of scientific thinking. The next portion will describe the fascinating negotiations between Hollywood producer Frank Capra and the Bell Telephone Laboratories, which hired him to produce several science films. The resulting films, widely seen on television and repeated later in schools, are heavily laden with religious and specifically Catholic allusions. A third chapter investigates a dispute over the implications of space travel that animated science fiction presentations during the decade. Was the penetration of the heavens best understood as a secular or a religious endeavor? This question was also a defining element of the animated debate about unidentified flying objects, a discussion scientists tried but failed to control.

A third section of the book also begins in the 1950s but inquires into the activities of intellectuals and academics. Two organizations of particular importance were founded during this era: the Society for the Scientific Study of Religion and the Institute on Religion in an Age of Science. The first group, primarily joined by sociologists and psychologists, made a penetrating inquiry into a principal intellectual problem of the day: Was social science compatible with religious belief and practice, or was it merely a dispassionate survey of behavior? The second group began as an adjunct of the Unitarian Church but quickly grew into an important center for reconciling science and religious metaphysics. In effect it attempted to create a second modernism. Eventually it became host to the expression of a variety of contemporary scientific cosmologies.

The final chapter offers an occasion to conduct an inventory, a moment to take stock at one of the important public sites for the interaction of science and religion: the Seattle Century 21 exposition of 1962. Although the fair ostensibly celebrated the great virtues and promise of modern science and technology, other important players demanded and won important roles, including the Moody Bible Institute with its creationist films. Behind the scenes, the delegation to nonscientists of authority for designing exhibits imposed other serious limits on the presentation of science to the public.

By the mid-1960s, at the end of this book, the period of scientific cultural dominion had begun to end. For a great many reasons, including a further intensification of democratic suspicion of expertise as well as growing self-doubts among the scientific community, the postwar era began to close. But nothing had really been settled; science had not emerged as the sole fixture in the cultural firmament. Religion as a cultural element had prized open a large place for itself, despite the brilliant accomplishments of science and technology. It maintained a central place; it had grown, reshaped itself, and above all persisted as a vital element of culture.

In the course of writing this book three themes have come to occupy an unexpected place in my thinking. The first is the entangling alliance between notions of democracy and the contest and conversation between science and religion in this period. It now seems impossible and even fruitless to try to separate democratic ideology and practice from arguments about religion and science. Discussing religion and science within the mainstream of American culture—where this discussion belongs—makes this consideration of democracy an obligation, though I certainly did not begin with this intention. It explains the significant fact that countless individuals who were neither theologians nor scientists helped as much as the experts to define the meaning of religion and science in American culture.

A related issue suggests the importance of the perennial contest over cultural authority: Who shall speak for science and religion? Much of the energy expended in arguing about science and religion, from the Scopes trial to the Velikovsky controversy in the 1950s to teaching creationism in the public schools today, actually has to do with the credentials of speakers and the communities they hail from. When science and religion encroach on each other's interpretations of the world—as they always must—they light backfires of controversy that scorch both sides.

Finally, I am intrigued by the infectiousness of both science and religion as ways of thinking. The most remarkable moments in this exploration come when either side crosses over, when party allegiances become confused, when scientific professionalism on the one hand or religious yearning on the other intrudes to change styles and trends of thinking.

A related theme that emerges throughout this book suggests that even the distant reaches of American culture manage to have considerable commerce with each other. In fact this is a book about the surprising intersections of ideas, discussions, and lives that created a web of dialogue around what so many men and women took to be a central issue of their day. I confess to an extraordinary joy in discovering these relationships, to be able to count up the figures who knew each other or worked together in the enterprise of cultural creation. But I have tried to moderate my enthusiasm about these interactions for one principal reason: it is really the point I wish to make. For this is the way American culture is created: not by isolated subcultures operating according to their own rules in self-styled obscurity, but by groups and individuals reacting to questions that discharge like sheet lightning across the sky. That they produced cultural products that sometimes look, sound, and feel different is no argument against the role of the same central imperative: to find the ideal relation between science and religion in a society of immense flux. This book explores the consequences of trying to do so.

The energie of the uni-

verse is constant while en-

tropy [randomness] strives

toward maximization.

Rudolf Clausius

Chapter 2

WILLIAM JENNINGS BRYAN, SCIENTIST

William Jennings Bryan never wrestled a lightweight. His opponents over the decades had been organized business interests, the banks, the corrupt East, the Republican Party, World War I, and German militarism. Now, at the end of his life, he faced the most clever and subtle force of all: the science of evolution. Never one to shirk a momentous encounter, he wrote, "In this fight I have the most intolerant and vindictive enemies I have ever met and I have the largest majority on my side I have ever had and I am discussing the greatest issue I have ever discussed."[1]

With the end of the war, Bryan had become a national voice for Fundamentalist Protestants. Shortly before his death he had been engaged as a tour leader to conduct a group of Protestant pilgrims on a trip to the Holy Land. Known widely to his supporters as a political figure of high principles and to detractors as a man of quixotic faith in lost causes, Bryan had increasingly moved, with the rural political laity he represented, from radical to conservative populism. A critical element in tempering this change was the rapid growth of Fundamentalism, based on a profound social and intellectual split in American Protestantism just before World War I. A man of many causes, Bryan articulated the anxiety of the legions he led into an aggressive religious contest with modern American society. It is wrong to dismiss Bryan or the larger causes he represented as the aftershocks of modernization. At least two of his principal ideas recurred in a new form in the late 1930s and then continued for the next three decades. They include the assumption that one test of scientific theory is its intuitive clarity, its appeal to commonly understood experience. The second is the democratic suspicion of elites. Both issues almost invariably combined and reinforced each other, particularly in popular culture.

The specific cause that most preoccupied Bryan was the crusade to exclude Darwinian science from the public schools. Meeting with considerable success in the South, Bryan helped convince the Florida legislature to pass a resolution in 1923 against teaching evolution in the schools. His handiwork showed in the antievolution law of Tennessee.[2] But he was most comfortable leading intrepid legions of Fundamentalists into battle in July 1925 at Dayton, Tennessee, in the famous Scopes trial testing the validity of that state's antievolution law. Almost immediately after its conclusion he died: some said of a broken heart and the loss of a lost cause.

The traditional telling of this story is certainly the most dramatic. Bryan mustered an army of believers who, to their anguish and outrage, listened with horrified incredulity to his betrayal on the witness stand of their rockhard, literal interpretation of Genesis. Bryan's confusion before the bar was their undoing too, and his sad defeat in death brought the decline of organized resistance to evolution. The high-flying standards of parochialism were lowered as most Americans subsequently accepted sophistication . . . and modern science.

A more recent version of this historical encounter at Dayton is less conclusive. True, the Scopes trial was a journalistic disaster for Fundamentalism and a triumph for lawyer Clarence Darrow of the defense and the Baltimore pundit H. L. Mencken. But the cultural meaning was less certainly clear. Fundamentalists continued to press, successfully in some cases, for the passage and enforcement of antievolution laws. To a degree they went underground or, better, stepped out of the public spotlight. They continued to construct arguments and assemble constituencies against Darwinian science, and they successfully discouraged the teaching of evolution science in the public schools for two generations. When they resurfaced in the 1960s and 1970s as a powerful force in education and politics, they surprised only the inattentive.[3]

Yet there is another story still to be told with William Jennings Bryan as its leading player. Not only does this demand a reassessment of Bryan's role and intentions, it requires a reexamination of the meaning of science and religion in American culture—of how these words were used and what aspects of culture they designated. Bryan's actions and writings at the penultimate moment before the trial suggest that his greatest mistake was to take for granted an unchanging and unchallenged compromise between science and religion established in the nineteenth century. He wrongly assumed that the heart of American culture was whole. Instead he revealed a fault line between popular and professional science, ready to break open during times of stress in American culture in the 1920s and again in the postwar period.[4]

On 30 December 1924, William Jennings Bryan paid his five dollars to join the American Association for the Advancement of Science (AAAS). This old, distinguished organization of scientists was the bedrock of respectability, and Bryan's act proclaimed his assumptions about the relation of amateurs and professionals. In effect, he affirmed the reputation of the organization as hospitable to independent membership by men merely interested in science or peripherally associated with research. The AAAS was an umbrella organization of the American science establishment and devoted much of its energy to popularizing modern scientific theories, yet it remained open to men like Bryan.[5]

Bryan designated Section D (Astronomy) as his chosen area of specialty. Earlier, he had sent in his application but neglected to sign the check. Now he "returned it with the season's greetings." As he told the amused men of the press, he was "only one of several thousand members who harbors doubts on the subject of evolution."[6] The announcement of this surprising affiliation interrupted the annual meeting of the AAAS in Washington, D.C. A highly publicized feature of the gathering was a thorough and critical scientific refutation of Bryan's position on evolution theory presented

Figure 2.1   The savants of the American Association for the Advancement of Science greet their surprise new member, (astronomer) William Jennings Bryan. Cartoon by Clifford Berryman, *Washington Star,* 4 January 1925.

by Edward L. Rice, a biologist from Ohio Wesleyan University. As *Science* magazine reported shortly afterward, Rice's address had been a model of temperance and toleration, calling for the judicious consideration of all theories. Rice hoped that mutual respect between science and religion would enrich both, provided Bryan and his followers and some strident proponents of Darwinism would lower their shrill voices.[7]

Rice's quiet accounting of Bryan's scientific errors was devastating. One could only conclude that the "Great Commoner" did not understand scientific method or Darwin's writings. His position against evolution theory came from outside the normal standards of scientific debate. Bryan's charges constituted a crude lawyer's brief, a scattered shower of rhetoric that rained indiscriminate accusations on a theory that was in fact measured and reasonable, the very model of a careful analysis. Perhaps because of Rice's judicious warning, the AAAS was enough impressed with the threat that Bryan represented to organize a committee to promote the teaching of science and evolution in the public schools.[8]

But the larger question is, Why did Bryan join the AAAS in 1924? What was his motivation in pledging membership to the largest and most reputable scientific organization in the United States and one known, incidentally, for its vocal support of evolution theory? Quite clearly the answer has nothing to do with a run-up to the Scopes trial. The Tennessee antievolution law that created the case did not pass until the spring of 1925, well after he secured his membership. Neither the American Civil Liberties Union nor John Scopes had yet imagined initiating a test case for Darwinism. The explanation lies instead in taking seriously Bryan's assumption that he was, on his own terms at least, a scientist. Doing so reveals the sort of science to which he committed his soul and how, perhaps, millions of other Americans understood science.[9]

In the early 1920s Bryan pressed his case against modernism in religion and science with the steady nerves and energy of a convert, addressing meetings of antievolutionists, speaking from the pulpit, lobbying in the halls of state legislatures, and even venturing at times into hostile universities. One of the most pointed of his testimonies came when he addressed the state legislature of West Virginia on 13 April 1923 as an expert witness on evolution theory and modern science. He repaid the attentive legislators with an extended lesson in chemistry. For his text Bryan took an interpretation of the second law of thermodynamics that appeared to nullify any possible natural evolution toward more complex life forms. Everyone knew that the world of chemistry was constructed out of ninety-two elements, he noted. No force in nature could make these elements evolve; they simply were what they were. So, he continued, water consisted of its two constituent elements, separated or combined. There was no prewater, no vestigial water, no evolution of something into water. Between its constituent elements and water itself, there were no missing links, no intermediate forms. Water was water. Hydrogen and oxygen were hydrogen and oxygen. Thus, he concluded, chemistry "mocks the atheist and brings confusion to the evolutionist." "Is it conceivable that two such gases as oxygen and hydrogen should just happen?" he asked rhetorically. The implied answer was that only God could create something as useful and perfect as water from such base elements. Furthermore, as the second law of thermodynamics seemed to demonstrate, the world left to itself would degenerate into chaos.[10]

His second lesson from chemistry concerned the ideas of permanence and pattern. "Chemistry has taught us the properties of matter and the way to use them, but they are all stationary," he declared. If scientists could detect any change in nature, its direction would necessarily be toward degeneration and disintegration, never evolution into higher orders. Here he rested his case: God had created a world in which species, like the elements, were stable and unchanging. The essence of true science, he concluded, was the study of "classified Knowledge" and its organization into patterns and hierarchies; all else was speculation. All truth derived from God, "whether in the book of nature or the Book of Books." Neither guesses or hypotheses (which he equated) were themselves scientific. Only descriptive classification was.[11]

Going through the vast inventory of God's patent office of elements, creatures, and natural phenomena, the scientist would never find anything that contradicted the Bible. He could not discover exceptions to design and pattern in any of the splendid, sublime richness of creation. Nor could he ever find anything irrational, anything that contradicted common sense, for science was a universally legible revelation of God's purposes. The book of nature could not contradict the Book of Revelation because both hewed to the same laws, logic, and principles. Anything absurd to man's mind was just as surely absurd to God. A world without an ultimate reason, based on evolution out of nothing toward something, upon change from simple to complex, from plain to brilliant and beautiful, from the inanimate to the quick, from instinctual to intelligent, all conceived without larger purpose, was impossible.

Bryan affirmed this conception of science with every breath of culture he inhaled. His understanding of science was firmly grounded in a popular view that flourished from the early nineteenth century. At that time, under the influence and challenge of the Enlightenment, American philosophers and theologians, and especially the Scottish thinkers who influenced them, developed a theory of science that enthralled the democratic, evangelical fervor of the antebellum period. Based on Sir Francis Bacon's separation of science and religion, this theory granted to each realm a place in the glorification of God. Bacon's inductive methodology in science (that observation

Figure 2.2 William Jennings Bryan, shortly after he joined the American Association for the Advancement of Science, demonstrates how one might view a solar eclipse—to make a point about the transitory decline of the Democratic Party in the 1924 elections. Courtesy of the collection of the Library of Congress.

leads to theory) provided a commonsense answer to the difficult and complex problems stirred up by modern science and philosophy. Reasonable men agreed that observation was the method for acquiring truth, and reasonable men knew that what they observed was real and tangible.[12]

The philosophies of the Scotsmen Thomas Reid and Dugald Stewart, based on this commonsense view of religion, appealed to American Protestants who feared the radical, antireligious fringe of the Enlightenment. Forever explained by the compelling brilliance of William Paley's metaphor of the Watchmaker and the watch, the Creator and the created, this unity of science and religion inspired a generation of American scientists who emerged after the American Revolution.[13] What Paley did was to refashion an old argument that had long been part of Christian eschatology into a modern demonstration of natural theology. His philosophy of creation affirmed, in Aristotelian fashion, that God created a world of separate species, each with its own essence. By this formula (elaborated brilliantly by Saint Thomas Aquinas among others), human essence was of the utmost importance and difference, defined as it was by spirit, soul, and reason. Paley translated such notions into mechanical metaphors, uniting technology and theory into a persuasive and easily understood metaphor that was readily accessible to nineteenth-century thinkers.[14]

By Bryan's day the assumptions and language of this unity bore little direct resemblance to contemporary European or American scientific theories or philosophic systems such as pragmatism. But it persisted generally, even if its visible roots had long since disappeared. Commonsense science had dissolved into American culture until it had become simply common sense.[15]

Although he repeated these ideas as his own, Bryan's reasoning was contained within the essential outlines of the philosophy. The highest pillar of truth, he wrote, was the agreement of science and religion on one essential proposition: mankind was the center and purpose of the universe. Science and religion were just complementary methods of understanding God's design. A corollary that followed described science as democratic in character and meaning. Just as every person could read and understand the Bible, so each could understand and appreciate the workings of nature. To suppose otherwise would undermine the democratic nature of Protestant culture and invite in a priesthood of interpreters of science and maybe even religion. True science would naturally affirm true religion. The common man understood this unity that American society was based on. To deny it would undermine American democracy itself.

Of course Bryan was not alone in defending the democratic foundations and purposes of science, although he gave a special twist to these notions. Certainly in its public countenance, at least, mainstream science equally proclaimed its democratic and social service aims. From the mid-nineteenth century, this justification grew in importance as science began to professionalize and enter the university. Its links with social reform in the Progressive Era and its ties to pragmatism are well-known examples of this orientation. The question was not whether or not democracy, but the definition of science in its social setting. Because Bryan used the same language of the democratic persuasion as did mainstream science, his arguments were both powerful and insidious, even as his populist politics clashed with the growing elitism of the science establishment. Both he and they appeared to be speaking the same language when in fact they were not.[16]

To Bryan there were deniers and false prophets. Using a deceptive science like evolution, scientists plunged toward their final destructive con-

clusions. World War I, with its merciless killing, its death by technology, illustrated perfectly such inevitable destinations: the absolute dangers of un-
bounded intelligence in the service of evil. In this appalling instance,
intellect alone guided nations, and "learning without heart" pushed civilization toward the barbaric suicide of universal war. In this instance Bryan
was voicing his dismay that Darwinism had been used to justify the German
war machine, that the "survival of the fittest" had translated into "might
makes right."[17] To oppose this philosophy meant to dam up its sources in
the hypothesis of evolution. Even in present-day America, Bryan warned,
false science threatened the republic. Some five thousand strong, the scientific establishment planned to "set up a Soviet government in education,
and, although public employees, demand the right to teach as *true,* unsup-
ported guesses that undermine the religious faith of Christian taxpayers."

With this argument Bryan raised his last challenge to modernist science.
The taxpayers, to use the crassest formulation of the argument, had the democratic right to determine what was taught in their schools. If information
contradicted the knowledge of the Bible and the custom of their culture, it
was clearly the right and duty of citizens to reject it as false. Bryan did not
demand a specifically Christian education, he cautioned, only the exclusion
of any non-Christian science, or the teaching of notions that would shake
the Christian pillars of society.[18]

Using these tools, Bryan placed the keystone to his considerable edifice
of anti-Darwinism. He revealed the nature of his definition of science. As a
citizen in a democracy, he felt qualified and compelled to judge and guide
the direction of social change. As an informed voter he had learned enough
about both modern science and religion to adjudicate their conflicting
claims in society. The preservation of democracy demanded that he oppose
the establishment of any elite: corporations, banks, corrupt politicians, and
now scientists, who would impose their esoteric reasons and secret purposes on the world. He could not accept the word of an expert over his own
conscience if it contradicted common sense or shared culture. To do so invited reproducing the German experiment of World War I, a system of mil-
itarized ruthlessness. Better to recognize the limits and boundaries of
knowledge; better to consult the books of God and nature in their splendid,
literal concordances than worry about inconsistencies.[19]

Nor was Bryan the only critic of modern science and its opaque theorizing. During the controversy over Albert Einstein's theory of relativity that
smoldered after World War I, lasting until 1924 or so, charges of elitism and

obscurity were common. A few eminent scientists such as the astronomer Robert Millikan sought to integrate older scientific notions of a mechanistic, Newtonian world with modern theory, all the while holding firm to their belief in Christianity. Millikan's assembly of religion and science was published in 1927 as *Evolution in Science and Religion.*[20]

But Bryan gave no indication he was aware of this complex discussion of modern theory. Perhaps he joined the AAAS as a public gesture, designed to advertise his position or maybe as a defiant declaration of principle: from a saint in a laboratory coat. There is nothing inconsistent about either reason when seen within his peripatetic crusade against Darwinism. Responsible citizenship insisted that he apply his rich, beautiful voice to the rising chorus of democratic prophecy against apostate science. Common sense, derived from common culture and experience, made him, as much as anyone else, an interpreter of popular science. Recording his membership in the greatest scientific organization of his day was an act of informed patriotism.

In the moments before the Scopes trial in July 1925, Bryan clearly anticipated the gravity of the confrontation and the considerable stake he had in its outcome. He continued to remark upon the undemocratic underpinnings of the science establishment and to excoriate elitism and exclusivity. Even if all 11,000 members of the AAAS were counted, that still constituted "a pretty little oligarchy to put in control of the education of all the children."[21] But clouds of uncertainty were building. Asked by the Christian Fundamentalist Association to aid the local prosecution of Scopes, Bryan labored to shore up his arguments, to call on a counterscience implied in Fundamentalist religion. On one occasion he appeared to borrow a tactic from the scientists themselves. Referring to the AAAS committee on science education, he proposed his own "Board of Advisors" to inform the country "that our side was prepared to hold its own against their committee of scientists." Our experts will match your experts! There was also talk of opening a Fundamentalist university to teach the proper relation of science and religion (founded in 1925 in the soon to be hallowed town of Dayton).[22] To muster support, Bryan wrote to several notable opponents of evolution to persuade them to testify at the trial. There he encountered unexpected difficulties. Although an enthusiastic enlistee in the larger cause, geologist and well-known critic of Darwin George McCready Price, author of *The New Geology,* declined to travel to Dayton. Another prominent antievolutionist, James M. Gray, president of the Moody Bible Institute of Chicago, also regretfully refused an invitation to testify. But he declared his allegiance to Bryan's cause and affirmed his willingness to serve on the advisory committee should it be formed. He also sought to bolster Bryan's understanding of the issue, sending him a copy of his pamphlet "Why a Christian Cannot Be an Evolutionist."[23]

Bryan responded by sending Gray his own pamphlet, "Indictment against Evolution," and asking advice on how to square the two different accounts of creation in Genesis. Gray's reply was politely instructive but cool. He first denied that there were two accounts of creation. The initial "account" described the creation; the second developed the "story of the things which follow their creation." As for Bryan's pamphlet, it was "weak and inadequate" because it only skirted the central issues of evolution and did not engage them. These, Gray informed his new pupil, revolved around the absence in evolutionary theory of a "personal Creator, Director and upholder of the universe."[24]

It is possible that Bryan suspected the inadequacies of his acquaintance with science and theology, as this correspondence might have suggested to him. There had been other early warnings. Several times in 1924 Bryan's literary agent had warned him that his column "Bible Talks" was supercharged with theological controversy and therefore hurting sales to newspapers.[25] Still, the trial began with a major victory when the judge excluded expert witness for the defense. That had been Bryan's point all along: that the issue of Darwinism could not be settled by scientific elites. Chicago lawyer Clarence Darrow (who fancied himself something of a scientist) would not be allowed to shift the trial to an elevated and complex discussion of science and so had to send his experts back to their university laboratories. So when Bryan agreed to testify and submit to cross-examination, he did it as an informed citizen, speaking to other citizens about their common culture of science and religion. Whatever his foreboding about his own lack of specific knowledge, he proceeded incautiously in the cause of democracy. That of course was his error, for Darrow had every intention of demonstrating Bryan's inadequate knowledge of the Bible. Prepared to attack the Darwinian hypothesis as bad science, Bryan was suckered into defending the literalness of the Bible—something he had serious private doubts about.

During this devastating cross-examination, in which the "Great Commoner" revealed what James Gray surmised, Bryan became befuddled. After bungling his defense, contradicting himself, and worse, offending many attending Fundamentalists, Bryan penned a revealing, heartfelt but feeble

Figure 2.3   William Jennings Bryan makes a point at the trial of John Scopes in July 1925 in Dayton, Tennessee. Courtesy of the Bettman Archives.

self-defense. In this document Bryan opened his wounds to the world and then, in what must be seen as a defiant act of self-medication, stitched up his self-esteem again. In his short public relations release titled "Mr. Darrow's Charge of Ignorance," he shunned his tentative role as a scientist and theologian to justify himself with the only expertise that remained to him. He was not "ignorant" as Darrow charged, even if the niceties of scientific theory and biblical exegesis eluded him. He was an expert in democracy, a citizen representing the considered opinions of other citizens. Admittedly, his reading of science had only been general; he was not a close student of geology, paleontology, or philology. "My life has been spent in the study and discussion of economic, social and governmental problems," and he had tested this learning before the general population, not among scientific elites. As if to regain his bearings, he recounted a short biography of his humble origins and mustered a roll call of his famous acquaintances and accomplishments. Writing more vigorously and now restored in dignity and self-confidence, he puffed: "In a trip around the world, I was given audience by a number of kings, emperors, and prominent public men, and have been cordially received by presidents of Latin America and high officials throughout both the eastern and western hemispheres." Now he returned, finally, to assault evolutionary science again. But gone were the learned references to chemistry, to the inadequacies of scientific theory, to missing links, to questions of order and classified knowledge. Stripped of rhetorical confusion and emotionally lean, his reason was elemental. Acceptance of evolution, he wrote, "changes the philosophy of life and tends to chill spiritual enthusiasm."[26] Evolutionary science threatened the system of beliefs around which Bryan constructed his identity. It undermined American democracy and American history as well as the traditional alliance of science and religion. It challenged the culture in which Bryan lived and whose beliefs he articulated. It threatened his very being, as Christian, as citizen, as scientist, as American. He was the object lesson of its pernicious progress.

I'm going to sing a song
about Old Man Atom
I don't mean the Adam in
the Bible datum,
I don't mean the Adam
that Mother Eve mated,
I mean *that thing* that science liberated.

"Old Man Atom," from a
Talking Blues film
by Vern Partlow (1947)

Chapter 3

The Republic of Science

The advent of the nuclear age in 1945 conferred a precarious moment of opportunity on America's atomic scientists. The ambiguity of their position, as creators and destroyers, enormously augmented their public notoriety. The impact of their esoteric talk and the alarming outcome of their research in nuclear physics vicariously enhanced the reputation and importance of American science in general. But where there was great prestige, there was also censure. The other side of the liberation of atomic energy was increased discussion of controlling the activities of scientists and worry about the meaning of technological advance in American society. In the postwar age of big science, flush funding, and seemingly miraculous discoveries, scientists attained a status that convinced some of them to seek national, even international, leadership. But as a priesthood of knowers, a group that understood the dark, liberating secrets of nuclear power, they were criticized by the same arguments that William Jennings Bryan had raised in his attack on the science establishment. By the end of the 1950s the atomic scientists had seen their hopes for a world government founder on the shoals of American culture: on suspicions of elitism, their failure to popularize a clear message about the implications of nuclear science, and a growing critique of science from a moral and religious perspective.

After the 1930s, when it had suffered an eclipse in funding and prestige—a time when public and private funding levels declined—science experienced a huge and sustained burst of public support and interest, primarily because of nuclear research. The group that historian Daniel Kevles calls the "Los Alamos Generation" occupied a position of immense prestige from which it could intervene in the most important policy discussions of the nation.[1] Despite this position, science—particularly the big science of the Cold War—found itself stained with indelible misgivings that spread into the whole modern scientific enterprise. Were the social and moral responsibilities of the science profession the same as those of the community that supported it? How did the religious underpinnings of society relate to these questions?

The specific arguments swirling around Bryan and the Scopes trial certainly did not reappear in considerations of atomic science, but notions of responsibility and morality did. In his presidential address to the AAAS in 1951, geologist Kirtley Mather mapped the short, spectacular history of science since 1945. Opinion had shifted abruptly from "one in which scientists could bask in the sunshine of widespread admiration, respect, and even awe, to one in which the storm clouds of suspicion, recrimination, and fear endanger the intellectual progress and continuing welfare of mankind." He continued, "Science discloses the imperative need; something that transcends science must assist man to respond to the challenge of our time."

There are several reasons to pay close attention to these remarks. Mather clearly believed that devotion to the procedures of science established a higher calling of truth seeking. Yet he also believed that principles outside science should be brought to bear on its applications. Science was, he argued, morally neutral even if it was intellectually superior.

Coming from Mather, these were important thoughts. The geologist had been an active opponent of Fundamentalism in the 1920s and had submitted a brief at the Scopes trial in support of teaching evolution theory. But Mather, like a good many other scientists, was a profoundly religious man and spent considerable time in the 1950s and 1960s pondering the possible outlines of a religious cosmology. Whereas Bryan challenged specific theories of science for contradicting literal Scripture readings, Mather pointed to another and vaguer misgiving about science—its purported moral neutrality. But that could be just as unsettling for a society that increasingly depended on a vast science enterprise.[2]

The clash of views about science became acute immediately after the war, centering on the issue of atomic science. When scientists appeared before the Senate's Special Committee on Atomic Energy in early 1946, their greatest concern was the freedom of scientific research. Testifying before Connecticut senator Brien McMahon's committee, they, politicians, and other witnesses tried to develop a policy and a language suited to the role of atomic science—and all science—in American society. Not surprisingly, in these deliberations there emerged several positions about the role of science in the atomic age.

How should science operate in modern society? How free should the scientist be to pursue research and interchange with other scientists in other nations? Were they privileged? Did they have unique responsibilities? Of what polity were they citizens? How did their work fit the moral and religious traditions of American society? Most of the scientists who appeared answered these questions by confidently asserting their membership in a unique international community of researchers. They were bound up in a special culture defined by the methods of science. The virtues of this community were derived from the universal commandments of research: Absolute intellectual honesty was necessary to advance knowledge. Respect for the work of others was inevitable. Truth was the highest virtue.

Chemist and Nobel laureate Harold C. Urey, for example, argued against military control of atomic energy research and in favor of openness. "Nearly all scientific work," he noted, "proceeds by one man making a discovery, moving the subject forward by a small amount, publishing his data, presenting it at a scientific meeting, everybody discussing this thing, and someone in the group goes home with an idea of his own that might be slightly different from that of the man who presented the paper."[3] Consequently scientists needed the freedom to choose what they would publish or not publish, unrestricted by outside censors or bureaucratic authorization. They belonged to a special community that existed beyond the borders of nationalism and above parochial cultures; they should determine the fate of their ideas.[4]

To many of the senators this open community with its free discussion was a dangerous suggestion, and they were far less sanguine about the special status of atomic scientists. With the Soviet Union very much in mind, Senator Millard Tydings of Maryland chided Vannevar Bush, head of the federal Office of Scientific Research and Development, for his suggestion that science somehow operated outside ordinary culture:

> SENATOR TYDINGS: Do you think it is possible to accomplish in the world a free exchange of scientific knowledge—in a world that does not permit the free exchange of religious knowledge?
>
> DR. BUSH: Science, Senator, has always been more or less free; it has always had a flavor of internationalism, you know.
>
> SENATOR TYDINGS: So has religion.[5]

In questioning Harvard astronomer Harlow Shapley, the senators reiterated the critical point: Could you have scientific freedom in a society whose culture and politics were totalitarian?[6] The very question revealed disbelief that science could represent a community that lived by its own elevated rules. Science, like any other human endeavor, was guided by the same rules of conduct and open to the same quirks of behavior as any other aspect of society.

Of course the senators were not spinning out cultural theory here; they were primarily concerned by the dangers of the Soviet Union's acquiring the atomic bomb. But the implications of their argument were important and eventually resulted in a law establishing the Atomic Energy Commission, which, while it held the military at arm's length, cautiously regulated and surveyed atomic research. Although many scientists agreed with some restrictions and others embraced defense research, they still chafed at the notion of military controls.

There was a third voice at the hearings that presented a wholly different interpretation of science—one akin to Bryan's commonsense, democratic critique. The witness was Mrs. Harper Sibley, one of only two women on a long list of experts, politicians, and scientists. Mrs. Sibley was the president of the United Council of Church Women, and she and her organization supported the more liberal bill before Congress that would create a civilian oversight agency to guide nuclear research. Her reasons were grounded precisely in the other internationalism that Senator Tydings had referred to: a universal religious morality that should guide the behavior of all nations. To her, keeping a monopoly of nuclear information was tantamount to "blasphemy."

The real import of her testimony, however, lay in the long quotation she read from the War Department's official press release describing the 16 July 1945 test in Alamogordo, New Mexico—a document she cited to support her view that religion should be mentor to science. This remarkable document portrays the observers as speechless because scientific language could not convey their reactions. So the release used two traditional rhetorical devices to articulate their response. The first drew on portents, widely used by Shakespeare to signal a happening that turned the world upside down. In this case preparations for the atomic device were "accomplished amid lightning flashes and peals of thunder." The announcement continued: "A significant aspect, recorded by the press, was the experience of a blind girl near Albuquerque many miles from the scene, who, when the flash of the test lighted the sky before the explosion could be heard, exclaimed, 'What was that?'" Even the blind could see![7]

But Mrs. Sibley was drawn to General Farrell's final words that echoed not Shakespeare, but the Bible:

Atomic fission would no longer be hidden in the cloisters of the theoretical physicists' dreams. It was almost full grown at birth. It was a great new force to be used for good or for evil. There was a feeling in that shelter that those concerned with its nativity should dedicate their lives to the mission that it would always be used for good and never for evil.

She ended with his last sentences:

Thirty seconds after, the explosion came first, the air blast pressing hard against the people and things, to be followed almost immediately by the strong, sustained, awesome roar which warned of doomsday and made us feel that we puny things were blasphemous to dare tamper with the forces heretofore reserved to the Almighty. . . . It had to be witnessed.[8]

The scientists and senators allowed Mrs. Sibley to record her organization's vote for a more liberal bill and then ignored her larger argument. Yet she expressed two of American culture's most dynamic resources for understanding and assimilating modern science: its long and deep literary and religious heritage. The atomic scientists had recognized the political power of organized religion and solicited aid from groups like the one Mrs. Sibley represented. But her insistence on seeing a religious dimension to scientific discovery was as much a challenge to the heavily guarded castle of science as to senatorial skepticism about scientists.

For much of the 1940s and 1950s the prestige of atomic science was the decoration that confirmed the special rank of science in American culture. One of the leaders of the atomic scientists movement, James Franck, who penned the nuclear scientists' petition of June 1945 pleading with President Truman not to use the atomic bomb, believed that scientists were "a kind of international brotherhood, comparable in many ways to a religious order."[9] Arthur Holly Compton, another leading atomic scientist, argued that the modern enterprise of highly organized group research could be a social model for reorganizing American society. "If co-operation," he wrote, "is thus the lifeblood of science and technology, it is similarly vital to society as a whole."[10]

In 1943 Mark May of the Yale University Institute of Human Relations, addressing the Conference on the Scientific Spirit and Democratic Faith sponsored by John Dewey, put these ideas in an older guise traceable back to the turn of the century. "I believe," he declared, "that the moral code practiced in the fellowship of science is distinctly superior to that practiced in the most civilized societies." This moral code included absolute honesty, fearless search for the truth, and universal proclamation of the results.[11]

The two writers who probably did most to establish the vision of a scientifically transformed society in the public mind after World War II also affirmed this notion of the special place of science in modern society. Vannevar Bush's 1945 report to the president, suggestively named *Science, the Endless Frontier,* was in its way a latter-day frontier thesis, arguing the pioneering role of science in the Cold War world. In his case for government funding of research, Bush attached his argument to this traditional cultural metaphor, one repeatedly linked to science, research, rocketry, and space exploration in the next several decades. The scientific frontier promised boundless opportunity and heroic stories as well as a driving force for economic development. It was the perfect expression of the optimism and vision from a man who wished to persuade the government and the nation to embrace science, the scientific method, and the defense of the United States against the Soviet Union.

In his book *On Understanding Science* (1947), James Conant, president of Harvard University, shared Bush's optimism as well as some of his Cold War commitments. Conant wanted sufficient public awareness of science to achieve social and political unity. "We need a widespread understanding of science in this country," he wrote, "for only thus can science be assimilated into our secular culture." With that achieved, we would approach a "unified, coherent culture suitable for our American democracy in this new age of machines and experts." Although there are certainly strong intimations in his book that America's political and social elites and decision makers should thoroughly understand science, Conant also wanted the nation as a whole to recognize the accumulating momentum of scientific discovery. Unlike other forms of knowledge, science was neither a set of ideas nor a pattern of beliefs but a dynamic, advancing inquiry. To accept this definition would encourage the nation to apply a secular, rational discourse to solving social problems.[12]

As Conant and many other scientists argued, the heart of their case lay in differentiating modern science from common sense. In the nineteenth century the image of the scientist as inventor, using ingenuity to solve a problem, had blended well with the democratic ethos of that age. But by the twentieth century even the terms of technological advance had changed to more group-oriented laboratory and corporate models. For theoretical physics especially, the changes grew even more distinct. Experimentation in everyday life, as opposed to experiment in science, Conant wrote, differed because of the assumptions that guided each. Common sense used practical experience to design the terms of experiment. Modern science, however, employed hypotheses drawn from and related to other theories of science. In fact there was no single scientific method, but rather a trained awareness of the dynamic implications of hypothesis, observation, and new hypothesis. As the philosopher of science Ernest Nagel put it, science was the by-product "of inquiries conducted in accordance with a definite policy for obtaining and assessing evidence."[13]

If science was not common sense, neither was it magic or wizardry. Modern scientists neither performed miracles nor practiced magic: science was not invocation; it was not incantation. Yet with the development of atomic energy and hints about the possibilities of space exploration, such thinking and descriptive terminology returned in a rush, providing popular culture with metaphors to engage scientific theories that seemed beyond comprehension.[14]

To counter such ideas, scientists, as they had long done, promoted their own version of popularization and sought to explain theories to the public in their own terms. Still, they had few illusions; not Everyman or Everywoman could become a scientist. As Michael Polanyi has written, "Laymen normally accept the teachings of science not because they share its conception of reality, but because they submit to the authority of science." As Harvard physicist P. W. Bridgman warned bluntly in a speech to the American Association for the Advancement of Science in 1946, the right to impose responsibility on the scientist represented "the right of the stupid to exploit the bright."[15] The campaign to promote science understanding after World War II was intended to raise universal respect for the science endeavor, to unclog the veins of discussion about pure science research, and to increase the flow of funding.

Part of the message of popularization entailed generating support for what was called pure science. The public could easily understand and sympathize with inventors or scientists whose work could be applied to medicine or engineering. But sympathy for theoretical research or abstract intellectual inquiry was harder to generate. As Margaret Mead and Rhoda Métraux discovered in their survey of high-school students in the early 1960s, the scientist was usually pictured positively, but with eccentric attributes: "A man who wears a white coat and works in a laboratory. He is elderly or middle aged and wears glasses. He is small, sometimes small and stout, or tall and thin. He may be bald. He may wear a beard, may be unshaven and unkempt."[16] Behind this peculiar image lay the notion that the theoretical scientist was ill equipped to deal with real problems. It implied that his otherworldly gaze marked him as a victim of impracticality.

All these issues complicated the drive to create a national science foundation, which began during the war and finally came to fruition in 1950. Two problems seriously complicated its establishment: the type of projects to be funded and the control of the agency.

In the late 1930s the National Academy of Sciences created the National Science Fund to explore ways to support fundamental scientific research. Among its members were a group of prominent science advocates—scientists and academicians who promoted the interests of science, such as Karl T. Compton of Massachusetts Institute of Technology, Frank B. Jewett, president of the National Academy of Sciences and chair of the board of Bell Laboratories, Robert A. Millikan of California Institute of Technology, and Harlow Shapley, director of the Harvard Observatory. In early 1945 Shapley met in Washington with some of the leading proponents of a national science foundation. "Through the connivance of Henry Wallace," he reported to Frank B. Jewett, "I was brought into a prolonged luncheon meeting the other day with the Director of the National Budget and Mr. Will Davis. . . . There is a pretty important ferment stirring in Washington with respect to the future of scientific research. It is both pure and applied research that is under discussion, especially the former."[17]

Shapley's remark pinpointed one of the key issues in the creation of a national science foundation: its dimensions and expanse. Would it fund only research that promised no immediate benefit but might reap huge rewards later? Should it also support applied science, which might involve using scientific thinking to resolve social, economic, and political problems? Applied science could imply social science: was this truly science and worthy of government support?

The other key issue had to do with control of any federal grant-giving science agency. Some of the early thinking about the National Science Foundation crystallized into a proposal that placed oversight of the agency in the hands of eminent scientists. This was acceptable neither to a great many of the congressional supporters of federally backed scientific research nor to President Truman, who vetoed a national science foundation bill in 1948 because it lacked executive department oversight.

In fact it took five years to pass acceptable legislation setting up the National Science Foundation. The resulting agency was designed by compromise and initially limited to the natural sciences. Its functions were narrow in terms of setting national science policy and were leashed to the executive branch of government through the power of the president to appoint its director. Its emphasis in the beginning was pure science, although its functions were expanded in the 1950s to include applied and even social sciences.[18]

The protracted debate buffeting this legislation exposed the broad crosswinds of opinion about science in this period. The issue of political control over money lavished on science was one important consideration. But even deeper, there was a fundamental disagreement over the nature of science itself. On one side, some scientists believed in the superior ethics of the science endeavor based on the defining tenets of professionalism. The special code of truth telling, the very procedures of science, they argued, would guarantee the scrupulous award of funding to deserving projects, if only scientists were placed in charge. As Robert K. Merton, one of the founders of the sociology of science, put it: "One sentiment which is assimilated by the scientist from the very outset of his training pertains to the purity of science. Science must not suffer itself to become the handmaiden of theology or economy or state."[19]

The notion of scientists as leading citizens of a virtuous republic was passionately contested by opponents of a national science foundation. A particularly interesting and sharp testimony in congressional hearings came from John W. Anderson, president of the National Patent Council, which in 1949 opposed the NSF. Anderson charged that the legislation had been "spawned somewhere within the long leftist shadow of Henry Wallace." Harlow Shapley, "recently named as active in organizations identified by Congress as subversive," had, he noted, also helped to draft and design various NSF bills.[20]

This attack and various efforts to attach a loyalty oath to every grant represent more than the sniping of conservatives or the unthinking reflexes of anticommunists. The larger issue had been raised before in questioning the special position of science in American culture. The specter of communism and the Soviet state's centralized bureaucracy of science had provoked Bryan twenty years earlier. Now, government-sponsored science invoked deep concern. For those who knew the details, Soviet science had been sullied by the grimy paw of politics. Centralized direction of research and its application to social and economic problems challenged the freedom of the individual and, of course, the private market of ideas and products. There also remained the broad suspicion of Soviet science, and therefore anything that resembled it, for its lack of concern for the religious traditions of Western culture. Science, freed from such moral restraints, could behave in monstrous ways—not only in the anxious imaginings of science fiction, but in the very real and reprehensible behavior of scientists in Germany during World War II and in the Soviet Union. One could interpret this experience in two ways. Scientists were forced, by the bureaucratic power of the state, to act contrary to their ideals and best interests—to betray the ethics of science. Or one could argue that crude experiments and vicious technology developed because the Soviet Union and Germany denied the moderating power and principle of religion and constructed totally secular enterprises—with inevitably disastrous results.

There is evidence that Americans looked with considerable confusion on claims of scientists' special status. Sometimes they were wildly optimistic. The period after World War II had more than its share of scientific hoaxes, hopeful fictions, and delusionary experiments. Promises of skies thick with private helicopters, atomic trains and watches, and miracle cures were made and then quickly retracted. As Martin Gardner, a watchman for such incursions upon the scientific endeavor, has written, "The sudden success of atomic research hitherto the subject matter of science fiction, is certainly a major factor in this trend."[21] Several historians of science have seen this enthusiasm within a larger trend in the development of popular scientific ideas. Spencer Weart, for example, writes that "nuclear energy had become a symbolic representation for the magical transmutation of society and the individual" in what was a reiteration of an old cultural notion of the passage "through destruction to rebirth." Arguing from a somewhat different framework, and in a very pessimistic frame of mind, John Burnham concludes that after World War II science became increasingly infected by the misleading demands of the mass media. The result was a decline into superstition as mysticism and the dramatic formats of film and television popularization overwhelmed the complexities of science and the difficulties of explaining it.[22]

A 1958 report for the National Association of Science Writers, prepared by the Survey Research Center at the University of Michigan, caught the divided mood that brought science its ambivalent reputation after World War II. The survey found overwhelming confidence in science and high prestige for scientists, yet very few of those Americans interviewed could define scientific methods with much understanding. About a third believed that scientists should not stray into any work that might conflict with religion. Almost half said that faith—not science—should be the model for social organization. On the practical issues of science, researchers found that those who did not trust scientists had a vision of the group as odd, irreligious, and not interested in practical results.[23]

Summing up almost a decade of endeavor to educate the American public about atomic energy, Edward Shils wrote in 1957, "It is a paradox that the past decade during which the uproar of anti-intellectualism and of distrust for scientists was louder than it has ever been in America, was also the decade of the greatly enhanced influence of scientists within public bodies."[24] The sociologist's interpretation of this fact was not what might be presumed. He believed that the suspicion was a repressed function of admiration, an expression of jealousy, and a bugle call announcing the retreat of the enemies of science.

Shils's identification of atomic theory as the basic ingredient in the sweet-and-sour reputation of scientists suggests the leading role atomic science played in American culture during the postwar period. This influence is clearly visible in the fate of efforts to make international science a vi-able model for social reform. The efforts of atomic scientists to institute a "republic of science" snared them in the recurrent American misgivings about science.[25]

Seizing the ambivalent prestige of the Manhattan Project, the scientists who worked on the atomic bomb sought greater influence in the councils of policy making. More than almost any other group of scientists, they deemed the scientific ethic to be the model for social reconstruction. The standards of truth telling, universal methods, and the internationalism of the scientific community at first suggested the possibility of creating a world government superior to any single nation in scientific matters at least.

Dismayed at the terrible destructiveness of Hiroshima and Nagasaki, and aware that this devastation was only a down payment on a note that might exact much greater penalties in the future, a group of scientists from the Manhattan Project founded the atomic scientists movement. Their initial aim was to secure civilian control and reasonable freedom for scientific research. Several groups organized to lobby around different aspects of the problem. The Federation of Atomic Scientists (replaced in 1946 by the Federation of American Scientists) appeared in the fall of 1945 to work for international control of atomic energy. At the same time, a larger group including nonscientists formed the National Committee on Atomic Information, designed to promote a reasonable understanding of atomic energy and its social implications. A third group, affiliated with the Federation and called the Atomic Scientists of Chicago, published the *Bulletin of the Atomic Scientists* beginning in late 1945.[26]

The scientists were united about the dangers civilization risked in pursuing military applications of atomic energy. As the clock hands on the cover of the *Bulletin* warned, midnight (or nuclear war) was increasingly a danger. The scientists knew that the Soviet Union would sooner or later develop atomic weapons, increasing the danger of nuclear war. Consequently they pushed hard for world government, first through the tentative steps suggested in the Baruch-Lilienthal plan of 1946 for United Nations control of atomic research and then in a larger and more extensive campaign to place the destiny of peace itself in the hands of an international body they helped design.

In part such ideas flowed as a natural consequence of the internationalism of atomic science itself, where major discoveries in Germany, Denmark, France, England, Italy, and the United States contributed to the theory and technology of the first weapons. In part it depended on the identity of the atomic scientists, many of them refugees from war-devastated Europe. In a curious way, the Manhattan Project itself, despite its rigid military compartmentalization, had elements of a kind of international university of modern physics. Under the extreme pressure to develop a bomb and win the war, the atomic scientists had created a prototype of international cooperation in science that might be translated into a movement for world government.[27]

The failure of the Lilienthal plan at the United Nations in 1946 seriously undermined practical approaches to a first step to international government, but it did not necessarily dampen the enthusiasm of scientists and other supporters of the idea. With the backing of important intellectuals such as Max Lerner and Dorothy Thompson, as well as physicist J. Robert Oppenheimer, the United World Federalists was launched in April 1947. Another key and parallel organization, headed by Robert M. Hutchins, president of the University of Chicago, was the Committee to Frame a World Constitution (1945).[28] Just how scientists related to this impulse is captured by the words of physicist Leo Szilard, one of the principal scientists of the Manhattan Project. "All this presupposes," he wrote of the control of atomic energy, "that we are really making the building up of a world community the cornerstone of our national policy, and that the world could count on the continuity of such a policy on the part of the United States. This probably cannot be achieved without making changes in the Constitution."[29] Eugene Rabinovitch, editor of the *Bulletin,* put it boldly in an article in 1947: Scientists must remember how they came to realize the necessity of world government. "Their special task," he continued, "which none else can perform with equal authority and chance for success, is to lead others along the same path."[30]

In fact, scientists were extraordinarily busy at this time talking about the perils of atomic energy across the country. As Professor Selig Hecht noted, writing of the history of the Emergency Committee of Atomic Scientists at Princeton: "At practically every university and research center in the country informal groups of scientists became associated into organizations, dues-paying organizations, with speakers' bureaus and discussion forums. Some of the men spoke as often as five times a week." When this proved insufficient, "Scientists again took the initiative. They went to Washington and they talked to anybody and everybody."[31]

Much of the original enthusiasm and bustle of speechmaking and conference giving eventually diminished. As David Inglis wrote to the *Newslet-*

ter of the Federation of American Scientists in March 1949, "Our part in politics as scientists was much more clear in that first year of the life of the Federation when we had, as the result of our special experience, a message that was new. By now the torch of truth which we carried has been glimpsed by man, forgotten or perverted by most of these."[32] Inglis went on to argue that scientists could not go it alone and that if they wanted a world government they should endorse the program of the United World Federalists.

There was notable support even in Congress during the late 1940s for some form of world government based on the activities of atomic scientists and world federalists. Senators Claude Pepper of Florida, Wayne Morse of Oregon, Frank Graham of North Carolina, and Charles W. Tobey of New Hampshire spoke with varying enthusiasm for a stronger United Nations. As Senator Pepper noted, twenty-one states had "passed resolutions approving a world federation of one type or another." This "rapidly expanding, popular demand," he declared, affirmed the faith of Americans in building a strong United Nations.[33] Yet Pepper, Morse, and Tobey were scarcely in the conservative Senate mainstream on such matters, and events of the Cold War quickly overwhelmed what little public support remained. The explosion of the first Soviet test atomic bomb in 1949, the revelation of spying by Klaus Fuchs in 1950, the beginning of the Korean War also in that year—just to name a few events—emptied the life out of internationalism.

Robert Hutchins wrote a postscript for world government activism in April 1949 in a speech given at Spokane, Washington. Four years ago, he said, "We all ran for the nearest exit, shouting, 'There must never be another war; we must have world government right away." Even the mass media seconded these doomsday warnings. "But apparently you can get used to anything," he concluded. "We have now returned to our normal occupations and preoccupations. . . . We have succeeded in forgetting what we all know, that the atomic bomb alters the whole outlook of life in America."[34]

The failure of the atomic scientists to achieve political leadership or translate the scientific ethic into a new world order underscored the very assumption they had denied: science, whatever its special intellectual demands, turned out to be subject to powerful cultural and political constraints. However universal their methods, scientists belonged to a national cultural with its parochial restraints. The rest of the 1950s would accentuate that point repeatedly as suspicion, distrust, and despair incited by the Cold War turned the loyalty of the scientists from an assumption to a question.

Another demonstration of the enormous difficulty in popularizing their position came in January 1947 with the screening of the Metro-Goldwyn-Mayer film *The Beginning or the End?* In a letter to the office of the Atomic Scientists of Chicago in July 1946, Bernard Iddings Bell counseled an appeal to the American public through mass culture. "What we need is a campaign of shameless propaganda," he wrote. "What we need for our purpose now is slogans, shibboleths, comic strips, motion pictures centering around glittering stars and crooners."[35]

Bell's "shameless" proposal was more than realized in the MGM film. The atomic scientists approached Hollywood and the Motion Picture Association in mid-1946 with proposals that the industry educate the American public to the realities of atomic power. The Chicago scientists stressed two general points: that civilization was at stake in an arms race and that the only effective control of nuclear energy would come in the guise of world government. Fred Eastman, representing the atomic scientists, even suggested teaching conferences for motion picture producers conducted by scientists. Scientists had already met with publishers, clergymen, and the radio industry. "The Federation of American Scientists will be glad to have one with the policy-makers of Motion Pictures, if you wish it," he concluded.[36]

The atomic scientists got more than their wish. Sam Max, who produced the MGM film, visited both the Oak Ridge Institute of Nuclear Studies and Harry Truman and received the president's nod to make the film. He then turned to leading nuclear scientists for advice. As Max intended it, the film would dramatize the development of the atomic bomb and the decision to use it, portraying real participants like Groves, Truman, Oppenheimer, Einstein, Fermi, and Szilard. But the screenwriter who developed the script added melodramatic and romantic flourishes. Such a brimming stewpot was likely to boil over, and it did. A number of scientists, as well as Groves, vigorously objected to depictions of themselves or to invented incidents, and they chided MGM for its gross scientific errors.[37]

Individual scientists demanded changes, but the political pundit Walter Lippmann articulated their dissatisfaction most clearly. In a letter to the Emergency Committee of Atomic Scientists in October 1946, Lippmann reported seeing the partly finished film. It "bears out your own apprehensions. You will be surprised to learn that in spite of Nils [sic] Bohr's saying that he must not be impersonated, he has been impersonated.... Apart from that, the basic theme of the film is not the problem of the atomic bomb in the world, but the success story of the Americans, particularly General Groves, in making the bomb."[38] There were other gross falsifications such as a fabricated scene between General Groves and President Truman. Lippmann succeeded in having that excised. Einstein and Szilard also gravely objected to the plot and registered their complaints with MGM.

In justifying its alteration of science and history, MGM invoked dramatic pragmatism, in Hollywood a far higher value than truth. As Sam Max wrote in early 1946 to Norman Cousins, editor of the *Saturday Review of Literature*, several of the scientists, especially younger ones on the Manhattan Project, were anxious about the content of the film. "They are worried that we will not make a picture which will be a big, long speech for world government," he wrote. "Quite frankly, they are right." The film would make its points through melodrama, not with scientific lessons or statements.[39]

Advance publicity for reviewers in the form of a promotional booklet suggested an emotional and ideological itinerary to follow through the film. A publicity shot featuring the four main characters of the film, all fictitious, pictured them looking up to the sky against the backdrop of a mushroom cloud. As if to explain their inattention to the blast, a quotation beneath the print explained that they had more important things to consider: "The timeless moment that gives all of us a chance to prove that human beings are made in the image and likeness of God." Such religious overtones played throughout the film. As Max explained in the booklet, "After further research at such atomic centers as the University of Chicago and Columbia University, and a discussion of the film's religious aspects with Cardinal Francis J. Spellman," he reported, "he had found the most amazing and most human story he had ever heard."[40]

That story, invented by Hollywood, featured a young American scientist, Matt Cochran, and his friend Jeff, an assistant to General Groves. The young scientist's wife and the assistant's girlfriend completed the dramatic quartet. The movie began with the ceremonial opening of a time capsule in 2446, placed five hundred years earlier. Among the objects was a film, purporting to be a newsreel about the beginning of the atomic era. In fact there were several plot lines to the film. One was the history of the Manhattan Project. A second, wholly invented but designed to signal the reluctance of scientists to engage in destructive work, focused on Cochran, who expresses serious doubts about his work. As in many Hollywood films, the voice of conscience has to pay with his life. Matt prevents one of the atomic

Figure 3.1 This promotional still from *The Beginning or the End?* (Metro-Goldwyn-Mayer, 1947) depicts the message communicated by the film. The main characters pictured here are so absorbed by religious thoughts that they pay no attention to the atomic blast in the background. From the pamphlet *Facts about the Making of M-G-M's Remarkable Motion Picture,* produced to accompany the film. Courtesy of the Department of Special Collections, University of Chicago Libraries.

bombs from exploding and exposes himself to deadly radiation. He saves "40,000 Americans"—a figure that sounds close to the initial casualty count at Nagasaki, as if to expiate dropping the bomb. A third plot concerns family building.

The last scene united all these strands under the shadow of the Lincoln Memorial in Washington. Matt has died of radiation poisoning, and Jeff brings his last letter to read to his pregnant wife. From death, Matt's words justify the bomb: "God has not shown us a new way to destroy ourselves. Atomic energy is the hand He has extended to lift us from the ruins of war and lighten the burdens of peace." This is not the end, but the beginning, "the timeless moment that gives us all a chance to prove that human beings are made in the image and likeness of God."[41]

If the movie horrified many of the atomic scientists depicted in the film and amused critics, who dismissed it as boring and inaccurate, there was an important lesson to be learned. The atomic scientists, thinking they could gain access to the mass media and employ them for their special message, were thwarted by Hollywood. Instead of using the film industry as an instrument, the atomic scientists entered the maze of popular culture and lost their way. Hollywood could hardly be expected to produce a film that denied its formulas of success or its reading of American culture. Shortly thereafter the movie industry developed a special idiom for presenting atomic science in modern society. Nothing could have been more damaging to science and scientists than the science fiction monster films that followed—most of them picturing scientists as inept, careless, and unable to control the forces they unthinkingly unleashed. In a way *The Beginning or the End?* pointed to that road, soon to be taken.[42] The atomic scientists had simply been unable to speak to the American public with an authentic voice through the mass media.

Distortions were bad enough, but charges of treason and disloyalty deeply wounded the atomic scientists. As early as 1947, the AAAS Council had created a special committee on civil liberties for scientists—a sure sign of the growing public malaise about scientific research and especially the disagreements around maintaining nuclear secrets. By the early 1950s the *Bulletin of the Atomic Scientists* was publishing special issues on loyalty oaths, visa problems created by the Internal Security Act of 1950, and other offenses against scientific freedom of speech.[43]

Public expressions of suspicion about the direction and impact of science on society came in large measure from contradictory interpretations of its success. The Manhattan Project was only a first step in developing the vast destructive potential of nuclear energy. As powerful tests and destructive devices streamed out of physics laboratories, there were increasing doubts about the endeavor. Were scientists acting responsibly? Could they be trusted with the secrets they created? Were some of them communists? How could the ordinary man or woman be expected to understand even the rudiments of modern science? If scientists could unleash the miraculous energy of the atom, was it not possible that esoteric forms of knowledge would reveal interplanetary visitors or unseen forces that controlled human destiny?

Philosopher of science Ernest Nagel saw a link between the developing intellectual critique of science and popular suspicions. As he wrote in 1954, "Intellectual historians join hands with preachers and publicists" in blaming the ideological ills of the world on a positivist, scientific philosophy. This, he said, was a "debasement of the scientific enterprise that would have extraordinary consequences.[44] In effect, what Nagel so clearly enunciated here was the precipitous decline of the scientific ethic as the model for redeeming and reconstructing society. It meant the decline of what many intellectuals and reformers since the Progressive Era had assumed: that science offered a method of arranging knowledge and exploring and resolving social problems. Somewhere along the way, natural science had lost its didactic power. It was no longer considered the foundation of democracy.[45]

Another question was the responsibility of scientists for redefining science by the quantum of destruction it could release. Perhaps the public was wrong to blame scientists for the destructiveness that flowed from their research. Yet as the *Christian Century* politely editorialized in 1948, it was untenable to say that "any increase of knowledge is a good thing." A scientist who did not exercise social responsibility was not much different from "a piece of laboratory equipment." A slightly later piece in the same periodical called "Scientists—Our Modern Mercenaries" exchanged etiquette for sarcasm. The anonymous scientist who wrote the article (known as "One of Them") claimed that scientists were "almost wholly devoid of humanitarian impulses, they consider their cold and analytical search for scientific knowledge more important than any current affairs of mere mortals."[46]

When they revisited the role of science in American society, James Conant and Vannevar Bush recognized the dangerous new discord around science. In 1952 Conant warned of a growing tendency to "equate science with magic" that could be "seen on almost every hand." Science was not magic, however. It was a complex orientation to the world that depended in part on observation and in part on generating explanatory theories. In the end, other ways of understanding the world would have to make their peace with science. Religion in particular needed to reconcile itself to the conclusions of science and even adopt the scientific method. This reconciliation could be achieved when "all documentary evidence in support of the doctrines of Christianity or Judaism or any other religion is subject to the same critical examination as the boldest would apply to the scientific explanations of man's origin and development."[47]

Vannevar Bush, writing ten years later in his *Science Is Not Enough*, extended this appraisal. A decade of meeting the communist challenge, of overromantic praise for scientists and accusations of disloyalty, had left the public confused about the meaning of science and the role of the scientist. In fact, many scientists had behaved without grace and good sense. But the religious person need not despair. "He can accept the aid of science, which draws for him a wide universe in all its majesty, with life in all its awe-inspiring complexity. He can accept this knowing that on the central mysteries science cannot speak."[48]

If atomic scientists faced extraordinary public and political confusion about their relation to society, much of this had to do with the important role that religion played in the cultural mastery of nuclear science. Religious commentary accompanied the birth of the atomic age. Immediately after the dropping of the bombs on Hiroshima and Nagasaki, Protestant and Catholic churches began intensive debates over the discovery and meaning of nuclear energy. A number of mainline Protestant groups condemned the use of the bomb, and in March 1946 the National Council of Churches issued a report affirming this position. The Catholic Church also issued strong protests against atomic weaponry. Evangelical groups were sometimes more circumspect, incorporating the bomb into end-time language and apocalyptic thinking, which increased rapidly in the United States after 1945.[49]

At the beginning, scientists had recruited religious organizations as allies. During the acrimonious debates over military control of atomic research in late 1945 and early 1946, the atomic scientists successfully enlisted important religious groups to speak for their autonomy, for freedom of research. In their anxiety to warn the public about the dangers of nuclear warfare, atomic scientists found religious groups were effective friends. In their struggle to direct research toward civilian projects and away from military needs, they received support from Protestants and Catholics.

But joint lobbying on the morals of research and war played only a part in the religion-science dialogue surrounding the bomb. A great deal of the hesitation about science had to do with its purported amorality or, worse, its pretension to substitute for traditional morality. Atomic science opened access to the secret powers of the universe. Here was a discovery, a branch of science, that come upon the world suddenly, without a language, without a history, and unsecured in any cultural context. To religious thinkers, and in a culture saturated with religious traditions, this presented a challenge to interpret the new science inside religious language and Christian allegory. Many of the atomic scientists eventually recognized that their discoveries would be placed in this framework. It was not possible, they discovered, for science to communicate through science alone.

There were also significant individuals who, in their lives, tried to straddle the boundaries between atomic science and religious culture. One of the most interesting of these men was William Pollard, a scientist who worked on the Manhattan Project and then became director of the Oak Ridge Institute of Nuclear Studies after the war. Three years after being appointed to this important position in 1947, Pollard began training to become an Episcopal minister. When his intention first became known, he reported, "The most common explanation for my action interpreted it as a reaction to the guilt of my involvement in the development of atomic weapons." But his goal was actually to reconcile science and faith. He concluded, "I decided that a person could, without violating his intellectual integrity, both think within the framework of a Judeo-Christian view and believe all scientific knowledge of the structure of the world."[50] There was nothing very new in this accommodation to an old and powerful impulse in American culture: to study nature as a means to celebrate a God of creation. Only the issue was new.

Pollard's experience illustrates the complex weave of relationships with religion at the time when scientists appeared to be the sole masters of progress and invention. There were several issues that could not really be separated. First, there was the imputed guilt about the use of atomic bombs. However much scientists rightly claimed to protest their use, they had created fission weapons: they were responsible. But what resources did they have within scientific culture to guide the direction of science? Was the scientific ethic sufficient to make the huge moral decisions about the direction of research and warfare? On what scientific basis could they even argue against employing the atomic bomb? Furthermore, how did the discoveries of the atom and the immense power it granted humans affect the place of mankind in the universe? Was playing God with the fate of civilization a godlike act?

Catholic theologian and neo-Thomist philosopher Jacques Maritain, who had a great deal to say on the reconciliation of science and religion, denied that science could go it alone. Invited to comment on a submission to the *Bulletin of the Atomic Scientists* that stressed the superiority of the scientific ethic to all other cultural constructions, Maritain strongly disagreed. "I think that, as a result of the impact of the application of science on the destiny of mankind," he wrote, "the scientist can no longer be entirely satisfied with his merely scientific work. He is reminded that he is both a scientist and a man, with his responsibilities as a man." He invoked an oft-repeated dichotomy to explain what he meant. Science provided the means, but wisdom and religion defined the ends toward which science should be turned.[51]

The atomic scientists movement paid careful attention to critiques of religious thinkers, and the *Bulletin* periodically published discussions around the moral and ethical problems created by nuclear research. The religious argument was predictable: science had no moral gyroscope; alone, it could lead nowhere. Archbishop Richard J. Cushing of Boston made this very plain in his address (reprinted in the *Bulletin* in 1948) before science clubs at Boston University. The elevation of science in the modern age could be an undiluted evil. Scientists had lost their ears for culture and their eyes for nature. "Such men are tone-deaf and colorblind in the world of certain aesthetic values," he warned. The results were well known: "It is a tragic fact that the worlds of Prussian science, of Nipponese science, of Soviet science and let us be honest, of Democratic science have produced men equally insensible to the world of moral values."[52]

Some scientists appeared to agree with this charge. The *Bulletin* printed a number of articles from the late 1940s through the mid-1950s that repeated this argument or its variant that scientists required some form of faith to resist the demand of governments to pervert their work into offensive military weapons. This latter position had for many years been associated with Albert Einstein, and he articulated it often. As he put it in a speech in 1950, "Let me then make a confession: for myself, the struggle to gain more insight and understanding is one of those independent objectives without which a thinking individual would find it impossible to have a conscious, positive attitude toward life."[53]

That the *Bulletin* hoped for some sort of reconciliation with religion, particularly the Catholic Church, is revealed in its discussion in 1952 and 1953 of Pope Pius XII's conciliatory words about science. This became possible when the pope spoke of the theory of evolution and repudiated a necessarily literal interpretation of the creation story. In 1951 he praised modern astrophysics for revealing new theories of the origin of the universe.[54]

In March 1955 the *Bulletin* published two important articles that drew the line between the realms of science and religion. A long essay by Pierre Auger of the Natural Sciences Department of UNESCO argued unabashedly for the supremacy of the scientific way of looking at the world and its superior community of international ethics. Auger anticipated the opposing arguments and the criticisms of his position. But, he countered, modern humans must end their adolescence and recognize "the disappearance of the antique cosmos, and its replacement by the scientific universe." We could, he concluded, no longer ask the sorts of questions that would lead to answers of faith and magic. Only a genuine engagement with the natural world in which humanity gave up "common sense" for the hard and often surprising research of modern science would be appropriate. It would take courage to do so, for it meant losing "the wonderful gifts of imagination and the natural taste" of adolescence for the hard reality of adulthood.[55]

Protestant theologian Reinhold Niebuhr's response was acerbic. Auger, in proclaiming his belief in the triumph of scientific method, was in fact only reviving an old argument from nineteenth-century French social theory (Comtian positivism). Auger shared, he said, "one of the pathetic illusions of our culture," propagated mostly by social scientists, that history could be interpreted and guided scientifically. This wrongheaded conclusion depended on the assumption that science could manage human behavior. This, Niebuhr concluded, had long been discredited "by the obvious fact that they are akin to illusions by which the present despotic potential managers of history, namely the Communists, are inspired." Such harsh words were not an accusation that scientists held radical political opinions. Niebuhr always carried the communist example in his portfolio because to him it expressed the essential distinction between science and religion. Science, he argued, must finally return to religion, because left to itself it invited arrogance and destruction, Soviet style.[56]

If the atomic scientists quickly learned the strength of American politics and the temperament of culture when they attempted to shape research policy or express their hopes for a world government infused by scientific principle, they had only realized what others repeatedly recognized, forgot, and then learned again.[57] Science in American culture could not be just abstract theory and experimentation; it meant that plus a comet's tail of social, political, and religious implications. In their encounter with the anomalies of culture, scientists found that religion was a ready competitor, consisting of a net of deep-seated moral ideas to capture and hold science.[58]

There was one more reason scientists after the war discovered religion to be a cousin to their efforts. This has to do with the background, upbringing, and beliefs of scientists themselves and the long-term affinity of scientific exploration and American Protestant culture. A number of sociologists and other observers of the time commented on the heavy overrepresentation of scientists with a Protestant background in the United States during this period and before. For some historians this was more than accidental, for, they argued, science and Protestantism had a mutually sustaining, friendly relationship during and after the English Enlightenment extending through the seventeenth-century Puritan revolution. The division of labor created by Francis Bacon and other thinkers ensured the independence of scientific thinking. This tendency simply carried over to the United States.[59]

There are elements of truth in this historical judgment, although the relationship between religion and science in the United States has been as contentious as it has been smooth. In particular, Darwinism and various twentieth-century theories of physics have created antagonism between scientists and some religious groups. It also remains true that Protestants made up the bulk of American scientists as late as the 1960s. Scientists have been drawn disproportionately from the Quakers, Unitarians, and Church of the Brethren. A second large group includes those from from Jewish backgrounds. Catholics, on the other hand, had a lower representation than expected. Of institutions that turned out the highest percentage of practicing scientists, western and midwestern schools were the most productive. Of leading scientific schools, City College, Brooklyn, Queens, Yeshiva, Brigham Young, Utah State, and the University of Utah were the front runners, followed by small midwestern Protestant colleges.[60]

The preponderance of scientists with Protestant backgrounds at the center of the American scientific enterprise may or may not indicate the hospitality of certain forms of religious sects for laboratory research and scientific speculation. But it does suggest the relevance of Protestant culture for the encounter of American science with issues of religion. The very

familiarity of scientists with forms of Protestantism suggests that their response to challenges to the self-sufficiency of science and the ethics of the
scientific community would be explored along Protestant lines. This does
not mean, of course, that Catholic and Jewish versions of the struggle between science and religion were unimportant. Nothing is less true. Indeed,
all three religions were deeply engaged with the issue after World War II.
But the most dramatic encounters were set upon the stage of a Protestant
heritage within American culture. On this stage scientists declaimed their
superior ethic, their exemption from the historical and cultural authority of
traditional morality and politics. But from here, offstage voices chided
them for their arrogance and prompted them to speak on more modest lines
about the benefits of modern science and more favorably of religion. As
Lewis Mumford wrote in 1942, "Man does not live by machine alone." It
was a prophetic Americanization of the old biblical proverb for the time.[61]

The elaborate reverence of even religious thinkers before the pretensions of science is a measure of the decadence of our culture.

Reinhold Niebuhr (1954)

Chapter 4

A World without John Dewey

John Dewey was one of the most important and accomplished social philosophers of science in the twentieth century, yet he and his ideas are either absent from or the source of controversy in discussions of science and religion during the 1940s and 1950s. In fact, the most important organization to sponsor a dialogue between science and religion in this period established an agenda that specifically rejected Dewey's pragmatic vision. This effort, carried out by the ongoing Conference on Science, Philosophy, and Religion in Their Relation to the Democratic Way of Life, founded in 1939 at the Jewish Theological Seminary in New York

City, underscored a crucial polarization among intellectuals before and during World War II. It also specified the terms for an enduring dialogue among members of America's East Coast academic elite about the relation of science to religion during the postwar period.

Although we might assume that the seeds of this modern dialogue about science and religion were sown in the midnight sun of atomic energy and raised in the glare of its aftermath, we are in fact looking at a harvest of ideas in the 1940s and 1950s, not their semination. Some of these criticisms and hesitations accorded to the proposals and reputation of the Los Alamos generation had already been widely rehearsed even before the heyday of postwar big science and atomic energy.

For a variety of reasons—some international, some indigenous—the 1930s were a time when Dewey's scientized social philosophy and its European counterpart in logical positivism aroused worry and opposition among religious and idealist thinkers in America. Dewey himself confessed to feeling besieged, and attacks on him were frequent and serious. Even if Dewey was only the pretext, the symbol for complicated and ambiguous attitudes toward the prevailing norms of social science and democratic theory, the ruckus was genuine and the effects were severe.[1]

To John Dewey, the 1930s were the best of times and the worst of times. By all accounts he traveled in the fast lane of influence, called on not just to impart wisdom on philosophy, aesthetics, and social science but to judge the political situation. Yet in the mid-1930s he asked despairingly: "What is the cause of the sudden decline of faith in the method of free, experimental inquiry and of the recrudescence of dogmatic authorities, backed by physical force?"[2] A revolt against science, he worried, was gathering in almost every field. This sudden philosophic uprising was based in a false distinction between pure and applied science—as if technology could somehow be separated from the experimental method that explained it.[3] Another destructive division proposed to separate science from ethics, with science and its method of empirical inquiry consigned only to mundane practical matters, while loftier questions awaited an audience in the antechamber of theology.[4] The most costly divide, he noted at a Conference on Methods in Philosophy and the Sciences in 1937, affected education. "The retreat from reason is the penalty we are paying for an inherent dichotomy in the way we educate people," he noted. The reason: statesmen and men of letters understood almost nothing of the technical forces shaping society, and scientists appeared unconcerned about the consequences of their research.[5]

These were developments that made the movement for the Unity of Science attractive to Dewey. Organized in Vienna and Prague in the early 1930s by scientific philosophers Otto Neurath, Philipp Frank, and others, the movement represented a modern form of the great Enlightenment encyclopedia movement. By proclaiming the virtues of positivistic science and pushing toward the unification of sciences, the movement hoped to close the gap between science and philosophy. At various conferences in the 1930s, scientists gathered to shape this emergent unity and end the departmentalization and excessive specialization among scientists. They proposed universal scientific axioms and sought to coordinate scientific language. It was, as Neurath said, an attempt to unify science while preserving all its different emphases. The unity of science would never impose some external philosophy on the various sciences but would distill from them their elements of similarity and coherence.[6]

Dewey contributed one of the first articles to appear in the movement's *International Encyclopedia of Unified Science* in 1938. His essay focused on unifying science through practical problem solving. He was persuaded that scientific thought manifested itself in all walks of life: a farmer, a mechanic, a chauffeur, an engineer—each applied scientific thinking. The "enemies of scientific attitude," however, attacked this universal method by appealing in their own self-interest to the obscurities of routine, prejudice, and dogma that had always dirtied the lens of traditional philosophy. The proper course was for science to organize around eliminating social problems. There it could reveal its fundamental unity—between life and thought, between common sense and theory.[7]

Implicit in the philosopher's arguments were acute moral and aesthetic sensibilities that he had absorbed from the historical roots of American religious tradition.[8] But to his critics Dewey appeared to collapse all such concerns into an omnibus scientific method, with a single method of inquiry replacing the entreaties of faith and social science substituting for ethics. To his religious adversaries, Dewey's mortal sin was trespass. His philosophy claimed relevance to arenas to which religion and idealist philosophy laid exclusive claim. More than most of his contemporaries, Dewey was a scion of the Enlightenment and a proponent of secularism.[9]

Opposition to Dewey's philosophy arose from many quarters—the communist left and traditional Catholic and Protestant theologians—but some of the sharpest barbs were hurled from the castellated walls of the University of Chicago. Long since departed from the university, Dewey

nevertheless maintained considerable influence in the philosophy department, a presence that two men in particular hoped to efface. They were the
philosopher Mortimer J. Adler and John Maynard Hutchins, the new president of the university.

After a stint at Yale Law School, Hutchins became president of the University of Chicago in 1929 at the age of thirty. The son of a Presbyterian
minister and by training a legal scholar, he pushed for a radical reform of
higher education to modify the contemporary emphasis on electives and
scientific training. His curriculum stressed hierarchy, great works of literature and philosophy, and the permanent truths of civilization. Hutchins's
task was not easy, nor was the road clear. Frequent sallies at convocation
speeches and in papers disputing the sufficiency of the scientific method
provoked an uproar among the faculty. For example, in 1934 he denounced
the philosophies of mere "facts." William James and John Dewey, he
argued, were the leading anti-intellectuals of "our time." This anti-
intellectual position "must be repudiated if a university is to achieve
its ends."[10]

To aid in developing a new curriculum, Hutchins hired Mortimer Adler,
a young philosopher from Columbia University. While at Columbia, Adler
had taught with poet Mark Van Doren in a great books honors course where
he could indulge his preference for the history of ideas. He had also studied
philosophy with Dewey. Hutchins hoped that Adler could wean the philosophy department from the influence of George Herbert Mead and other
Dewey sympathizers, but Adler failed and left the department in 1931. Beneath these academic squabbles, Hutchins and Adler were developing their
great books curriculum. Failing to win acceptance at Chicago until 1943,
the curriculum was installed at St. John's College in Maryland in 1937.[11]

When Hutchins published his reform proposals in *The Higher Learning
in America* in 1936, Dewey wrote a scathing review. Hutchins, in attacking
democratic education and the idea of progress, claimed that excessive faith
in science had undermined the house of intellect. "Somewhat strangely,"
Dewey wrote, "the natural sciences are regarded by Mr. Hutchins as the
cause and the mirror of this [destructive] empiricism." Yet Hutchins's proposal to reinstall "ultimate first principles" represented an authoritarian
counterrevolution. His admired sages, Aristotle and Saint Thomas
Aquinas, might be competent advocates of first truths, but their prestige
rested solely on the "authority of a powerful ecclesiastic organization [the
Catholic Church]."[12] Dewey made no effort to disguise the source of his

anger: no "truth" established outside experience and science could be universalized except through authority or force. This undermined democracy, and Dewey made no apology for implying that Hutchins was its enemy.

Undaunted by these attacks on his associate, Adler published two books in 1940 that expounded his viewpoint, based on the works of the great medieval theologian Thomas Aquinas. In these works Adler gave subtle recognition to unspoken tension with Dewey over the Roman Catholic Church. Dewey was usually careful to avoid overt attacks on the Catholic Church, and as a Jew Adler was certainly not defending it. But the choice to argue over Aristotle and Saint Thomas on both sides was not accidental. Eventually this dispute would break out into open warfare, with both sides hurling exaggerated accusations.[13]

The first of Adler's works, on hierarchy, explored the deep chasm dividing modern science from philosophy. Paraphrasing Harvard astronomer Harlow Shapley, Adler recounted the results of his famous experiment. While measuring various objects in the universe, from "the smallest atomic particle to the largest galaxy of stars," Shapley observed that mankind seemed to fall somewhere in the middle. The scientist deduced nothing from this find, but Adler leaped to a momentous conclusion. If you replace respective size with a concept of hierarchy, he argued, then mankind occupied the middle—the center. This was a working demonstration of design in a God-created order.[14]

Just as there were hierarchy and fixed species in nature, so knowledge itself was organized in ascending order, he continued. It flowed upward from "history [the lowest] to science, from science to philosophy, from philosophy to theology, to mystical wisdom, and ultimately to the vision of God."[15] By pushing science down, near the base of the pyramid of knowledge, Adler hoped to truncate its influence. Science was empirical; its knowledge was accidental. Philosophy, on the other hand, contemplated the essential. Science was merely a way of knowing things in their variety and according to their changes—not by their fixed nature. Science might study nature but it could never know it as philosophy did.[16]

If this position appears dissonant with the reputation of Chicago in the 1930s as a modern center for scientific and sociological learning, it was in another sense a reaffirmation of the university's religious roots. Its first president, William Rainey Harper, had been a biblical scholar, and the early days of the institution saw considerable effort to establish a holistic view of religion and social science. Faculty members such as the physicist Robert

Millikan preached the compatibility of religion and science in the chapel. Still, the faculty remained deeply skeptical of Hutchins's and Adler's attempts to reform the curriculum.[17]

In his memoirs Adler recounts that he and Hutchins became deeply discouraged toward the end of the 1930s. They had not installed their program of academic reform at Chicago. Attacks on them continued, and John Dewey's philosophy still seemed entrenched. Worse, said Adler, the excesses of scientific faith had contributed substantially to the grave social crisis of European fascism. Thus when Adler received an invitation to serve on the steering committee of the first Conference on Science, Philosophy, and Religion, he carried the dispute with Dewey with him, hoping to use the conference to advertise his own position. In so doing, he injected Chicago's academic politics into a national discussion of religion and science. He also posed a question that almost destroyed the conference before it began: If philosophy and theology were superior to science, if they claimed to measure questions of ethics and metaphysics not accessible to science, shouldn't the conference say so? Shouldn't it accept his hierarchy of disciplines and confine science to the bottom?[18] This blunt question posed by Adler became a kind of defining theme in the history of the conference.

Adler and Hutchins were not alone in attributing the political and social crisis of the 1930s to a crisis of faith and tradition. For quite different reasons, Rabbi Louis Finkelstein of the Jewish Theological Seminary in New York City developed a similar analysis. A member of the administration of the Theological Seminary in the late 1930s and then president after 1940, Finkelstein was a leading light in the Conservative Judaic tradition in America. Founded to bridge the gap between tradition and modernism in Jewish adjustment to American life, the Conservative movement, since the late nineteenth century, had remained a peripheral theological and organizational force under the leadership of such men as Solomon Schechter and Cyrus Adler. Finkelstein was an activist, however, who sought to push Conservatism into the forefront and to inject Judaism into the mainstream of American discourse about its most precious traditions of democracy and freedom.[19]

In the late 1930s, Finkelstein aggressively pursued these twin goals. Under his sponsorship the seminary created the Jewish Museum in New York and began the radio program "The Eternal Light." In 1938 Finkelstein organized the Institute for Religious and Social Studies (originally the Institute of Inter-Denominational Studies), which welcomed ministers and

graduate students of various Christian denominations to study with a mul-
tidenominational faculty. It initially proposed to provide Christian theological students and clergymen with more intimate knowledge of Judaism. As
Finkelstein explained in a history of the organization, it also organized a
united front against fascism and communism. "These ministers," wrote
Finkelstein, "are thus searching out for especial emphasis those elements in
their traditions which go back to the Prophets of Israel, but belong essentially to all groups of American theistic religion"—in other words, the
Judeo-Christian tradition.[20] This interfaith effort quickly evolved to another purpose: to find agreement between religion, science, and democratic
practice.[21]

Finkelstein's effort to write Judaism into the history of American
democracy, his advocacy of a vibrant Judeo-Christian/American heritage,
inspired his activities for many years. This was intensified by the urgent tug
of events in Europe and the sour atmosphere of anti-Semitism in the
United States during the late 1930s. As William Albright (professor of Se-
mitic languages at Johns Hopkins University) recalled of the founding, the
catalyst was the radio priest Father Charles Coughlin's growing strength in
the Catholic Church. Many thoughtful Jews, he wrote, "and our president,
Dr. Finkelstein, became more and more conscious of this danger." Finkelstein's proposed to relocate Judaism within the American patrimony, as the
philosophical basis of liberal democracy. As Paul Weiss, a member of the executive committee of the conference, told the group in September 1940,
"The religion of modern democracy has a Hebraic as well as a Christian
strain; but the Hebraic is more deeply grounded, nearer to the core of
things, at the very source of whatever is religious."[22]

Finkelstein was not unique in discussing the Judeo-Christian tradition,
but he was one of its principal early advocates. Just across Broadway, at
Union Theological Seminary, Protestant theologian Reinhold Niebuhr also
began to speak of the same tradition at about the same time. To Niebuhr the
tradition emphasized the concepts of sinfulness, faith, and prophecy
against a corrupt Protestantism tainted with Enlightenment science and
Greek secularism. To some degree Finkelstein shared this orientation.[23]

But why his preoccupation with science, why sympathize with Adler in
his dispute with Dewey? Finkelstein, despite his own sympathies for science, worried deeply about rampant skepticism in the late 1930s. He interpreted the world crisis initiated by Germany, Spain, and Italy as a situation
generated in the darkness of secularism and spread by the imperial claims of

science. A social science world, he worried, would inevitably surrender to the potent force of human depravity and greed. The best response to this threat, he believed, was to bring together scientists, philosophers, and theologians to restore unity to the divided modern mind. What better way than to establish a new concordance of science with religion? For Finkelstein this was no stealthy effort to slip under the wire into the camp of liberal Protestantism or to join the modernists who had brought science and religion together in a celebration of progress. Finkelstein vigorously opposed the religious compromises that granted John Dewey an eminent position among Protestant liberals. The democracy he sought to join grew from the soil of religious tradition, not science.

Finkelstein had confided his hesitations about modern science as far back as the mid-1930s to President Henry Sloane Coffin of Union Theological Seminary. To explore the problem, he initiated a series of lectures on science and religion at the Institute of Interdenominational Studies. He succeeded in attracting important scientists and theologians. In one significant address in 1938, University of Chicago physicist Arthur Holly Compton spoke to students of the compelling interrelation between science and religion.[24] Finkelstein hoped to make this dialogue a permanent, ongoing feature of the seminary, but by early November 1939 he unveiled a new plan. He convinced a group of important scientists, theologians, and public intellectuals to attend a planning session for a conference of scientists, theologians, and philosophers to confront—and perhaps resolve—the dangerous divisions of knowledge and faith in American culture.[25] In a confidential memorandum written before the meeting, Finkelstein was frank. "The decay of religion which, in the opinion of so many observers including Professor Albert Einstein and Bertrand Russell, is largely responsible for the moral debacle lying at the root of our troubles, is at least partly the result of the supposed antagonism between Science and Religion."[26]

The group met on 3 November 1939 in New York at the seminary and included several figures who emerged as leaders of the ongoing conference. They included Coffin, Compton, Dr. Hughell E. W. Fosbroke, Protestant theologian from the General Theological Seminary, John A. Mackay, from Princeton Theological Seminary; Thomist scholar Father Anton Pegis of Fordham University; Harlow Shapley, Jewish historian Alexander Marx of the Jewish Theological Seminary; Protestant theologian and biblical scholar Frederick C. Grant of Union Theological Seminary; and Harold

Figure 4.1   Rabbi Louis Finkelstein, Harlow Shapley, and Father Gerald Phelan at the eighth Conference on Science, Philosophy, and Religion, held in 1947. Courtesy of the Joseph and Miriam Ratner Center for the Study of Conservative Judaism, Jewish Theological Seminary of America.

Lasswell of the William Alanson White Psychiatric Foundation in Washington, D.C.

The discussion opened with tentative assertions, a mutual sounding of depths to make the measure of differences. Scientists Compton and Shapley were edgy about relating science and religion, yet both acceded to the general proposition that divisions of knowledge and the warfare of clergy, philosophers, and scientists had deeply injured modern society. The sense of crisis was palpable. MacKay told the group, "[we are experiencing a] major calamity of our contemporary civilization." This dire situation occurred for one of the "first times in history for many centuries at least." There could be no hope unless "we can evolve some basic idea to which people of intelligence in the different spheres of life would pledge."[27]

Response to two questions united and divided the participants. To what extent could it be said that Judaism and Christianity were historically necessary to the development of modern science? In other words, what was the historic relation between Western science and religion? The second problem posed a variant of the same question: What similarities and differences united and divided contemporary science and religion as ways of knowing and acting?

Rabbi Finkelstein insisted on describing religion (Judaism and Christianity) as the soil in which American democracy and scientific culture blossomed. Arthur Compton agreed: "You relate it, and I believe quite properly, to the Jewish and Christian culture, as incubating the scientific period." Although Shapley wondered out loud how Compton could concede such a point, Compton stood his ground. The historical connection was crucial, all the more so because it was never "adequately considered by the scientific men."[28]

Finkelstein pushed the group to accept a public statement announcing the establishment "of a school for the advancement of religion, science, and democracy. It is our opinion that this school will further the spiritual life of the whole American people." Its intent was to strengthen denominations, "deepen religious faith, and in this way serve as a bulwark for democratic ideals."[29] What Finkelstein had in mind was unmistakable in a discussion document that he produced. American democracy, he declared, "stands on the firm rock of belief in God, and in human brotherhood and dignity." The United States was no bland melting pot, but rather a federal system of religions and prophetic faiths. Yet totalitarianism abroad and confusion at home had created "spiritual decay." Our civilization might produce an Einstein, an Edison, and a Ford, but not a great writer or a memorable philosopher. "We must face the fact," he warned, "that humanity today is suffering from a general breakdown of character."

Finkelstein's cure extended his metaphor of crisis. The echo of malaise inside the United States resounded with the European catastrophe. Excessive belief in science provoked a similar dangerous situation in America. Paganism and atheism abroad and scientism at home were acids that ate away the spiritual basis of society. A restored ecumenism would bind members of the three great American faiths—Catholics, Protestants, and Jews—to modern science; spirit would alloy with science. "The literature and doctrinal teachings of each faith will be used to strengthen all faiths. The investigations and techniques of science will be brought into the service of religion. Out of this effort and similar undertakings there may emerge a better appreciation of the religious foundations of America's democratic institutions."[30]

The group responded to Finkelstein's entreaties and agreed to organize a continuing conference. The phraseology was opaque and understated Finkelstein's frank attempt to put religion at the core of American values. The purpose seemed more general and entirely noncontroversial: simply to encourage a joint effort to advance democracy. But one development hinted at discordant dynamics within the group. Shapley insisted on reversing the words in the title. It must be a conference on science, philosophy, and religion—in that order.[31] The group quickly agreed.

On the substance of how to relate method and knowledge in religion and science nothing was settled, but a prolonged discussion of the issue suggested the outline of problems that would later arise in the permanent conference. Compton and Pegis, for example, debated whether theology could be considered a science—the Thomist scholar suggesting that it could be and Compton denying this because it "did not rest upon experience."

Harlow Shapley, despite his testiness about the analytical validity of theology, mused about the potential of religion to respond to large spiritual questions. He struck a disingenuous pose: "I am entirely naive as to what the job in religion is, but it seems to me that it is something about man's relationship to the universe."[32] The astronomer did not choose his words well or make his thoughts very sharp, but his position was clear. He was an unrepentant scientist: he rejected traditional theology, theologians, and philosophers because he believed in the sufficiency of the experimental method. Yet there were yearnings of the cosmos in his response. Life was pregnant with meaning; evolution of the universe might reveal God or some sort of perfectibility. He simply wasn't sure. This stance as the religious naïf thrust Shapley into the inner circle of the conference and under the influence of Finkelstein, with whom he long remained associated. It confirmed him as a seeker, a joiner of conversations and organizations devoted to exploring the potential fusion of religion and science. It was a belief he never achieved yet persisted in pursuing.

Shapley's religious quest was shaped in a life of remarkable social mobility and change. From a small town in Missouri, he went to Princeton University as a graduate student of the astronomer Henry Norris Russell. In 1913 he found a position at the Mount Wilson Observatory in California. His important work revised estimates of the size of the Milky Way, and he produced a comprehensive catalog of galaxies. By the late 1930s he had moved east to become director of the Harvard Observatory and founder of the Graduate School in Astronomy at Harvard. He was the most widely cited astronomer in America during this decade. Shapley also won recognition as a public intellectual and a determined popularizer of science. Widely quoted in the press, he sought out discussions about science and science policy. A political radical during the 1930s, he advocated government funding of scientific research and worked to bring anti-Nazi scientists to the United States.

Some of Shapley's astronomical works had a direct impact on the argument between religion and science, and he was conscious of their implications; indeed, he probably overdramatized them. In 1917 and 1918, working at Mount Wilson Observatory, he made the measure of the galaxy and found that the "solar system is off center and consequently man is too." This discovery amounted to the "overthrow of the Copernican theory." Not even the heliocentric compromise worked. It was time for a "Fourth Adjustment," for mankind to realize that humans are not even at the center of a minor galaxy.[33]

Imagining himself a kind of Copernicus, Shapley exhibited both the pretense and misgivings of a scientist whose faith remained in the scientific method and yet who entertained the possibility of religion. Engaged in practical science, he joined organization after organization devoted to bringing together science and religion—organizations in which he played the skeptic drawn close to the light of belief. He might write about "anthropomorphic culprits who misuse cosmic terms in their chatter about the silly affairs of a short-lived species on a mean planet." Then, a few pages later, he could say: "We see in the new astronomical revelations the stuff that philosophic dreams are made of. We see the stars as providers of human interest of the deepest kind—as feeders of the inherent religious hunger."[34] This was the Harlow Shapley who helped organize scientists to attend the continuing Conference on Science, Philosophy, and Religion. Here was an enthusiastic supporter of Rabbi Louis Finkelstein, a fellow seeker for religion in a world of science. The organization would have been very different without him.

Together Finkelstein, Shapley, and the other assembled participants in the November 1939 meeting issued a call for a formal conference on integrating science, philosophy, and religion, planned for the fall of 1940. "It is our opinion," they offered, that such a conference would enlarge the "appreciation of the meaning of life and culture" and contribute to the "foundation of a true civilization." This was not a group that took itself lightly or hedged its ambitions. In times of dire need, they affirmed, intellectuals had to find a unity of purpose and possibly even method. Civilization itself rested on their deliberations.[35]

Given the daunting task of reversing the secular bias of American intellectual life, strident debate broke out even before the first public meeting of the conference in September 1940. A maelstrom of controversy swirled around the hardheaded elitism of Mortimer Adler. Early in 1940 Finkelstein wrote to Adler asking him to join the conference and then traveled to Chicago to consult with him.[36] Spring found Adler thick into the planning, where he pushed hard to shape the speeches and the audience. In April he wrote to Finkelstein expressing concern about "the wisdom of inviting the logical positivists to the Conference." I hope, he said, that you have no intention of allowing the meeting to "degenerate to the [low] level of an American Philosophical Association meeting." Losing on the count of exclusion, he retreated, threatening to stay away himself. The meeting, as planned, would speak at cross-purposes and in great confusion. Worse, he concluded, "I'm an impolite sort of fellow and am likely to insult my colleagues if they talk as stupidly as they usually do."[37]

Reassured that he would be heeded, Adler sent a deliberately provocative "contract" to Finkelstein for agreement by other planners of the conference. This he titled "On the Fundamental Position" of the conference. For truth to prevail, he declared, hierarchy must rule. The conference should unanimously "repudiate the scientism or positivism which dominates every aspect of modern culture." This intellectual oath pledged intolerance for error. Most important, it declared that "religious knowledge, because supernaturally generated, must be superior to philosophy and science as merely natural knowledge."[38]

In large measure Finkelstein agreed, although he worried about Adler's tone—arrogance perhaps would be better. "I agree with you absolutely, and unreservedly, in your strictures about the fundamental problems of American education." We cannot solve this without "a vivid, philosophical, and profound faith in God, which must permeate our whole field of thought," he responded. But the conference could not abandon those men who had a "fragment of knowledge about the reasons for the decay of our civilization," so the invitation list had to remain fairly ecumenical. Still, Finkelstein was reassuring and even conspiratorial. The vast number of Adler's critics, he noted ("and I have heard from quite a number of them during the course of last year"), hadn't the slightest idea what the Chicago scholar was talking about. Come early to plan strategy, he urged. "It is vital that our purposes in this should not be misunderstood; and that we should not permit the mischief makers, who seek to increase the confusion of American intellectual life, to misinterpret us."[39]

One critic who heartily seconded Adler's (and Finkelstein's) position was the literary critic Van Wyck Brooks. For several years Brooks had worried over a separation in American letters between the despairing view of modernism and the firm, deeply felt literature of middle America. Others who agreed with Adler (to some extent) included some of the Catholic theologians invited to the conference. Many of the scientists and social scientists were outraged, however, and expressed themselves with abandon at the preliminary planning session that met in August 1940. When Adler insisted that philosophy and religion rule the conference, Harlow Shapley responded that the purpose of the conference was "exploration." The British-American sociologist Robert MacIver was even sharper: Adler's demands would ruin the conference. Adler persisted: "The aim of free speech is not to go on being free." The purpose of knowledge is to move through chaos and "the contemporary corrupt liberalism" toward certainty.

The intellectual heat continued to rise. William Albright voiced what many in the room thought: Adler's methods smacked of fascism. This assertion brought a rush to compromise. Finkelstein in particular claimed that science, philosophy, and religion represented different orders of knowledge—none was inferior to any other. But Adler would not bend: "Either philosophy is superior to science, as knowledge, both theoretically and practically, or it doesn't exist." Shapley couldn't contain himself. He retorted to Adler: "I wish you would read a little science some time. You make such a dogmatic statement."[40] And so erupted the very sort of dispute that Finkelstein had hoped to avoid. Yet his sympathy with Adler persuaded him to insist that he be included. The group rejected Adler's memorandum as an intellectual superstructure for the conference, but the philosopher promised Finkelstein he would deliver an address that would repeat these strident ideas.

Before the public conference several of the founding members issued press releases that, taken together, added up to a strangely discordant call for philosophic unity. The official announcement declared unity and equality among disciplines: "There is no suggestion that any discipline should become subject to another; nor is there any thought of reducing the various religious traditions to a common denominator." Press release after release, however, contradicted this compact of equality. The chair of the Harvard sociology department, Pitirim Sorokin, proclaimed the subordination of science to the "control of goodness and beauty." William Albright contributed another version of the inadequacy of science. "The positivistic faith," he contended, "may content the religious humanist, but it does not satisfy a world of men and women who, deprived of the old faith in God, make themselves new gods in the image of Hitler." Louis Finkelstein dressed his position in more moderate language: "The truth is, of course, that the more science we have, the more character building religion is demanded." Scientist Arthur Holly Compton agreed with this analysis. The terrible divisions of the world could be cured only by recognizing God's ultimate reign. "This is the central theme of Christianity. It is prominent also in the teachings of Judaism." But Harlow Shapley argued the contrary. Science could not be faulted for the contemporary crisis even if there had been a severe decline in morality. The remedy was more science, not less. "To make the moral achievement implicit in science a source of strength to civilization," he said, "the scientist will have to have the cooperation also of the philosopher and the religious teacher."[41]

The first conference, held one month later, 9–11 September 1940, at the Jewish Theological Seminary, extended the dispute. The first day was spent in executive session as the founding members met to discuss the public conference. Although Adler did not appear, his presence attended. Shapley in particular fumed at the philosopher after reading his paper. "My first feeling about the paper and the attitude is that it is absurd." He was so angry that he asked to criticize Adler's accusations off the record. Shapley had warned Finkelstein earlier; he would try to contain himself so that the room would not have to "be fumigated."[42] During the afternoon session, philosopher Sidney Hook denounced Adler: his speech should not be given in public because it was so inflammatory and abusive.[43]

When the public sessions convened the next morning, Van Wyck Brooks's remarks on American intellectual life set a critical tone. In his critique of American letters he warned, "the writers have ceased to be *voices of the people.*" Worse, they have become self-consciously "high brow," with the result that literature had become *off-center.*" What the people once possessed—and writers had now repudiated—was a "core of unity," an agreement on "certain *religious and philosophical* postulates" that enriched their understanding of science and literature.[44] Brooks insisted on restoring harmony among the various disciplines and collaboration between forms of knowledge inside the rich moral tradition of American democracy and culture. Although this was not quite Adler's point, it expressed the spirit of the philosopher's hierarchy of knowledge.[45]

Adler disappointed no one who knew about his speech in advance. As expected, his paper "God and the Professors" outraged much of the audience, especially those who harbored sympathy for John Dewey. The problem of contemporary society, he declared, was its cultural decadence. This sorry state sprang from the disordered minds of teachers and intellectual leaders. The proof was demonstrated in the terrible reviews accorded Robert Hutchins's book, *The Higher Learning in America,* of which John Dewey's had been the worst. In a particularly risky statement Adler concluded, "Democracy has much more to fear from the mentality of its teachers than from the nihilism of Hitler." A world without hierarchy meant a planet in chaos. "Science contributes nothing whatsoever to the understanding of Democracy," he continued in another thinly veiled swipe at Dewey. "So, perhaps, the Hitlers in the world today are preparing the agony through which our culture shall be reborn." We need to be saved not from them "but from the professors."[46]

Sidney Hook, as a representative of the very scientific pragmatism Adler had denounced, replied with fury. In his memoirs, he recounts the disorderly scene. Finkelstein chaired the session where Adler spoke and "tried to cut me off several times during my relatively brief but vigorous criticism of Adler's remarks by stamping hard on my foot under cover of the low wood partition that separated us from the audience." Hook linked Adler's remarks to neo-Thomism and the broad attacks on Dewey by the Catholic Church and Protestant Fundamentalists during the 1930s—all of which seemed to come to a head at this moment.[47] His most telling point, however, cut with the sharp edge of common sense: "We have just been told that American democracy is in greater danger from its professors than from Hitlerism. Such a statement is not merely false but irresponsible, and, at the present time doubly so." Beyond that, he concluded, John Dewey was right about President Hutchins because the latter had "abandoned the field" in his exchange with Dewey.[48]

Although Adler's intemperate remarks produced both smoke and fire, his position was not unique among the philosophers and theologians who attended the conference. He tapped a swell of pent-up resentment against science and the growing prominence of secular social science. Others besides Adler and Brooks took up the call for a more religious orientation in culture. Harvard Sociologist Pitirim Sorokin proposed a rejuvenated, "more Godly, nobler," civilization based on the spiritual reality beyond the sensate world. Lyman Bryson, of Columbia Teachers College, responded from the opposite perspective. All the men he knew who approached life "in the highest term" were "devoted to science and none of them are devoted to philosophy."[49] Sorokin, however, would not be dissuaded. The "best formula of democracy which I know of," he continued, "is given in the New Testament in the Sermon on the Mount."[50]

Remarks by the French Catholic philosopher and leading neo-Thomist Jacques Maritain initiated another bid to subordinate science to religion. Before the first meeting, Finkelstein and the French philosopher had corresponded extensively about the principles that should guide the conference. Maritain worried that some of the founding members were persons "imbued with positivistic prejudices, misinterpreting philosophy and theology and making of experimental science the supreme standard of thought." This error, he said, would set back the cause. So he suggested excluding "a priori" those who denied autonomy to philosophy and theology. In August he urged Finkelstein to change the public announcement of the conference because it implied that no discipline was superior to any another. Maritain objected. Subordination was the point, hierarchy the structure; anything else entailed error and chaos. Most important, he persuaded Finkelstein to drop a proposed paper by Yale philosopher Brand Blandshard. Blandshard later protested that this "censorship" amounted to a "Catholic veto against public criticism of church policy."[51]

At the conference Maritain likewise argued for a hierarchical system of knowledge, with religion premier and philosophy and science entitled only to lesser portfolios. Edwin E. Aubrey, a University of Chicago Protestant theologian, rejected Maritain's theocratic vision and insisted instead that religion and science were too distinct to conflict. Philosopher Harry Overstreet of the City College of New York pulled the discussion back from the brink. Maritain was wrong about a hierarchy of disciplines. How could a conference devoted to unity of knowledge propose such a devastating delusion? How could it say, "But we philosophers, you know, are superior to you poor scientists who are only dealing with phenomena"?[52] The paper by physicist Philipp Frank rushed to defend scientists: the most ideologically incorruptible students in the university were "students of mathematics, of physics, of astronomy." Everyone knows that, he asserted.[53]

So it went, back and forth, with Catholic theologians defending hierarchy and scientists avid in their opposition. Finkelstein continued to guide the meeting toward consensus, although he clearly sided with theology. The proof for his position, he declared, was the changing nature of science, where concepts and theories could always be superseded. But philosophy and theology were either true or false: "Certain statements of theology for the people who believe in them are permanent truths."[54]

When the conference came to a halt on the afternoon of 11 September, Van Wyck Brooks gave something of a summary. The meetings had assembled men and women for two or three days, but the participants remained "feeling somewhat perplexed, if not disappointed, and baffled, particularly those who sought for certainties and final answers."[55] Science and religion remained at odds and, more important, scientists and theologians were still divided.

Brooks was only partly right. Despite the intense rancor over Adler's proposition and its echo in the discussion of Maritain's thesis of hierarchical knowledge, the conference opened a dialogue that most of its participants welcomed. The founding members, even before the public sessions, planned another meeting the following year. Their enthusiasm rested on faith in the power of intellectuals to shape culture and public policy. Such a republic of intellectuals would fail, however, unless they could stop bickering about method and establish some grounds for a concerted effort to save civilization. The agreed-on structure of unity borrowed a concept: "corporate thinking." This notion, derived from the model of scientific team research, became the blueprint for the next year's sessions. Local discussion groups were to organize around important issues in philosophy, social science, and psychology and bring their conclusions to the next conference.[56]

The conference turned a more positive face to the public than was warranted by these discussions. The primary objective, to reconcile science and religion, had failed. But Finkelstein's other personal objective was a resounding success. The conference adopted his conception of a Judeo-Christian tradition and affirmed its crucial role in modern science and democracy. Behind the scenes the Jewish theologian had begun to cement permanent ties to important Catholic theologians, linking them, through him, to eminent scientists such as Harlow Shapley. Here was the outline of a functioning democratic intelligentsia, united in its belief in the power of

Figure 4.2 Rabbi Louis Finkelstein, Simon Greenberg, Philipp G. Frank, Harlow Shapley, and William G. Constable at the Conference on Science, Philosophy, and Religion. Courtesy of the Joseph and Miriam Ratner Center for the Study of Conservative Judaism, Jewish Theological Seminary of America.

ideas. Given the acute distress of world war and rising anti-Semitism, this was a substantial achievement.[57]

Finkelstein spoke to these several purposes and accomplishments through press notices that emphasized different elements of the discussions. One recognized that scientists and philosophers had redefined their differences: "The scientists who presented papers were able to issue a common statement of their views. The philosophers narrowed the area of disagreement among themselves. Thomists recognized the position of logical positivists in the field of science, though they denied its value in other fields. Logical Positivists seemed to recognize the right of Thomists and other philosophers to carry on their speculations."[58] Another called the conference a "united intellectual front." It quoted Van Wyck Brooks's aspiration:

"Our efforts will not have been in vain if some conception of God, as the Creator and End of morally free persons, could be accepted by all as the ultimate basis for any theory of Democracy which involves inalienable rights and inescapable duties." Even to consider unity around such ideas would have been unthinkable ten years before, when the scientist labored in his laboratory "as scornful of the philosopher as the philosopher, deep in his scholarly retreat, was indifferent to the scientist." But fascism had forced the knowledge makers of society into dialogue. The conference was their first achievement.[59]

In this assessment Brooks was right; the first conference had set a new framework for discussing intellectual issues. Its even greater success was in attracting a large audience of academics from the East Coast and the Midwest, most of them drawn from Harvard, Columbia, and Chicago and their satellite schools. At the time, these three universities represented the predominant scientific schools in the nation; each also had important theological seminaries attached to it. All were committed to promoting the scholar as public advocate. The consequence: a grandiloquent academic style and the prestige of the nation's leading institutions defined the conference.[60]

The second conference in 1941 renewed the search for a unified method of science, philosophy, and religion. Without Mortimer Adler there were fewer fireworks, only sputtering claims and counterclaims. But a dispute erupted over theoretical priorities and innuendos of a relation between science and fascism. Added to this were deepening shadows of discouragement. Held two months before Pearl Harbor, in a time of anxious anticipation, the session on the state of American letters was particularly pessimistic. Poet Mark Van Doren invoked Adler's theme: "The most important way of understanding man," he claimed, "is to have a definition of God, and to think that it is worth while defining God and worth while discussing God." Van Wyck Brooks read his paper "Primary Literature and Coterie-Literature," a bitter attack on contemporary writers for their nihilism, for failing to return to their native democratic soil. There was also considerable discussion of Archibald MacLeish's recent article in the *Nation* titled "The Irresponsibles," an attack similar to Brooks's denunciation of American writers. Poet Stephen Vincent Benét best summed up the mood. "Having asked for very little from their writers, in the past thirty years, those who read them now ask much. They ask for faith and hope and greatness of spirit."[61] Apparently they failed to find them.

A spirit of recrimination continued to dwell with the purported misuse of science. As Charles W. Morris, a philosopher from the University of Chicago, put it during the second day, "There was on the first day, yesterday morning, and through this present paper [by John A. MacKay] an implication that the logical affiliation of naturalism is with totalitarianism." Morris could not, however, imagine any way to "identify Dewey with totalitarianism." On the contrary, it was religion and metaphysics that produced fascism. Totalitarian movements flourished in "countries in which the Catholic or the Protestant traditions have been very strong."[62] Physicist Philipp Frank supported Morris, but that in turn elicited strong rebuttals from several of the Catholic theologians present. Even the next day, Dewey remained an issue. William O'Meara, professor of philosophy at Fordham University, denounced Dewey for denying the necessity of God. On the contrary, he claimed, "The truth that God exists in my view is thus an indispensable element in all science."[63]

Despite the strong attacks by theologians on pragmatism and naturalism—indeed, on science itself—their cause advanced little. Many of the invited scientists failed to attend sessions on theology, philosophy, or literature and so missed these critical words. Other participants chided the conference for not advancing beyond vague speculation. The most powerful of these voices belonged to the anthropologist Margaret Mead. When informed that Harlow Shapley's Harvard discussion group had committed itself to the supremacy of the individual, she asked: So what? "I assumed that we were going to get down to serious business this year." It was 1941, she continued, and time to act. Her suggestion was to apply social science to the problems of society. We want power, she appeared to say, "to apply the insights of science to human relationships."[64]

When the founders of the conference met to consider next year's program, they adopted Mead's suggestion for more specific, utilitarian discussions. A few objected strenuously, arguing that the meeting should return to its original large purpose of relating science, philosophy, and religion. But both Finkelstein and Shapley, who was emerging as a key player in the conference, proposed that the meetings shift in scope, away from vague first principles and toward consideration of specific social and cultural problems. The conference agreed.[65] In a sense Finkelstein's original agenda had been altered. But he had accomplished much, if only because of the language adopted in the meetings. For example, scientist Harold Urey proposed that religion be taught in the public schools because the "Hebraic-Christian tradition . . . is the most important thing in our democratic ideals today."[66]

The historical significance of the Conference on Science, Philosophy, and Religion remains obscure unless placed alongside a rival, ongoing meeting of intellectuals grouped around John Dewey that convened, beginning in 1943, to defend the scientific paradigm of democracy. The anger and fears of these intellectuals about the alliance of Finkelstein with Catholic, neo-Thomist intellectuals and religious scientists highlighted a deepening split among American intellectuals. Dewey's side rejected any possibility that organized religion could serve as the model for social organization or democracy. Because of this, Dewey's forces remained impotent in a culture permeated with religion. Despite spirited rejoinders by the New York intellectuals gathered around the *Partisan Review*, inside the newly formed Committee for Cultural Freedom, and in Dewey's own Conferences on the Scientific Spirit and Democratic Faith, the pragmatists were ineffective and poorly organized. Whereas Finkelstein's conference ran annually for decades, Dewey's gatherings bloomed for a short season and died. Nonetheless the dispute between these groups revealed important polarities of thought about religion and science emerging anew in American society. Most important, it identified the captains of each opposing team: Catholic theology and pragmatism.

In his initial planning, Finkelstein twice wrote to Dewey inviting him to attend the proposed conference. Each time the philosopher declined. His reasons challenged the very basis of Finkelstein's endeavor. It was a fundamental mistake to force cooperation when science, philosophy, and religion were necessarily different, wrote Dewey. "The actual conduct of the [first] Conference," he told Finkelstein in April 1941, "did more than confirm me in my belief." He could not see "how any person of intellectual respect who is not ecclesiastical can take part in another such conference." Dewey sent this sharp rebuke to Finkelstein and then wrote to Sidney Hook to suggest developing an opposition. "Personally," he noted, "I wouldn't object to a manifesto of protest against the Finkelstein methods."[67]

Another of Dewey's allies also engaged in an acrimonious correspondence with Finkelstein. Horace Kallen, former student of William James, author of important works on American pluralism, and champion of Dewey, quizzed Finkelstein about his judgment in inviting Adler to the first conference. He also reminded the theologian of the controversy over Einstein's participation. In the summer of 1940 Einstein wrote a paper declaring that religion and science could cooperate, provided religion relinquish concepts of the supernatural. Finkelstein publicly disagreed, and Kallen saw this as a rejection of serious scientific thinking. As a Jew, he recognized the vast importance of "active toleration." "Your conference," however, "made the painful impression of an active intolerance, commented on as such in Protestant publications." Although he did not admit it openly, Kallen feared that Finkelstein had made a devil's pact with the Catholic Church.[68]

During the 1930s Dewey, Hook, and Kallen had increasingly focused on the Catholic Church as the enemy of pragmatism. These thoughts surfaced in several organizations: the Committee on Cultural Freedom, founded in 1939; various small meetings such as the Conference on Methods in Philosophy and the Sciences, first held in 1937 at the New School in New York; and the ongoing Conference on the Scientific Spirit and Democratic Faith first convened in 1943 by the Humanist Society.

Continuing feuds between Hook, Dewey, and Kallen and other intellectuals grew during the late 1930s. High on the list of opponents were Lewis Mumford, Adler and Hutchins, Van Wyck Brooks, Mark Van Doren, and other writers who expressed doubts about the effectiveness of the scientific method in solving social problems. To respond to this opposition as well as to defend Dewey was the purpose of the first Conference on Methods, held in May 1937. Kallen was the organizing force behind the group, but Dewey was the featured speaker. When he addressed the opening session, Dewey reminded the audience of a critical need to understand science and its consequences. Without recognizing its effects or its methods, society stumbled into a "retreat from reason." Hook, in his commentary on the talk, spoke harshly of the muddled views of Adler and Hutchins in proposing education defined by fixed principles or eternal truths.[69]

To Kallen the enemy was, and had long been, the Catholic Church. Although his animosity reached back into the 1920s and his encounter with the Irish Catholic opponents in the Sacco and Vanzetti case, he found growing evidence that the Catholic Church had bullied its way to power in American life and culture. In a way he was right. Catholics, through the New Deal coalition and urban machines—through sheer numbers—were moving aggressively into the American political mainstream. Kallen dated this activity to the campaign for Al Smith in 1928. "Since then," he wrote, "the totalitarian intent of the church has become extraordinarily aggressive and activist." To Kallen this ominous development and anything like the Conference on Science, Philosophy, and Religion that granted respectability to neo-Thomism or other Catholic doctrine threatened democracy.[70] Kallen's strategy was a redoubled defense of Dewey and his own rational pluralism, expressed in an unseemly stridency about the Catholic Church. He carried his attack to the National Conference of Christians and Jews, urging the organization to expose anti-Semitism among Catholic friends of the radio broadcaster Father Charles Coughlin. Kallen worked for a while with the organization Christ's Mission, which published the *Converted Catholic* magazine. He wrote several letters to the Committee for Cultural Freedom urging investigations of Catholics. For example, he confided to Ferdinand Lundberg of the committee in 1939 that "most persons guilty of crimes of violence and fraud have had fundamentalist training and are Catholics, etc." To revisionist historian Harry Elmer Barnes he suggested that the committee "do something with regard to the Catholic assault on secular education." Could the organization check on "the relation of religious affiliations or parochial school training, Sunday school training, etc., with juvenile delinquency, criminality, etc., etc.?" To *Christian Century* editor Charles Morrison he proposed that the Protestant journal explore the "impact of Catholicism" on the production of motion pictures."[71]

The event the jelled the opposition of Kallen, Dewey, and Hook to the Catholic hierarchy was the Bertrand Russell case. Russell, the famous British philosopher, had been hired by President Nelson Mead of City College to teach for three semesters. The Board of Higher Education in New York City approved the appointment in February 1940. Then came an attack by Episcopal bishop William T. Manning, George A. Timone of the Knights of Columbus, and Norman Vincent Peale of the Marble Collegiate Church. For a month the sides jockeyed for position until a lawsuit stopped the appointment. In April Mayor Fiorello La Guardia excised Russell's line from the city budget. Despite appeals, rallies, and other maneuvers, Russell was never hired.

To Kallen, Dewey, and Hook, this was a belligerent swagger of Catholic political power. Despite editorial support from city newspapers and protests by the American Civil Liberties Union and the Committee for Cultural Freedom, prejudice against the British philosopher prevailed. Russell's crime was his personal life and his attitude toward science and religion. As Kallen wrote for the *New Leader* in March 1941, the Catholic Church was fighting a scorched-earth battle against science. It was trying, by the naked exercise of power, to "keep religion going." Many Protestants and some Catholics, he wrote, were modernists who accepted science as a method for developing religious insights. But the Russell case exposed the reactionary purposes of the church.[72]

Kallen, Hook, and Dewey were so exercised about the event that they rushed *The Bertrand Russell Case* into print in 1941. In his contribution, Kallen remarked that Russell had deeply offended religious sensibilities by marrying three times. This explained the powerful alliance against him among politicians, the Catholic Church, and rogue Protestants such as Norman Vincent Peale. This unholy coalition actually aimed to discredit science. "The ecclesiastical assault on Bertrand Russell," he concluded, "is but the current phase of a warfare waged by priestcraft against men of faith and science since science first began to penetrate the dogmatic walls of churchly doctrine."[73] Kallen then repeated his charge that church membership actually damaged moral sensibility. Crime and delinquency, he reported, were directly proportional to "intransigent dogmatism."

Both Kallen and Sidney Hook also read the attack on Russell as part of the Catholic effort to subvert public education by securing release time for religious instruction. In his essay Hook took another swipe Hutchins and Adler for promoting metaphysics and theology in institutions of higher learning through their curriculum of highbrow fundamentalism. This belligerent reaction was epitomized by the sorry performance of Adler at the Conference on Science, Philosophy, and Religion.[74]

Kallen, Hook, and Dewey were uncompromising proponents of the scientific study of society and a rationally organized social order. They saw a serious split among American intellectuals over democracy itself, and they drew a defensive line around their beliefs. Finkelstein's conference and its broad appeal to fears of a Western spiritual decline, plus the Conservative rabbi's informal alliance with the Catholic Church, which itself was moving into a position of power in American culture, deeply concerned these men of science. The only alternative, they decided, was to organize their own side into a conference to promote science as the foundation of democracy.

Plans for the liberal conference began in early 1943 under the direction of a Unitarian minister, Rev. Edwin H. Wilson, editor of the *Humanist*. Since its establishment in 1941, the *Humanist* had taken the lead in defending Dewey's educational philosophy and spiritual humanism. Writing to Kallen in January, Wilson proposed a meeting of interested intellectuals including Hook and social commentator Harry Overstreet, together with a group of Unitarians. It would be a planning session for "Professors, liberal ministers and rabbis, scientists, ethical leaders and others" who believed in the empirical and naturalistic approach. The outcome was a formal organization, a title for the conference, and an honorary chair, John Dewey.[75] The public conference was set for the end of May. In their official announcement, the organizers articulated their intent to challenge Finkelstein's group. The *Humanist* meeting would be "more inclusive of certain viewpoints in religion and other fields than the Conference on Science, Philosophy and Religion." As Kallen wrote to Abraham Flexner, his group proposed to take up "candidly" the issue of free thought and "democratic religions vs. authoritarianism."[76]

When the conference assembled in May 1943, the participants stressed two crucial points. Science, by definition, was a democratic faith. As Mark May of the Yale Institute of Human Relations put it, the fellowship of science was an "international culture." It practiced a moral code far superior to the mores of most civilized societies. Other speakers agreed that science could thrive only in a pluralist society. As Herbert Schneider remarked, there had been a revival of "apocalyptic" gospels like Reinhold Niebuhr's neoorthodoxy. Such movements, together with neomysticism and neo-Thomism, had adopted a pseudoscientific cast to appeal to the contemporary confusion, but they were not scientific.[77]

Kallen delivered the most uncompromising speech. The democratic faith, he asserted, was the extension of "the ethic of scientific method." Only in a nation that treasured cultural pluralism could science prevail. This was the opposite of the "spiritual" fascism practiced by the Catholic Church. "Behind the authoritarian assault on democracy," he warned, lay claims to a monopoly on truth and wisdom. Only the contemporary Protestant state, with its openness and toleration, offered protection against this ambition. "Men of science are of a faith more loyal and devout. They do trust their truths and even put them to the test of free competition on merit, without fear or favor."[78]

Although some considered the conference a success, afterward Kallen hoped to "put it in the hands of other people than the rather namby-pamby Humanist crowd." Over the summer his wishes were fulfilled, and the conference moved to the Ethical Culture Society, with Jerome Nathanson taking a lead in its continuation. Plans to publish the speeches of the first conference took shape in the fall, but even this was discouraging. Edwin Wilson wrote to Kallen in November asking him to delete from his paper those portions referring to the Catholic hierarchy, which were "too hot for use." Kallen shot back: he would resign if his original words were censored.[79]

Despite Kallen's insistence on preserving his intemperate remarks, sales were tepid when the volume appeared in 1944. The conference met four times, until 1946; a few regional committees were also set up to expand the work of the national meeting. But the organization never made the impact that Kallen, Hook, and Dewey anticipated. Only three of its proceedings were published. In part this came from divided attention, as Hook became far more concerned with the communist threat than the internal subversion of antiscience movements. Dewey was unable to assert leadership of the organization because of his age, although he engaged in a spirited exchange with Alexander Meikaljohn over the great books curriculum in the pages of *Fortune* magazine in 1944 and 1945. Kallen, even toward the end of the 1940s, appeared to be strangely frozen in his position as a sentry on the lookout for attacks on science and education by the Catholic hierarchy. Inevitably the group could never compete with the larger, more impressive organization begun by Finkelstein. Finally, despite their criticism of Finkelstein's group for promoting a conservative, limited dialogue, what Kallen and his allies produced was even more single-minded and uniform—defined, as it were, as a rescue mission to the besieged fortress of Dewey's philosophy.[80]

Finkelstein's third conference was held in late summer of 1942, and it devoted considerable attention to the philosophic and religious origins and sustaining ideas of democracy. Much of the dialogue revisited old haunts along familiar intellectual itineraries, however. The sense of catastrophe and crisis remained, but so did the fundamental disagreements between theologians and scientific thinkers. The theme of "unity in diversity" that came to be the watchword of many speakers proved unsatisfying. Harry Overstreet (who also attended Dewey's conference) gave an optimistic twist: "I take it that the grandest thing this Conference can do will be to serve as a central stimulating agency" for diverse intellectuals to find a common universe of discourse. But others disagreed that there had been any movement toward such a platform or even a recognition of what that might look like. Indeed, at the very first session F. Ernest Johnson of Columbia University Teachers College worried that the conference might degenerate again, with the pragmatic group accusing the transcendentalist group of playing into the hands of fascists (and vice versa).[81]

During the rest of the war and well beyond, the conference continued its deliberations. Finkelstein, Shapley, and the other leaders of the group continued to explore means for strengthening the impact of their discussions, forming local groups and meeting frequently during the year. They even considering establishing a permanent academy. As the topics of the conferences pointed more and more toward social problem solving, the specter of religious and scientific disagreement still hovered over the meetings. The sharp divisions in American intellectual life expressed in 1940 continued. For example, when Van Wyck Brooks tried to organize a session of literature for the 1944 meeting, he encountered so much resistance that he advised abandoning the project. The response of James T. Farrell was not untypical. The author of *Studs Lonigan* wrote that he disagreed with any attempt to bring science and religion together. The only consequence would "be that of strengthening the Holy Roman Catholic Church."[82]

In 1947 Finkelstein was clearly worried that the conference had failed in its original mission. He wrote to Brooks to invite him to a discussion about disbanding the group. The "issues which evoked the Conference in 1939 are still with us," he wrote. But the conference had so far failed to meet the challenge. "We may even have to confess that the original goals may not be attainable."[83] Finkelstein wrote in the same tone to Robert MacIver that same year. "I do not, of course, mean to disparage our work," he said, but he added that it might be just to say that the discussions had become "tangential to the goals we had originally set before ourselves."[84]

In fact, during every one of these first ten years of the conference, soul searching and stocktaking were the order of the day. This frustration resulted in sporadic attempts to shift the purpose of the conference, as in 1945 when Harold Lasswell suggested a much more structured governing body to develop ideas that could be turned into policy.[85] Theologian Anton Pegis wrote to Finkelstein in the same year, but with a plan that tugged in the opposite direction. The conference had become too unwieldy; it had been sidetracked from its original purpose of merging religion and science. It must return to this initial impulse. "In the course of its history," he wrote, "the Conference gave up this objective" of bringing scientists and religious thinkers together for the easier aim of "legislating for others." Yet moral unity still lay ahead, unattained but as important as ever.[86]

In the postwar years the contradictions in purpose that had always divided Finkelstein's best intentions continued to polarize the conference. Annual meetings shied away from continued, open confrontations between science and religion and focused instead on practical problems for democracy such as race relations and the usefulness of the social sciences. If anything this signaled a broadening ecumenism in the group. Shapley in particular emerged as an energetic force behind the conference and in promoting summer meetings at the resort on Lake Mohonk, New York, for the purpose of continuing high-level discussions and planning forthcoming conferences. Local groups such as the New York and Boston affiliates held frequent discussions centering on the social and philosophic problems of reconciling faith and science and in writing statements and contributions for forthcoming conferences.

By the early 1950s various reorganization plans had been discussed. It was finally agreed, in 1951, to create a more formal structure with a list of one hundred fellows from various geographic and academic regions and disciplines, together with a second tier of members or associates. It became, in other words, more policy oriented, aimed at social science applications and problem solving, and more academic. The heavy representation of Catholicism and lay neo-Thomism gradually diminished.[87]

One reason for the continued stalemate was Finkelstein's resistance. He had long opposed too practical an agenda for the conference. Its purpose, after all, had been to reconcile science and religion first and solve social problems second. But this task proved enormously difficult and contentious as annual conference *Proceedings* warred in the same trenches and ventured onto the same no-man's-land. The tenth conference, which looked back on earlier meetings, concluded as much and continued to see theology and then science, by turns, offering themselves without resolution as models for organizing knowledge and developing social models.

If the Conference on Science, Philosophy, and Religion could never accomplish its primary goal of intellectual integration, what was its effect? Why did it remain so attractive to leading East Coast intellectuals for this considerable time? In the early years it tended to recruit from elite universities like Columbia, Harvard, Yale, and the University of Chicago, along with religious institutions such as Union Theological Seminary, Fordham, Notre Dame, and the Jewish Theological Seminary. Its leading members represented a particularly weighty section of the American intelligentsia. But this group did not represent the whole of American intellectual life. Obviously missing were the defenders of John Dewey, the avant-garde Jewish intellectuals of New York, and their more cosmopolitan émigré allies. The early unrepresentativeness, however, suggests the importance of the project. One purpose was to foreground and bolster the role of the public intellectual. Not only was this a popular incantation at conferences, but many of the leaders of the group had long advocated an enhanced role of idea men in setting the direction of American culture. Hutchins, Adler, Van Wyck Brooks, Norman Cousins, and Lewis Mumford contended that the cultural critic should be the guiding conscience of the society. In this sense the conference was an inviting platform for the public intellectual whose influence in this period was, in fact, declining in value and importance.[88] As a conference participant, Richard McKeon realized in 1945, "We were scientists, philosophers and religionists . . . shocked by the fact that intelligent consideration of the world situation really made no difference."[89]

But the conference did achieve two notable successes. It cemented the Judeo to the Christian inside the academic and political language of the period. If science and religion could not be integrated, Judaism and Christianity were woven together in a parlance that filled each conference meeting and spread into discussions in religious journals and college classrooms during the 1950s. It reinforced the studied ambiguity of President Dwight Eisenhower in 1954 when he said of American democracy: "Our form of government has no sense unless it is founded in a deeply felt religious faith, and I don't care what it is. With us, of course, it is the Judeo-Christian concept, but it must be a religion that all men are created equal." Behind this bland religiosity lay efforts of the conference to create a new ecumenism of American religions. This had been one of Finkelstein's deepest purposes, and his success was impressive.[90] The conference also succeeded where it failed. A number of participants, their appetites whetted for discussing science and religion, went on to join other organizations devoted to the same general purpose but under different auspices and with different emphases. If the meetings lacked clarity and unity of outcome, if the moral center of modern technological society could not be discovered in three days' sitting once a year, the issues themselves developed a long life and buzzed energetically around the classrooms and offices of American universities and colleges for many years.

Although science and religion could not be forced together, commitment to trying accomplished much the same purpose. Scientists and theologians never agreed on the respective roles of science and religion in society, except on one crucial point: that science and religion were both necessary to democracy. In a different way the atomic scientists had discovered the same truth about American culture. To Finkelstein, Shapley, Adler,

Lasswell, and the others, the science-religion dialogue was the starting point. From the perspective of John Dewey and supporters of a secular faith, however, this amounted to a fatal concession to religion. Members of Finkelstein's group were merely negotiating the surrender of science and its exclusion from discussing the major social and ethical problems of the day. To the pragmatic intellectuals the whole discussion was fatally flawed from the start. That science and religion represented different approaches to the world was certainly accurate, they agreed. But to contend that religion and science dealt with discrete realms of human thought and action was an enormous concession to religion, for it reestablished separate spheres of thought and experience that the movement had struggled to join. Where was there room in this spiritually based culture for the secular, humanist thought of John Dewey?

And—in the name of all
the legendary sergeants
who went through this
alma mater of mechanized
assault—what is the Army
coming to when they make
you go to church?

Gilbert Bailey, *New York
Times* (1947)

Chapter 5

"A MAGNIFICENT LABORATORY,
A MAGNIFICENT CONTROL ROOM"

In the fall of 1949 Wayne A. Hebert, a travel-
ing evangelist for the Moody (Bible) Institute of Science (MIS), reported
back to headquarters on the completion of a tour showing three creationist
science films—*God of Creation*, *God of the Atom*, and *Voice of the Deep*—to
thousands of American servicemen and their families. The program had
spread quickly throughout United States military camps and to installations around the world. "The Moody Film program," he noted, "is mandatory for all military personnel. Aboard battle ships, destroyers, hospitals,
army posts, air force bases, and in military schools, men are seeing all three
productions." Even jaded Washington was abuzz with talk about the inspirational films: "In the Pentagon Building, Washington, D.C., the main con-

versation," he confided breathlessly, "from Secretary of Defense Johnson down to the smallest janitor is: "Have you seen 'God of Creation,' 'God of the Atom' and 'Voice of the Deep'?"[1]

Although prone to exaggerate the success of his mission, Hebert nonetheless could take legitimate satisfaction in a very busy schedule of showing the Moody religion-science films to American servicemen, particularly in the air force. The "churching" of these servicemen was part of a larger project undertaken by the American military under the rubric "Character Guidance," which had as one of its aims the promotion of religious belief. Beneath its bland designation, this program represents an extraordinary involvement by the American government in the religious lives of soldiers. For several years toward the end of the 1940s and well into the 1950s, American servicemen viewed these films, sometimes during basic training, but more often as part of special programs directed by military chaplains. How the promotion of creationist science by the Moody Institute of Science and the training mission of the American military united in this remarkable program is the subject of the next two chapters.[2]

At various times in its long history the American military has become intensely interested in the moral and religious well-being of its recruits. The period following World War II and extending into the first years of the 1950s was such an era of spiritual concern. To many close observers the moral qualities of the young men inducted into the armed services during the war and afterward seemed abysmal—emblematic of a generalized spiritual crisis gripping the United States. As Brigadier General C. T. Lanham, special assistant to the chief of staff, told the Small Business Men's Association in 1949, "Somewhere, somehow, a perverted philosophy had found its way into our national blood stream." We had been careless entering World War II, he noted, overly sure of American values and their universal acceptance. "In mid 1941," he said, "these complacent assumptions came down like a house of cards. For in that year we found that the young men in our expanding Army were divided and confused."[3] The postwar world was just as devoid of shared values. As Rabbi Solomon B. Freehof of the National Jewish Welfare Board told President Truman's Committee on Religion and Welfare in the Armed Forces in 1948, "We cannot let our young generation sink into the forgivable and understandable but nevertheless tragic pagan negativism which their literature reveals." American young people suffered from a mood that was "dangerous to themselves, bad for religion and not good for the United States of America."[4] These young men proved exemplars of the spiritual malaise identified by the Conference on Science, Philosophy, and Religion in its early years. Descriptions of their inadequacies echoed the more sophisticated analyses of American culture pronounced by Adler, Brooks, Maritain, and Finkelstein in the early 1940s.

Beyond their general moral shortcomings, American soldiers earned two other serious demerits in the eyes of their superiors. One was a very worrisome incidence of venereal disease, a constant and indeed obsessive concern of the military for generations. Army air force general Curtis LeMay was only blunter than most when he demanded that all personnel take seriously the threats he hurled. Because of a sudden high incidence of new cases in November 1947, the entire air force was at risk, he warned. Venereal disease was a willful act of delinquency. Even loose talk endangered the service: "Those who in any way," he warned, "brag about or encourage immoral conduct are as seditious to the moral integrity of this command as those who advocate desertion of duty."[5] He promised to investigate and act.

Sexual misconduct was only one form of delinquency that blemished the postwar record of American soldiers. Reports streamed back to the military command in United States from Europe, noting other forms of misbehavior. As noted by Major General John H. McCormick, director of military personnel, "We were having a peculiarly difficult time" in Europe in 1945 to 1947. "The moral tone of the troops in the occupation was quite low." Consequently, "We took some drastic action."[6]

To the military command, questions of morals invariably deepened into more serious problems of morale, thereby threatening preparedness and long-range planning. This had long been the assumption, and its omnipresence helped give rise to the chaplains movement, especially in the twentieth century. By bringing ministers, priests, and rabbis onto military bases or adjacent to battlefields, the military had hoped to provide spiritual inspiration without compromising the fighting spirit of the troops. At first this had been voluntary. During the Civil War, for example, the budding evangelical minister Dwight Moody preached to Union troops under the auspices of the Young Men's Christian Association. During World War I the military initiated greater morale training, although the YMCA still played a major role in supplying chaplains. In 1917 Congress accepted the appointment of representatives from religions other than Protestantism. A chaplains' school was organized and then, during the next three decades, the chaplaincy edged toward professionalism: no longer would it be sufficient for the

Knights of Columbus, the YMCA, and the Jewish Welfare Board to supply volunteers.[7] Immediately after the First World War, several religious organizations that abhorred the slaughter sought to withdraw the chaplaincy from the armed services. They failed, but relations between civilian churches and the military remained troubled for decades. During the 1930s chaplains were primarily charged with ministering to recruits, although their most important public function was to lecture on venereal disease and sexual morality.

This narrow responsibility persisted even into World War II. At the outset the chaplains movement remained relatively ineffective, being poorly organized and marginal, so the Department of War set up several new institutions inside its own command structure designed to inculcate values. In 1940 the army established a Morale Division, and in March 1941 this was moved to the War Department Special Staff. Much of this sudden activity right before the war derived from a *Life* magazine article deploring the low morale of new draftees and the ominous popularity of the graffiti "OHIO" (over the hill in October, suggesting desertion). *New York Times* editor Arthur Sulzberger commissioned an investigation by reporters and turned his shocking results over to President Roosevelt. The exposé provoked another flurry of reorganization. In January 1942 the Morale Division was renamed the Special Services Branch. By 1943 this body had been divided into a Special Services unit that supervised recreation and a new Information and Education group that oversaw news, orientation, and troop attitudes.[8]

After the war, as the military began the more complex task of fighting the Cold War, demands for moral and ideological instruction increased. The military responded with its Character Guidance program, established in early 1947. Incorporated as a fundamental part of training in the army in mid-1948, this program suggested a permanent interest of the military command in the moral, ideological, and spiritual well-being of its recruits. In another change it asked the chaplaincy to oversee the program, thereby making military chaplains an essential part of the fundamental training of soldiers.

That chaplains could respond to the request to supervise moral and ideological instruction in the late 1940s is evidence of the continuing professionalizing of the movement in the postwar era. Chaplains had already undertaken a greater role after the war with a series of lectures in 1946 on the religious and moral aspects of citizenship—dubbed natural theology. By

1947 a special Chaplain's Hour was set aside on military bases as a time for talks and lectures that were eventually published in 1950 as *Duty, Honor, Country.*[9] As the chaplaincy became a crucial presence in the American services, it took on the development of moral and political orthodoxy among recruits, not just religious instruction and counseling.[10]

The imperative behind the acceleration in these programs of education and moral and religious instruction inside the armed services came from political necessities that had little to do with the real needs of soldiers. Moral and religious instruction became a key part of the public relations program to sell the American public a program of universal military training (UMT), which the War Department very much desired. Simply put, moral and religious instruction became a tactic aimed at the American home, at the parents of sons who would presumably enter one of the services at age eighteen. To convince mothers and fathers that their sons would not be hardened by military service, the War Department made such instruction a key part of replicating the home environment in military camp. During their training, recruits would continue to receive religious and moral admonishment. Perhaps there would even be significant numbers of conversions. Gently led by chaplains of their own faith, these young men might become properly churched. What mother could deny the government its needed manpower in exchange for such a bargain?[11]

There is another sense in which this policy reflected what must be considered a sea change of sentiment following the war. The splendid success of mobilization, its feats of organization and planning, persuaded many policymakers that organization and mobilization should become permanent features of the republic. Ideological and religious organization were for some an irresistible feature of this infectious appeal. Not even the military was immune.

Even if this policy was merely (at first) primarily a public relations tactic undertaken to ease the passage of very controversial legislation (UMT) requiring every able-bodied boy of eighteen to spend six months to a year in the military, the religious program was widely adopted and taken seriously by commanding officers on bases and particularly by the chaplains themselves. Not only did it give the chaplains a crucial, ongoing part in basic training and camp life, in many cases it opened the military base to evangelism. Individual chaplains used Character Guidance and the ambience of government-sponsored spirituality to urge more than just caretaking or substitute parenting. To some the military services offered a springboard for reform and regeneration of the rest of society. As a Colonel Croker told President Truman's Committee on Religion and Welfare in the Armed Forces in 1950, "We have begun down at Maxwell Field an organization that we call Christian Brotherhood of the Air Force, and it's most unusual. We have everything from a major general," he exclaimed. "He's an oldtime pilot, the Deputy Commanding General of Air University. Down to privates. There are about 40 officers and airmen. You might say they sprang up spontaneously."[12]

The movement for universal military training that inspired much of the moral and spiritual awareness of the armed services in the late 1940s, and that placed the chaplain at the center of ideological orientation of troops, emerged toward the end of World War II at the highest levels of the Congress, the executive office, and the military. The initial legislative proposals for UMT came from Republican congressman James W. Wadsworth of New York in early 1943. Then Congressman Andrew May, Democratic representative from Kentucky, introduced a bill to the House in August 1943 calling for universal training. In the spring of 1945, a House Select Committee on Postwar Military Policy held hearings, and when it reported later that summer it recommended universal training. Working diligently outside government, the American Legion also supported a slightly different form of the bill.

Major impetus for the universal draft came from such military men as Generals George Marshall and Dwight Eisenhower. They sought a citizen army, trained in high-technology weaponry, ready for mobilization to meet the swift challenges of modern warfare. In effect, preparedness and advance training became necessary because of the growing technological complexity of modern weapons: a scientifically literate soldiery seemed imperative. President Roosevelt also announced support for a version of universal service in late 1944. His variant, however, initially looked like the Civilian Conservation Corps experience of the 1930s, when young men were mustered into national service for peacetime purposes and provided with education and organized by nonmilitary discipline.[13] But even Roosevelt relinquished this vision by 1945 and came to support the military program for universal service.

His successor, Harry S. Truman, proved an even more determined friend of universal military service. In October 1945 Truman, in an address to the House and Senate, proposed passage of a universal military training program. For about a year congressional sponsors maneuvered to secure passage of a bill, but serious obstacles emerged. The deployment of the atomic bomb suggested a need to rethink the nature of potential armed conflicts. Perhaps in the future all wars would be fought between air forces without time or opportunity for mass mobilization. For those who advocated peace and disarmament—and there were many important church organizations, labor unions, and politicians who did so—a huge army represented a provocation. For others the idea smacked of militarism. Finally, major leaders of the Republican Party such as Robert Taft of Ohio were hostile to the idea.[14] Unable at the moment of its greatest potential to secure passage, Congress fell back upon the more limited and acceptable peacetime conscription of a smaller armed force.[15]

Stymied by such powerful figures and ideological obstacles, Truman decided to appoint a civilian advisory commission on universal military training. In doing so, he created a forum for advocates of moral and religious training inside the armed forces. Simultaneously, the army created a public relations prototype of universal military training at Fort Knox, Kentucky. This experiment was given wide publicity and applause by the President's Advisory Commission on Universal Training.

In choosing members for his commission Truman named public figures—scientific, corporate, and religious leaders—known to be sympathetic to universal military training. Key advisers in pushing for the commission included James Conant, president of Harvard University, and Rev. Edmund A. Walsh, vice president of Georgetown University. The most noteworthy appointee was Massachusetts Institute of Technology president Karl T. Compton. One of the nation's leading scientists and educators, Compton had long served presidents as a science and technology expert. Part of the famous family of Elias Compton, a Presbyterian clergyman, and brother of Arthur Holly Compton, he helped guide defense spending policy after World War II. Compton was designated chair of the commission during its first session in December 1946. That he received this appointment is testimony to the importance Truman placed on creating a scientifically sophisticated military.[16]

Other evidence of the significance Truman accorded the commission was the presence of his close associate, adviser, and administration UMT point man Samuel I. Rosenman, and of Joseph E. Davies, former ambassador and an important Washington lawyer. Others designated included Harold W. Dodds of Princeton University and Daniel Poling, president of the World's Christian Endeavor Union and editor of the *Christian Herald*, a Protestant publication sympathetic to universal military training.

Although the principal impetus behind universal military training came from a desire for preparedness articulated by the War Department, the navy, and the executive branch of the government, other aims of the program became more central as the commission met and took testimony. President Truman's language in announcing the commission is fascinating on this score. In metaphors he often invoked on momentous occasions, he cited ancient history to illustrate his vision of a citizen-republican army. "When the Romans and the Greeks and some of the ancient Mesopotamian countries turned to mercenary defense forces, they ended," he noted in his published remarks to the commission on 20 December 1946.

Behind this tortured analogy lay the president's desire to mobilize the entire nation—or better, continue its mobilization into peacetime, with its dangerously smoldering Cold War. The question, said Truman, was not "military" training, but citizenship training. "I want it to be a universal training program, giving our young people a background in the disciplinary approach of getting along with one another, informing them of their physical makeup, and what it means to take care of this Temple which God gave us." A nation that failed to encourage this would succumb, he predicted, to the total warfare invented by the twentieth century.[17]

A desire to see comprehensive scientific and moral training undoubtedly inspired Compton to accept the chair of the commission. The hearings were filled with references to federal support not only for military training, but for specialized instruction in modern technology and for improved general science education. During the time when American scientists were mounting a concerted effort to establish a national science foundation to fund research, the commission carefully related universal training programs to the program for government sponsorship of science. In fact scientific figures such as Vannevar Bush testified before the group claiming that UMT would supplement enhanced graduate education in the sciences. If, he said, "we had in this country under supervision men in every town who had at one time, not too far in the past, been part of the military machine, it would be much easier to institute emergency controls." A draft of the commission's final report dealing with scientific research proposed training scientists as well as improving general education "basic to the security as well as the future progress and prosperity of the Nation." In other words, Bush and Compton saw universal military training as part of a concerted federal effort to create a scientifically literate population alongside its vital defense research endeavor.[18]

This doctrine of total mobilization of American society extended far beyond training in science and mathematics. Although the UMT recruit was assumed to require familiarity with modern technology and advanced weaponry, the commission increasingly focused on moral and religious training. A report submitted to the commission by the Office of Education in April 1947 underscored this point. "We stand today," it announced, "on the threshold of the atomic age. Accustomed as we are to a mechanized and highly technical civilization, we nevertheless face the future of scientific development with some misgiving." This situation could be remedied first by understanding science itself. "If the people of a free society are to control the use of science and to direct it to humane ends, they must understand something of its method and its possibilities." But even this knowledge remained insufficient, for science offered no guidance in a world of real, clashing values. Compton resolved this problem in his ambitious goals for UMT: "The security of the country depends not only upon military preparedness but also upon the physical, mental, spiritual, and moral fibre of the youth of the nation."[19] Universal training would reinforce all of these aptitudes for modern life.

Beyond these lofty goals there were concrete, immediate problems facing the commission. As Walsh noted in January 1947, the problem of venereal disease in the armed services had come up repeatedly in correspondence to the commission. "Mr. Wilson [Charles E., president of General Electric and a commission member] has reference to the fact that during these days, as Dr. Compton said, we have all been bombarded with protests from mothers, sisters, and wives."[20] This was another compelling and ancient reason to provide moral instruction to young recruits.

An immediate problem was the accusation, made widely in the press and by opponents of universal training, that Truman's plan would saddle American democracy with the heavy burden of militarism. It would burden the republic with the weight of a standing army. This was substantially the point made by the Retired Methodist Ministers' Association, one of the vocal critics of UMT. Compulsory military training would compromise the spirit of the founding fathers and betray "every concept of true democracy." Furthermore, it would "utterly destroy one of our most cherished and sacred freedoms—religious freedom."[21] In response, General George Marshall proclaimed that this was exactly the opposite of his understanding of universal military training. UMT was not equivalent to the European system of general conscription "but is its antithesis, and its purpose is not to build up a larger standing Army and permanent Navy, but to keep them at a minimum."[22]

The reasons for the moral and religious emphasis in the plans for military service after the war thus had complex origins and spoke to multiple problems encountered by the armed services. General C. T. Lanham, chief of the Information and Education Division of the War Department, clearly outlined changes the army planned to make with or without UMT. There would be mandatory training of the minds of soldiers. The modern military would instruct them in motivation, spirituality, democratic ideals, and individualism. Father Walsh enthusiastically endorsed this endeavor. In February he told the other commissioners, "In other words, the thing is clarifying in our minds as to what they [the army] are finally willing to accept as a training program. The military aspect really becomes only one element."[23] As Compton summarized the whole project in May 1947, the president had given the commission a very broad charge. The members had concluded that universal training could be justified only by important military considerations. But if such a program became necessary, they wanted to be sure that it included careful attention to "character development."[24]

Despite the testimony and extensive deliberations, the decision to embrace moral and religious training as a key element of universal military training had actually been made even before the commission's hearings began. Based on several months of planning, the army opened an experimental program in universal military training at its base in Fort Knox, Kentucky. The program that began on 5 January 1947 had been suggested initially in the fall of 1946 by Dr. Arthur L. Williston of Dedham, Massachusetts, and developed by the War Department. Williston was head of the New England Citizens' Committee for Universal Military Training, and he suggested a special project to enhance knowledge of electronics. The War Department accepted the suggestion but transformed it into a prototype for universal training.

When the Universal Military Training Experimental Unit opened on 5 January 1947 with its 657 "UMTees" and 553 officers, teachers, and trainers, the project anticipated an extraordinary change in the atmosphere of basic training. The commander, Brig. Gen. John M. Devine, maintained the traditional eleven-week program of physical and military instruction, but everything else changed—so much so that soldiers in nearby units dubbed the recruits "the Lace Panty Brigade."[25]

Facilities at the base hardly resembled the spartan functionalism of most training camps. Trainee conduct was regulated not by standard military discipline but by an experimental trainee court system. Facilities for spare time pursuits included hobby shops, film and game rooms, and "a music room with deep rugs and a civilian attendant in charge of the classical records." Opportunities for field trips and outside study and for leisure activities such as choir practice were frequent. As a UMT promotional film noted, "Every Wednesday and Saturday afternoon, U.M.T. groups visit nearby points of historical interest. The boys are studying America. They are learning about their country and its people." Even the traditional rough language of boot camp was discouraged, although new soldiers were allowed an occasional "damn" or "hell."[26] As Gilbert Bailey wrote for the *New York Times,* the army fussed over the "beardless wonder" like "an anxious parent," providing him with all the comforts and distractions of home: "shows, educational films, movies, tours, games, athletic events, hymn sings, choir practice," and so on. The UMTee could try out for an athletic team or glee club, try his hand at painting, or join a church.[27] The corps also published its own newspaper, the *UMT Pioneer.*

Recruits for the experiment were drawn from a cross section of potential trainees. All were at least eighteen years old, and none had previous military experience. All were volunteers. Several local outside groups were given input into the experiment. A Louisville Civilian Advisory Committee, made up of local citizens, organized to assist the military authorities and monitor the off-duty activities of UMTees. Every bartender and package store clerk in Louisville was instructed not to sell liquor to recruits, all of whom wore a special identifying badge indicating their unit. Subcommittees of the Louisville advisory group reported on nonmilitary base activities of recruits in several vital areas: education, entertainment, health, and in particular religion. Outside experts were called in to advise the army and assess the results. They included such individuals as Helen Hamilton Woods, deputy director of the Women's Army Corps (WAC), many of them friendly to the cause.

The most innovative feature of this new basic training regimen for universal military service was its outright advocacy of religious commitment. When a new recruit arrived at Fort Knox he was initially interviewed by one of the base chaplains. The chaplain explained the availability of religious resources in the area and tried to persuade the youth to "come in for a period of instruction on Religious fundamentals."[28] If he belonged to, or identified with, one of the three major religious denominations (Protestant, Catholic, or Jew), he was assigned to a religious orientation group. If he did not, he could choose one or substitute a lecture series on ethics. During the first week, the recruit attended the mandatory "religious orientation talk" of his choice. Then for the following four Sundays he went on mandatory "church parade"—in effect compulsory church attendance, again with exemptions for those who chose ethics lectures.

Almost unnoticed by most observers of the experiment was the religious pluralism to which it unobtrusively claimed adherence. If the World War II military experience did not dramatically advance racial equality, it did affirm the religious pluralism of the United States in its tripartite constituency: Protestants, Catholics, and Jews. This pluralistic democracy not only made possible the general prescription of religion in the Fort Knox experiment, it also hastened the professionalizing of the chaplaincy as part of the military establishment. When Dwight Eisenhower uttered his famous aphorism about American religious democracy in 1954, he was only affirming what had, in the military, become ordinary experience because of such exposure as UMT pluralism.

The staff report on the Fort Knox experiment for the President's Commission explained that "the Chaplain's program is one of the most striking innovations of the experimental training at Fort Knox." During the six-month training period, UMT chaplains had twenty-nine separate, compulsory contacts with the trainees.[29] These periods combined discussions of religion with citizenship training lectures such as "The Meaning of Citizenship," "The Citizen and His Way of Talking," and "The Citizen and His Worship." After three months the army chaplains could be proud of their accomplishments. More than 20 percent of the new recruits reported on arriving that they had never attended church; statistics at the end of the period reported that seventy-six Protestants had been baptized and forty Catholics were undergoing religious instruction. This meant that close to 20 percent of the recruits made some sort of religious commitment. After this initial conversion, religious instruction continued in the "Service Men's Christian League," a "soldier organization" set up to continue religious self-education where men could talk about such practical problems as "The Relation of Science to Religion."[30]

This program of religious encouragement and propagation by the army was both one of the most striking alterations of basic training it undertook in the Fort Knox experiment and one of the most widely discussed and approved changes. The report of the Louisville Sub-committee on Religious Instruction enthusiastically praised the effort. It was essential, the committee reported, to emphasize ethics, morals, and spirituality even more strongly "in the army than in civilian life, because the young people are away from the normal controls of home and church." The message here clearly alluded to problems of promiscuity and venereal disease. But on broader questions the UMT training in spirituality and citizenship made military service seem not like preparation for combat, but like education for any emergency the nation might encounter. The army was not a Sunday school, the committee remarked, but it attempted to "preserve the ideals of the good life which the boys bring from home and church" while teaching the techniques of war.[31]

The President's Advisory Commission on Universal Training enthusiastically supported the Fort Knox experiment, with its heavy dose of religious instruction. (The commission had encouraged the army to give more time to religious instruction, so it was praising one of its own initiatives.) As Daniel Poling wrote in his notes on UMT, Fort Knox "gives to every trainee spiritual leadership from his own church and strengthens him within his own faith. Beyond this, it offers to men of no church and no faith, those fundamental principles of religion, from which all moral values stem."[32] This feature became one of the program's strongest selling points to a skeptical American public.

The War Department cranked out considerable publicity for the experiment. Helen Hamilton Woods and Alan Coutts from New York University traveled around the country giving speeches in favor of UMT. Woods worked in particular with such groups as the Advisory Council to the Women's Interest Section of the War Department publicity section. This section, begun in 1941, included women's groups ranging from the Red Cross to Auxiliaries of the CIO and the National Catholic Women's Organization. In 1947 the Interest Section distributed 3,500 copies of a "Report on the Fort Knox Experiment with Universal Military Training." Wood also persuaded groups of mothers, parents, and ministers to visit the base, many of them associated with the Women's Interest Section or active in charitable, patriotic, or educational activities. In all, almost five thousand military and civilian visitors (including commission members) toured the camp during the six months of the experiment.[33]

UMT trainees observe Easter Day.

Chaplain Maury Hundley administers Communion to a group of Protestant trainees.

Bottom right: Members of the Kentucky Citizen's Advisory Committee show a keen interest in UMT while talking with trainee Earl G. Fox. The Louisville clergymen are, left to right: Rabbi Joseph Rauch, Father Charles C. Boldrick and Dr. Homer W. Carpenter.

Chaplains of both faiths interviewing trainees. In foreground: Chaplain Maury Hundley; in background: Father Charles Murphy.

Figure 5.1   UMT trainees receive their religious instruction. These two photo composites were published in the *Cavalcade of UMT*, 6 January to 6 July 1947. Courtesy of the United States Army Military History Institute.

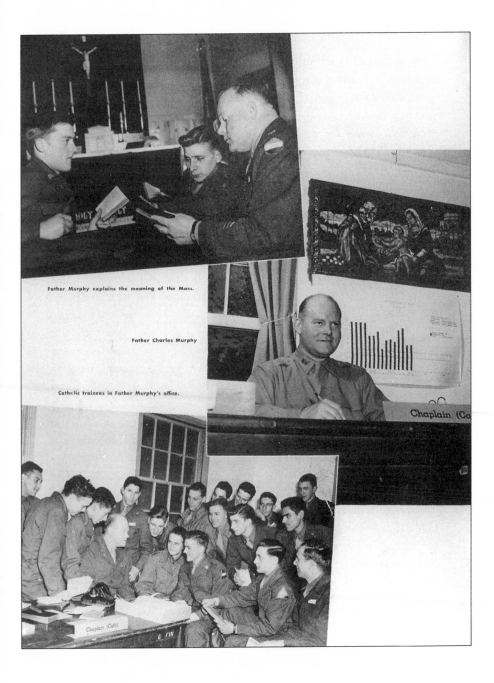

Father Murphy explains the meaning of the Mass.

Father Charles Murphy

Catholic trainees in Father Murphy's office.

All of this advocacy, plus the expense of bringing organizational representatives to Louisville by military transport, caused a small furor in Congress, where those who opposed UMT seized on what they denounced as government-financed propaganda. During the summer Forest A. Harness of Indiana presided over hearings of a special subcommittee convened to investigate illegal executive department expenditures. Harness and others accused the War Department of misspending taxpayers' funds to advocate a government program—a clear violation of statute. When the committee met in June, it interrogated Helen Hamilton Woods about her work for the project. Congressman Henry J. Latham of New York asked if she had indeed "told some of the girl Scouts and mothers groups that there were great spiritual benefits to be derived" by the recruits at Fort Knox. Woods's answer danced around the claim she had no doubt made to these groups: that the army would improve the spiritual life of recruits. The "spiritual benefit," she told Latham, was striking. "The record of church going has been phenomenally high," she continued. Latham interrupted: Was it some sort of "evangelical set-up down there?" Not exactly, continued Woods, but chaplains had been made a crucial part of training. Was it better than "in their homes?" Latham pursued. Not exactly, replied Woods again, but it wasn't "easy to get children to go to church."[34]

Although no one on the congressional committee voiced the slightest uneasiness about the army's encouragement of religion, most objected to its propaganda for UMT. In particular, the committee questioned the promotional activities of Woods and the expenditures for travel, particularly a whirlwind side trip of educators organized during a national National Education Association convention in Chicago. The committee also queried the publication of the *UMT Pioneer* (with large numbers of surplus copies intended for nationwide distribution). In particular the committee challenged the propriety of the speaking tour of T/5g Henry S. Fingado, a recruit from Fort Knox, who traveled around the country from April to June speaking in favor of UMT at American Legion posts.[35]

When the committee reported in July 1947, it accused the army of illegally using United States funds for propaganda. Special trips, publications, and employees agitating for UMT, it concluded, were all illegal. One immediate result of the hearings was the termination of many of the War Department's publicity activities for UMT. Helen Woods and Alan Coutts both resigned as consultants. In January 1948 the inspector general of the army investigated the unit and determined that the use of soldier-speakers had been illegal.[36]

Neither the Fort Knox experiment nor the "Report of the President's Advisory Commission on Universal Training," issued in the summer of 1947 (the Compton Report), persuaded Congress or the American people of the necessity for universal military training. For a year or so the movement languished. Opposition from important Republicans like Robert Taft, from mainstream religious organizations, and from labor unions made passage of a bill all but impossible. But several important changes had occurred during the course of the hearings and experiment. The War Department had arrived at an important policy decision: the spiritual and moral training of recruits was now deemed an important component of basic training. Furthermore, it had placed responsibility for this ideological and religious training squarely on the shoulders of the chaplains movement. This decision in turn set the stage for the next intensive attempt to introduce religious instruction into the military: the President's Committee on Religion and Welfare in the Armed Forces, appointed by Truman in October 1948.

This renewed effort to promote religious worship and moral well-being in the armed forces stemmed in part from the failures of the Compton Commission. Since it was unable to swing Congress or the nation over to support for universal military training, the commission's suggestions for upgrading religious and ideological awareness among recruits were not a priority in the new conscription legislation of 1948. President Truman, however, considered this aim important enough that he convened a new committee to promote national awareness of spiritual needs in the armed forces. As he confided to Poling, one of the most loyal UMT supporters: "As you know, the formal safeguards and the religious guidance program recommended by the Compton Commission [issued in a supplementary document in September], of which you were also a member, not only had my support but caused me to reconvene that Commission when the draft law did not include them." The president, then, saw the new committee as a continuation of Compton's efforts. So did its new head, Rabbi Frank C. Weil, who noted that "it flows from the continuity of the Compton Commission."[37]

Just as Truman's purposes had not altered significantly, so the problems he and his advisers in the military foresaw continued to mount. On 3 December the president and Defense Secretary James Forrestal met with Weil

Figure 5.2   Harry S. Truman and his President's Committee on Religion and Welfare in the Armed Forces. Courtesy of the Harry S. Truman Library.

and other committee members in the White House. There, off the record, the president declared his firm support for universal military training and its significance for training a young man's moral being. Secretary Forrestal seconded Truman's statement and asked the committee to be tough in its criticism of the "Military Establishment."

Truman hoped for a better reception this time. Public opinion, still led by the *New York Times*, worried about the conduct of draftees and their apparent lack of moral inhibitions. In addition, the Fort Knox experiment had proved popular with some elements in the press and in the military, and certain aspects of it seemed worthy of general incorporation into basic training. Finally, the United Service Organizations (USO), dedicated to providing a range of services to soldiers, fell into disarray during this period and even shut down briefly. Thus, as the Cold War intensified the provision of moral and spiritual leadership within the military by the chaplains movement seemed even more apt—and politically expedient.[38]

The continuity between the two advisory committees was established by the carryover of three members who served with the first group: Truman Gibson, Daniel Poling, and Edmund Walsh. New members included Weil; Basil O'Connor, president of the American Red Cross; Ferdinand Powell, a civic leader from Tennessee; Dorothy Enderis, a Milwaukee educator; Dr. Lindsley F. Kimball, president of the USO; and Mark McClosky from the Federal Security Agency. The president gave the committee clear instructions by executive order: "It is hereby declared to be the policy of the Government to encourage and promote the religious, moral, and recreational welfare and character guidance of persons in the armed forces."[39]

Despite similarities to its predecessor, the committee mounted a very different operation. Although its ultimate purpose probably remained molding public opinion into support for universal military training, that was not its publicly stated aim. Instead it concentrated on the question of religious instruction in the armed forces and therefore paid substantially more attention to the chaplains movement and the Character Guidance program. Because of this focus it had far greater success than its predecessor in attracting support from mainline civilian religious groups, although there were still vociferous critics. It was also more aggressive. It issued quarterly reports to the president, and in late May 1949 it held a large conference in Washington to promote its ideas. It also remained in existence longer, picking up where the Compton Commission left off in 1947 but extending well into the period of the Korean War.

One of the committee's first actions was to join with the newly reorganized USO to create a national program for organizing leisure and community activities for soldiers. It also stressed the central importance of religion in upgrading the moral quality of recruits. Its first report, issued in March 1949, focused on the problem of local church opposition to the draft. This, explained the committee, deeply wounded morale. The report bluntly posed a choice: Will soldiers become "bitter, cynical, mercenary, and disillusioned? Will they return holding clearer concepts of the ideas of religion and democracy?" Although the armed forces had upgraded its chaplains to officers and had constructed "appropriate edifices for religious worship"— all with public money—the community churches and religious organizations still had an obligation to reinforce the official program. Separation of church and state demanded caution in dealing with shared responsibilities, the document continued. Therefore off-base, civilian programs continued to be crucial to the men and women undergoing military training.[40]

To proselytize for this community-federal effort, the committee persuaded the president to call a National Conference on Religion and Welfare in Washington for 25–26 May 1949. Groups invited included a wide range of religious and civic leaders, fraternal organizations, veterans' groups, education associations, and trade unions. As always in such endeavors, the purpose was complicated. The committee wanted to inspire local groups to greater efforts on behalf of servicemen and servicewomen. So the call it issued stressed the need for broad public programs for those in uniform "to contribute to maintenance and preservation of our democratic traditions and our religious ideals." They also hoped to stimulate greater support for Truman's policy of military buildup. As Chairman Weil told the gathering, "The President's Committee is unique in American history." It was the first time any president had created such a group—"a committee on religion and welfare in the armed forces, consisting of civilian representatives representing the lay and clerical community."[41]

Charles H. Tuttle, chair of the Discussion Group on Religious Needs, explained what the content of that religious spirit should be. He recalled the New York World's Fair of 1939 ten years before and the risk that sectarianism had posed during its planning. In exhibiting the "World of Tomorrow" and showing the role of religion inside that world, compromise had developed as the only solution to competition among groups. Catholics, Protestants, and Jews had built a single temple "erected for all and dedicated by all to the Fatherhood of God and the brotherhood of man." This "moving" experience could serve as a model for religion in the armed services—distinct among American institutions because of its ecumenism and its fundamental loyalty to democracy.[42]

Tuttle was certainly not unusual in his sense of the momentous possibility of the renewed religious emphasis in the military. Rev. G. H. Whiting of the National Baptist Convention argued that the whole nation, not just soldiers, needed to be raised up. "I feel," he told the assembly, "that we not only need a revival of religion in our peacetime servicemen and women, but we need a revival of religion in over 100 million citizens of the United States."[43]

That was also Daniel Poling's conclusion after a trip to Pacific installations of the armed forces. American communities had raised soft and passive sons: "a parasitic type of human who has formed the habit of allowing other people to provide his entertainment and diversions. He is a radio-listening, game-attending, movie-going, auto-riding, television-watching creature who is rarely called upon to operate under his own power." This rehearsal of alienating devices in modern mass culture seemed, at least to Poling, to demand a revival of old-time character training.[44]

During the next year of its existence, the committee continued to take testimony, issue reports, and work toward a consensus over spiritual and ideological instruction appropriate for the armed services. It became particularly exercised about the serious lack of interest on some bases in the Information and Education (I&E) programs, the "Information Hours" during which Character Guidance and ideological instruction were to take place. There was some improvement in I&E during 1949, but the different services tended to use it differently. In its final summary report on Information and Education in December 1949, the committee proposed a weekly program in each of the services to discuss democratic principles and American ideals. This was necessary to garner civilian support for the military, for without democratic "experiences to replace those normally acquired in the home, school, church, or civilian organizations," the soldier would be denied crucial citizenship training. Reaching back to Tom Paine's "The Crisis," written to justify the American Revolution, the committee called the modern recruit a "citizen-serviceman" and demanded that he be trained accordingly.[45]

The content of proposed lectures emerged in testimony before the committee. In the army, chaplains hoped to strengthen a sense of personal responsibility. Lectures were designed to contradict the belief that an individual was "a 'trousered ape' or a little 'tin god'" by stressing directly and indirectly that he is a creature of God." Chaplains recognized that three major faiths could be present in any military audience. To ensure that Jewish soldiers would feel included, "such examples as are needed to give flesh and bone to the talks are chosen only from the Old Testament, as far as the Bible is concerned."[46]

The only sharp change in the tone of the committee discussions came after the beginning of the Korean War in the summer of 1950. In October the group issued a statement asserting the undiluted dependence of American democracy on religion in "a time of unparalleled struggle for the minds and souls of men." To prevail in this conflict, the committee demanded that religion take a larger role, that the nation's religious organizations minister to men and women in the armed services. The statement was sent for approval to Catholic Cardinal Spellman of New York, Rabbi Bernard J. Bamberger, president of the Synagogue Council of America, and Bishop John S. Stamm, president of the Federal Council of the Churches of Christ, then presented to President Truman at a public ceremony.[47]

Further evidence of the public relations possibilities of the committee centered on yet another effort to pass universal military training. At a meeting on 26 October Poling suggested that the committee endorse UMT now that war had started. Although committee members agreed that universal training was an excellent idea, they declined to support it publicly for fear it might compromise their other mission to upgrade the moral and spiritual experience inside the military. Recognizing the difficulty of advocating universal training, the committee continued to focus on improving the religious life of millions of recruits brought into the services by the Selective Service system.[48]

Perhaps the most significant work of the committee came with its advocacy of the military chaplaincy. Much of this effort aimed at smoothing relations between civilian churches and military chaplains. Staff members of the committee met with various church groups and chaplains' organizations to deal with broader philosophical questions and practical problems of staffing chaplains' posts. This became a significant practical problem in early 1950 when the USO was deactivated. The committee, at least for a time, tried to fill this void by organizing local civilian groups around training bases to provide basic leisure services and facilities. At the end of 1950 it also urged the establishment of a unified chaplains' school for the army, navy, and air force to upgrade the quality of religious leadership.[49]

One of the most impressive witnesses before the committee, and a powerful force in the upgraded chaplains movement, was Maj. Gen. Charles I. Carpenter, chief of the Armed Forces Chaplains Board. Carpenter, a Methodist chaplain and religious adviser to President Truman, became chief air force chaplain after that service separated from the army in 1947. Long an advocate of a separate air force chaplaincy, he had consistently criticized the quality of chaplains and facilities and had much to do with upgrading the Character Guidance program. These actions responded to the grave problems of a new service in the midst of rapid demobilization after World War II. Because of his success, he became head of the Defense Department's Board of Chaplains in 1949.[50]

One of Carpenter's first acts as chief chaplain of the air force was to im-

plement the recommendations of a study of the ethics of air force officers.
The study, undertaken at the Air University, was headed by Chaplain Wallace I. Wolverton, a philosopher trained at the University of Chicago.
Wolverton in turn hired academic consultants to design the study. Included
on the team were T.V. Smith of the Maxwell School of Politics and Citizenship at Syracuse University and Horace Kallen of the New School in New
York City. Administered to more than four hundred officers at the Air Force
Academy, the questionnaire developed a moral profile of the men. Displaying the effects of "dissident behavior" by some air force officers, the study
revealed "noticeable and disturbing" nonconformance with power and the
free reign of "appetitive" behavior. Wolverton suggested "a manual for use
in the indoctrination and education program of the Air Force." His report
could, he concluded, become the basis for designing such a guide. Carpenter accepted this suggestion and noted that the top brass of the air force was
currently considering a new program of ethical standards applicable "in any
echelon, from General Vandenberg down to the corporal who commands a
group of men under him."[51]

Further testimony by Carpenter revealed just how seriously the air force
took religious instruction. At Lackland Air Force Base, a principal intake
center for new recruits, there were twenty-two chaplains on duty, including
one Jew, five Catholics, a Christian Scientist, a Mormon, and fourteen
Protestants of various denominations. "Those men," he continued, "are in
constant contact with the young recruits from the first 50 minutes after they
enter the base until they leave." On arriving a recruit would receive "religious literature provided by the government: Protestant, Catholic and Jewish testaments and prayer-books." Then each recruit underwent a personal
interview in which the chaplain bluntly asked him to "straighten out your
thinking in relationship to God." Often the youngster would sadly respond
that he should have settled such questions before leaving home. Then, Carpenter continued, "you give him training for church membership and you
carry out a baptism."

Beyond this, Carpenter indicated that the "Air Force is interested in a
preaching mission program"—in effect, the evangelizing of the corps. Various faiths were asked to submit names of preachers, priests, or rabbis who
could spend four or five days on a mission to the base. This volunteer service, Carpenter noted, was an ideal place to bolster the cooperation between
the civilian community and the armed services.[52] What Carpenter did not

Figure 5.3   The National Jewish Welfare Board, part of the religious ecumenism of the chaplains movement, operated centers wherever there were large concentrations of troups. Courtesy of the Harry S. Truman Library.

specify was the importance of this mission program as the rationale for inviting the Moody Institute of Science to begin its extraordinary creationist science evangelical program in the air force.

In its final report to the president on the military chaplaincy in 1950, the committee followed many of Carpenter's suggestions and recommended a serious reinvigoration of the religious movement in the armed forces. Religion, it concluded, offered a key to the struggle between totalitarianism and democracy. Victory could come only through a "program of adequate religious opportunities for service personnel [as] an essential way of strengthening their fundamental beliefs in democracy." Religion also could ward off militarism because it represented a crucial civilian safeguard that could be brought into the service. Military life should, as far as possible, "reproduce civilian life."

Much had yet to be done, concluded the report. Facilities were often bare or nonexistent. The number and training of chaplains was insufficient. Local communities sometimes were indifferent or intolerant toward the military's religious endeavors. Selection and training had to be upgraded. But the report expressed optimism about the potential for improving the quality of the religious experience in the military.[53] In terms of public relations, the committee had not convinced the American public to support universal military training. But that was never its overt mission. It had, however, focused public attention on efforts made by the military services to ease the transition from civilian to military life. In doing so, it became part of federal definition of Cold War policies and politics.

By the early 1950s, when the President's Committee finished its work, the chaplaincy in the armed forces, and particularly in the air force, had a clearer mission. It provided the basic religious orientation, instruction, and oversight of recruits. It carried out the new Character Guidance program with weekly lectures on morals and citizenship. As Charles Carpenter concluded, "It is absolutely a necessity that the military and the civilian agencies join to save the American youth of today for the American manhood of tomorrow." This meant serious application of all the programs in the armed services devoted to recreation, leisure, off-base activities, and religious and moral guidance offered to the young recruits. The military experience would then reinforce and reinvigorate the best values and experiences of civilian life. But Carpenter asked for more. He wanted a national revival of "the agencies in American life that build morality and spiritually"—schools, homes, and churches. In this way "we may begin to come back to the days when we teach those things that will make Americans idealists, and moralists, and believers in God." The answer was a national crusade, an evangelizing of civilian as well as military life. As General Lanham told the President's Committee in 1948, in the armed forces we have "a magnificent laboratory, a magnificent control room to try to build some of these things that need to be built in a civil community."[54] The armed services had decided that, applied to the military, "modern" meant both scientific and technological enlightenment and intensification of religious belief. This endeavor set the stage for one of the most remarkable programs for the propagation of religion ever undertaken in the armed forces. Exploiting this opening for evangelical work, the Moody Bible Institute of Science spent several exhilarating years, from the late 1940s into the early 1950s, performing demonstrations with its portable creationist science laboratory and showing its spectacular science films to thousands of American soldiers. In doing so it introduced them to a very particular version of the conversation between religion and modern science taking place in American culture.

Here at Moody Institute of Science, faith is our most important product.

Publicity Department, Moody Institute of Science

Chapter 6

Churching American Soldiers

In March 1950 the Christian Brotherhood, an evangelical Protestant group organized at Maxwell Air Force Base in Alabama, designed a special program titled "Religion in the Modern World." Scheduled to run over several weeks, the seminar planned to open with a showing of *God of the Atom*, supplied by the Moody Institute of Science (MIS) and devoted to "the place of atomic power in Christians' world today." Two weeks later a second Moody film, *God of Creation*, would be featured. In mid-April there would be three sermons taught by a "nationally-known religious figure." The seminar would then end with two sessions. The first would be with an atomic scientist: "Effort is underway to secure Dr. [Arthur or Karl?] Compton." The last week would be a discussion with lay leaders such as Elmer Roper and Stuart Chase.[1]

This evidence of the remarkable progress of the Moody Institute of Science toward legitimating its science evangelism program was based in part on the receptivity of the armed services to religious proselytizing during the late 1940s. But the popularity of the Moody science films must also be credited to the energy and talent of Rev. Irwin Moon, the originator of the program.

Moon began his long career as a science-religion evangelist in the late 1930s, but his concern for demonstrating the compatibility of science and religion originated with the Scopes trial of 1925. There Bryan's attempt to convict Darwinian science resulted in an apparent defeat for commonsense philosophy of natural and biblical correspondences. In fact Bryan had warned that this moment would be a turning point; the nation would have to choose between false science and religion. There were indications that summer of a remarkable victory for science and modernism. Following the trial, with its adverse publicity and the sudden death of Bryan, this might well have seemed true. Bryan's university project limped along, short on students and funds. Universal Pictures made a triumphant Darwinist film in 1931, *The Mystery of Life,* with Clarence Darrow as narrator.[2] It appeared that Fundamentalists would have to choose between the book of nature and the Bible—but in this case the book transformed through the new medium of film. As Bryan himself had recognized, the contest of ideas in modern society implied a competition of images. He told the Visual Instruction Association of New York that "the motion picture is the greatest educational institution that man has known and it won't be long before every school in the country will use the motion picture because there isn't anything good [or bad, he might have added] that can not be taught by film."[3]

Irwin Moon recognized this potential as well as the importance of combating Darwinism through the modern mass media, and he devoted his life to this cause. Although he never expressed himself theoretically, he understood that in aiming at the visual senses, modern communications technology provided a means of reconstructing a commonsense interpretation of the world. He realized that the magic of the camera could dress the tenets of Old Testament science in the garment of virtual reality.

Irwin Moon was born in 1907 in Grand Junction, Colorado. As a young man he was fascinated by science and experimentation as well as by the Bible. A tinkerer and mechanic by aptitude, he underwent an abrupt religious conversion while in high school and thereafter made his way to the

Figure 6.1   After a lengthy exposition of "the book of nature," Rev. Irwin Moon appeared on camera at the end of *God of Creation* (1946) to read from "the book of God." Courtesy of the Moody Institute of Science.

Moody Bible Institute in Chicago. This led him to further study at the Bible Institute of Los Angeles and the Los Angeles Baptist Seminary. After he assumed the pastorate at Montecito Park Union Church in a Los Angeles suburb in 1929, he began experimenting with illustrated lectures and sermons. He quickly realized their effectiveness and soon turned to the problem that had always distressed him: the yawning separation of science and evangelical religion opened up at the Scopes trial. By the early 1930s Moon began to experiment with preaching the similarities between scientific theory and Scripture. Using a pawnshop microscope and a home-made telescope, he developed a demonstration called "The Microscope, the Telescope, and the Bible," which he performed for his congregation in 1931. He expanded his lectures, and his equipment grew to include "electronic, photographic, stroboscopic and sonic devices." He also began to offer his services to other churches and schools. In 1937 he resigned his pastorate to become a full-time lecturer, and his organization became a nonprofit corporation in California.[4]

In an interview shortly after this, during one of his science preaching missions, he elaborated on the confusion surrounding the dispute between science and religion. "There are two great books which do not disagree and these are the Bible and the Book of Nature." Unfortunately there were "infidels" among scientists who denied this simple observation, but they were unscientific in their approach, he asserted. "A true scientist knows that he is only searching for truths which always have been there" because of God. Religion, he noted, sought "truth in another direction and only the old-fashioned see conflict between science and God."[5]

Although Moon did not directly address evolutionary theory in his demonstration lectures, his presentation compelled the conclusion that close attention to nature revealed God's handiwork, not random selection or survival of the fittest. The discovery of patterns, laws, and hierarchies reaffirmed the argument made by the eighteenth-century thinker William Paley in his famous work *Natural Theology*. A watch without a designer was unthinkable; a natural order without God was inconceivable.

Moon's growing reputation among evangelical groups brought him a visit in 1937 from Dr. Will H. Houghton, president of the Chicago-based Moody Bible Institute. Houghton attended a presentation of Sermons from Science at the Church of the Open Door in Los Angeles. As Moon explained, his "burden was not to minister to over-fed Christians in Bible conferences, but to reach those who would never be reached by ordinary methods, particularly high school and college young people." Convinced that this was not "gadget evangelism," Houghton persuaded Moon to join the Moody Institute Extension Department.

Moon's showmanship—for that is what it was—fit perfectly into the long history of the Moody Bible Institute's adaptation of technology, advertising, and theatrics as modes of evangelism. As far back as the 1870s and 1880s its founder, Dwight Moody, had preached in theaters and circuses, using hymns written by Ira Sankey that echoed popular music styles. During his famous World's Fair campaign of 1893 in Chicago, shortly before his death, Moody advertised his ministry in the amusement columns of newspapers. He preached in notorious city theaters, in tents, and in public auditoriums as well as in churches. He outfitted a portable horse-drawn gospel wagon to be pulled through the slums for impromptu services. At the end of his life he had begun the "Colportage Society," which, like the Sears, Roebuck catalog, sent its messages into countless rural homes.[6]

After Moody's death in 1897 the Moody Bible Institute continued to exploit the technologies of popular culture for gathering in souls. In the early 1920s it began to experiment in radio broadcasting. Houghton himself had briefly worked on the vaudeville circuit early in his life and clearly understood the effect popular presentations had on mass audiences. In the 1930s Irwin Moon's scientific-evangelical road show offered another way to reach new groups. Most important, it promised to establish the presence of evangelical Protestant Christianity at the cutting edge of the new technique in science popularization—film.[7]

Under extension auspices Moon continued to operate his equipment and evangelize for the next two years, until in 1939 a remarkable opportunity to reach a larger audience opened up. While the San Francisco Golden Gate Exposition was being planned, the San Francisco Christian Business Men's Committee decided to sponsor Moon and his lectures. They financed and built a special auditorium, a "streamlined building," for the science presentations. Near the "Carnival fleshpot" on Treasure Island in the midway section of the fair, Sermons from Science featured polarized light, demonstrations with helium and liquid air, fluorescent minerals, ultraviolet rays, and the million-volt transformer Moon used to spray electricity from his fingertips toward the heavens.[8]

During the two successive summers of the fair Moon held forth with his sermons to thousands of observers. Then, when the fair closed, Moon took his demonstration into auditoriums, church halls, and eventually army bases. When World War II began, with its huge numbers of new recruits streaming through basic training, Moon volunteered his services to the armed forces and began to tour with his equipment, often taking Houghton with him. An early publicity release reports on his efforts at the army installation at Camp Shelby, Mississippi, and suggests something of the tone to his presentation. Moon challenged the assembled soldiers with his Fundamentalist message: "If any man can prove to me that any statement in the Bible is untrue, I'll gladly give him all this apparatus."

Apparently a hit with the commander and much of the audience, the demonstrations had to be presented twice. As the camp publicity noted: "In case you don't know just what kind of a show it is, Mr. Moon takes two tons of scientific apparatus worth about $20,000 and proves the Bible to be literally accurate with it. He isn't fooling, either." Finally, the release concluded, soldiers enjoyed the show because "it was good entertainment of a kind many of them had never seen, and secondly, it gave them an entirely new slant on their religion."[9] As another publicity release proclaimed, Moon had joined the show business hoofers on the USO circuit: "Into those camps all over the world went Moon right behind Entertainer Bob Hope."[10]

Moon's illustrated science sermons drew lessons that servicemen could use to understand their own situation as combatants. During the (dangerous) electric finale of his presentation, Moon would comment that he was obliged to obey the laws of electricity. "It brings me immunity from almost certain death," he continued. "Just so, by following God's spiritual laws as clearly stated in the Bible, we may have immunity from certain and eternal spiritual death."[11]

Moon was brimming with ideas about the possibilities for science evangelism, and during their joint trips around army bases he and Houghton discussed the difficulties of modern evangelicals. In early 1941, during one of these conversations, he suggested that the Moody Bible Institute initiate a conference of evangelical scientists to help ministers and evangelists comprehend modern scientific theories. More substantially, Moon began to work with film and produced his first religious-science documentary in 1944, designed for screening before servicemen, which he titled *They Live Forever.* Backed by the Moody Extension Service, he offered his assistance to the armed forces and showed this film and his Sermons from Science demonstrations to soldiers about to embark for duty abroad.[12]

In discussions with Houghton, Moon proposed another project he had long considered: a film studio/science laboratory to develop his concept of demonstrating God's miracles through science. This could extend his Sermons from Science to a national audience and bring his voice to millions of unchurched Americans. Houghton agreed and persuaded the Moody Bible Institute to appropriate money to buy a building and begin production. In 1945 the Moody Institute of Science purchased the former Masonic temple on Santa Monica Boulevard in West Los Angeles in the vicinity of the major Hollywood studios. With scientific backing from the American Scientific Affiliation, which grew out of Moody-sponsored annual conferences of evangelical scientists, Moon set up his studio—what he called his scientific laboratory—in the old three-story brick building.

The Moody Bible Institute, the Moody Institute of Science, and the

Figure 6.2   During World War II, Rev. Irwin Moon entertained thousands of troops with his Sermons from Science. Courtesy of the Historical Collection, Moody Bible Institute Library.

Figure 6.3   An old Masonic temple became the first headquarters of the Moody Institute of Science in a location near Hollywood in Los Angeles. Courtesy of the Moody Institute of Science.

American Scientific Affiliation shared two principal beliefs that united them in this visionary enterprise. They agreed that religion and science were in accord—and that this harmony should be proclaimed and demonstrated. Scientific observation revealed a conspicuous design in nature that could be explained only by religion and a creator God. Lacking such an understanding, there could be no satisfactory explanation of the underlying regularities of life and nature. By definition this conclusion condemned theories such as Darwinism as merely false speculation. Evolution was an unproved and irresponsible theory, whereas creation remained obvious and demonstrable. Theirs was nonetheless a soft-line approach to the conflict between religion and science. Moon and his allies could accept most scientific theories and experiments, including those of astronomy with its vast estimates of time, without prejudicing their fundamental beliefs. Every sound theory was in Moon's eyes a demonstration of the continuing miracle of creation.

But why did the Moody Bible Institute commit such large resources to science proselytizing? In part, the memory of Scopes still had to be vanquished. Even more important, Houghton, urged on by Moon, recognized the growing importance of science and technology in modern American culture. To sit back and allow scientists to explain science in their own terms was to surrender the relevance of evangelical religion to modern life. Given the growing complexity of scientific theory and its inaccessibility to the intuition of ordinary men and women, science had to be explained by someone. Better the Moody Bible Institute than the spiritually sterile laboratories of universities and colleges; better the evangelical American Scientific Affiliation than the American Association for the Advancement of Science.

When Moon set up a movie studio and called it a scientific laboratory, he was not being disingenuous. He merely employed a definition of scientific experiment that differed from what scientists of the day would normally have considered laboratory work. In no meaningful sense was this establishment an astronomical, biological, or physics research center. The MIS possessed neither the equipment, the trained personnel, nor the interest in undertaking advanced investigations. Nor had it any research agenda—at least none identifiable with existing scientific paradigms. Instead, its purpose was demonstration and education, conveying simple scientific concepts in a biblical context to mass lay audiences. By interpreting the patterns of nature through scientific experiments, Moon was doing science in another guise—in the evangelical sense of demonstrating God's truths to human beings. The purpose was not to extend knowledge into the unknown but to teach what had already been discovered to the unknowing and to place that science in the context of eternal religious verities. In short, the Moody Institute of Science was a movie studio devoted to presenting a religious interpretation of science through film.

Freed from the protocols of research, Moon and his associates concentrated on visual techniques. Their film equipment, constructed primarily in the Institute, was up-to-date and innovative, much of it initially built out of World War II surplus. Over the next few years the Institute effectively experimented with new techniques of time-lapse and microscopic photography. In the 1950s it even found itself in a dispute with *Life* magazine over which was the first to photograph a beating human heart during surgery. As one MIS publicity statement put it, the purpose of the MIS productions was to present "first-century gospel with twentieth-century illustrations."[13]

What shaped these films more than anything was the growing technological and scientific literacy in midcentury America. Overt preaching with a few examples drawn from science, as Moon had discovered in his travels throughout the United States, would not gather in the unchurched. The audience had become sophisticated in two ways, and the Institute had to respond. First, most Americans knew something about modern scientific theories, if only key words like "relativity" and "atomic particles." More important, audiences accustomed to Hollywood movies expected accomplished film presentations. Primitive animation, amateurish photography, and inept editing would repel them, but imaginative production qualities would provide a gloss of modernity and technological expertise to the biblical message without corrupting its timeless truth. This was the key to persuading schools, movie theaters, television, and the armed forces to accept the MIS films as legitimate documentaries.

After a survey of educators in the late 1940s, the MIS confirmed that it was wise to proceed cautiously with inspirational messages. It was not deemed controversial, its survey found, to mention God in science films, although synonyms such as "Designer," "Architect," and "Creator" were more acceptable. Anything specifically promoting Christianity, however, seemed to incite accusations of sectarianism. In an internal memo, the MIS fretted over the evil effects of the Darwinian controversy. Scientific materialism had engulfed a generation, making it "almost devoid of faith in God with the ensuing lack of spiritual ideals." But prudence and caution could overcome even this terrible obstruction.[14]

The MIS continued its discussions of strategy for several years. As F. Alton Everest, a close associate of Moon in the Institute, told a 1954 meeting of the American Scientific Affiliation, the filmmakers had profited from the challenge of presenting religiously inflected science to secular audiences. Secular schools and universities taught exclusively materialist science, he noted, although this orientation clashed with religion learned in churches and homes. But one unguarded entrance opened into these secular bastions of learning. The way to convey religion into the classroom, the MIS had discovered, was through the "weak message." To the unchurched, this understated presentation of biblical ideas went off "like a bombshell." The strategy—suggested in Moon's approach—had been to open his presentations with visually spectacular demonstrations of the miracles of nature and then close with the inevitable conclusion that earth, man, nature, and the universe were joined in a divine blueprint of salvation. Exposing young minds to theologically oriented science, even if the word Christianity was never uttered, would prepare the ground for great works of evangelism.[15]

The MIS also recognized the need for trained evangelist-technicians who were adept at showing the films in out-of-the way places and under difficult conditions. Almost immediately after the Institute began film production, it also undertook missionary and technical training. As Moon wrote in 1947, "If the radio, the airplane, and the camera are to be used effectively in the mission field, there must be thorough training on the part of those who use them." Consequently the Hollywood laboratory began to offer flight training and instruction in radio technology to missionary trainees.[16] Under these auspices Moon recruited two important associates, Wayne Hebert and Keith Hargett, who later became regulars on the air force Character Guidance circuit as "missionary technical specialists." The spiritual justification for this attention to modern technology was providential. "God has given us the needed tools—radio and the airplane—that will enable us to get the job done." The specialist was "a licensed communications man, a pilot, pilot mechanic, photographer," and a real missionary in every sense. With these skills he could meet the challenge of the huge demographic explosion of "heathen."[17]

The first five MIS films proved to be the most successful productions of the Hollywood laboratory and the prototype for many of the scientific documentaries that flowed from the studio over the next ten years. The first endeavor, *God of Creation* established a striking general format for the four specific films that shortly followed. Finished in early 1946, this forty-five-minute documentary featured dramatic and unusual photography revealing the "hidden miracles" of nature, the normally unseen processes of biology captured through innovative photography. Using time-lapse shots, the studio captured the various life stages of a butterfly, the growth and flowering of poppies, the quirky movements of paramecia. But what is most unusual about this film is its self-conscious preoccupation with using technology to enhance ordinary vision. Moon employed microscopes, unusual photographic techniques, and the telescope at Mount Palomar Observatory to increase the audience's range of sight. Armed with these augmentations, the viewer could "see" the magnified patterns in nature. By making nature accessible in this visual fashion, Moon could reveal the concept of design and praise the works of the creator God.

In his voice-over explanation of the scientific footage, Moon was relentlessly anthropomorphic, probing the simplest observations for the moral purpose they illustrated and for their relation to human concerns. This led naturally to the sermonized ending. During the last few minutes of the film Moon appeared on camera, dressed not as a scientist but in a conservative suit. Reading from the Bible spread before him, he asserted what had become obvious: the patterns illustrated in the film represented traces of God's larger design of nature and his concern for mankind.[18] Above all, the films sought to establish these ideas as commonsense experience. Here was Moody's and Moon's response to Darwinism and its soulless scientific construction of the universe—a popular film designed for a nation intrigued by the gadgetry and technology of advanced industrialism, puzzled by modern counterintuitive scientific theories, and increasingly used to learning about the world through the medium of film. *God of Creation* ingeniously blended Hollywood production values and an appeal to American know-how, with biblical literalism, a fusion that claimed the prestige of science for evangelical Protestantism. That this self-styled professionalism represented the key to evangelical science strategy is underscored by publicity photographs taken for the MIS and published in the *Moody Monthly* and distributed to the press. In these photographs Irwin Moon appears wearing a white coat—the popular symbol of science—seated in front of a sizable piece of scientific equipment. It represented a denial of the amateurism that had betrayed Bryan.

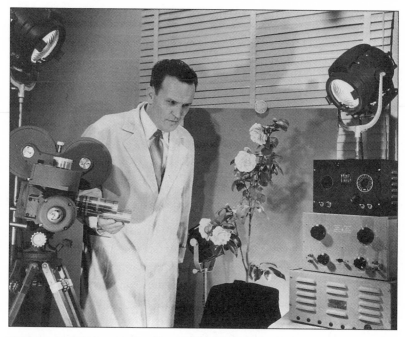

Figure 6.4   Part of the genius of the Moody Institute of Science films was time-lapse photography. Rev. Irwin Moon dons a scientist's white coat for this publicity photo demonstrating the technique. Courtesy of the Moody Institute of Science.

A similar format and purpose inspired the next MIS films. The atomic bomb in particular featured in these films because of its obviously potent symbolism and its puzzling and complex science. *God of the Atom,* released in September 1947, followed the general scheme of the first film: the technical story developed "along with the spiritual, is obviously a TEACHING role for Irwin, with photogenic 'props' to prevent the necessary minimum of pedagogy from breaking down."[19] That lesson was clear. *God of the Atom* invoked the monstrous power of the new science to awaken spiritual sensibility. Featuring Larry Johnston, a research assistant at the radiation laboratory at the University of California and a student of atomic energy, the film included shots from Hiroshima, Nagasaki, and Los Alamos, many of them gathered by MIS employees on research trips. Footage in the Berkeley laboratory was also taken by the MIS staff. This cooperation between Moon and the scientific community even led to hopes for endorsements from mainline scientists. As one member wrote to publicity department, "We thought perhaps we could go ahead and make a special deal with Larry Johnston for a private showing of 'ATOM' in the Radiation Lab of UC Berkeley. Maybe you could even get some quotes from such physicists as E. [Ernest] O. Lawrence etc., for promotional purposes." "We really owe them a lot," he continued, "and it would be a wonderful opportunity for witnessing, and getting top strata reaction on the technical story plus the spiritual application."[20]

This was not the only professional advice or endorsement that the Moody Institute of Science sought in these early, heady days of filmmaking. In 1947 the Institute sought expert instruction in editing and cutting from "a hot shot MGM editor." Both *God of Creation* and *God of the Atom* were thoroughly analyzed. The editor advised "merciless cutting" in both documentaries. But apparently this "Godless Hollywood character says the film has a tremendous message—even saying 'it touched him.'"[21]

Another innovative film was *Voice of the Deep*, made in 1948 and devoted to exploring the undersea world. Based on the wartime discovery that fish uttered sounds, the documentary largely grew out of F. Alton Everest's experience and expertise at the Navy Radio and Sound Laboratory in San Diego during the early 1940s. The lesson underscored by Moon made a perfect religious analogy. Human beings had been ignorant of the vocal world under the seas until science discovered it. So too were humans ignorant of the world of spirit until it was revealed to them by sacred Scripture. Armed with science and the Bible, mankind could now hear fish communicate as well as receive inspiration from God. As Moon concluded, "Yes, there are two realms . . . not only in the physical world—but in the spiritual as well." Those who denied the unseen physical and spiritual worlds were ignorant. The boundary between natural man and his spiritual realm could be bridged only when the individual became a "new creature [a born-again Christian]."[22]

F. Alton Everest made the theology and evangelical program behind the MIS films transparent in an article in 1947 for the *Moody Monthly*. As much as anything, the piece urged a presumably reluctant evangelical community to accept the validity of using science to convert souls. He began by discussing Baconian science as the fundamental methodology for the study of nature. Although he conceded that this age-old approach required some modification, it underlay all of science. And what Bacon had presumed, modern man must continue to believe. God intended humans to discover the facts about the world through observation and induction. The ultimate purpose of this knowledge, Everest concluded, was to honor God. Two years later, in a book titled *Dust or Destiny*, timed to coincide with the release of another MIS documentary of the same name, Everest repeated his Baconian formulation together with his argument for God from the design of nature. The MIS could combine science and religion in this extraordinary fashion, said a publicity release at the time, because at Moody, "miracles are accepted there as photographically suitable for the Institute's motion picture work."[23]

Everest's most elaborate exposition of the MIS strategy came in a book published in 1951, titled *Hidden Treasures*, again published to coincide with the release of a new film. Everest revealed two tactics. First, he grounded his science explicitly in the eighteenth-century works of William Paley. Science, he quoted Paley, should be "a continued act of adoration." Translating this old dictum into modern terms, the Institute had "made it the main business of the Moody scientific films to point men from His handiwork in nature to His handiwork in redemption." Speculating on the meaning of contemporary scientific discoveries, he borrowed Harlow Shapley's notion of humans as the median point of matter and renamed it "the median point in His creation." The telescope had revealed a huge universe, shrinking man into insignificance, but the microscope discovered a vast miniature world that reestablished the stature of humans. Between these two worlds, mankind occupied the very center of creation and God's attention.

Everest made another point to support his merger of science and religion. For each film produced by the Institute Moon and Everest relied on legitimate academic science—not for the biblical conclusions they imposed on their experiments, but in the use of up-to-date equipment and scientific theory. Because science usually remained silent about larger issues of religion and generally showed little curiosity about arguments over God's existence or the design of nature, it was possible to borrow almost any theories and procedures from this vast lending library. Only a few important theories had to be avoided—such as Darwinism. Still, a huge variety of scientific principles remained to illustrate the religious program of the Institute.[24]

During the next years, the MIS produced several more films for its series, including *Red River of Life* on the human bloodstream and an anticommunist nature film, *The City of Bees*. During this time Moon's associate Alton Everest became more important in the MIS, moving from associate director (1945–53) to director (1953–70). To devote himself to full-time filmmaking, Moon relinquished most of his traveling Sermons from Science presentations to George Speake, a mechanical engineer and navy veteran recruited by the Institute as a missionary technical specialist. During the heady earliest years of film releases, there were even brief negotiations initiated by MGM Studios about the possibility of commercial distribution of the MIS films.

The Institute kept careful records of the success of its science films, for their purpose was always proselytism. A letter from the Princeton Evangelical Fellowship in the spring of 1947 documented an extraordinary event in that progress of saving souls. The center showed *God of Creation* two times. The second showing was in the campus chemistry auditorium before two hundred students, professors, and townspeople. "Among those who came," reported the Fellowship, "was Albert Einstein, and the audience, which saw him come in was greatly impressed by the reference to him that was made in the film. Afterwards over seventy Gospels of John were distributed."[25]

A general accounting in the MIS records for 1947 and 1948 noted 8,967 showings of *God of Creation* in churches and schools, an attendance of 1,400,000, and 2,400 conversions. For its three films the Institute counted a total audience of 2.5 million with almost 4,000 conversions. Despite the tiny percentage of direct conversions recorded, the Institute believed its evangelical work was successful. During the 1950s it branched out into producing special films for school use, in which the religious message grew even more muted. In 1957 and 1958 thirteen programs under the name Sermons from Science were released as a television series and shown in a number of major markets including Detroit.[26]

The greatest achievement during these years, without a doubt, was the evangelical work in the United States Air Force and the widespread adoption of the first four Moody films as a staple of the Character Guidance program.[27] The needs of the air force and the ambitions of the Institute formed the basis of a partnership that operated for at least a decade. When the air force became a separate service in 1947, Charles I. Carpenter became chief of chaplains. Carpenter had worked since the beginning of World War II to professionalize the chaplains movement and succeeded in 1949 in separating the air force chaplains from the command of the army. Carpenter also established an audiovisual program and experimented with radio services for soldiers. The foundation for this energetic new chaplains movement in the Air Force built on the new Character Guidance program.[28]

Another of Carpenter's innovations was the "preaching missions" begun in the fall of 1948. The purpose of this program was to send ministers, priests, and rabbis to distant bases around the world. Ready with evangelical technicians, the Moody Institute of Science sent out missionary specialists through this program to demonstrate Sermons from Science and to show the new MIS science-religious films it was producing.[29]

Wayne Hebert recorded a perhaps apocryphal account of the original showing of the MIS films for the air force. While resting from a speaking trip for the Moody Extension Service in late 1948, he claimed, he chanced on a newspaper report of the forthcoming reinstatement of the Selective Service system. Hebert instantly recognized the potential of a huge new audience for the MIS films. He wrote to the Chicago headquarters for permission to begin a national tour of military camps, taking with him *God of Creation, God of the Atom,* and *Voice of the Deep.* "My first meeting in the military camps," he recounted, "was at Fort Ord, California. At the very beginning the Lord started blessing. In the very first service 96 men came forward and accepted the Lord Jesus Christ."[30] Such successes confirmed the format and set the agenda for years to follow. Hebert would fly from one camp to another showing the MIS films and accepting conversions in private afterward.

Carpenter, who was looking for just such a program, met with Hebert several times in late 1948. Given the interest of Truman, his President's Committee on Religion and Welfare in the Armed Services, and Gen. Hoyt Vandenberg, chief of the air force, in beginning an effective Character Guidance program, the Moody films and Hebert were perfectly positioned. After sending an aide to view the films, Carpenter invited Hebert to Washington to preview one of them for his colleagues. As the evangelist recounts: "Everyone received the film with open arms—wanted to get copies for overseas use immediately." As Carpenter later commented, "When I found Moon I found all I wanted."[31]

Carpenter received permission from Maj. Gen. Robert W. Harper, in charge of United States Air Force training, to initiate showings. The program began almost immediately as chaplain Col. Glen J. Witherspoon scheduled a United States trip for Hebert "in a B25 fully equipped with two pilots, crew, chief, etc." Stops were set for seventeen air force bases, most of them in Texas and other western states. At each base Hebert showed the three films to officers and afterward counseled those who desired further religious instruction. "I could use ten copies of each [film]," he wrote to the vice president of the Moody Bible Institute, "and keep them busy constantly getting 30 definite gospel messages out daily." But the best news was that the air force had invited him to make several more trips throughout 1949. "I praise God for this great opportunity," he concluded.[32]

Hebert's next report in September came following an extended tour in which the showings were opened to enlisted men. The first began in March and covered sixty-five bases in the United States. He estimated an audience that numbered about 67,100 servicemen and dependents. Under the auspices of the Character Guidance program, the evangelist could not preach openly. "However, I was able to deliver a challenging message after each film, explaining the plan of salvation completely." He would then invite men to consult him about their spiritual problems. Even more impressive, the air force had apparently incorporated the Moody science films into its basic training format. At the intake station at Lackland Air Force Base in San Antonio, the "biggest tool that the Air Force has for its training program is 'God of Creation,' 'God of the Atom' and 'Voice of the Deep.'" The first thing recruits encountered on the base was *God of Creation*. "They see this film before they are given complete uniforms. After this film, the Chaplain interviews them," he reported.[33]

Later that year Hebert was again escorted on a whirlwind tour of military bases, this time in Europe. In November 1949 he was invited to show four Moody films in Tripoli, Athens, Rome, Wiesbaden, and Paris, and at Lagens Field in the Azores. Again, the United States Air Force paid the expenses of transporting Hebert and the equipment.[34]

Reports from the air force about the showings confirm that they represented an official policy of the command. For example, at the Air Force Reserve Training Center in Reading, Pennsylvania, Hebert showed two Moody films. As the *Reading Eagle* reported, Col. John I. Moore, commander of the base, "explained that these scientific color films are designed to explain the relationship between science and religion, and to assist in forming a combined religious-educational program which is now being carried out at all air bases of the Continental Air Command." A report from the Ninth Air Force in April 1949 also noted that a visit from Hebert was considered part of a special initiative from headquarters to carry out the new Character Guidance program.[35]

Carpenter's enthusiasm for the Moody films grew as commendatory reports flowed back from bases Hebert visited. For example, on 22 March Lt. Col. J. R. Propst of the Bedford, Massachusetts, base wrote to the commanding general of the First Air Force about reactions to the three "exceptionally fine technicolor films." "The reaction of the men," he wrote, "was one of awe and intense interest. They were held almost spell-bound during the entire showing." "We all learned many things," he continued, "which we never before realized in regards to the greatness of God and the mysteries of life and the universe." It was the unanimous opinion of "all personnel" that these were the best films they had ever seen. In addition to being religious, they were also "of a scientific nature."[36]

As Brig. Gen. Harry A. Johnson wrote to William Culbertson at Moody after Hebert's tour, "I have been well pleased with the splendid reports which have been received from our Commanding Officers." Ordinarily, he said, religious films were not particularly popular. "In this case, however, we have received repeated requests for further films of a similar nature." Wherever Hebert had showed the films there were enthusiastic reports back to the command. Both the First and Ninth Air Force commands wrote of the very positive reception of the films, and they requested more showings.[37]

To acquaint the air force chaplains and religious leaders with the accomplishments of the new Character Guidance program, Carpenter addressed a July 1949 conference of the Air Force Association, held in Chicago. Delegates representing various Christian and Jewish groups attended, as well as experts on youth training. As the *Chicago Daily News* reported, Carpenter informed the group that "among the many methods being used to give members of the armed forces moral guidance are films produced by the Moody Bible Institute."[38]

There were times, however, when the Moody Bible Institute seemed to want to move too quickly and presumed too much about its role in the air force. After the release of a careless statement in December 1949 quoting Charles Carpenter as saying that the MIS films were the "backbone" of the air force's indoctrination program, Carpenter quickly responded. The publicity was wrong on several counts. The air force headquarters in Washington, D.C., had only recommended the films to various commands. Chapel attendance had not increased dramatically as the publicity also claimed. Most important, the MIS films were only one part of the indoctrination program. "We have other very vital programs in indoctrination and the films are only part of our attempt to make the program effective," he noted.[39]

In fact, however, this probably represented the only rough moment in negotiations that finally resulted in the widespread adaptation of the MIS films for Character Guidance in the air force. In early March 1950 Carpenter requested a meeting at the Moody Bible Institute to smooth out difficulties in the science film project. Carpenter was distressed because the films were being shown in a haphazard, uncoordinated way. Apparently the Institute had been asking various air force commands to host the films and a representative of the Institute, thus bypassing the Washington command headquarters. This could not continue, said Carpenter. "In the final analysis this office is held responsible for all religious programs in the Air Force." The head chaplain assured the Institute that the service was pleased with the films, but he emphasized that more coordination was necessary.[40]

The meeting took place on 8 March 1950 at the Moody headquarters in Chicago. Carpenter seemed delighted by the results. The Institute agreed to clear all activity relating to the air force through Carpenter's public relations officer. In turn this initiated a closer working relationship between the Institute and Carpenter's office that bore fruit over the next several years. In December 1950 Carpenter invited E. A. Scott, the Moody public relations man, to a conference in Washington with "Public Relations people of the Training Command." This would promote smooth joint public relations. As Carpenter closed, "I feel that Moody should receive every type of publicity advantage in this situation but would like the planned program worked out jointly." In effect Carpenter had reined in the freelance evangelism of the Institute and firmly placed the use of the films under his oversight. In exchange, the Moody Institute of Science had become a major supplier of films for the United States Air Force.[41] Carpenter had also cleared the program at the highest echelons at air force headquarters. Hoyt Vandenberg, chief of staff of the air force, commented very favorably on the films in 1949: In my opinion," he said, "these films and the story they tell are the best instruments to accomplish the character building program for the servicemen." And surprisingly, there appeared to be no objection from other religious groups (Catholics or Jews) to the particular Protestant, evangelical message that the films preached or to its New Testament message.[42]

The year 1950 was extraordinary for the partnership between the air force chaplains and the Moody Institute of Science. In early summer a breathless article in the service publication the *Chaplain* spoke of the amazing reconciliation of modern science and religion, which had burst apart as a result of the Scopes trial. The "impossible" seemed to be happening, "for science and religion have put away their boxing gloves for a working partnership." The Moody science films reached hundreds of thousands of Americans. "At least one command reports an increase in chapel attendance and decrease in V.D. rate among its men," the article continued. So successful were the showings that the films had become "part of the U.S. Air Force personnel's indoctrination." This result signaled a revolution in religion and its relation to other institutions in American life. Churches that once opposed showing any movies now welcomed Moon's documentaries. "Service camps, universities and colleges that once believed religion and science were divorced for eternity are one by one changing their hypothesis and saying the two are united." Most comforting of all, chaplains of all faiths acclaimed the films.[43]

This heightened year of evangelism saw a major joint effort by the chaplains and the Institute to bring the films to air bases. In February a schedule was drawn up for showings of *Dust or Destiny* at seventeen bases throughout the western United States. On every base there would be two showings at least. During duty-hour presentations, only officers would be allowed to attend. In the evenings the movie would be open to the whole base. An even more ambitious program began in June when the secretary of the air force invited Moon on a fifteen-day tour with his Sermons from Science presentation to various air bases in Alaska. The air force agreed to fly Moon and his equipment and to pay the necessary costs.[44]

In October 1950 Carpenter's office drew up an elaborate schedule for showing the Moody films during the next eight months. In fact the Institute and the air force had come to an exclusive arrangement. The MIS films made available to the armed forces could be shown only on military installations and not in (nearby and competitive) civilian churches or assemblies. The four MIS films were each to be shown at sixteen air bases in round-robin fashion. Since no one from the Moody Institute of Science would accompany the films on this particular circuit, it was necessary to keep them moving on schedule.[45]

In December the air force established another program to ferry Moon and his Sermons from Science to twenty air bases in the spring and summer of 1951. Expenses for the presentation were entirely assumed by the Air Training Command. The production group would include two "scientists, representatives of the Moody Institute of Science," who would arrive by trailer truck with their equipment. Each stay was to last four days on each base, with shows Sunday through Wednesday nights. The Moody Bible Institute provided the science caravan and technicians at cost, saving the Air Training Command a huge sum. Advance notices sent to the bases suggested that the sermons be presented in a gymnasium or an empty hangar in order to accommodate as large an audience as possible. Base chaplains were assured that the scientists realized the audience would consist of Catholics, Jews, and Protestants, so their posture was ecumenical: "The basic theme of the production is to present scientific facts of life which in themselves substantiate the existence of reason, orderliness and planning in the Universe." In other words, the instructions concluded, "proving the existence of God, and the need for orderly, moral living."[46]

As the MIS science films became more integrated into the air force Character Guidance program, the two organizations became further entwined. The Armed Forces Public Information Office in Los Angeles worked closely with the Moody Institute of Science on publicity for the productions. Speaking of the Sermons from Science demonstration, the *Air Chaplains' Monthly Newsletter* revealed in early 1951 that plans were being made "for a national campaign using newspapers, magazines, radio, and television to publicize this unusual show and its contribution to the Character Guidance program in the Air Training Command." Somewhat later it was proposed to redesign Sermons from Science to "meet the full aspects" of the air force Character Guidance program.[47]

Appraisal of the 1951 tour of the Moody presentations showed that the Sermons from Science production had been presented 239 times to a total audience of 187,028. The Air Training Command paid the MIS $8,000, and individual bases contracting for other showings contributed another $3,975 for a total of almost $12,000. Robert W. Harper, commanding general of the Air Training Command, suggested that the project be repeated because of its outstanding success.[48] In fact, over the next several years MIS tours, with Moon or another representative of the Institute, became a regular feature of the air force Character Guidance program. Response to the program continued to be enthusiastic. After a Sermons from Science lecture by Keith Hargett at Ellington Air Force Base, in May 1951 the colonel in command wrote to the wing chaplain at the base that the presentation had been extraordinary. The commander was particularly impressed by Hargett's humility. "I am of the opinion," he wrote, "that in a 'rebirth of character,' which General MacArthur contends is a necessity for permanent peace, an essential element is a de-emphasis of pride and a stressing of genuine humility."[49]

In June 1952 the Air Force Chaplain's Office announced another tour of Sermons from Science. This entirely new series boasted a heavily revised format. Instead of four shows there would be only one to ensure that most personnel could see it together. Keith Hargett, the presenter, promised a new chemistry laboratory and a breakthrough in microscopic projection. "All in all," Hargett declared, "we feel that we have a *new* and dramatic show designed to forcefully demonstrate the existence of God, inspire purposeful wholesome living, emphasize the worth of character and a good name." Hargett's carefully chosen words suggest that the Institute had learned to shape its Sermons from Science to fit better into the Character Guidance program by stressing character and behavior. Indeed the word "wholesome," generally used to refer to the problem of venereal disease, was always a serious concern of the chaplains but of little special interest to the MIS.[50]

Tours of the Sermons from Science continued in 1953 and 1954—indeed throughout the 1950s. As late as 1963, George Speake of the Institute reported visiting major air force bases with his scientific equipment and religious lectures. A Moody news release of that year also reported that the MIS had just shipped five hundred film prints and five hundred filmstrips to the army and the air force. That meant that a total of three thousand prints were currently circulating within the armed forces.[51]

Over the years, however, events gradually reduced the importance of the Moody films. Carpenter retired as commander of the chaplains in 1958 to assume the chaplaincy of the new Air Force Academy in Colorado Springs. Other groups such as the Catholic Church began to produce numbers of filmstrips and other visual materials. Denominationalism and sectarianism appeared to become more rather than less significant in the later period, and this compromised some of Moody's ecumenical efforts. Commercial filmmakers such as Warner Brothers also began to produce Character Guidance materials to compete with Moody.[52]

In 1963 the American Civil Liberties Union began an investigation of the chaplains' functions, challenging government expenditures for religious purposes. In 1966 the same watchdog lawyers' organization protested the use of MIS films in the Spokane public schools. There were also limits to audience appeal. In 1965 S. E. McGregor of the Beltsville, Maryland, Agriculture Research Branch wrote to the publicity manager at Moody about an unfortunate showing of an MIS film, *City of the Bees.* He had presented the film to a group at the Smithsonian Institution in February. The assembly included "old and young, male and female, beatniks and elite." They were completely unprepared, he admitted, for the evangelical coda to the film. "Perhaps my introduction did not properly prepare them," he reasoned, "or possibly Washington is a more wicked, atheistic city than I realized." Unfortunately "there was booing, hissing and open guffawing during this portion, with some rather sarcastic comments afterwards that left me shocked."[53]

Despite these growing limitations and the gradual separation of Moody and the air force chaplains movement, the partnership created in 1949 and lasting through the mid-1950s was an extraordinary event in the promotion of religion by the federal government. It remained a successful experiment because of two fortuitous developments. One was the agitation for universal military training that emerged from World War II and the continuing need, after the late 1940s, to promote an impression of the armed forces as a nonthreatening extension of home, community, and church. The Cold War and the Korean War intensified the preoccupation of the armed forces with Character Guidance and ideological instruction. Religion was as much an arm of preparedness in the military as it was in American civilian life at the time. The Moody films and Sermons from Science presentations fit this need perfectly because they presented a modern view of evangelical religion—modern because of its science context. Whereas straight religious exhortation would have evoked controversy or, worse, no reaction at all, the films and presentations appeared to be noncontroversial and up-to-date. They represented a modernization of traditional religious concepts in an acceptable and understandable format. But they did not, like theological modernism, tamper with the basic pieties of traditional American religion and commonsense Baconian science.

The second fortuitous happenstance was the preoccupation of Moon and the Moody Bible Institute with the outcome of the Scopes trial and the recognition that the message of scriptural literalism required updating, modernizing, and popularizing. Without question this could not be undertaken by theological means alone. But Moon accurately gauged the persua-siveness of science as a vehicle for presenting traditional ideas. He easily transformed a dry experiment into a religious miracle, adopting the lan-guage of religion to the description of natural events. If this represented an updating of eighteenth-century scientific theory, it was not recognized as such by most of the audience that saw these films. Moreover, the bril-liant experimental photography on which the Institute prided itself gave the cachet of the most contemporary scientific method. In fact, however, what was modern was the presentation, not the content of ideas, some-thing made quite clear when, at the end of the films or in the Sermons from Science presentation, Moon appeared to read the Bible and argue for the design of nature, the existence of God, and the need for conversion. But Moon had discovered that brilliant photography and compelling visual material encouraged a healthy suspension of disbelief. Finally, Moody was fortunate that Charles I. Carpenter, chief of the air force chaplains, be-came a strong supporter of these evangelical films and presentations. Without him Moody might have made limited inroads, as it did in the army and navy, but nothing on the scale of the air force partnership that developed.

Did this extended preaching mission "church" the unchurched recruits of the armed forces? Did it change their notion of the relation of religion to modern science? Despite efforts of the Moody Bible Institute to find out by counting conversions and donations, there is little evidence that it led to anything like large-scale conversions. The mission's greatest importance was as an example—an important instance of how the confrontation of sci-ence and religion was modified during this important period—and as a con-tribution to American culture. Seen by millions of Americans, the Moody films were to some degree real competitors with Hollywood. At the same time they represented an appendage of the Hollywood dream machine. They reflected the mass culture convention that dressed traditional ideas and themes in brilliant modern techniques. Like so much popular culture in America, these films mediated between old and new.

The Sermons from Science and the MIS films constitute one of the most crucial elements in a developing religious popular culture, something that never quite made it into the pages of *Variety* magazine but that nonetheless became part of the texture of American culture in these remarkable years af-ter the war. *God of Creation* and its progeny helped infuse American mass culture with religious sentiment; they challenged the viewpoint that religion and science clashed. If for a while they knit up the gap rent by the Scopes trial, they did so with a very special argument. Science and religion need not compete, promised the Moody Institute of Science, so long as science remained inside the context of evangelical Protestantism.

When the time comes that
evangelicals do something
in science to the extent
that they become estab-
lished authorities again
and the writers of ac-
cepted textbooks, the evolutionary structure of
scientific thinking will
have to give way to the reasonableness of a sound
Creationism cloaked in
scientific responsibility.

*Journal of the American
Scientific Affiliation* (1956)

chapter 7

Rendezvous at Rancho La Brea

The American Scientific Affiliation, orga-
nized in 1941 under the auspices of the Moody Bible Institute, was conceived in crisis and nourished on controversy. Designed to reconcile
religion and science—or better, professed religion and the profession of
scientist—the ASA foundered on this very problem, suffering a series of
changes and splits that, by the early 1960s, seriously weakened the organization and compromised its mission. Yet its dynamic and unstable amalgam
of ideals and purposes led it through choices and disputes that illuminated
the deeply troubled dialogue over science and religion in the postwar world.   147

At a time when the prestige of science swept through all the energetic places of American culture, the ASA sought to discover if science and conservative evangelical Protestantism could be reconciled. Was it possible to be a respectable scientist and still profess something close to the inerrancy of Scripture and the biblical account of creation?

In 1941 the fertile imagination of Rev. Irwin Moon and the practical energy of Will Houghton, president of the Moody Bible Institute, combined to lay the groundwork for the ASA, although Houghton and Moon had little to do with its eventual history. As with his Sermons from Science, Moon fervently believed that evangelical religion should reach new audiences, not the "over-fed Christians in Bible conferences," but "particularly high school and college young people."[1] He persuaded Houghton to plan a conference of scientist Christians who might come together to advise ministers on the validity and application of scientific propositions and draft a handbook for college students to prepare them to resist the secular temptations of the scientific laboratory. Houghton then wrote to F. Alton Everest, then an assistant professor of electrical engineering at Oregon State College, to invite him to help organize such a body.[2]

In fact, Moon and Everest had already discussed the project during a meeting in Oregon in 1940, so Houghton's letter merely formalized a process already under way. Other scientists they approached included John P. Van Haitsma, of Calvin College, Peter W. Stoner, a mathematician from Pasadena City College, Russell Sturgis, a professor of chemistry at Ursinus College, and Irving Cowperthwaite, a chemist employed at the Thompson Wire Company. This group, together with Moon and Houghton, met in Chicago in early September 1941.[3] Almost immediately Everest began to solicit members, writing to friends to ask their cooperation in locating scientists and professors "who really love the Lord."[4]

From the beginning, the organization adopted a professional posture and looked to the scientific world for approval. Moon had written to Everest before their meeting to suggest that they base their structure on an existing scientific organization. Everest responded by examining several constitutions including that of the American Association for the Advancement of Science. Based on this study he drafted what he anticipated would be "suitable for such a society of Christian men of science."[5] By early 1942 a framework had been developed that promised to "correlate the facts of science and the Holy Scriptures." The membership statement that all members needed to affirm was self-confident and assertive: "I believe the whole Bible

Figure 7.1 F. Alton Everest, organizer and leading intellectual force behind the American Scientific Affiliation, poses here beside the symbol of up-to-date science: the model of a molecule (in this case an amino acid). Courtesy of the Wheaton College Archives and Special Collections.

as originally given to be the inspired work of God, the only unerring guide of faith and conduct. Since God is the Author of this book, as well as the Creator and Sustainer of the physical world about us, I cannot conceive of discrepancies between statements in the Bible and the real facts of science."[6]

Yet as Everest later recalled, those at the initial meeting in Chicago exuded neither confidence nor clarity of principle. All of us, he remarked, "were very conscious of the poor image evangelicals frequently project in scientific circles." No one doubted the significance of reconciling science and religion within a general context of Protestant theology, but the contentious issue remained how to interpret Genesis in the light of modern scientific discoveries. Even if the words of the Bible were literally true, there remained subtle shades of meaning. Was there any "give" in Scripture for interpretation? Could modern science be accommodated through the paraphrase of eternal truths? If so, how far could interpretation stray beyond the eighteenth-century notions of William Paley or from the axioms of belief defined by the early twentieth-century fundamentalists? As Everest noted, the group could not agree on first principles. The members conformed on basics, he wrote, but also tolerated different interpretations. Most important, the organization resisted the "temptation of adopting a 'standard' ASA interpretation."[7] This compromise planted the seeds of dissension as well as the perennial hope of accomplishing the larger task of professionalizing evangelical science: to make it serve two masters.

In many respects the founding moment of the ASA was the culmination of a wave of organization following the Scopes trial that repositioned evangelical Protestants and prepared them for a new effort to combat modernism.[8] Although this effort assumed many guises and forms, the inspiration of the ASA took a turn away from Bryan's populist conception of science of 1925. The "Great Commoner" had seized the mantle of the amateur scientist, a hero of his age of individualism. Everest and his allies intended from the first to establish a credentialed organization that could compete in the world of professional science and corporate organization. This ASA strategy required a watchful eye to ward off amateurs and zealots from the inner reaches of the organization. Yet this tactic created a dilemma, for much of the audience it fervently hoped to attract was in fact zealous and nonprofessional. It decided to accept such people as members, send them tracts and journals, and admit them as participants in conferences, but never to let them be decision makers. Leadership remained a monopoly of the experts. From the beginning the tug of respectability was as tenacious as the pull of Scripture, and the ASA tried to accommodate both.

This position inevitably disrupted smooth relations with the Moody Bible Institute, although the greatest acrimony and conflict came with creation-deluge scientists who sought to enlist the organization for their unique explanation of the faults of Darwinism.[9] The Noah flood, this theory posited, could explain all the geological anomalies that enticed scientists into believing in natural selection.

Although apparent from the beginning, this aim of the deluge geologists to capture the ASA did not really become controversial until after the World War II. In the meantime the ASA incorporated itself in the state of California in 1943 and held preliminary meetings throughout the war years. Its first national convention was postponed until 1946. F. Alton Everest himself spent the war years at work at the Naval Laboratory in San Diego, and Rev. Irwin Moon concentrated his evangelical work on the armed forces. When the war ended, Everest quit his research post and decided to devote full time to Moon's film project. He became the leading technical adviser for the new Moody Institute of Science. As he noted, the purpose of the group "will be to provide a virile Christian testimony among students, the scientific world, and other intellectual spheres that are practically untouched today."[10] This was but one, if the most ambitious, Moody initiative to reconcile science and religion conceived at this time. The Moody radio station also broadcast forty talks by Arthur I. Brown called the "Miracles of Science," devoted to scientizing Fundamentalist belief and arguing against Darwinism.[11]

This general strategy matched the early aims of the ASA, which used its scientific expertise and connections to bolster the credentials of the MIS. The Moody films cited mainstream scientific establishments and persuaded leading institutions to allow them to shoot films at their facilities. Furthermore, Everest persuaded the ASA to act as the informal scientific panel to advise Moon's Hollywood studio on the scientific content of their films. As early as November 1945, Everest wrote that "last Tuesday evening, an ASA committee reviewed Moon's new film, 'The God of Creation' and recommended approval to the executive council."[12] Nonetheless, Everest did not want the ASA to be closely identified with the Moody science operation or, for that matter, with the Bible Institute. He intended it to stand alone, independent of any identifiable evangelical organization.[13]

This more secular purpose clashed with the efforts of the deluge geologists to develop a united front against Darwinism on the fringes of the scientific profession. Everest and the Moody Bible Institute certainly recognized a common purpose with the deluge geologists and accepted their support, but they remained wary of the single-mindedness and absolutism of the science credo that bolstered this particular interpretation of Scripture.[14]

Everest and most of the directors of the ASA accepted deluge members because they hoped to change their minds. They were, after all, neighbors on the continuum of orthodoxy and creationism. Yet the flood geologists insisted that a united front entailed agreeing with their particular creationist science, and Everest was from the first unwilling to tie the organization down to a particular interpretation. This was indeed a narrow path to tread! As Everest wrote in 1944, at about the time the deluge group proposed a merger, the ASA already had a creed in place. Members had to subscribe to "inspiration of the Bible in the literal sense." But what, practically, did that mean? Was it narrow enough to satisfy the deluge group? Was it wide enough to include practicing mainstream scientists?[15]

Organization of the deluge scientists had begun formally in 1938 with the formation of the Society for Study of Deluge Geology and Related Sciences. Publication of the *Bulletin of Deluge Geology* began in 1941 and lasted through the war years. Many of the deluge members were Seventh-Day Adventists and based their beliefs on such books as George McCready Price's *The Modern Flood Theory of Geology*. Price, a consultant for William Jennings Bryan in 1925, a longtime opponent of Darwinism, and the author of a college geology textbook, had for years struggled to gain scientific respectability for his theory that the fossil and geological anomalies discovered by geologists could be explained by the biblical flood that swept all living things in its wake. In this respect the deluge geologists must also be seen as potential competitors with the ASA. Common cause with them meant taking the risks of association with a jealous ally.[16]

This risk first surfaced in early 1944 when the Deluge Society offered to organize a united front to "smoke out" Darwinism "for a public licking." In a letter to a colleague in the ASA, Everest warned such an initiative would make "a laughingstock out of both parties. Remember the Scopes trial." But Everest planned a gentle response. He wrote to Dudley Joseph Whitney of the Society that the ASA fully shared the group's aims. But he asked, "Can we perform any useful service to the church by stirring up such debates when we are not agreed among ourselves?" Whitney replied with extravagant confidence, offering to put up a $500 war bond as a forfeit if he failed to "show conclusively that deluge geology is better science than ages [Darwinian] geology." The debate could be judged by a committee of experts and then published. This plan did not appeal to the ASA, which had fixed on a strategy of quiet persuasion.[17]

Relations with the Adventists became even more difficult in 1946 at the first annual convention of the ASA. Although the organization guarded against "spiritual apostasy in its membership by having the doctrinal statement sent out to each member for signing annually," the opposite risk of tendentiousness was identified with the deluge geologists. The convention discussed whether even to allow Adventists into the organization and, if so, on what basis. As a safeguard there were discussions about establishing a two-tiered form of affiliation, with full members who were established and reputable scientists and associates who might belong to the organization but could not vote.[18] Adventists did in fact join the ASA, but the Association refused any formal organizational ties with the Deluge Society.[19] In this way the ASA sought to negotiate between professionalism and amateurism in science and between versions of anti-Darwinism.

The immediate postwar task facing the ASA was to prepare a science handbook for college students—one of the initial purposes of the organization. The world had greatly changed, and as Everest wrote, we need "positive plans of action." "All the universities were once Christian," he continued; "now none are." This disestablishment had occurred over many years; to restore religion might require even greater time and effort, he concluded.[20] But the task must begin.

The difficulty began with a recognition of the diversity in modern science and the multiplicity of the languages that articulated its fields of study. No general approach could inject a Christian viewpoint into all of science: each branch required its own discrete discussion. This meant a book divided by field into biology, astronomy, geology, and so on. Everest initiated work on the handbook early in 1943 when he circulated position papers throughout the ASA for commentary. As he wrote to C. Stacey Woods, general secretary of the Inter-Varsity Christian Fellowship in November, this vetting by experts would help establish the highest scientific scholarship as well as "a Christ honoring interpretation of Biblical passages." Although the overall purpose remained an evangelical appeal, "we will feel repaid if students are stabilized in their Christian faith."[21] If this approach dimly recalls Bryan's assault on the teaching of evolutionary theory in 1925, it also suggests the changed circumstances of the postwar world: immunization, not quarantine, had become the strategy to achieve a healthy modern Christianity.

The handbook, titled *Modern Science and Christian Faith* and edited by Everest, finally appeared in 1948, with a revised second edition in 1950. The purpose of the work, as Everest wrote, was twofold: to demonstrate a harmony between the Bible narrative and observations of the physical world, and to persuade readers that this doctrine could be accepted by reputable men of science. Did Christians perform different work than secular scientists? the book asked. The answer was yes and no. Elaborating on how religious belief modified science, most of the articles focused on the implications of evolutionary theory for various disciplines and bore such titles as "Biology and Creation," "Astronomy and the First Chapter of Genesis."[22]

The central piece confronted the deviation of modern geology from the

Genesis story. The author, Edwin K. Gedney, laid out a number of standard objections to evolutionary theory: the lack of transitional species, the incomplete fossil record, the sudden appearance of life. He then took up several possible theories to account for a lengthened geological record that scientists had estimated. These interpretations included such notions as progressive creation (creation in several stages). None of these was entirely satisfactory, but the author swore to the truth of the Bible. Evolution, he summarized, was based only on faith, whereas creation as described in Scripture amounted to true science.[23]

Such a cautious (and ambiguous) position on evolution could be expected. But Peter W. Stoner, writing on astronomy, took a more radical view. Genesis and astronomy, he began, agreed entirely. Radioactive dating now proved that the universe was immensely old, from 2 to 10 billion years. This concession to modern science did not disprove Genesis but actually confirmed it, because it demonstrated an actual beginning time of the universe. "Every star is losing energy and mass—therefore, there is a beginning," he concluded. Stoner then went through the Bible verse after verse to indicate how modern science could be reconciled with Scripture.

This particular argument stirred deep controversy. Certainly not all members of the ASA accepted carbon dating or welcomed estimates of the vast age of the world. But there was a familiar argument here that even Bryan and other earlier creationists had employed. Stoner returned to the second law of thermodynamics to prove his point. To demonstrate the validity of biblical creation, he invoked the theory of cosmic devolution. This ingenious acceptance of the ancient age and evolution of the universe continued to animate the discussions of the ASA and to foment disagreements and splits among its members. Stoner in particular led a faction that proposed to accept as much modern science as possible. In so doing, his group stretched the story of creation into a series of extended-time metaphors— in other words, toward accepting a theory of theistic evolution.[24]

Yet the most basic, elementary assumption of the ASA and its gathering of scientists remained the insistence that science and religion must agree, even if, as modern disciplines and manifestations of belief, they seemed to represent opposite orientations to the world. The great error of the modern world—supposing that science and religion must disagree—had to be refuted. The task of the ASA, then, was to reconcile scientists and scientific theory to scriptural truth. This undertaking had nothing to do with dividing knowledge into separate scientific or spiritual realms. Nor did the ASA insist on a specific form of reconciliation. Instead, the organization wanted scientists to situate their profession inside a Christian context. As Harold Hartzler, future president of the ASA, wrote in 1953, "I would say our ultimate aim is the evangelization of men of science, but we do not openly state that aim. You see we would rather first get the confidence of men of science, and then lead them to a saving knowledge of faith in the Lord Jesus Christ."[25] The ASA was, in other words, an ecumenical science organization with evangelical purposes.

When organized initially in 1941, the ASA elected F. Alton Everest as its first president. He served during the war years, but a serious, full-time commitment had to wait until 1945. Still, signs of life were apparent. A number of local groups sprang up before 1945. The first national convention met in 1946, beginning a lively series of annual meetings. In 1949 the ASA published the first issue of its new *Journal of the American Scientific Affiliation.*

As Everest steered the organization through its first promising early years, by the 1949 convention it became apparent that a number of issues had hardened into difficulties that required address. This turned out to be a decisive moment in the history of the organization and a fundamental turning point. When the members met in Los Angeles that year, they spent considerable time on several field trips: a visit to Mount Palomar Observatory, a tour of the Los Angeles County Museum fossil exhibition, and a particularly noteworthy visit to the La Brea tar pits in the city near Wilshire Boulevard. During the 1940s the area had been landscaped as a park with an observation station built underground to view some of the thousands of skeletons of Pleistocene epoch animals trapped by the tar—many of them long extinct. This was precisely the visual evidence of evolution that required attention and explanation.[26]

All of these group excursions, but particularly the one to La Brea, reveal how important questions of origins, evolution, and the age of the world remained for the ASA members. The urge to visit such anomalous sites seemed irresistible. From the first, the group had been deeply concerned about materialist interpretations of evolution; it would be no exaggeration to say the organization was founded to provide an alternative, scientific version of Genesis, a workable version of creation science. This was its deepest, most abiding commitment yet its most difficult challenge, for defining just how science might explicate Scripture became an increasingly difficult and divisive issue. Nonetheless, from 1946 to 1949 reconciling Genesis and science was the most frequently discussed subject of the conventions. The trip

Figure 7.2   Members of the American Scientific Affiliation (MacRae, Voskugl, Monsa, Sutherland, and Everest) visit the La Brea tar pits in Los Angeles during the 1949 convention. The giant extinct sloths modeled here presented the sort of evidence that intrigued and divided the organization. Courtesy of the Wheaton College Archives and Special Collections.

to La Brea and other fossil grounds at subsequent conventions represented field trips into temptation.[27]

Everest had long planned the visit to La Brea. In 1944 he wrote to inquire about the museum there. "I was just toying with the idea that the ASA group might visit whatever there is to visit, although I am not sure that anything but the pits remain."[28] When the group did make its way to La Brea the issue of evolution had reached its peak of interest. Everest recalled a "memorable scene" from a meeting of the Los Angeles convention, with "George McCready Price quietly sitting in the front row as geologist J. Laurence Kulp presented his critical paper on 'Flood Geology.'"

Kulp took the opportunity at this session to dissect and refute most of the major premises of deluge geology in front of one of its greatest advocates. The problem, said Kulp, derived from the entirely unscientific assumptions of deluge geology. To believe Price and his followers, one had to assume the suspension of major scientific laws. Kulp noted that the attack on accepted theories of geological "uniformitarianism" had been popular

Figure 7.3 This could have been a scene from a 1950s science fiction film, but instead it pictures American Scientific Affiliation members on a field trip during the Los Angeles meeting in 1949. Mount Palomar had become an almost universally recognized symbol of modern science and the mysteries of the universe. Courtesy of the Wheaton College Archives and Special Collections.

among some Christians, but this amounted to a quarrel with the truth. Flood geology misconstrued the age of the world and ignored the findings of geology. It was entirely "inadequate to explain the observed data in geology." Worse, the "major propositions of the theory are contradicted by established physical and chemical laws."

Kulp's most damning assertion came toward the end, when he explained his aggressive tone. "This paper has been negative in character," he concluded, "because it is believed that this unscientific theory of flood geology has done and will do considerable harm to the strong propagation of the gospel among educated people."[29] Allies in the cause of reconciling science and religion had deeply compromised the cause. This was a serious charge, and it offended many members of the ASA, even beyond the flood geology contingent.

Plans to take on Price had begun as early as 1947 when, in preparation for the 1949 meeting, Everest wrote asking Kulp to deliver the attack on deluge science. "I wish you would present us with this clear refutation of the Flood geologists' position as soon as possible. I *know* [his italics] they are all 'wet,' but I cannot refute them with my background in another field." The group represented "a real threat." "Boy," he concluded in exasperation, "this Southern California is the breeding place of every ism, it seems."[30]

At the bottom of his letter, Everest also explained his attitude toward Darwinism and his tacit acceptance of some of its elements. There was no need to attack the theory of evolution; only its materialistic implications needed to be challenged. Hoping to separate the reality of geological change from the interpretation given it by other scientists, Everest defined a crucial but elusive goal. It was necessary, he wrote, to guard the ASA against "scientific and intellectual mediocrity." Indeed, as he told a meeting of the executive council members at the same time, the real threat to the ASA came from its best friends, who imposed their own unscientific agendas on the organization. For this reason he advised the council (and they agreed) not to establish a speakers' bureau. How could they, he asked, maintain control "on what is said"? How could they, he left unspoken, earn the respect of mainline scientists if they were publicly represented by deluge geology?[31]

Everest had in mind a long-term strategy concerning Darwin, and the 1949 Los Angeles convention also debated its possibilities. As early as 1948 he began work on what he hoped would emerge as a definitive project, a volume to commemorate the one hundredth anniversary of Darwin's *Origin of Species*. The difficulties and attraction of such a project were immediately apparent, for all the members of the ASA rejected at least some aspect of the Darwinian equation, yet many accepted one or another piece of evolutionary theory. To accommodate these nuances of belief and satisfy a divided membership would require the effort of a decade. In the meantime, the ASA conventions increasingly took up the broader issues of evolutionary evidence: radiocarbon dating, the striated placement of fossils, the length of geologic ages, the possibilities of limited evolution after an initial creation, the development of specific organs such as the eye, and of course the deluge geology solution.[32]

As the deadline for the Darwin volume approached in 1959, the debate widened to include other issues in science. Two men, Russell L. Mixter and Harold Hartzler, served as president of the organization during these crucial years of growth and contention, although Everest remained an active member of the group. As more sophisticated geological debates preoccupied the ASA, so did new issues (and distractions) raised by social science begin to loom larger.

One of the most active protagonists in the evolutionary dialogue was Marion Cordelia Erdman, geology instructor at Wheaton College in Illinois. Erdman held an amalgamated view of geological science and creationism. Clearly, she noted in an article for the *Journal* in 1950, the Grand Canyon and its striations contained "a sequence from what have been denoted 'simple' forms to those which have been denoted 'complex.'" Whether this constituted evidence for Darwinian evolution, however, was another matter. As she noted in a later contribution, "fossils give absolutely no ground for losing faith in the inspired character of the Genesis chronicle. Neither do they provide startling confirmation of it."[33]

Cautious articles by Erdman and others explored such anomalies as the development of the eye—an evolutionary problem often cited by teleologists, who claimed that without a preexisting plan natural selection could never result in a specialized organ exclusively devoted to vision. The horse was another example, for it seemed to evolve out of earlier and smaller life forms but then to achieve its contemporary existence as a beast of burden designed especially for humans.[34] Despite such hesitant explorations, by the end of the 1950s a considerable number of the ASA leaders had come to accept radiocarbon dating and what it implied: an ancient earth. As Edwin A. Olson of Columbia University wrote for the *Journal* in 1959: it now "seems reasonable to measure man's tenure on earth in terms of tens of thousands of years." This was evidence of the progress of theistic (or guided) evolution, a position that Hartzler noted in 1957 was held by "perhaps 90% of the theologians of this country" and that to his (skeptical) eyes looked very much like "naturalistic evolution."[35]

The implications of this movement surfaced as the Darwin centennial volume took shape. While President Mixter, a zoologist, served as editor, Everest chaired a committee to oversee the publication and in this capacity exchanged frequent letters about the contributions with other fellows of the organization. For example, Everest wrote to J. Frank Cassel in 1951 recommending that the ASA exercise extreme caution lest it admit that "evolution is a fact." Cassel responded that biblical conservatives should admit the existence of evolution privately, if only to study it better: "At least among us girls," he continued, "let's call it by name, talk it over, and then do something about it."[36]

When the manuscript was finally assembled, Everest and Mixter attempted in vain to interest a secular press. They recognized that a mainstream imprimatur would greatly increase the odds of attention from other scientists. Perhaps it would also grant the work entrée into the general discussion of Darwinism expected during the centennial year. But they succeeded only in persuading a religious publisher, Eerdmans, to take the book, and it appeared in September 1959 under the title *Evolution and Christian Thought Today*.

The articles in the edited volume were written primarily by scientist members of the ASA; several were already familiar voices in the organization. One by one they examined the impact of Darwinism on biology and on the larger questions of the origins of life and the character of change in nature. Age-old problems remained unexplained: the fixity of species, the origin and descent of mankind, the problem of interspecies links, the age of the world, the fossil record. and so on. Toward each subject the guiding principle seemed to be salvage, if not salvation: How much of the biblical account of creation could be maintained inside a scientific world that completely accepted Darwinism? Who would take seriously the compromises proposed by the ASA? Was anyone listening beyond the band of Fundamentalist scientists?

Although there was considerable disagreement among the authors about precisely where to mark off the claims of religion and science and how to define a creationist science, most of them took a large measure of modern science for granted—as fact. Incorporating this into a scriptural narrative became, then, an exercise in compromise and the occasion to stretch metaphors. Each major detail of evolutionary theory was examined for what had to be accepted and what could still be doubted, an intellectual process that gave the collection a tenuous, argumentive tone. Perhaps the most optimistic note was struck in the last article by theologian Carl Henry, editor of *Christianity Today*. The volume, he concluded, "looks to a sequel, in which the reality of divine revelation in the cosmos and in Scripture is coordinated, and in which Jesus Christ, and not evolutionary process, is seen as the only adequate index to cosmic activity and purpose."[37]

If *Evolution and Christian Thought Today* was intended to bridge a gap between theology and science, it stood too close to one side to be visible to the other; in fact it really addressed only one audience. Its obvious constituency remained the evangelical Protestant public and those laymen with enough scientific understanding to follow the arguments. There was little in it that might interest a scientist as scientist, for the book was an argument that turned on itself, part religious polemic, part a plea for further consideration. In reality it probably impressed neither audience: those who wanted a decisive argument against Darwin or those who might have been interested in how religion could add to what science already knew about evolutionary theory.

As the Darwin centennial approached toward the end of the 1950s, the ASA also accelerated toward another decisive turning point in its history. Irving A. Cowperthwaite, in an article for the *Journal* in 1960, pointed to an inevitable change. At two recent annual conventions, in 1957 and 1958, "there appeared to be a growing conviction that inexorable pressure of expanding knowledge is about to force us to accept some formulation of the theory of evolution." J. Frank Cassel, writing in the same issue, went further in discussing the most recent convention in Chicago. Clearly the scientists of the group were drifting toward some form of evolutionary theory. But more orthodox members remained adamantly opposed and, according to Cassel, poured on a "tremendous heckle." I believe, he concluded, "I can question some of my long-cherished interpretations of the Bible without being damned by doing so or being led astray by Satan in the process." Obviously, others remained unconvinced.[38]

Another contentious issue was the burgeoning importance of social science in American society, particularly after 1960. Social science had long existed at the periphery of the ASA as a dimly lighted path that it was dangerous to follow. But some members of the ASA enthusiastically claimed social science for Christianity. This banner was carried high by sociologist David O. Moberg, from Bethel College, who joined the organization in the mid-1950s. He spent considerable time persuading the group to support religious social science research. In an article for the *Journal* in 1958, Moberg argued that sociological study had discovered a tantalizing preliminary result: holding "orthodox or Conservative Christian beliefs is related to good personal adjustment in old age." In other words, he argued, sociology could be used to confirm religious belief. Moberg wanted to move too fast, however. When he proposed a joint meeting in 1961 with two organizations, the Society for the Scientific Study of Religion and the Religious Research Affiliation (with which he was associated), Hartzler rejected the notion. The "aims of these [sociological] organizations," he wrote, "are quite different from ... our own."[39]

Still, in early 1960 planning for the annual convention incorporated a serious social science agenda with four separate commissions—specializing in the history and philosophy of science, natural science, social science, and psychology—defining the program. Not every member approved this move to accept social science, nor did the disapproval come just from religious conservatives. "Some of the natural scientists in the A.S.A.," wrote chemist Walter R. Hearn to a colleague in 1960, "think we have gone too far in welcoming social scientists." The nature of the ASA might be changed "for the worse if large numbers of sociologists, economists, etc., join."[40]

Members of the ASA had always been disputatious, and the issue of professionalism inevitably exacerbated these internal differences. Splits and disagreements regularly occurred on both extremes of the issue. For example, in 1953 an informal coalition of New York members petitioned the ASA to widen and loosen the stated purpose of the organization: correlating science and Scripture was simply too narrow a goal. In their brief position paper the group asked the ASA to commit itself to genuine science, not Christian apologetics. The only route to respectability, they continued, was to control papers given at conventions. In particular, they objected to anything relating to flood geology. "To seriously discuss such nonsense on the formal program puts us in the category of those that still debate [the] validity of the dowsing rod or the witch doctor or flying saucers as space ships from Mars" was their unkind characterization.[41]

Several other informal caucuses appeared to agree, including one formed in California and another in the Midwest. But the ASA leaders declined to push ahead with a split. As future president Harold Hartzler wrote in 1954, the very existence of the ASA was at stake. "Do we want to go down the road of just being another scientific organization, or do we really want to stick to our guns and be a real witness for the Lord?" Hartzler wanted both, but he recognized the impossibility of satisfying every faction.[42]

This discussion could not be resolved by a few position papers, letters of objection, or disputes at annual conventions; after all, it related to the essential definition and purpose of the organization. In the mid-1950s several resignations occurred that threatened to cripple the organization. In his withdrawal, linguist Eugene Nida wrote that he was "very much disturbed at what seems to me to be the trend of events in A.S.A." These included primarily the continued adherence of the organization and its journal to anti-scientific positions. Council member John R. Howitt commented on this situation to Hartzler in late 1956. "Ever since the Wheaton Convention I have felt some misgiving that all was not well in the body politic of the A.S.A."[43]

To maintain control over the roiling debate within its membership, the ASA enforced its peculiar compromise of openness to competing ideas by maintaining control of the organization in a small, close-knit group of like-minded leaders. This was accomplished with two strategies. The ASA council defined (and redefined) distinct categories of membership and severely restricted voting privileges—primarily to practicing scientists. The council also regulated ordinary affiliation in order to prevent any large group from attempting to seize control of the organization or its annual conventions. Although this kept deluge geology under control, it gradually pushed the organization toward mainline science.

These experiments with restriction first appeared when the constitution was amended in 1951 to establish a two-tiered membership list. Although the organization still circulated its Fundamentalist doctrinal position to be affirmed by everyone, there were distinct differences in responsibilities and privileges of members according to their professional standing in the scientific community. The superior position was fellow, defined as a member with high academic and scientific standing who also subscribed to the basic tenets of Christian faith. Fellows could be elected only by the other fellows and possessed voting rights and policy-making responsibilities. All were expected to present papers at the annual conventions. Associate members, on the other hand, included professed Christians who had some scientific training. Associates could come to annual meetings but could not vote.[44]

Despite this change, rumors of constitutional change continued to bounce around the organization throughout the 1950s. The impetus came primarily from scientists who wished to lessen the doctrinal rigidity of the organization and also eliminate the embarrassing presence of deluge associates. In 1953 a three-category scheme was proposed consisting of fellows (still the highest), members, who had undergraduate degrees in the natural or social sciences but no voting privileges, and associates, currently majoring in the natural or social sciences, who could come to meetings but could not vote. A next step occurred in 1955 when the program committee of the annual convention decided to screen all papers submitted for presentation.[45]

The most serious attempt to change the constitution came in the mid-1950s when several of the fellows attempted to revise the membership affirmation—and hence redirect the organization itself. A questionnaire sent around to the members showed this to be a very controversial suggestion. Nonetheless a new constitution was approved in 1959 that simplified the doctrinal statement (vowing belief in limited inerrancy) and expanded the membership categories to four: fellows, honorary fellows (without the vote), members, and associates. As Walter Hearn wrote that year, the ASA had profoundly shifted its orientation, and this would greatly disturb the older members of the organization. But, he added, "I think it has put us in a good position to be of service both to Christians and to scientists."[46] In essence the strategy increased the distance between practicing scientists and amateurs while trying to keep them under the same ecumenical umbrella.

This tilt toward professional science placed the ASA at odds with part of its own membership and weakened the alliance it had struck with the Evangelical Theological Society, an organization that Everest reported in 1950 would be a "partner organization to ours."[47] Toward the end of the 1950s the ASA held several joint meetings with the Evangelical Society, presumably in hopes of convincing this more strictly creationist group of the validity of limited evolution. The effort brought mixed results. A report on the 1957 conference maintained a judicious tone but gave a pessimistic survey of the encounter. Each side, the theologians and the scientists, needed instruction in the methods of the other, but clearly the ASA members concluded that in these circumstances discussions were difficult. The meeting in 1958 grew even more testy, as the Evangelical Society protested the "weighty" presence of Drs. Ramm and Kulp, who planned to defend uniformitarianism versus catastrophism. As anthropologist James O. Buswell of the ASA liaison committee wrote, he intended to avoid "another squabble over geology and the flood."[48]

The early 1960s finally brought the oldest controversy in the organization to the breaking point. The ASA had always been ambivalent about whether to allow Seventh-Day Adventists to join. As early as 1945 Marion Barnes, later editor of the *Journal*, wrote to admonish Everest: "I feel that the admitting of SDA's to membership is to attach to the A.S.A. a stigma."[49]

The most difficult blend of membership came not from the theology of the sect, but from the popularity of deluge geology among many of its members. From the beginning this group had challenged the direction of the ASA and promoted its flood interpretation of geological discoveries. It succeeded because of the open forum style of the organization. Finally, however, Everest's strategy backfired. He hoped to energize new and more scientifically acceptable modifications of creationism; instead he stirred up a polarized fight with dogmatists. As he concluded: this approach, "with its toleration for and encouragement of a wide spectrum of views, has nurtured a tidy number of literal creationists." Not everyone admired this harvest of believers, and in 1955 he wrote that inclusiveness had become a noticeable problem, with Laurence Kulp "saying scurrilous things about [flood geologists] Price and Whitney."[50]

Among those not as tolerant as Everest, complaints mounted over the burgeoning fight between deluge geologists and sympathetic Fundamentalists versus a growing group that tentatively accepted aspects of evolutionary theory. John R. Howitt sent President Hartzler a memorandum on the developing schism in late 1956, referring to the "Crisis in the A.S.A." Howitt was defending the conservatives against those who, despite their declaration of adherence, had diverged from "faith in the Word of God." To allow this to continue would threaten the organization itself. It hurts me, Howitt concluded, "to hear fundamentalists ridiculed by members of the A.S.A. I am also amazed when I hear a leader of the A.S.A. express the fear that the new Darwin centennial volume may be anti-evolutionary." Would this book, written by Christians, actually glorify Darwin, he asked in horror?[51]

Publication of the Darwin centennial book finally precipitated a split in the organization along the old fault lines of flood geology. As Walter Hearn wrote in 1960, the organization remained committed to evangelical Protestant principles, but "some of our extremely conservative members are disappointed that our book is not another anti-evolution polemic."[52] Nonetheless, Hearn believed that the more open, questioning position of the book expressed the better nature of the organization.

The decisive event was the publication in 1961 of *The Genesis Flood*, written by Henry M. Morris and John C. Whitcomb Jr. Morris had been an early member of the ASA and had amassed a considerable following among fellows of the organization. In the early 1960s a significant group of these ASA fellows, including Morris and six others, plus (nonmember) Duane Gish, founded the Creation Research Society. As Everest commented, this "polarization within the ASA (actually a rejection of the open forum principle) percolated over the years and eventually resulted in the formation of the Creation Research Society." Relations with the Evangelical Theological Society also were strained to the breaking point because many members of the latter organization favored flood geology. In fact a considerable portion of the correspondence between fellows and ordinary members of the ASA revolved around manuscripts claiming the absolute validity of Genesis and denouncing Darwinian evolution but rejected for publication in the *Journal*.[53]

Although Everest played down the effects of the split on the American Scientific Affiliation, it remains a turning point in the history of modern evangelical theology-science relations and, in one sense at least, a symbol of an interrupted dialogue. The principal audience of the ASA scientists turned out to be the conservative evangelical community, in which the deluge geologists were an important and growing segment. Inability to convince them to keep at least one foot inside mainstream science lessened the opportunity to play middleman to science and religion, which had always been the intent of the ASA. From its beginning the organization had lived a paradox, keeping tight rein over its inner circle but allowing considerable freedom of expression in its journal and conventions. The fellows recognized the dangers of allowing amateur scientists and theologians to determine policy. This principle of guided democracy kept the ASA open to diversity and to considering the impact of the newest ideas in science and their potential influence on traditional theology. But a sizable segment of the membership was never comfortable with openness. Just as evolution had been the pretext for organizing the ASA, so it precipitated the split that occurred twenty years later. Everest and most of the other fellows had accepted much of the evidence for Darwinian evolution, even if they still could not countenance the underlying hypothesis of random selection. They acknowledged the great age of the earth and accepted evolution within limited circumstances. This progression toward theistic evolution remained completely unacceptable to strict Fundamentalists.[54]

But did the creeping professionalism of the ASA improve its standing among mainstream scientists? Did the half-open door to evolutionism bring any rewards of recognition or any increase in prestige for the evangelical purposes of Everest and the other theologically conservative scientists who gathered every year to listen to papers on evolution, biology, and social science and to tour local geological sites on field trips? Despite the earnest efforts of the ASA to carry its message to the mainstream, this potential audience remained indifferent or hostile. Like the deluge geologists, mainstream science rejected the ASA's ambivalence about first principles and spurned the ambiguities of their compromises.

In a retrospective article on the history of the ASA published in 1959 in the *Journal,* zoologist William J. Tinkle argued that the organization had not been sufficiently forthright or tough-minded. An open forum was interesting but limited in usefulness. "We ought," he concluded "to settle some principles, then go out and make converts among other scientists." Their purpose must be to "correct the mistakes of scientists which have lessened faith in the Bible."[55] Such a strategy suggested that some members were willing to give up the effort to merge religion and science, abandon the free play of mainstream dialogue, and go all out for evangelism.

The most obvious sign of respectability would have been membership in the American Association for the Advancement of Science (the same organization Bryan had joined immediately before the Scopes trial). The ASA first applied for group membership in 1951 and received a polite but pointed rejection. The AAAS was inclusive and ecumenical in its interests in science, but it could not include any "strictly religious doctrines." It would "be disastrous," wrote the AAAS representative frankly, "if we became identified with any partisan attitude on any subject in any field."

The ASA asked again in 1954 and received much the same response. The scientific establishment rejected the application and suggested that the ASA wait some time so that the "clarification of the objectives of the Affiliation should occur." In 1959 Walter Hearn suggested another tactic. Individual members could join the AAAS. In fact, he noted, since their journal *Science* "has begun to deal more and more with broad philosophical issues, I almost feel that *most* of our members *should* belong to the A.A.A.S" (his italics).[56]

The campaign for respectability also extended to publishers. It remained very much in the interest of the ASA to secure a mainstream house to bring out its publications. Everest had initially been optimistic about getting the premier publisher, Macmillan in New York, to take the student handbook prepared by the ASA after the war. After Macmillan rejected the manuscript, Everest wrote again in September 1946 saying that the publication would be aimed at college and university students. We feel, he confessed, "a publisher already established in the publication of scientific books would be a wise choice." Would there be any financial arrangements under which Macmillan might take the book, he asked? The publishers responded in October, after a lengthy discussion, that they could not accept the manuscript even with a subvention by the ASA.[57] In all, Everest canvassed eight standard "secular houses" including Harper and Doubleday, but none was interested. The manuscript was finally published by the religious press Van Kampen, in Wheaton, Illinois. After similar efforts almost ten years later, the organization settled on a religious press to bring out its Darwin centennial book.

At the same time that it sought recognition from the mainstream, the ASA remained cautious and standoffish toward mainstream theological movements, which shared to a limited extent their suspicions of materialist science. In particular, the organization voiced opposition to Protestant neoorthodoxy, a movement that stressed the predominance of faith but that looked to members of the ASA like nothing but disguised modernism.[58]

The organization was also wary of what looked like pseudoscience. When Immanuel Velikovsky's much commented on book *Worlds in Collision* appeared in 1950, several members asked for an extended discussion of the work at the next convention. When the group met in August, however, several fellows including Hartzler, Stoner, and Kulp "all mentioned it unfavorably." "It appears," wrote Mixter, "that there is very little modern science in it. Whatever can be proved by folklore seems to be its chief merit."[59]

Toward other Christian academic groups, the ASA turned a cautious face, wishing to carry on any joint activity on its own terms. Thus the ASA continued polite relations with such groups as the Society for the Scientific Study of Religion but declined to undertake joint meetings. On the other hand, the organization was clearly thinking of organizing a federation of Christian scholarly societies in 1959 under its own aegis. Such an organization might encompass such groups as the Christian Association for Psychological Studies, founded in 1953.[60] Other ASA outreach programs included displays at national science fairs (1957, 1958) and the distribution of information at the 1962 World's Fair in Seattle.

By the early 1960s the organization had assumed a consistent shape and program, with an ongoing journal and a growing membership. Like the Conference on Science, Philosophy, and Religion, it had confronted the intellectual problem of reconciling science and religion but had chosen a far different path by following scriptural orthodoxy. Yet it too was deeply influenced by some of the same tugs of professionalism. It too responded to the rising tide of social science in the late 1940s and 1950s. It too tried to negotiate between audiences, to prevent marginalization, and to maintain ties with the principal scientific and theological discussions in the United States. It too saw in the philosophy of John Dewey the dreaded competitor of materialist ethics and non-Christian humanism.[61]

But the American Scientific Affiliation had set itself a more impractical, even impossible, goal. Maintaining an open forum of ideas about science under the aegis of evangelical Fundamentalism pleased neither mainstream scientists nor conservative theologians. Neither group responded in large numbers, except by their pointed absence, and the ASA failed to develop into a convergence of science and Protestant theology and became simply another group asserting another position. It published a lively journal and maintained a long-term organizational presence, but its original ambitions diminished. Such as they were, its inroads into science were made among the already converted, a marginal group confined to peripheral university and college teaching programs. The science community rejected all efforts to conduct science from within the fold of religion. And unlike its parent institution, the Moody Institute of Science, it developed no strategy to attract a mass audience.

Keeping tight rein on the contending attractions of science and Scripture, the ASA nonetheless edged closer to mainstream scientific positions than other creationist groups. Professionalism compelled this direction, even though hesitations by its leaders prevented too rapid or complete a triumph of the scientific mode. Perhaps this limited success confirms the appeal of extremism. Only commitment to the paradigm of science or, conversely, the paradigm of creation science could energize a mass audience and awaken the influence the ASA valiantly strove to achieve. Yet there were other alternatives in the restless American search for a new accommodation between religion and science. Scientists might develop religious insights based on mainstream scientific theories, using astronomy and physics to define a new cosmology. But such a radical undertaking was for others, not the American Scientific Affiliation.

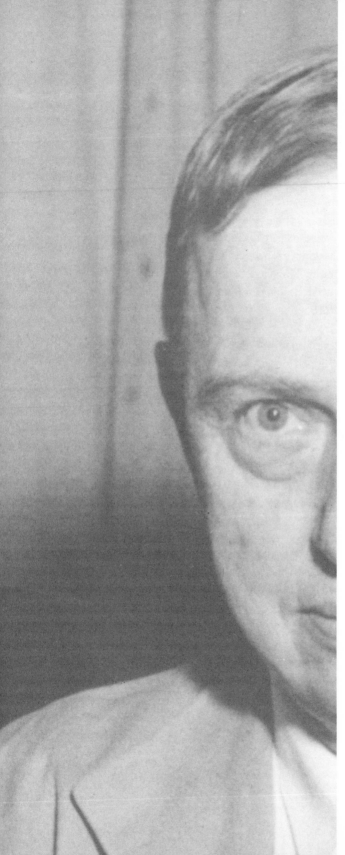

I am myself so impressed
by what Dr. Velikovsky has
had to say and the way in
which he has established
his hypothesis that I feel as
eager as he is to have it un–
dergo the crucial test
which the spectroscopic
analysis he suggests would
do.

Horace Kallen to Harlow
Shapley (May 1946)

Chapter 8

Two Men of Science

And Joshua spoke before the host of Israel,
preparing them to do battle with the Amorites, saying: "Sun, stand thou still
upon Gibeon; and thou, Moon, in the valley of Ajalon." And the sun did
stand still until the Israelis had dispatched their enemies. And there was
never a day before or afterward like this day, when the Lord heeded a man's
voice and fought for Israel.

Depicting several natural miracles of the Bible in historical times, this
account of the running battle of Joshua and his band also involved a hail-
storm of stones called upon the enemy and a huge rolling boulder commanded to seal up a cave where rival kings were hiding. This avenging
slaughter by Joshua and his soldiers, exacted by God, has provoked far less

controversy and debate for its cruelty than for the suspension of natural law the prophet describes. At this and other great formative moments of the Israeli people such as the exodus from Egypt, the Lord intervened to upset natural history. The Israeli people were thus born and sustained in geological catastrophism.

How, in the eyes of modern science, could such stories be anything more than obscure myths, etched in a cave of ignorance by primitive people, their relevance now faded with age? In a natural world ruled by uniformitarianism, which demanded that natural history unfold generally in a slow, regular development, how could such suspensions of natural law occur? Creation science in the guise of flood geology had appeared in an effort to explain those anomalies of modern science such as fossils, carbon dating, and astronomy that seemed to contradict Genesis. But what about events in the historical era portrayed in the Bible itself, where God seemed to contravene the laws of physics and biology? Did these miracles happen? If so, did God temporarily suspend natural law, or might there be ways to explain miracles in terms of special variants of natural law?

Worlds in Collision, Immanuel Velikovsky's best-selling work on astronomy, ancient myth, biblical history, and anthropology, published in 1950, provided a powerful answer. If, as he argued, the Hebrew Bible was a true account of the founding of the Israeli nation, there might be scientific explanations for these momentous events without miraculous exceptions to the laws of nature. Velikovsky devised a narrative account of how this might have occurred. In doing so he touched off one of the great controversies about the meaning and limits of science in twentieth-century America. As the *Harvard Crimson* quoted astronomer Harlow Shapley in September 1950, it was "the biggest uproar in scientific circles since Newton and Darwin."[1]

Behind the scenes as well as before the court of public scrutiny, two important men of scientific culture, the astronomer Shapley and John Dewey's great defender Horace Kallen, labored to shape the popular reception of Velikovsky's theories. The story of their bitter competition demonstrates how fragile were the boundary markers set around the dialogue between science and religion in postwar America. At stake were the most elementary definitions in this interchange: Who should speak for science? What were the limits of scientific theory? What were the rules of scientific discourse? What was the nature of science popularization? Shapley did not exaggerate: the answer lay in the definition of science itself and in rearguing the fundamental issues that erupted at Dayton in 1925.

Figure 8.1 One of the four illustrations by science fiction painter Chesley Bonestell for the article by Gordon Atwater that appeared in April 1950 in the *New York Herald Tribune*. The original caption read "Egypt, lashed from the sky by a comet during Exodus: One of the basic events in a controversial new book, 'Worlds in Collision.'" Courtesy of Space Art International.

One of the leading practitioners of science popularization in America, Harlow Shapley also demonstrated his keen interest in the conversation between religion and science in encouraging the activities of the Conference on Science, Philosophy, and Religion. His opponent, Horace Kallen, was a leading philosopher of scientific humanism, an adversary of religious sectarianism, and an apostle of William James and John Dewey. But their positions in this contest belied these identities and made them unexpected and uncompromising rivals. Although they shared an intense belief that religion was important in society and culture, they articulated fundamentally different definitions of science.

In a long, rambling poem written for the *Humanist* in 1950, Kallen poured out his philosophy of religion and pluralism in verse. Imagining himself alone on a ocean beach, he falls into a terrified reverie in which all the major religions march before him as "Fear-created masters of creation," the "quaking, shaking spirit of every age and nation." He awakens in the final stanzas, experiencing a "cleansing" of his heart as he imagines a seafarer approaching the coast of the United States, guided free and unhurt to its shores by the Sankety Point light on Nantucket.[2] Much might be said about this short work's caricature of contemporary religion and about the redemptive associations made with America. But in a more serious way the poem exudes the emotional energy of Kallen's theory of pluralism and his commitment to a vision of American culture in which all religions participated equally to enrich individuals: a world where no dogma ruled—not even science.

Horace Kallen was, himself, an immigrant (a seafarer) and an exemplar of his well-known theory of American pluralism. Brought from Poland to the United States by his family at age five (in 1887), he quickly assimilated to American culture. Never completely at ease with his Orthodox rabbi father, Kallen rejected the supernatural elements of religion and pursued a secular career in learning. He graduated from Harvard College in 1903 and then taught while completing doctoral studies in philosophy in the famous Harvard philosophy department. His mentor William James had then reached the height of his international reputation and had attracted his own pluralism of students: the Jew Kallen, the African American W. E. B. DuBois, and the writer and art connoisseur Gertrude Stein. During these prewar years, Kallen also studied at the Sorbonne and at Oxford, where he had a number of important discussions with a fellow student and later figure of the Harlem Renaissance, Alain Locke. There, he said, in his talks with Locke, "I first used the phrases that have become clichés—'right to be different,' 'cultural pluralism,' and 'pluralistic society.'"[3]

Present at one of the most exciting times and places in the development of American philosophy, Kallen absorbed much of the theory and orientation of James (becoming his posthumous editor). Unlike James (and like Dewey), Kallen was most interested in the practical application of the pragmatic notion of pluralism to politics. Whereas James in his most famous book, *The Varieties of Religious Experience,* had turned pragmatism into an inquiry into and verification of religious experience, Kallen applied himself to understanding the puzzle of American culture. How could the United States create one culture out of the many contending immigrant cultures? To Kallen the popular contemporary metaphor of the "melting pot" meant either the dominance of Anglo-Saxon traditions or the degradation of culture into ephemera (the "ready-made," "factory-made," "boiler-plate," "standardized," "syndicated Hokum") of popular culture. He proposed instead a theory of pluralism that maintained cultural distinctions between religions and ethnic cultures, allowing them all to contribute to the rich, harmonic mixture of Americanism.[4] This form of multiculturalism contradicted the assertive atmosphere of contemporary Anglo-Saxon supremacy, burgeoning racism, and anti-immigrant sentiments of early twentieth-century America. Kallen was not afraid to give offense in defending this vision. For his views he was dismissed from teaching at Princeton University and then, during World War I, forced out of the University of Wisconsin for defending the rights of pacifists. In 1919 Kallen joined the faculty of the New School for Social Research in New York City as one of its founding members. He remained there the rest of his career among a distinguished group of dissident academics and men and women of letters.

Cultural pluralism justified enthusiastic support for Jewish culture, and throughout his life Kallen participated in a variety of organizations such as the American Jewish Congress, devoted to enhancing Jewish culture and life in America. He was a confirmed and early believer in Zionism. Summarizing his views, he called himself a Hebraicist. But he was also a "scientific humanist" in the sense that he believed in the primacy of a scientific, pragmatic exploration of political and social problems and rejected all forms of philosophic and religious dogmatism. Here too Kallen blended Judaism with pragmatism. He repudiated what he called the Greek philosophic ideal of absolutism and formalism and celebrated the Hebrew notion of freedom and process. To allow for flux, "to insist on the concrete instance rather than on the general law," was the essence of the Darwinian approach to learning. It also meant giving "an overwhelming scientific background to the Hebraic as against the Hellenic visions of the nature of reality."[5]

Kallen also applied this pluralistic theory to the world of science, reflecting and updating some of James's own distaste for excessive scientism. Kallen believed that all fields of endeavor should be open and diverse. True science, in so many ways the fountainhead of this pluralism, was itself open, changing, and self-adjusting. Its essence was not law or regularity, but a method that sustained dialogue. It could tolerate no orthodoxies. From the Enlightenment onward, it had been defined by change and growth. As he told a meeting of the Fifth International Congress on Unity among the Sciences at Harvard in 1939, he supported a "common language of science but not a common synthesis." Science was science and not some other discipline precisely because it "yearns for no finality and no fixity to come to rest in." To believe otherwise was to abandon the essence of secularism and redefine science as a religion.[6]

Inevitably, this attitude pushed Kallen to construe "science" rather broadly. Like James he was intrigued by psychic research, maintaining a willful skepticism, although he confessed "there is much that is coercive." On occasion he corresponded with the American Society for Psychical Research, in one instance in 1941 to inquire about a supposed communication between (the departed) William James and his (living) friend James Hervey Hyslop.[7] More important was his broadly catholic, inclusive vision of the scientific profession. The religion of science and democracy, he wrote in 1951, "concedes no greater power or privilege to its experts in the sciences of man and of nature than to the laymen of the faith." This populist vision made Kallen sympathetic to scientific amateurism and hostile to the elitism of the scientific establishment, which he defined as occasionally stubborn and wrongheaded.[8] If science and democracy crossed swords, Kallen chose the side of pluralism.

At the same time, Kallen was vociferous in his rejection of religious dogmatism, a position that placed him at odds with contemporary creationists. Having decided early on that Protestant sectarianism was far more compatible with pluralism than Roman Catholic unity, Kallen had fought hard, with Dewey and Sydney Hook, to prevent what they all saw as encroachment on the separation of church and state (specifically religious instruction in public schools). Kallen opposed the Conference on Science, Philosophy, and Religion for this reason. He was horrified by the slashing neo-Thomist attacks of Mortimer Adler. He urged on the Committee for Cultural Freedom to defend Bertrand Russell's right to teach in the New York City public university. He believed that sociological study would reveal the dangers of Fundamentalist beliefs and their tendency to induce crime and other forms of antisocial behavior. He helped organize the watchdog Institute on Church and State in 1948 and devoted considerable attention to its efforts to prevent religious intrusion into public education.[9] He defended the reputation and philosophy of John Dewey after World War II during their plunge. That is why his championing of Immanuel Velikovsky is so deeply puzzling.

The first contact between Velikovsky and Kallen appears to have been in late 1939. Velikovsky wrote to Kallen regarding an academy of sciences that he and anthropologist Franz Boas planned to establish in Jerusalem, then part of the British protectorate of Palestine. Velikovsky's remarkable peripatetic life began in Vitebsk in Russia. His father, like Kallen's, was a Hebrew scholar. Immanuel, however, went to secular school in Russia to study mathematics. Later he traveled to Montpellier in France (which would accept Jews) and then on to Edinburgh to study medicine. Completing his medical degree in 1921 at the University of Moscow, he left once again, living in Jerusalem and then in Vienna, where he practiced psychoanalysis. In 1939 Velikovsky arrived in New York, carrying with him a manuscript ("From Exodus to Exile") that correlated the stories of the Old Testament with historical incidents in ancient Egypt. He also intended to push forward on plans that would "unite the Jewish scholars, to exhibit the high standard of the spirit of our race, to promulgate the sciences, to prepare the necessary atmosphere for the establishment of the University in Jerusalem" (the Hebrew University).[10]

Armed with a recommendation from Zionist leader Judge Morris Rothenberg, Velikovsky took his manuscript to Kallen, who read it quickly. In mid-March he wrote to Velikovsky that his "argument seems convincing." The book would be of "extreme interest to all persons of general culture."[11] Kallen quickly become Velikovsky's informal literary adviser and mentor, and for the next several decades he worked to secure the Russian immigrant an academic position and struggled, usually in vain, to win him a hearing among scientists.

Urged on by his friends, Velikovsky waited for a possible book contract.

During this period, he explains, he suddenly realized that only a great geological catastrophe could explain the historical peculiarities he had uncovered. As he later recounted, all of his books "were conceived in a single year from the spring of 1940 to the spring of 1941," with "all the implications of catastrophism for history, folklore, religion, geology, theory of evolution, astronomy and physics." In the same letter, Velikovsky fretted because he had "not met my Huxley," implying that he was a figure of Darwin's stature and eminence searching for an amanuensis and defender. (Kallen perhaps?)[12]

During the next few years Kallen worked diligently to open the scholarly academy to Velikovsky, while the Russian scholar sought a publisher for his work. By 1944 Velikovsky had completed his manuscript "Ages in Chaos" and submitted it to Oxford University Press with the suggestion that Kallen be solicited as a reader. Oxford complied, and Kallen's report, returned in August, was an enthusiastic recommendation for publication. "Every library will need one," he wrote, "and the reconstruction of Jewish history and the vindication of the historicity of the Bible . . . should provide an extensive general market."[13] Despite this endorsement, Oxford eventually declined the manuscript.

Kallen and Velikovsky continued their dialogue for several years as Velikovsky gradually revealed his emerging theory of catastrophism and biblical history. At first the Russian émigré refused to be explicit, until one day the two met by accident in the New York subway. "To my perennial question he replied with another: 'Which miracle in the Old Testament do you regard unbelievable?'" Kallen answered, "Elijah's being taken up to heaven in a fiery chariot." He was expected to say "Joshua's stopping the sun," but as Kallen later recounted it, this was beyond even the "conventionally miraculous" and beyond Kallen's world altogether. Yet this was the very miracle Velikovsky intended to explain.[14]

In the spring of 1946 Velikovsky sent Kallen the first part of his new work, "Worlds in Collision," after he had approached Harlow Shapley at a meeting in New York in April with a request that the astronomer read the work. Shapley agreed to do so if it received a recommendation by a reputable scholar. "Among the tasters mentioned to protect Shapley from intellectual poisoning," Kallen recounted, "I was one."[15]

Shapley's version of the encounter was somewhat different. Velikovsky accosted Shapley at a meeting in a New York hotel. "He sought my endorsement of his theory. I was astonished. I looked around to see if he had a keeper with him." Hearing the gist of it, Shapley tried to explain to Velikovsky that if the earth had stopped (to accommodate the miracle of Joshua), then "it would have wrecked all life on the surface of the planet; it would have denied all the laborious and impartial findings of paleontology." The "theory" had nothing in common with science.[16]

Nonetheless Velikovsky followed up his visit with two letters asking Shapley if he would undertake an investigation of the atmospheres of Mars and Venus to prove his catastrophic theory. Shapley declined and suggested that Velikovsky approach two other scientists to make the test. Kallen intervened, however, again asking Shapley (the two had become acquainted at Harvard) to make the spectroscopic analysis. Velikovsky's theories, he said, show "a kind of scientific imagination which on the whole has been unusual in our times." If his theory was valid, astronomy, history, and the social sciences would all require dramatic revision; even if wrong, this "would still be one of those very great guesses." Shapley responded that Velikovsky had proposed changes in the structure of the solar system during historical times that would falsify the laws of Newton. "If Dr. Velikovsky is right," he concluded, "the rest of us are crazy." In other words, the ideas were preposterous.[17] Not to be dismissed, Kallen again petitioned Shapley, arguing about the implications for Newtonian physics, but then he wrote to Velikovsky saying that Shapley's reaction was "to be expected." There was a lesson in this curt dismissal: Velikovsky must learn to translate his ideas into the language of the natural scientist. "I suspect that you will need to complete your final study," Kallen warned, before the scientific community would pay attention.[18]

Velikovsky was not entirely warned off Shapley by his rebuff, however, and he persisted in trying to interest the astronomer in his work. In 1947 he sent Shapley a manuscript, "Cosmos without Gravitation." Shapley dismissed the work, but Velikovsky responded again asking several questions about planetary magnetic fields and confessing that in his manuscript he had not yet been aware of the "implications of my historical cosmology." Now, however, he was preparing a new work that would demonstrate these implications.[19]

Shapley's hostility to Velikovsky's catastrophism portended the difficulty the philosopher would have in gaining a hearing from scientists and, at first, even finding a publisher for his work. Obviously, scientific journals were reluctant to accept works that relied on historical events to validate scientific theories. Velikovsky did publish two short works in 1945 and 1946:

Figure 8.2   Horace Kallen.
Courtesy of the American Jewish Archives.

"Theses for the Reconstruction of Ancient History" and the piece he sent
to Shapley, "Cosmos without Gravitation." But it was becoming clear that
access to the public would have to be gained through general publishing and
not the organs of a skeptical scientific community.

Kallen continued to promote Velikovsky's career and ideas during the
next few years, and the author began to cultivate other friends. Among these
he counted Albert Einstein, although exactly what the great physicist really
thought of Velikovsky remains unclear. Gradually pieces of the theory began to appear in print. In the summer of 1946 John J. O'Neill, science editor
of the *New York Herald Tribune*, published an enthusiastic summary of
some of Velikovsky's ideas. Clifton Fadiman of the Book of the Month Club
also expressed interest. But the turning point came in 1947 when Macmillan gave Velikovsky a contract for *Worlds in Collision*.[20] The stage was set
now for one of the most acrimonious and important public fights of

the twentieth century over the nature of science and religion in American culture.

Kallen's role in promoting and then defending Velikovsky after the debacle surrounding *Worlds in Collision* requires some explanation. As an eminent man of scientific culture, an opponent of Fundamentalism and the literalism of religious sectarianism, and a defender of strict separation between church and state, by his actions Kallen nevertheless ranged himself alongside amateurs, crackpot scientists, and religious Fundamentalists. Velikovsky's theory gave aid and comfort to creationism while it undermined the most elementary theories of modern (and ancient) science, including Darwinism and Newtonian physics. Such a perilous challenge to the mainstream could be justified only by extraordinary circumstances.

Part of the affinity between Velikovsky and Kallen rests on their shared heritage and beliefs. Both were committed Zionists. They were both men of immense and catholic learning and interests. They were both immigrants and outsiders, suffering the attacks of establishment orthodoxy—Kallen because of his politics and Velikovsky because of his science. They also became friends. Beyond all these reasons, however, the subtext of Velikovsky's book spoke directly to the calamity of the Holocaust. Nazi aggression against the Jewish people in Europe attempted to eliminate even the traces of their culture, their very historical existence. After the war, quickening aspirations for a homeland in the British protectorate of Palestine made the history of Israel even more pertinent. To transform the Old Testament of the Bible into historical record, to explain its miracles as natural history as Velikovsky did, represented a dramatic empowerment of a people. Although the author never drew the religious and Zionist implications from his story, they were present—powerfully so—and obvious.

This argument coincided with the aims of Kallen's pluralism, and he recognized them as such. A cultural history bolstered by science, a new nation supported by a sacred and secular history, reestablished the importance of Judaism in a world that had very nearly destroyed it. And beyond even these arguments, Velikovsky's ideas appealed to Kallen's understanding of science; indeed, they illuminated it as well as the Jamesian pragmatism it was based on.

Following his pragmatic bent, Kallen demanded an open hearing for Velikovsky, a serious examination of his theories by reputable scientists. As they engaged his ideas, truth would emerge. Just as James had pursued religious experience and followed experiments in psychic research, Kallen also implored the scientific establishment to tolerate the exploration of marginal ideas. This did not happen, however, because of what he condemned as the "religion" of science, meaning the infection of science by dogmatism and the priestly rigidity of men like Shapley. "Scientists," he wrote, "work at their vocations as organization men, serving the vested interests of their establishment, and defending the diverse orthodoxies on which they rely in their personal rivalries for place, power and prestige." Inevitably this entailed the denunciation of new ideas as heresy and the isolation of their authors as crackpots and charlatans.[21] If this opinion effectively placed Kallen on the side of the amateurs and social critics of science—of men like William Jennings Bryan and F. Alton Everest—that was not his intention but his fate.

For Harlow Shapley the issue was much the same, although he construed science and his own role within it quite differently. By 1950 Shapley was sixty-five years old and had long passed his most active days of scientific research. Indeed, by this time he had become most widely known as a science statesman, a popularizer of science, and a participant in debates about American foreign policy. An instrumental figure in proposing a national science foundation and then fighting successfully for it, Shapley also advocated international scientific cooperation, even after World War II and the beginning of the Cold War. During the 1930s he had established close links with Soviet astronomers. For his efforts he was investigated by the FBI and in 1946 was called before the House Un-American Activities Committee. His most controversial act was probably participation in the Waldorf-Astoria Conference on Science and Culture in 1949, which invited American and Soviet scientists and intellectuals to discuss issues of cooperation and peace. The conference incited a huge controversy with charges that it was communist sponsored and dominated. One of the leading opponents, Sydney Hook, claimed that Shapley collaborated with the Communist Party and even defended the Soviet purge of scientists in the 1940s. Hook also charged that Shapley's "authoritarian streak" was demonstrated by his attitude toward Velikovsky. For his efforts in promoting internationalism, Shapley was subpoenaed by Senator Joseph McCarthy.[22]

By 1950 Shapley's efforts in favor of science and science popularization included his support of the National Science Foundation, service on the board of directors of Science Service, and active participation in the American Association for the Advancement of Science and countless other organizations. He was an active journalist and speaker on behalf of science and science funding. At the same time, Shapley revealed a strong religious bent, which he had disclosed in his participation in the Conference on Science, Philosophy, and Religion. He developed this concern even more extensively in the 1950s. As a recognition of these activities, he received an honorary doctorate of divinity from the Meadville-Lombard Theological School at the University of Chicago in 1969.[23] Yet Velikovsky's theory was not what Shapley meant by religion or anything he could consider as science. Indeed, it insulted both definitions.

Yet *Worlds in Collision,* when it appeared and for several decades afterward, attracted considerable attention from Shapley. Each side in the ensuing controversy became an example of the faults and blindness of the other. Never accepted in any respect by mainline science, the book (joined by subsequent works by Velikovsky) maintained a haunting presence at the edge of modern astronomy, with its fervent advocates, its angry disparagers, and its periodic revivals.

Velikovsky launched his book by invoking the image of a devoted but beleaguered Baconian scientist. "I opened and closed the library at Columbia [University] for eight or nine years (certainly I was the greatest exploiter of that institution)." A scientist, he continued, studies, thinks and then expresses an opinion. He collects and orders neglected facts. The validity of his conclusions must then be tested by the reader, who should have the courage "to trust in his own ability to think. He should read the book and look into the references and make his own conclusions." This brief discussion of method redefined science; most important, it broadened the science community to a democratic party of common sense.[24]

Science, Velikovsky announced, must look at the past through anthropology, history, and religion because only these disciplines bore traces of the great catastrophes of the biblical ages. Hence *Worlds in Collision* compiled and correlated myths, religious stories, and primitive historical accounts of the era of the Old Testament. Velikovsky assembled ancient myths and religions, oral traditions, poetry, and other writings from around the world. Only in this way could the author lift the "collective amnesia" that humans had mustered to repress the trauma of celestial catastrophe. By correlating hints of catastrophic events among early peoples, he pieced together a narrative of natural history that appeared to validate the accounts of the Bible, including the stunning and problematic miracles of the books of Exodus and Joshua in which the Red Sea parted, manna fell from the heavens, and the sun stood still in the sky. To explain these events, Velikovsky developed a theory of catastrophism. The natural history of the world, he wrote, was not the smooth, gradual unfolding of timeless events, but rather the result of sudden and violent revolutions.

The most powerful of these, and the event that lent his work its title, was the near collision of worlds that occurred twice during recorded history. About 1,500 B.C. a new comet, expelled from the planet Jupiter, swept close enough to Earth to part the Red Sea with its gravitational pull. As Velikovsky put it, "When Venus sprang out of Jupiter as a comet and flew very close to the earth, it became entangled in the embrace of the earth. The internal heat developed by the earth and the scorching gases of the comet were in themselves sufficient to make the vermin of the earth propagate at a very feverish rate." Hence the biblical plagues. Fifty years later another approach of the comet rained rocks on Joshua's enemies and caused Earth to change its rotation—thus "stopping" the sun. As the author sermonized, "The celestial body that the great Architect of Nature sent close to the earth, made contact with it in electrical discharges, retreated, and approached again."

Earth was finally released from these periodic visits when the comet collided with Mars sometime around 747 B.C. The comet was then wrenched into a regular orbit, and Mars shifted to its current position. This ended the bizarre planetary warfare between Earth, Venus (the comet in orbit), and Mars that resulted into the geologic catastrophism of the past and remained imbedded in hundreds of eyewitness accounts in civilizations throughout the world. Having the most important record of this natural story, Israel became a "nation chosen to bring a message of the brotherhood of man to all the peoples of the world." By synchronizing natural history and the collective wisdom of the world's civilizations, Velikovsky had validated the Hebrew Bible, reinvented the history of the Israeli people, and given them a new purpose.[25]

The run-up to publication of Velikovsky's book included a considerable publicity campaign. Advance commentary included an expected endorsement by Clifton Fadiman of the Book of the Month Club. He wrote to Velikovsky that his book might "well turn out to be as epochal as *The Origin of Species* of Darwin or the *Principia* of Newton." James O'Neill of the *Herald Tribune* called it a "magnificent piece of scholarly research [that] raises world history to a level of superlative interest." Gordon A. Atwater, head of the Hayden Planetarium at the Museum of Natural History in New York City, suggested that "the underpinnings of modern science can now be re-examined."[26] Advance excerpts from the work also appeared in *Harpers* and *Collier's*.

A *Reader's Digest* summary and comment on the book appeared shortly before publication and, as much as any other publicity, reached a huge American audience. The article "Why the Sun Stood Still" directly linked Velikovsky to William Jennings Bryan and the Scopes trial. "How strange all this would seem to Clarence Darrow and equally to William Jennings Bryan, if they could know," wrote Fulton Oursler. What they would realize, he implied, was that Velikovsky had confirmed Bryan's position: Earth had passed through cataclysmic change during historical times as recorded in the Bible. The story was a tale as fascinating as something concocted by Jules Verne, "yet documented with a scholarship worthy of Darwin or Jeans [Sir James Hopewood Jeans, the astronomer]." So now, Oursler concluded, "To science, *Worlds in Collision* opens up a vast new debate; to millions of true believers in the Old Testament, it will come as an unintended and reassuring answer to the rationalist criticism of the last 75 years."[27]

In fact the debate predicted by Fulton Oursler in the *Reader's Digest* had already begun, although it took an unexpected and injurious turn. In early 1950 Harlow Shapley, based on the excerpt published by *Harpers* in January, realized that Macmillan was about to produce the book. To the astronomer, the issue was the prestige this distinguished science publisher might lend to Velikovsky's book. So he fired off to Macmillan a letter that contained the suggestion of what later became a threatened boycott against the publisher. "What books you publish is of course no affair of mine," Shapley wrote. But he added that he had consulted a number of scientists, including James Conant and all the members of the Harvard Observatory. They were, to a person, "not a little astonished that the great Macmillan Company, famous for its scientific publications, would venture into the Black Arts without rather careful refereeing of the manuscript." In closing, Shapley declared the Velikovsky thesis "the most arrant nonsense of my experience, and I have met my share of crackpots."[28]

Macmillan editor James Putnam responded, thanking Shapley politely for his interest and responding only obliquely to the astronomer's innuendos. Instead, he revealed his own stake in the book: "I have been working with Dr. Velikovsky on his book, *Worlds in Collision*, for several years." Furthermore, the publisher was not placing the book in its scientific series. "Obviously," he concluded, "it is a most controversial theory, and we have long since faced the fact that there will be a great diversity of reaction to the book."[29] Macmillan remained enthusiastic about *Worlds* and anticipated large sales. It calculated that through advance publicity millions of Americans had already heard of the book or read excerpts from it.[30]

But Shapley persisted. Answering a letter in early February 1950 from George Brett, president of Macmillan, he said he had searched through his files and found Velikovsky's "Cosmos without Gravitation." He had misplaced it in the "curiosa" section, "where we put the writings of the Flat Earth Society, the product of the over-throwers of the theory of relativity, the flying saucer reports and the like." (Brett had quietly sent the manuscript out to four more readers, only one of whom advised against publication.) Shapley also embarked on his own version of prepublication publicity. An article in February in *Science News Letter* and one in March in *Reporter Magazine* by Shapley's colleague, Dr. Cecilia Payne-Gaposchkin, denounced Velikovsky's theory as incoherent amateur science.[31]

The hottest contest, however, appeared after the distinguished literary periodical, *Harpers,* published its excerpt and a summary of the book written by Eric Larabee. Letters to the editor were sharp, ranging to very critical and incredulous. Yale anthropologist George P. Murdock bluntly concluded: "Harpers has been had." Harvard astronomer Donald Menzel wrote that the thesis did a grave disservice to science, history, and religion such that it might "reopen the war between science and theology." Like Shapley, Menzel also pursued a less public role, meeting with Larabee at the Harvard Club of New York to convince him of his error in siding with Velikovsky. Remembering the encounter, Menzel lamented that it was "a complete loss of time, of money, and of cocktails. For Larabee took the position that, having hitched his wagon to Velikovsky's comet, he was bound to Velikovsky henceforth and forever more."[32]

When it appeared in late March, *Worlds in Collision* dropped into a turbulent stream of arguments between the scientific community and Velikovsky supporters. Garnering enormous attention, although very mixed reviews, the book quickly became a best-seller, confirming what Putnam and others at Macmillan had predicted. Velikovsky was widely mentioned in newspaper articles, on the radio, and in journals. The Hayden Planetarium planned a sound and light demonstration of his theory, tentatively called "Our Battle-Scarred Earth." But from the beginning his work was never seriously entertained or even examined by the regular scientific community, largely because its methods completely contradicted normal scientific procedures: history, religion, myth, and legend tainted the normal protocols of observation, and Velikovsky challenged the laws of Newton and the theories of Darwin.

Led by Shapley and others, the scientific community, especially astronomers, considered a boycott against Macmillan's science book list. Given the near unanimity of the scientific community about Velikovsky, the publisher appeared to have no choice but to drop *Worlds*. It did so despite the book's appearance on the best-seller list for twenty weeks. After only two months, Macmillan sold its rights to Doubleday. Then, in an act of contrition, Macmillan wrote to Shapley in early June noting that the house had canceled its contract with Velikovsky. At the same time, Shapley had to fend off accusations that he had organized the crusade. Writing to T. O. Thackrey of the *New York Daily Compass* (a friend but a Velikovsky supporter), Shapley refused any further comment in print on *Worlds*. Both sides, he said, should be pleased: the author's supporters had a best-seller, and Shapley had the assurance that no astronomer or scientist or scholar took the book seriously. Everyone, he said, was unrestrained in condemnation "of a once reputable publisher." The astronomer repudiated charges that he was behind "various hypothetical crusades." He then mused that the whole affair revealed "the rather black future, and obvious decadence of our times." Linking Velikovsky to Senator McCarthy, Shapley described both as manifestations of a credulous public and serious miseducation.[33]

Shapley's suggestion of the pall of McCarthyism (from which he was currently suffering) was an ironic invocation of the very fault he had been accused of. These were serious charges because of real consequences visited upon Velikovsky's advocates. In the aftermath of the threatened boycott of Macmillan, editor James Putnam was fired and Gordon Atwater of the Hayden Planetarium lost his job.

The case of the Planetarium is a particularly intriguing example of the politics of science popularization. Gordon Atwater had been selected to head the Planetarium immediately after the end of World War II, in part because of his work with the parent Natural History Museum in its cooperative ventures with the Naval Training School of Fort Schuyler, New York. Atwater was not an academic astronomer but a practical technician and was deeply interested in science popularization and issues of space travel. Intrigued by Velikovsky's catastrophism, he planned a spring show in April designed with the advice of Chesley Bonestell, the well-known science fiction illustrator.[34]

The Planetarium routinely engaged in speculative programs about space travel (shows like "The Conquest of Space" and "The End of the

World"), and it also commemorated both Christmas and Easter with special demonstrations of the heavens at those times of the year. None of these invited controversy, but the favorable attention to Velikovsky cost Atwater his job. In his published comments on the Russian scientist, Atwater admitted areas of disagreement. However, he concluded, "The greatest value of 'Worlds in Collision' is this: it sets up an unusual approach to one of the world's great problems." By the time these words appeared on 2 April, Atwater had already been forced to resign.[35]

As early as 9 March, Atwater had been instructed by Wayne M. Faunce, vice director of the Natural History Museum, to terminate any references to the "theories or explanations of Dr. Immanuel Velikovsky which are currently being publicized." On 10 March the Planetarium revised the anticipated show, "Our Battle-Scarred Earth," to excise all mention of Velikovsky. Whether these actions reflected the hidden hand of Shapley is difficult to know. He had held the position of trustee of the museum since the 1930s and continued to be active in its governance. The board could not have been ignorant of his widely published views. On the other hand, trustees such as Charles H. Smiley of Brown University felt strongly that Atwater had made a terrible mistake and said so vigorously to the higher administration of the museum.[36]

None of these suppressions quieted the controversy around Velikovsky; they merely compounded the issue to include the behavior of scientists. *Worlds in Collision*, rather than initiating a scientific discussion of theories of catastrophism and astronomy, began a debate about the fundamental nature of science, pitting the mainstream science community against amateurs in what was in effect a reprise of the arguments and issues at stake in the Scopes trial, between a narrow community of experts and the potentially enormous community of readers who proposed to make up their own minds about the meaning of science.[37]

Both sides recognized that the debate involved the place of science in modern society. In an interview in April, Velikovsky tried to maneuver to the high ground. "Science today," he said, "as religion in the past, has become dogmatic—in the East [meaning the Soviet Union] as in the West. A scientist must swear loyalty to the established dogmas."[38] The science establishment had contravened its own standards by condemning his work without exploring its scientific claims. This out-of-hand rejection had begun with Shapley's refusal to test the atmospheres of Mars and Venus. Velikovsky had been the victim of a science pogrom ever since.

This debate received one of its clearest statements in 1951 with a dialogue in *Harpers* between Velikovsky and James Q. Stewart, an astrophysicist at Princeton. Stewart charged that Velikovsky misunderstood the nature of science itself. His "observations" proved completely unreliable, and his conceptual scheme was wildly exaggerated. Velikovsky responded that in effect he could read simultaneously from the book of God and the book of nature. Comparing himself to Copernicus, he bitterly attacked science for adopting the worst elements of religious intolerance. By exiling him from their community, scientists had mistakenly divided the world of knowledge into acceptable science and frivolous humanism. But they were wrong. "They say," he remarked bitterly, "'The sky is ours,' like priests in charge of heaven. We poor humanists cannot even think clearly, or write a sentence without a blunder, commoners of 'common sense.'" Such guardians of scientific truth fancied themselves inerrant and brandished "bell, book, and candle," to enforce their beliefs and excommunicate heretics.[39]

Velikovsky's was not the lone voice condemning the scientific establishment. Horace Kallen agreed with his condemnation of the scientific elite. Behind the scenes, his words about Shapley became bitter and accusatory, and he joined Velikovsky in believing that the Harvard astronomer had developed an obsessive, personal stake in the controversy. Having encouraged Velikovsky to publish, Kallen now supported his efforts to gain a fair hearing. He was delighted with Velikovsky's sharp answer to critics in *Harpers* in the spring of 1951. "I think you are holding up your end with dignity and effectiveness," he wrote. Kallen also encouraged Velikovsky to become an associate member of the New School. In return, Velikovsky offered to teach a course on evolution and catastrophism. "Is the School liberal enough to offer such a course?" he inquired.[40]

Orchestrating public support for Velikovsky was a complex matter because, as Kallen recognized, some potential supporters could be highly controversial—even objectionable. In August Kallen wrote to Velikovsky that someone had approached him about organizing "pro-Velikovsky societies." Kallen shrank from this tactic: "You ought to discourage that. What should be encouraged is the formation of study groups that would consider objectively the pros and cons of 'Worlds in Collision.'" When Velikovsky offered to do this and include the philosopher, Kallen responded enthusiastically: "I should myself be happy to see the formation of a group to explore ideas under your leadership and I hope something can develop in that direction in the course of this year."[41]

After a hostile review in *Science,* the journal of the AAAS, Kallen offered to write a rebuttal, but Velikovsky personified the opposition in Shapley and considered a lawsuit charging defamation and slander. He eventually settled on another strategy, a published rebuttal of his critics tentatively titled "Stargazers and Gravediggers" (eventually published in 1983). The AAAS never did consider Velikovsky's theories to be worth serious scientific evaluation, and as late as 1970 Kallen wrote that in the organization "the Shapley animosity perdures and its infection continues to spread." When in 1974 the AAAS finally held a symposium on Velikovsky's works, the tone was anything but positive. Astronomer Carl Sagan's remarks were typical: Velikovsky was not a scientist; he was merely defending religion.[42]

Kallen continued to be a warm friend for the next two decades. On occasion he visited Velikovsky in Princeton, New Jersey, where the writer now lived. He continued to correspond with editors like Eric Larabee of *Harpers* and other friends about the controversy. Of course Velikovsky was grateful. In August 1952 he wrote to Kallen, "In two years since the publication of my first book only a very few scholars had the courage as you have." The following fall Velikovsky managed to get a limited hearing at a Graduate Student Forum at Princeton. The meeting went well, he told Kallen, although the graduate students had come to watch him stumble. Before the assembled group of scientists and their students, he had attempted to respond to Shapley's original charge that his theories rested on mere folklore. "Seven years later," he confided, "I write you this, to say that I try to meet the challenge."[43]

For a short time it appeared that Albert Einstein might become Velikovsky's most important recruit. While in Princeton Velikovsky had several conversations with Einstein, who was then at the Center for Advanced Study. These talks became a public issue in 1955 when historian of science I. Bernard Cohen published a posthumous interview with Einstein in the *Scientific American.* In it Cohen noted that Einstein had dismissed Velikovsky's theories. But, wrote Velikovsky to Cohen in July, "In the last eighteen months of his life, Einstein spent not a few long evenings with me discussing my work, exchanged long handwritten letters with me, read repeatedly my book ... and showed great interest in my ideas and gave me very much of his time." Cohen corrected his initial remarks later, but Velikovsky was still wounded. "Last I spoke to you," he wrote Kallen, "was on telephone when I was upset by the last of the attacks on my book, the meanest of all, because it was made in the name of a deceased." Velikovsky planned to

include details of this controversy in his "Stargazers" manuscript, plus letters from Einstein.[44]

During the next several years Kallen continued to support and advise
Velikovsky, while the latter gained adherents from groups dedicated to
spreading his theories. Velikovsky also published several new books, all of
them extensions of his theories of catastrophism. The question of his religious views became more important as the controversy over his ideas extended their long half-life. In late 1962 Velikovsky wrote to Kallen about the
possibility of a forum on the Catholic, Protestant, and Jewish responses to
Worlds in Collision. As for his own religious views, Velikovsky was cryptic. I
am not a believer "in the accepted meaning of the term. This I tell you, but
did not tell to my readers." But, he concluded, I have not denied "the events
that underlie the stories of Genesis, Exodus, Numbers, Judges, Prophets
and Psalmists."[45]

Kallen was just as opaque and indirect in his response to Velikovsky
about religion. He referred his friend to an article in the *Jewish Spectator* in
which he commented on his religious commitments. They remained, he insisted, a version of pluralism, what he called "orchestration" or the assembly of many religions and cultures playing harmonically together. This
arrangement would constitute a form of secularism or a religion of religions
"whose God holds all the different supernaturalist religions equal in rights
and opportunities. This is the theology behind the separation of church and
state." Inside this harmony, Judaism would play an important role, free to
express its culture and ideas.[46]

After the initial flurry of interest and debate surrounding the publication of *Worlds in Collision*, interest in Velikovsky's theories temporarily died
back except among devotees. Attention waned until the early 1960s, when
an article in *Science* magazine (1962) and a special issue of the *American Behavioral Scientist* (1963) reopened the debate over the validity of his theories and rehearsed the charges of an unfair and hostile reception of his book
by the scientific community. Velikovsky became greatly encouraged, and he
wrote to Kallen about enthusiasm for his theories sweeping the campuses.
"It looks almost as if the present 'revolt' on campuses is caused more than
by other things by the realization that the text books and the teachers are of
the relics of the Victorian age." The early 1970s saw another peak of interest with the foundation of discussion groups and a Velikovsky newsletter
called *Chiron*, in addition to two other small publications devoted to
spreading his ideas: *Kronos* and *Pensée*. In 1975 a Center for Velikovskian

Studies organized in the Department of History at Glassboro State College in New Jersey. During these last years, Velikovsky received invitations to speak at a number of universities and before other interested audiences.[47]

Toward the end of his life Kallen published a portion of his manuscript "Shapley, Velikovsky, and the Scientific Spirit" in a book edited by *Pensée* magazine. Kallen found himself in the company of an odd collection of Velikovsky disciples, but he insisted that the issue was in fact Shapley's suppression of his friend's theories, not the company he himself kept. Now that various *Mariner* space probes had visited the planets, he contended, Velikovsky's theories appeared more plausible. The truth, confirmed by the real scientific spirit, would eventually emerge.[48] Shortly before this piece was published, Kallen once more attacked Shapley in print. In his book *Creativity, Imagination, and Logic: Meditations for the Eleventh Hour,* published in 1973, Kallen denounced the persistence of belief in the face of contrary facts. Usually this blindness veiled the eyes of religious true believers. "But science," he said, "also has its instances, such as Lysenkoism in biology, and anti-relativity in Stalinism and Hitlerism, anti-catastrophism in Shapleyite astronomy." In this misbegotten list, Shapley took a prominent place in the list of the greatest antiscientific rogues of modern history.[49]

In fact, Kallen's correspondence with Velikovsky is filled with disparaging remarks about Shapley and repeated snatches at hope that Velikovsky would eventually receive his deserved public hearing (as if only Shapley prevented this). Velikovsky, on the other hand, bombarded Kallen with confirmations of the accuracy of his theories and predictions. For example, "You will be undoubtedly interested to hear that by 1961 enough substantiation—in archaeological, geological, and astronomical finds—came to light as to make my publisher desirous to publish 'Velikovsky and the Test of Time.'" Velikovsky also repeatedly urged Kallen to write to Shapley, follow up on his letter of 1946, and indicate how correct his friend had been in predicting recent astronomical discoveries: "A letter that you write him would become historical," affirmed Velikovsky; it would be poetic justice.[50] Kallen never did write that letter, but he joked to Velikovsky about the astronomer: "I trust you (and Mrs. Velikovsky) are both in good health," he wrote in 1970, "and that you are cultivating gay spirits and the prospectives of laughter in view of Shapley, et al. Maybe part of your Seder should be celebrating your liberation from the image of that theologian in astronomy."[51]

Shapley, Kallen argued, had instituted a lifelong vendetta against Velikovsky and soured the scientific community on his theories. Even when Velikovsky, with the help of Carl Sagan, finally breached the walls of the scientific community, he faced more ridicule and rejection. Sagan persuaded the AAAS to hold a session on Velikovsky and then, at the meeting, submitted his theories to a rough, serious treatment, pointing out scores of mistakes and unscientific assumptions. Guessing right on occasion meant random success, not scientific predictability, wrote the astronomer. In fact, he proposed, the miraculous intervention of God and the suspension of natural law constituted a far more satisfactory explanation for biblical events than Velikovsky's displaced planet-comet theory. There was nothing here, he concluded, but a desperate attempt to nourish "religious roots" and achieve a "cosmic significance for mankind."[52]

The final chapter in this extraordinary debate came with the posthumous publication of Velikovsky's *Stargazers and Gravediggers*. Written in immediate response to the Macmillan fiasco and revised over several decades, the book did not appear until 1983. It reproduced the Shapley correspondence with Macmillan, Kallen, and Velikovsky. It commented extensively on conversations between Einstein and Velikovsky in Princeton shortly before the great physicist's death. But it also revealed Velikovsky's uncompromising temper of mind and the relentless self-advertisement that infuriated scientists and intrigued the general public.

Reading the Shapley letters together does not quite make the case that Velikovsky intended. Clearly Shapley was vexed by Velikovsky's persistence, for following the unsatisfactory conversation with Shapley in 1946 Velikovsky sent him his publication "Cosmos without Gravitation" and then three further letters. Shapley obviously tried to brush him off, but Velikovsky (and Kallen) persisted. It was only when Shapley heard rumors that Macmillan would publish *Worlds in Collision* that he became distressed, and then only because it was America's most distinguished science textbook publisher that listed the book. Nor did Velikovsky make a convincing case that Einstein was moving toward agreement with his catastrophic explanations of world history. Einstein was clearly friendly toward Velikovsky and upset at his treatment by the scientific community, but this did not constitute theoretical agreement.[53]

There are, however, interesting suggestions of tone and meaning that emerge from reading this apologia. For example, Velikovsky marked the signing of his contract with Macmillan with the following statement: "That month the state of Israel came into being, and dramatic developments followed." This was also a period when the author published several pieces on Israel for the *New York Post*. As he wrote in commenting on a hostile review, "I know of only one way to serve science and religion—by pursuing truth." "And," he concluded, "it is certainly not to the detriment of Israel that the Hebrew Bible is shown to be an essentially true book." Furthermore, Velikovsky continued to construe his fate with scientific martyrdom, comparing himself to Galileo and Shapley to the Italian's persecutors.[54]

Most important, however, Velikovsky linked himself to what he believed was a larger argument in the history of science between informed, often heroic, amateurs and an aloof establishment. The truth would emerge from "the jury system"—from public opinion—which would apply common sense to the consideration of scientific issues. Against this democracy of opinion, he contrasted the autocracy of elite institutions like Harvard University, the AAAS, and the defenders of orthodoxy.

In many respects Velikovsky's outsider status, his antiestablishment stance, energized his relationship with Kallen. This distinguished man of American scientific culture had also lived at the periphery of academic life. He had suffered for his political positions. He defended a beleaguered John Dewey against the Conference on Science, Philosophy, and Religion, in which Shapley played a major role. He was an ally of Sydney Hook, who denounced Shapley as a communist sympathizer for his work in sponsoring the Waldorf Conference of 1949. To complete this transformation of Shapley into anathema, however, Kallen identified the astronomer with the sins of the Catholic Church. The scientific establishment, he wrote in defending Velikovsky, was like a church. "Such religions of science," he noted, "insist on their own orthodoxies, exercise their own censorship, maintain their own Index, and impose their own Imprimatur."[55] There were no graver charges in his vocabulary of denunciation.

Kallen imagined science in the Jamesian sense that the great philosopher had employed to validate religious experience. The content of belief mattered less than the act of believing and the observable effects of that belief brought before the individual soul and the public for evaluation. So too in science: what mattered was the pragmatic test among a plurality of ideas and theories. For Kallen the greatest crime of scientists like Shapley was dismissing Velikovsky's theories without opening his books. To affirm established theory over the democratic process of truth discovery was to give the scientific establishment the tools of inquisition, elevating it to an esoteric theology, granting it special status, subverting the elementary procedures of American democracy. As James had preached, the true religious spirit was close kin to true faith in science: "Religion is first and last," Kallen announced in a lecture in 1967, "the assurance that the unconquerable can be conquered, that the inevitable can be escaped. We are seeking this assurance."[56] For Kallen there was still another reason to abide with Velikovsky. As a fellow Zionist, a Jew who believed in a pluralistic vision of America, Kallen was intrigued by the secular confirmation of the sacred history of Israel that Velikovsky provided.

The religiousness at the base of Velikovsky's vision resonated through American culture. His science had little meaning or importance outside its religious context. It was not stellar catastrophism per se but catastrophism as confirmation of the historical validity of the Old Testament that made *Worlds in Collision* a best-seller in 1950. The book intervened directly into one of the most important science-religious dialogues of the century.

To Shapley the dispute with Velikovsky and Kallen presented an opportunity to untangle the misunderstood relations between science and religion in American culture. A modernist in his Protestantism, Shapley abhorred what he believed was the aggression of pseudoscience and Fundamentalist religion against the instruments of science popularization. Whether he overreacted to this challenge is inconsequential here. Why he reacted is crucial, and that is demonstrated by his charge against Macmillan, *Harpers* (one of America's most distinguished intellectual journals), and the Hayden Planetarium, a leading institution of American science popularization. In Shapley's account the Velikovsky affair took place in the context of a bruising political fight to achieve a national science foundation devoted to funding pure science, and of personal attacks on him by Senator McCarthy. For him the issue was in fact amateur science versus establishment science: science controlled by scientists, not politicians, amateurs, or crackpots. By implication this was a second Scopes trial in which the court of public opinion was entirely irrelevant to truth—an event that proved common sense to be the enemy of a modern science that had increasingly grown counterintuitive. For Shapley to read *Worlds in Collision* would have been completely irrelevant to the scientific theories Velikovsky promoted because they contradicted the very premises of science itself. To argue otherwise misrepresented the essence of science.

If there are direct parallels to be drawn between the Velikovsky affair and the Scopes trial in the sense that each attempted a scientific validation of the most difficult miracles of the Old Testament, there are also important diff-

Figure 8.3 Harlow Shapley pictured in one of his most important roles, that of public intellectual and science popularizer. Both were at stake in his long dispute with Horace Kallen and Immanuel Velikovsky. Courtesy of the Harvard University Archives.

erences. In particular, the Fundamentalist religious community remained generally cautious about, and then indifferent to, Velikovsky's hypotheses. The Foundation for Studies of Modern Science (founded in 1968), with Kallen as a board member, proposed to study Velikovsky's works in 1971 because "Velikovsky has proposed sweeping reconstructions of both natural and human history during the millennia preceding the birth of Christ." Yet the American Scientific Affiliation, as early as 1950, rejected Velikovsky's work as pseudoscience. Velikovsky in turn, in a radio interview, attacked Fundamentalists: "I consider any work written by a fundamentalist—say in geology or paleontology (there are books on the deluge, and so on)—as worthless."[57]

Other writers such as George McCready Price were more favorable, based on Velikovsky's catastrophism. *Reader's Digest* editor Fulton Oursler was also an enthusiast. In 1950, shortly before his death, Oursler conducted several interviews with Velikovsky. He determined that the Russian writer offered help in bridging the gap between science and religion, and he defended Velikovsky against the charge of some religionists that he had reduced God's miracles to obscure scientific explanations.[58]

Apart from these minor influences, Velikovsky no more won over the religious establishment than he conquered the scientific establishment. Most observers considered his works pseudoscience and interpreted the whole affair in terms of the struggle over science popularization. Based on the dispute, many of these interpretive histories have come to pessimistic conclusions about American culture, stressing the gullibility of the American public, with its toleration for science fiction and for pseudoreligions like that proposed in *Dianetics* (published the same year as *Worlds in Collision*). Historians of science have interpreted the affair as a classic example of the way science must defend its borders against the assault of charlatans.[59]

But as a historical event, as a barometer to the atmosphere of the period after the exhilarating, brief moment of scientific utopianism following World War II, the Velikovsky affair reflects and enlightens the dialogue between science and religion in American culture. The fundamental interest in Velikovsky expressed the religious overtones and enthusiasms of American society. Without the Bible narrative, his scientific theories stand as culturally irrelevant and uninteresting, a minor example of science fiction, not science thinking. Perhaps they might have remained unpublished. They gained attention because they addressed the vibrant religious sensibility in American culture. They maintained a large appeal because they revived the important argument that Bryan had tapped: the democratic community's right to decide the validity of scientific theory. This populist theme in modern American history empowered not just Velikovsky but the whole kingdom of Fundamentalism. Translated into a sort of Jamesian pluralism, it also appealed immensely to Horace Kallen. who, as an advocate of scientific culture, argued that the entire community, not just experts, should make judgments about truth. That, precisely, condemned both Velikovsky and Kallen in the eyes of Shapley. Science, he believed, by its very nature should never be molested by popular belief; it was the sole purview of those who understood it. At stake, then, was the most elemental relationship of religion and science to society and to each other, played before an audience that was deeply conflicted about the whole matter.

I simply must tell you of
my great pleasure at
watching "Our Mr. Sun,"
presented by you on TV
last night. It was not only
fine entertainment and
scientific education, but it
was a religious experience
as well! To combine all
three experiences in such a
program was a stroke of
some kind of genius, in-
deed!

Letter to Frank Capra
(April 1957)

Chapter 9

"Almost a Message from God Himself"

At a low point in his illustrious career, Hollywood director Frank Capra suddenly shifted to a new subject and a different medium. Abandoning studio filmmaking, Capra contracted with Bell Telephone Laboratories to produce several television documentaries illustrating the basic principles of modern science. For the television corporation this agreement followed a broad advertising strategy designed to interest young Americans in pursuing a scientific career and to enhance the image of Bell, but it was its first venture into science television. For Capra the films offered an escape from the frustrations of postwar moviemaking and a chance to revisit two early loves: science and Catholic religious culture.

Working through its advertising agency, N. W. Ayer in New York, Bell originally planned thirteen television specials, each highlighting a basic scientific problem. For Capra this task required a difficult balance. He had to satisfy Bell and Ayer that the science he portrayed was acceptable to the scientific community (represented by a panel of experts hired by Ayer). And he needed to create a style and presentation that appealed to an audience that had little knowledge of science and probably a low tolerance for uncertainty or the slow, complex process of discovery. He also invested considerable energy fighting for his personal vision of the relation of science to religion. The result was a constant but illuminating struggle between Capra, Ayer, and the science advisers to find a tone and format that would relate science and religion in a fashion acceptable to all the parties.

Four films eventually emerged from this process, each attempting to find a voice that met the minimum standards of the science establishment, the needs of popularization, and Capra's religious preoccupations. Each extended variations on an initial formula in search of a design with popular appeal. The result was an uneven but fascinating realization that picked elements out of the contemporary cultural air and combined them in a search for the right format. Capra borrowed from a host of television techniques ranging from cartoon characters and puppets to the sonorous commentary of cultural experts. There were frequent references to current science fiction films and to magic, and even overtones of the *Why We Fight* series of propaganda films Capra had made during World War II.[1] At the heart of everything he did there lay two purposes: a mission to reassure other Catholics that doing science was performing God's work, and a desire to resolve the deep-seated American controversy between amateurism and scientific expertise, which he interpreted as the source of animosity between science and religion.[2]

Frank Capra brought an unusual background to the documentary science series sponsored by Bell. Born in Palermo, Sicily, in 1897, Capra emigrated to the United States at age six and eventually took a degree in chemical engineering at California Institute of Technology in 1918. He remained affiliated with the Institute for several years as a director of the Cal Tech Associates. A self-made man in a world of highly mobile executives and creators, Capra became one of the most successful directors at Columbia pictures during the 1930s. Before this Capra worked as a writer on the *Our Gang Comedies*. In the late 1930s he produced several of the most original and acclaimed films of the decade, including *Mr. Deeds Goes to Town* and *You Can't Take It with You*. When war came, Capra enlisted in the effort with several widely noted documentary war films for the *Why We Fight* series.[3] After the return of peace, however, Capra became snagged in the perilous politics of Hollywood anticommunism. More damaging, his films seemed less fashionable in the tense Cold War affluence of the early 1950s.[4]

One recourse he took revived earlier interests. Capra began to promote two religious film projects, *Joseph and His Brethren* (which he pushed again in the early 1960s) and *The Trial*. Paramount Studios encouraged the latter project before canceling it at the last minute. The script, which Capra enthusiastically boosted, placed Christ on trial for failing human beings and ended with the conversion of his critics. The plot originated with several Palm Springs businessmen, who hoped to stage the trial as a means of attracting visitors to the resort.[5]

In 1950 he and script writer Charlie Stearns undertook another project, a science promotion film for Cal Tech to center principally on the work of the astrophysicist Robert Millikan. The initial Cal Tech project proposed to explore Millikan's widely proclaimed religious sympathies as well as his work on cosmic rays. But it was Capra's vision that defined the film. In a script dated May 1950, Capra expressed a justification for doing science that defined truth seeking as a religious function—a thought he repeated in all his science films: "Man is born with an insatiable desire to know what's on the other side of the hill—to know the unknown . . . . Why? Because man wants to know. Wants to know himself, his universe, his God."[6]

In June 1950, during the initial stages of the film, Stearns wrote to tell Capra that he planned to set up an editing center at Cal Tech. Then the following week Stearns said he intended to "case the Moody Institute of Science (or is it Institute of the Bible?) facilities to see what else we need soon."[7] This tantalizing reference suggests that Capra knew the reputation of Rev. Irwin Moon's bustling evangelical film studio in Hollywood and its efforts to unify Fundamentalist Christianity and science—and most important, that he considered the example worthy of study. All of these efforts were postponed, however, and Capra did not return to the cosmic ray film until several years later and in a different guise, under the auspices of the Bell Telephone Laboratory.

Did this interest in religion and science represent a detour in the director's work? Probably not. In Capra's films up to 1950 there had been suggestions of a consistent and abiding interest in religion. Even in his secular Hollywood films, some critics such as Neal Gabler have discovered a "theology of comedy"—a "secularized displacement of Christ's tale in which a common-man hero, blessed with goodness and sense, overcomes obstacles, temptations, and even betrayals to redeem his own life and triumph."[8]

In the Bell science series, however, we need not stretch to interpret or analyze metaphors to discover Capra's Catholicism. It existed explicitly, purposely, and controversially, even if Capra had to wage a guerrilla war to maintain the ambience of religiousness with which he sought to infuse the films. This may not have been Bell Laboratory's original purpose, but in hiring Capra it signed on a self-confident amateur scientist and novice religious philosopher. In neither role, it turned out, did Capra willingly compromise his views.

During the late 1940s N. W. Ayer, the well-known advertising agency, began to move aggressively into producing television programs. At first it confined itself to sports events, largely because of its Atlantic Refining and Lucky Strike cigarette accounts. In 1951 the agency began a series for Sealtest Dairy of one-hour live circus shows, "The Sealtest Big Top." In 1958 it created the NBC show "Shirley Temple's Storybook," and in 1959 it originated one-hour color telecasts of classical and popular music, the Bell Telephone Hour. Ayer's science film venture for Bell occurred in the middle of this prolific period, beginning in 1953 and continuing fitfully, after Capra left the production, until 1963.[9]

Interest in creating public service science programs originated in 1951 at Bell Telephone's parent company, American Telephone and Telegraph (the phone company). A variety of purposes defined this venture into trademark advertising. Science advocate Vannevar Bush, on the board of directors of American Telephone and Telegraph (AT&T), and Cleo Craig, president of the company, were both eager to embark on such a public service campaign. As Capra wrote in his published memoirs, "Mr. Craig insists that since science is what his company is selling, science is what the Bell System should sponsor."[10] AT&T commissioned its advertising agency, N. W. Ayer, to initiate such a project.

At first Ayer expressed doubts about attracting a broad audience for such productions and found that the television experts it consulted generally agreed with this appraisal. Nonetheless Bell pushed the project forward, and Donald Jones of the Radio-Television division at Ayer was appointed as its organizer. He immediately began to consult a wide range of prominent scientists, including Margaret Mead and Robert Millikan, and then approached Hollywood producers and hired several science writers to develop script ideas. Eventually the group produced outlines for a substantial number of half-hour and hour programs. At the same time, Jones searched for a producer to film the shows. Few of the Hollywood names he approached showed much enthusiasm—except Capra. Jones, formerly a film writer in Hollywood, knew and admired Capra's work. So when the director expressed interest in the project, Jones flew to California to negotiate with him.[11]

In his first conversations with Jones, Capra announced that his vision of the project included serious consideration of religious questions. Company officials were wary of this approach, and they became more so during production, but they accepted Capra's bias. Bell and Ayer were delighted to have such an eminent producer for the series, although they insisted on hiring science advisers to read and approve scripts and footage. Capra's description of the advisers was tough and slightly off-color, but accurate: the prominent scientists were being well paid "to act as a front, a shock absorber, an awning to keep pigeon droppings off Mother Bell's virginal image."[12] The partnership satisfied both parties. Bell wanted to experiment with television production, and Capra, as Don Jones told Ayer officials, had become "disgusted with the kind of pictures that Hollywood is making, and doesn't quite know what to do with himself."[13]

Capra was never shy about making his religious points, and he informed the science advisory board early on that his vision of a good film combined religion with science. "Gentlemen," he said on one occasion, "I don't think science is any more sacred than brick laying, farming, or dress-making. So you see, gentlemen, if I make a science film I will have to say that scientific research is just another expression of the Holy Spirit that works in *all* men." "Science," he noted, "is just another facet of man's quest for God—a seeking of the ultimate answer through studying nature's physical laws."[14]

In the first of several contracts (revisions occurred because of production delays and changes), Capra signed on with Ayer to produce thirteen shows for a series that would begin on 15 December 1952 and continue at four-week intervals through 1953. The agreement divided script approval. Scripts had to satisfy the general science advisers hired by Bell and Ayer—Warren Weaver, vice president of the Rockefeller Foundation, and Ralph Bowen, retired from Bell Laboratories—as well as project specialists brought on for each show. But Capra retained the final cut on each show.[15]

Jones and Capra decided that the first project should be a film about the sun, and the agency agreed to this subject. Once begun, the whole project

was then sealed up in secrecy, with Capra dramatically referred to in correspondence as "Mr. X" until formal public announcement of the series.

As Capra assembled his Hollywood production staff under the reincor-
porated firm Frank Capra Productions, he cast about for a script on the
sun. Ayer and Capra originally agreed to hire two prominent writers, the
novelist Aldous Huxley and the space travel advocate Willie Ley (Huxley
to be paid $5,000 for his treatment and Ley $900 for his). Huxley had been
in Hollywood for several years, where he continued writing novels and
worked on a number of film scripts. One of his most interesting recent
works had been *Science, Liberty, and Peace*, published in 1946. This
dystopian view of science warned that technological advance carried the
risk of increasing centralization of society and growing inequality. The solution, wrote Huxley, must be a decentralized world and a reinvigoration
of humanism. This was the message he brought to his treatment.[16] Willie
Ley, on the other hand, dwelt on the pinnacle of optimism about modern
science. A colleague and collaborator of the German (and American)
rocket scientist Wernher von Braun, Ley was a prophet of space travel and
eventually worked with Walt Disney Studios to create films for Futureland
at Disney World and with producer George Pal in his production *The Conquest of Space* in 1956.

Both men submitted scripts, although Huxley's was by far the more interesting and had more influence on the eventual production. It also represented considerable effort, as Huxley confessed to his brother Julian in
January 1953. The novelist wrote that he had to read 100 percent of the material to leave out 99 percent for a television audience, as well as expend "a
great deal of thought in regard to the ways in which information may be
conveyed in terms of photographic and animal-cartoon images."[17]

Huxley's finished script blended religious imagery and an apocalyptic
warning about unmanageable progress with the explanation of scientific concepts in a troubling and disjointed admixture. On the positive side, it developed features that eventually became part of the final script. These included
the personification of the sun as a character in the film—in this case he serves
as the narrator of his own story. Huxley collected much of his scientific material about the sun from Donald Menzel's recently published *Our Sun*. (This
book became the basis of the Capra production.) The most interesting Huxley touches came in the frequent references to religion. The author, in what
amounted to an attack on big science, glorified small-scale scientific research
for its purported kinship to a personal exploration of spirituality.

Some of these elements clashed with the intentions of Ayer and Bell and undercut their wholly positive understanding of science. The script offered a hesitant and even bleak vision of the future based on the insidious impact of science on human well-being. Huxley pronounced three jeremiads in succession. He warned against the disarming optimism of science and theories of progress. In a short parable, he described the rapid depletion of the earth's natural resources formed over eons of geologic history. "It isn't too difficult to be rich, when you're spending capital." warned the narrator-sun, "But when there isn't any more capital, what then?" Scenes of famine in India, eroded soil in Mexico, and devastated forests follow this warning. Huxley identified a second portent as atomic energy. While the narrator weighed this force as a possible solution to energy consumption, he stressed the risks of genetic damage and deformations in terms that almost invite comparison with the unruly radioactive monsters running rampant in contemporary monster–science fiction films. Finally, Huxley raised serious doubts about defense expenditures. But this vision of an exhausted planet, with squandered resources, set in a frame of pessimism and criticism of government policies, could never serve as the advertising tool Bell Laboratories sought. Even the ending was dark and enigmatic. Huxley proposed to conclude with sunset: "We could then close with the sun dropping between the horizon, night falling and the nocturnal creatures re-emerging—owl, bat, hyena, drunkard."

Within this catalog of unacceptable implications, one element obviously caught Capra's eye, for he incorporated it in the eventual production. This was Huxley's assertion of faith in the joint homage to science and religion by "St. Francis of Assisi on an Umbrian Hilltop, reciting his 'Canticle of Brother Sun.'" Huxley sketched a scene with the saint in reverential terms: "He is on his knees in an attitude of prayer—not looking at the sun when the sequence opens." Then he would turn toward the light to recite his prayer of praise: "Be praised, my Lord, in what you have created. Above all else, be praised in our Brother, Master Sun."[18]

Neither Huxley's dark treatment nor Willy Ley's much more pedestrian work proved completely suitable, so Capra decided to write his own version based on a presentation of Menzel's *Our Sun*. As a consequence, Menzel was brought in as the principal consultant for the film. He also became the major opponent of Capra's efforts to insert religious messages into scientific presentation.

Donald Menzel was no stranger to either science popularization or the struggle to steer public attitudes toward a favorable view of scientific research and away from religion and mystery. His book *Our Sun,* published in 1949 in a Harvard University series on astronomy, obviously sought a popular audience. Menzel began on a sympathetic note about the age-old worship of the sun by human beings. "The personification of the celestial bodies and of the forces of nature," he wrote, "were entirely understandable in the then [past] man-centered world." In fact, deification of the sun was normal for a certain level of civilization. Menzel's strategy, however, was to move quickly from mythology to modern science, explaining the latest theories about the age, composition, and function of the sun. From there he proceeded finally to the potential of solar energy. In the future, he concluded, "man may look to the sun not merely as the giver of light and heat, not with the blind superstitious mind of the astrologer, but with the firm scientific faith that—in the sunlight—coming events cast their shadows before."[19] This was certainly an optimist's credo.

As head of the department of astronomy at Harvard and a colleague of the much better known Harlow Shapley of the Harvard Observatory, Menzel continued to be highly critical, at least in private, of any pretension that religion should share the stage with science. As he wrote in his unpublished autobiography, "If prayer makes an individual feel better inside, if it tends to make him a better person, I most certainly have no objection to it." But the astronomer discovered no trace of God in scientific discoveries or of any designer in the laws of nature. There was, he believed, an inevitable clash between religious belief (as it existed) and scientific practice.[20] In these circumstances a forced marriage of religion and science in popular culture was not something he could support. Inevitably, he opposed Capra's repeated efforts to perform just this feat of matchmaking.

Menzel came onto the project in early 1953 after Capra had submitted his first script to Ayer. As Jones explained to the astronomer, "The script is still in its formative stages, and we welcome your comment on its tone, its quality as entertainment, [and] the scientific information contained in it." The purpose of the shows, Jones continued, was to present serious scientific subjects to a mass audience. After their television debut, the films would, AT&T hoped, become a staple for use in schools and before other special movie audiences.[21]

If Menzel proved hostile to the religious flourishes in the *Our Mr. Sun* script, other advisers on the project seemed more favorable. Warren Weaver, for example, commenting on the second version in February 1953, wrote that the script was admirable, even if it showed "a lack of pedagogical restraint." As for the religious touches—something Jones had specifically queried—Weaver said that "as a man who believes in formal religion," he approved of this sort of material. Jones reported the scientist's justification to Ayer: "He also reminded us that most of our audiences will have a quality of mind that is not logical but intuitive, artistic, historical, and literary." As Weaver himself put it to Jones, the script was a good one with (referring to Saint Francis) "a marvelous end!"[22]

Criticism by other special advisers fixed on nonreligious portions of the script. In his appraisal astronomer Otto Struve warned that Capra's mode of presentation might be offputting. He especially objected to anthropomorphizing Father Time and Mr. Sun into human cartoon characters. When Jones met with Struve on 16 March however, he pressed the astronomer on the religious question. Struve believed most scientists were not much interested in religion. Science did, of course, have a connection to religion, because "it brings one closer to the problems which human beings can't solve by logical processes," Jones paraphrased. "Struve says," he added, "the important thing on our program is to make the public understand that science is not opposed to religion."[23]

Astronomer Walter Orr Roberts expressed the same hesitations as Struve. As Jones summarized his conversation with the scientist, Roberts believed it was important to refurbish the image of the scientist: he was neither an atheist nor a "long-hair." Roberts was referring to a proposed conversation between Dr. Research (an actor who explained the scientific concepts to the audience) and the animated characters Mr. Sun and Father Time.

> MR. SUN: You know Mr. Research, I'm *beginning* to like you. (confidentially). But just between me and you and Father Time here, why do so many of your people—er—well, you know—sort of distrust scientists?
> RESEARCH: Well, unfortunately many good souls have a queer notion that scientists are long-haired *atheists*, who just make atom bombs.
> FATHER TIME: What's *your* definition?
> RESEARCH: Science wants to *know*. It's *right* that we should know, else God wouldn't have given man this driving curiosity, and acquiring new knowledge is doing God's work, too . . . Part of His plan for us to arrive at Truth.[24]

Roberts described this presentation as weak and ineffective: "if we are going to throw a sop to the antiscientists, let's not throw them a sop that is

Figure 9.1   Frank Capra and his crew at a filming of *Our Mr. Sun,* complete with "Magic Drawing Board" and the cartoon character of the sun. Courtesy of the Wesleyan University Cinema Archives.

phony." The alternative he proposed would emphasize the contributions of science to consumer products like washing machines. It should also argue that, despite the atomic bomb, scientists were neither "Godless nor immoral." As for the script itself, Roberts was delighted with much of it, particularly the "plug for God" at the very end.[25]

The "plug for God" ending was precisely the sort of interjection Menzel criticized, and his correspondence with Capra about such elements heated up over the early months of 1953. Commenting on the second script, Menzel conceded that he and Capra shared a similar general attitude toward popularization—it should borrow the tools of popular culture. Menzel sympathized with Capra's diverse methods of exposition including the anthropomorphism of the sun, and he approved the occasional moments of comic relief. But he could not countenance the references to God.

There were, he noted, two very rough spots where religion intruded in unnecessary ways. The first contained a passage about the change from Ptolemaic astronomy to Copernican astronomy:

SUN: In the Old Testament of Ptolemy, the *earth* was the center . . . In the New Testament of Copernicus, *I* was rightly placed at the center.

Menzel warned that implying the Old Testament was wrong and the new Testament right "could get you into religious arguments."[26] This was a minor quibble, however, compared with Menzel's dislike of the ending. Borrowing from Huxley's script, Capra introduced a long passage that paraphrased the famous prayer by Saint Francis. Even if the words of the prayer had been altered slightly, the allusions and language clearly revealed its identity:

> All praise be yours, my Lord,
> in all your creatures,
> especially Sir Brother Sun
> who brings the day;
> and light you give us through him.
> How beautiful he is, how radiant in his
> splendor!
> Of you, Most High, he is the token.[27]

Capra's version was also a prayer of gratitude to the sun:

> RESEARCH: We used to worship you as an unknown, whimsical god, but now
>   that we know you better . . . we love you as our great and good friend. . . .
> Thanks for all the radiant riches you shower down upon us. . . .
> Thanks for our daily bread . . . and all the fruits and flowers you grow for us.
> Thanks for feeding our animals. . . .
> And thanks especially for the glory and beauty of your "good mornings"—
>   . . . and your "good evenings." Thanks for everything, Mr. Sun.
> May God keep you shining forever.[28]

Menzel sarcastically dismissed this passage. Reference to a "whimsical" star was completely wrong; the very lack of capriciousness was what made the sun an object of primitive worship. The final sentences, he noted, "border on being pantheistic. Quit repeating the word 'thanks' at least after the first appearance of it. And I suggest that you say food instead of 'daily bread'. . . . Otherwise it sounds too much like the Lord's Prayer directed to the sun." Finally, the invocation to God to maintain the sun was "completely out of place." "Even God," Menzel noted caustically, "lives by virtue of his laws of Nature, one of which is that there is no such thing as perpetual motion. The sun will not keep shining forever and cannot keep shining forever, and this whole last sequence I find extremely grating, although I understand the basic reasons for it." If, Menzel concluded, "religion must be brought into this somehow or other," Ayer should hire someone "who is skilled in that particular field." The implication was that neither he nor Capra fit that description.[29] The astronomer closed by reminding Ayer that if his book *Our Sun* were the basis of the production, copyright payments would be owed to Harvard University Press.

Capra was enraged by this document and fired off a quick teletype to Jones as soon as he received it. Beyond the criticism of religion, Capra warned that Menzel would probably present Ayer "with several bills later on. Namely: for the use of his name, for the title, for any material that comes out of his book." Capra speculated, unkindly, that Menzel really wanted to be the scriptwriter and was in effect telling them, "You dopes, you should have gotten me to write this for you in the first place."[30]

Somewhat later, Capra answered more carefully. In a long response, Capra defended his view of science and religion. As I see it, he asserted, "one of the objectives of this program is to show that science is an integral part of the lives of everybody, and not just an esoteric pursuit of a select few in ivory towers who are indifferent to the laws of God and country." "I have no intention," he continued, "of glorifying a master race of Brahmins who consider faith in God and the moral laws as fairy tales for the untouchables." To refer to God's orderly laws is not ridiculous or out of place: "This is just to point out that scientists are doing God's work just as truly as carpenters, teachers, or social workers."

These were familiar themes for Capra, who had long believed that science and religion were twin aspects of the same endeavor and wholly consistent with Catholic teaching that reason and faith were dual roads to salvation. Capra was also self-consciously proclaiming his amateur expertise in presenting science material. He added to these another point that he knew would appeal to Ayer. The telephone company had obligations to the scientific community. "But when they go into millions of homes with their products," he concluded, "they have a greater obligation to the American people—the obligation to stress or at the very least to acknowledge the spiritual side of man's make-up—to acknowledge that all good things come from God—including science."[31]

This last general point may well have convinced Ayer and Bell that some religious references were probably inevitable, and they accepted Capra's insistence that religion had a role to play in the script. Still, Jones continued to mediate differences between Menzel and Capra right up to the end. In early 1956 he persuaded Capra to remove a reference to the "birth of Christ" as a legitimate date. On the other hand, numerous references to God adorned the script. Ayer, seeking to prevent further problems between Capra and the scientists, expanded the permanent advisory board for the series. Ralph Bowen of Bell Laboratories would be chair and Warren Weaver vice chair. Other consultants included distinguished biologists, chemists, geologists, and anthropologists.[32]

Ayer took one further precaution before final production of this first show. Jones quietly—and on his own—decided to present the script to religious experts to test Capra's theology. He sent copies to three experts in New York City: to the Jewish Theological Seminary, to the Catholic Archdiocese of New York, and to Reinhold Niebuhr at Union Theological Seminary. None made any objections to the discussion of religion.[33]

When finally produced, *Our Mr. Sun* included a mixture of science, documentary footage, low-key advertising, and animation contained within a religious-magical framework. The two human characters were Dr. Research (the television personality Frank Baxter) and the Fiction Writer (actor Marvin Miller). As the Fiction Writer explained, "your science and my magic" would present the whole story of the sun. The "magic" of the Fiction Writer was his drawing board of cartoon characters: Mr. Sun, Father Time, Thermo the Magician, and Chloro Phyll. Dr. Research, on the other hand, generally limited himself to explanations of scientific questions.[34]

Although a considerable portion of the film included footage of sunspots and other examples of solar photography, even these documentary visuals were contextualized in popularized form. For example, when Dr. Research discussed sunspots and the questions scientists still asked about their effects, the musical accompaniment was played on a theremin, an instrument widely employed in science fiction films to suggest otherworldly mysteries and danger. Every description of the sun was rooted in some anthropomorphic vision of nature: its positive or destructive impact on human civilization. With only brief mention of the Bell Laboratory and its investigation of solar energy, explicit advertising within the film was minimal.

Most striking, *Our Mr. Sun* began and ended with inescapable religious allusions. The opening shot revealed a sunrise as words emerged below it: "The heavens declare the glory of God: Psalms," accompanied by the rousing choral movement of Beethoven's Ninth Symphony. Music written especially for the production by Raoul Krashaar was titled "Celeste."

The final scene had been of particular interest to Capra, and he acquired a photograph of a famous statue of Saint Francis in Italy. The finale quoted Beethoven's music to accompany Dr. Research's paraphrase of the Saint Francis canticle. Despite Menzel's best efforts, the film still included a long prayer, although the vain wish for eternal sunshine was gone. Dr. Research, speaking offstage, invoked a catalog of "thanks" for the "glories we behold," for "green forests," for "wheat fields," for flowers, birds, insects, fish. He ended, "In the words of St. Francis . . . ("Statue of St. Francis SUPERIM-POSED over Sunset Sky"):

> Be praised, my Lord, in what you have created. Above all else, be praised in our Brother, Master Sun. . . .
>
> Sunset, and then, credits.[35]

Other strong allusions to Christian theology permeated the film. Several referred to the effects of creation: man could survive the greatest challenges because of his God-given "power source," "his mind." Furthermore, the sun and earth existed in a perfect relationship. Our planet had the right size, temperature, and atmosphere. As Father Time continued, "The right composition . . . everything just right to produce the biggest miracle of all . . . (Cue—INT. CRIB—new born baby crying.)"

The most important moment commemorated Capra's assimilation of science to religion. Father Time is given this significant speech:

> Inquire! Seek the truth. It's right that you should . . . know, or the Good Lord wouldn't . . . have given you that . . . driving curiosity. Measure the outside with mathematics . . . but measure the inside with prayer. Prayer is research, too! Study man as well as the world.[36]

With the experience of long and trying negotiations and production problems of *Our Mr. Sun* upon them, Capra and Ayer negotiated a new contract in the summer of 1954. The director threatened to pull out of production unless a better agreement could be signed—one that would allow Capra to ignore scientific advice should it compromise the entertainment value of the series. The subsequent agreement clarified relations between Capra and the science advisory board. Ayer also considerably scaled back its ambitious program and offered only three more productions in this phase of the series. The advisory board was assigned responsibility for selecting a single scientific adviser who, with the board, would affirm the accuracy and balance of the scientific material in each program. Scripts would be approved by the board and by AT&T to ensure they did not violate "internal or public relations policies." Should any changes recommended by the board "destroy [according to Capra] the entertainment value of the film," then the film would be abandoned and Capra's corporation would be paid a termination fee.[37] In effect this agreement confirmed the controversy in the process of the science series and allowed each side a veto over the other.

Despite its noncommercial aspects, Capra treated *Our Mr. Sun* as a Hollywood production and conducted an audience preview in Riverside, California, about a year before its broadcast. He got a mixed reaction. Most members of the audience said they might want to see it again, but many declined. A large majority favored more films of this sort. But there were scattered objections, particularly to the production gimmicks and "religious references." A few respondents noticed the "incompatible philosophy of science and religion."[38]

When the film finally appeared on CBS at 10:00 P.M. on 19 November 1956, this first showing reached about 24 million viewers in Canada and the United States. It received an audience rating of 25 and a 32 percent share of the audience. It attracted more viewers than the Robert Montgomery Show but lost out to Lawrence Welk's musical broadcast. *Variety* raved about it: "All hands on deck, particularly Capra and the magical animators at UPA, rate a bow for this one." Other press commentary was generally very favorable, but a number of reviews criticized the animation and other devices on the grounds that they detracted from the seriousness of the message. Of fan mail received by Ayer and Bell Laboratories, almost a thousand letters and postcards were favorable, and only a very few disliked the show. Of those who wrote in, 7 percent praised the religious theme; only about 1 percent criticized it.[39]

Capra garnered personal congratulations from a number of viewers; several of them noticed and approved the film's religious message. Among these was Rev. Irwin Moon of the Moody Institute of Science. "Dear Frank," he wrote: "Just a note to let you know we enjoyed your film 'Our Mr. Sun' very much . . . It is my opinion that this presentation will have a very great effect on television programming of the future and that once again you have pioneered in a new field with outstanding success." "Dear Irwin," Capra responded, "Thanks very much for your nice note on 'Our Mr. Sun.' Coming from one who has practically spent his life telling the world that the wonders of the universe are not accidental, this is high praise, indeed." He added: "I am sure you know what an inspiration your work has been to those of us who have tried our hand in this particular field."[40] The familiar tone of this exchange suggests that Capra had indeed followed up on earlier suggestions for a stop at the Moody studio and that the visit had been fruitful.

Of all the honors Capra collected for this first science film, none pleased him more or better fit his conception of the audience than the Smiley Award. Created by Sam Smiley, a twenty-eight-year-old employee of General Electric living in Cincinnati, the Smiley Award for achievement in the arts and popular culture had no public standing or institutional backing. That by itself indicated its virtue, and Capra seized on it as a confirmation of his version of science and the justice of his struggle against an advisory panel seeking to dampen his populist aesthetics and religious enthusiasms. Appearing out of nowhere, Smiley proved him right and confirmed his message.[41]

As production of *Our Mr. Sun* ended, work had already begun on the next three films of the series: *Hemo the Magnificent* (on blood); *The Strange Case of the Cosmic Rays*, and *Unchained Goddess* (on the weather). But negotiating these scripts proved just as difficult as with the first film. Aside from complex and detailed corrections on scientific matters, the advisory board continued to tone down Capra's religious leanings. In fact, when Ralph Bowen sent Capra summaries of the scientific commentary on the submissions to the board, he felt constrained to construe them in the best light. The "starkness and negative detail" completely "misrepresent the warm and enthusiastic reception which these superb shows met," he concluded.[42]

Negotiations over *Hemo the Magnificent* found the scientific advisory board prepared to accept some of Capra's religious idiosyncrasies. They willingly acquiesced in the spiritual context and argumentation that structured the plot. But they balked at a caricature of evolution in which Dr. Research answered a question put by the Writer: "Are you trying to tell me I descended from a little sea gnat?" In the proposed script, Dr. Research simply answered no. But the board proposed a stronger, more explicit response, a yes-but answer that ended in a vague coda of theology: "Physically we believe you descended from among an evolutionary line of lesser animals but at some point near the end of this evolution a miracle occurred and you became endowed with the human spirit which distinguishes you from all animals."[43]

When completed, the film extended the didactic formula and dramatic artifice that Capra had established in *Our Mr. Sun*. Dr. Research reap-

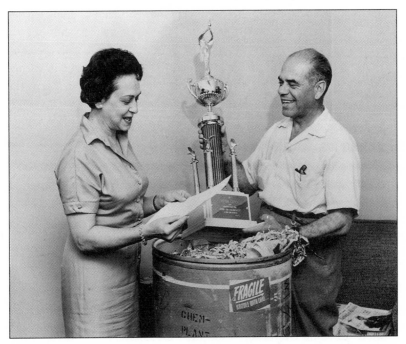

Figure 9.2 Frank Capra and his wife Lucile open the package containing the Smiley Award for *Hemo the Magnificent,* an honor the producer treasured as a sign of his links to common people. Courtesy of the Wesleyan University Cinema Archives.

peared, and so did the Writer (now played by actor Richard Carlson). Once again cartoons allegorized the scientific processes under study. As in the previous film there were long passages of documentary footage as well as animated explanations of concepts. Capra also continued to pursue his explanation of the relation between science and religion.

As before, the framework was explicitly biblical. To the soaring strains of Beethoven, the show opened with the words, "For the Life of the Flesh is in the blood," from Leviticus 17. The animated character Hemo (personifying blood) explained in introducing himself, "I am the sacred wine in the silver chalice [of the Eucharist]." In a long passage on evolution, developed in negotiations with the board, Research and the Writer explore the unique nature of human beings. Am I descended "from some kind of sea gnat?" asks the Writer. Research answers, "You have a human spirit that separates you entirely from the animal world."

Once again Capra raised the question of the legitimacy of doing science at all—the long-haired atheist problem. Humans sought truth in several ways, proclaimed the script: through art and through "spiritual revelation . . . through the power of prayer, love, mercy . . . moral laws, and in science we seek it through the study of nature and its physical laws." Further on the script again returned to the theme, asserting that science fulfilled many human aspirations:

> HEMO: Are you saying science is an art?
> WRITER: Sure it's an art. Thoreau once defined art as . . . that which improves the quality of the day. Well, what's improved our daily lives more than science . . . huh?"[44]

The final frames of the documentary called forth a vivid illustration of Capra's religiousness. Speculating about human longevity, the Writer predicts that scientists will solve the problems of disease. "What better way to love thy neighbor than . . . to heal him," responds Hemo, approvingly. Then, in a burst of anthropomorphic enthusiasm, Hemo exclaims: Birds and animals have their defined functions, but humans possess unlimited talents: "You're Creation's favorite!" exclaimed Hemo. "One of your greatest physicists, Max Planck, said that over the temple of science should be written the words: 'Ye must have faith.'" "Your great Apostle Paul wrote to his new church in Thessalonica: 'PROVE ALL THINGS: HOLD FAST THAT WHICH IS GOOD.' . . . A Scientist says, 'Have Faith.' A saint says, 'Prove all things.' Together they spell 'Hope.'" Instructions on the script deconstruct this finale: "Camera Zip Pans Right to: Painting of St. Paul, double expose over him a church cross and the words, (Dissolve in) 'Prove all things, Hold fast to that which is Good.' Camera Dollies back to MLS, both double exposed shots. Heavens light up as title zooms in—*Hope.*"[45]

Broadcast on 20 March 1957 over CBS at 9:00 P.M. (a better hour for a family program), *Hemo the Magnificent* captured the ratings contest with the NBC *Kraft Theater* and the ABC situation comedy *Ozzie and Harriet.* This was encouraging news to Ayer, and Jones wrote to Donald Menzel, who continued to follow the series, "We are encouraged by the results, and are now discussing plans for programs to follow the one on Weather and one on Cosmic Rays, which are in the final stages of completion." Capra was also heartened, particularly by some of the fan mail he began to collect.

Shortly after the *Hemo* broadcast, the director received a note from Father James Keller of the Christophers of New York. Keller informed him that he had been "cited for a double Christopher award for your outstanding work as producer, director and writer of 'Our Mr. Sun' and 'Hemo the Magnificent.'" This Catholic organization had organized to commend and encourage contributions to moral principles in films and other media. Father Keller was the author of the best-selling book *You Can Change the World,* and his organization represented an important effort within the Catholic Church to shape American popular culture. Capra was delighted with his notice and wrote back: "In this connection, I would like to mention the great public service the Bell Telephone System is doing in initiating and sponsoring this series. They have backed me up on the 'spiritual uplift' sections, even against the grumbles of a few (very few) of their scientific advisors."[46]

One explanation for Catholic attention to Capra's productions was a laudatory article published in the *Sign* (a Catholic periodical) and reprinted in *Catholic Digest* a month later. Appearing in June to coincide with the showing of *Hemo,* the tribute was written by Jeanne Curtis Webber, a freelance writer who had worked with Don Jones at Ayer to develop the series and then continued as researcher for *Our Mr. Sun.* Her account of the origin of the science series presents yet another version of its derivation. In an interview for this audience, Capra revealed his disappointment on discovering that his sons were not interested in pursuing a science career. The repute of the profession was low, Capra reasoned. "And scientists themselves complain they are thought of as strange ducks—men who speak a queer jargon, write only in formulas, and are probably up to no good." He determined to correct this impression.

Webber continued her paraphrase of Capra's views for her Catholic audience: "Capra believes that science is an expression of man's best aspirations. . . . Capra thinks it is an essential part of living, a way of serving God, for the more we know about the universe, he believes, the more we can appreciate its Creator." These values, Webber noted, came from Capra's college years when he formulated his "ideas about the relationship between science and his Catholic beliefs." Physicist Robert A. Millikan at Cal Tech provided his greatest inspiration. She continued to quote Capra: "'I noticed,' Capra explains today, 'that Millikan never gave a lecture without mentioning God. His lectures were truly exciting, inspiring accounts of what the mind of man could do. He saw no conflict between science and religion.'"[47]

Other Catholic groups pushed the films. William H. Mooring favorably reviewed *Our Mr. Sun* and *Hemo* in a column that appeared in forty-six Catholic papers throughout the United States and Canada. Capra also received a complimentary letter and an extensive introduction to a new Catholic organization, the Albertus Magnus Guild, founded in 1953 during the Boston meeting of the AAAS. This group devoted itself to promoting science among Catholics and "to assist[ing] Catholic scientists in relating the Church's teachings to the findings of science." Capra wrote to them: "I was also delighted to learn that there is such an active Catholic Society promoting the interests of Science. We both know science and religion are not incompatible and that they both glorify God."[48]

Father Patrick Yancey, S.J., editor of the *Albertus Magnus Guild Newsletter*, confided to Capra that "as a Catholic who has been working in science for over thirty years and, more particularly, in trying to promote a greater interest in the sciences among our Catholic people," he got "a big lift" from the producer's films. In fact, the founding of the Guild and Capra's films coincided with a more positive attitude toward the sciences inside the Catholic Church, based on the papal encyclical "Humani Generis," delivered in August 1950. In this document Pope Pius XII signaled greater encouragement of scientific enterprise. Even the notion of evolution, in some circumstances, could be integrated into existing faith. As he wrote, "The Teaching Authority of the Church does not forbid that, in conformity with the present state of human sciences and sacred theology, research and discussion, on the part of men experienced in both fields, take place with regard to the doctrine of evolution, in as far as it inquires into the origins of the human body as coming from pre-existent and living matter."[49] Capra's films echoed this doctrine.

Capra apparently allowed Catholic representatives to call on him at his office in Hollywood. One such visitor had praised the director for his film on the sun after such an encounter. "Your science films should do much 'candle lighting' in the minds of all of us and I hope, particularly in the minds of our younger generations coming along." "Thank you again, Frank," he concluded, "for your graciousness in receiving me and listening to the mission to which I had been assigned on Good Friday Morning."[50]

Capra himself promoted his films among other Catholics, sending a copy of *Our Mr. Sun* to the pope in 1957. Later that year Capra received praise from a member of the Franciscan Fathers seminary in Cleveland. What a pleasure it was, the correspondent noted, to see "the full picture of science and not leaving God out of the picture or shyly passing over the fact that God is controlling the Universe." "A hearty congratulations," he concluded, "for the way you came out and gave the Lord His proper place in these movies that are reaching a good number of people."[51]

Capra's last two science series films repeated the formulas of his earlier works while ever searching for new contrivances for popularization as well as the best language to express his soft religious message. *The Strange Case of the Cosmic Rays*, broadcast on NBC on 25 October 1957, was essentially a reworking of the script Capra had begun for the Cal Tech film on Robert Millikan. Negotiations over this program followed the pattern of earlier films as well, including serious problems with the advisory board over religious language as well as the outburst of a distrustful attitude Capra sometimes directed at scientists.

The format of *Cosmic Rays* was a concoction of styles, filled with allusions to the staple programs of early television and contemporary Hollywood productions. It combined a science fiction ambience, replete with a theremin and vibraphone (another musical instrument commonly used in science fiction films to suggest extraterrestrials) and the Bill Baird Puppets. In this instance the use of Richard Carlson (widely known for his science fiction roles) as the Writer borrowed his identification with that popular genre of Hollywood film. The puppets depicting Edgar Allen Poe, Charles Dickens, and Fyodor Dostoyevsky formed a "jury" called to award the "Edgar Award" for solving the mystery of cosmic rays from outer space.[52]

The first working *Cosmic Rays* script began with the motif. Originally it combined Capra's early sketches with a treatment by Jonathan Latimer that used the figure of Sherlock Holmes as the lead detective. The next revision introduced the puppet figures of Poe, Dostoyevsky, and Dickens as well as a long section about the Lord's Prayer written on the head of a pin (the purpose being to illustrate the size of molecules). Further revisions eliminated this illustration but continued to explore the religious justifications for doing science.[53]

The science advisory board reacted strongly to the tone and format of the script. The summary of their views sent to Capra protested his insistence on talking about religion. "The beginning text 'Science—the art of discovering what God created' grates on a majority of the group because (a) it unnecessarily mixes science and religion" and because "science is not at present concerned with God's creations in the spiritual world, only the physical." The board also "universally disliked the ending because of the sneering voice of Edgar, the implication that science has no motive and the sad ending."[54]

Capra took strong exception to this effort to censor his religious views,

Figure 9.3   Frank Baxter (Dr. Research) and the Writer, the always mysterious and menacing Richard Carlson, on the set of *The Strange Case of the Cosmic Rays.* Courtesy of the Wesleyan University Cinema Archives.

but he did promise to provide a more upbeat ending on science. "The keynote will be a glorification of the scientific method and of the great future that lies ahead. Also, we will convert Dostoevski from a scoffer who is bored by science at the start, to an enthusiast at the finish. One line will give you an idea: *"Dostoevski:* I had no idea science is for *people.* I thought it was just for longhairs." (Once again the long-haired atheist theme.)

As for the beginning lines, Capra conceded that the advisory board had the right to toss them out. But, he responded, the scientists were missing "an important bet" that Newton, Galileo, Boyle, Pasteur, and Millikan had all acknowledged. "If they are not studying God's work," he challenged, "whose creation are they studying? What does 'nature' mean—chaos or God? If it's chaos, can it make 'laws'?" And, he continued, "there certainly must be research going on in the spiritual, psychic and extra-sensory world, as well as the purely physical."[55]

Despite the excision of the opening, the religious message remained strong, as the final words of Dr. Research show. Following a sequence marking the enthusiasm of young students for science, the Writer celebrates the possibilities of a science career. Research responds:

> RESEARCH: Yes, and what a glorious opportunity to add to man's history . . . to harness these NUCLEAR fires for man's use! . . . To accept the challenge of Creation . . . and to use the gifts God gave us to explore the grandest of all frontiers . . . the Universe! For the more we know of Creation, the closer we get to the Creator![56]

Viewer interest in the NBC broadcast of *Cosmic Rays* fell back somewhat from the success of *Hemo.* Ayer continued to receive favorable letters and comments from listeners, but critical reviews began to mount, and some of them were harsh. Of forty-seven reviews, twenty-seven were favorable, fifteen mixed, and five unfavorable. John Crosby, the *New York Herald Tribune* writer, reproached the series for its simple-minded approach. Dick Klener, of the NEA Syndicate, wrote that the programs had received serious criticism from the beginning, yet "Undaunted, Capra & Co. are back with one that is in the same mold, 'The Strange Case of the Cosmic Rays.'"[57]

As Capra finished work on his last production, *The Unchained Goddess,* devoted to a discussion of weather, he had already begun to consider other film projects. At the same time Ayer moved to assert more control, particularly over costs, for any further films, because the $400,000 actual expenditures per production were far over budget. Capra did not end his relationship with Ayer quietly, however. He intimated in several letters that he was being pushed out of the series despite its extraordinary success.

Goddess animated the weather in the guise of a petulant, tempestuous, and irrational female character. In answer to a complaint about this sexist depiction from the ABC "Weather Girl," Capra replied, "*First* of all, I must tell you we decided that the weather goddess must be a woman because, I suppose, weather is so unpredictable, at times so beautiful, and at other times so terrifying." The caricature, in fact, structured the "plot": Meteora's growing love for Dr. Research. She ends the show by calling up a storm when he tells her he is already married. This comic relief contrasts with the usual more serious religious intent. As in every film, the same themes are revisited: the uniqueness of humans and the sanction of God for scientific discovery (complete with questions from Job: "Hath the rain a father? Who hath begotten the drops of dew?").[58]

Like *Cosmic Rays, Unchained Goddess* fell behind the performance of the first two films. In audience share, for its telecast on 12 February 1958, it lost out to two competing shows in the first half hour and one other in the second. More important, critical commentary in the press grew sharper and more dismissive. As Ayer informed Capra in March, "the newspaper critics seem to be about 42 per cent unqualifiably favorable, about 29 per cent fairly negative, and 29 per cent in between." Apparently this sophisticated public had failed to appreciate Capra's mixture of humor, drama, religion, and science.[59]

This end was probably inevitable. Capra had long chafed at the control Ayer exercised, and he disliked the growing efforts of the advertising agency to speed up production. As early as November 1954 he notified his agent that Ayer and Bell had become arbitrary about what they wanted: "I suddenly realized," he raged, "that the man who was making the pictures was low man on the totem pole as far as information was concerned. Everybody knew everything but the man who was supposed to make and deliver the films at a fixed cost. I looked in the mirror and saw a pigeon." Capra also claimed that Bell Laboratories did not appreciate his creative efforts. In response to a congratulatory note about *Unchained Goddess* from Harry Batten at Ayer, Capra responded. "I presume that the A.T. & T. group will feel the same way about it—although I haven't had the slightest comment from them, officially, on any of the films."[60]

Capra blamed Ayer, Bell, and the critics for the demise of his work on the series. As he put it in the unpublished portion of his autobiography, "The story of that science series was really the story of the response of TV critics. It can be told in 3 Acts: Act One: Love. Act Two: Disenchantment. Act Three: Murder." To some degree he was right. In their plans for future productions, there were suggestions that Ayer and Bell might eliminate the "offensive sugar-coating" in the series. Sanford Cousins of Ayer wrote to Capra in 1958 to say that no such action was planned. "You know us well enough to be confident that the sophisticated views of a comparative handful of critics will not cause us to panic." But, he continued, they would "stop, look and listen."

If anything, it was Ayer's increasingly stringent controls that forced Capra out. In 1958 Warner Brothers was hired to do several films including *About Time, The Thread of Life, Gateways to the Mind,* and *Alphabet Conspiracy.* Midway in this sequence, Ayer asked Capra if he might like to bid on the production of two of the films contemplated for the Warner project. Capra declined. Unhappy with the Warner relationship, Ayer eventually turned to Walt Disney Productions for *The Restless Sea.* The series finally ended in 1963.[61]

Despite Capra's obvious disappointment and his criticism of Ayer and Bell for their lack of support for the series, he also believed—rightly—that the total audience for his four documentaries was enormous and renewable. Not only were there two showings of each on national television, but the series enjoyed wide distribution in the public schools. As he noted in his unpublished autobiography, over 200 million viewers had probably seen the films. "For the past 13 years," he continued, "the Bell System has had *sixteen hundred* color prints of each film playing continuously in the schools, clubs, and churches of the U.S. and Canada." Furthermore, his efforts earned several awards, including an Emmy in 1956 for *Our Mr. Sun* and the Thomas Alva Edison Award in 1957 for *Our Mr. Sun, Hemo the Magnificent,* and *The Strange Case of the Cosmic Rays.*[62]

Writing to Frank Baxter, who had continued with Ayer in the Warner productions, Capra lamented a decline in quality after he left the project. "What I miss most in the continuation of the Series after I left," he remarked, "were the poetic and spiritual overtones that radiate from the physical world around us." This had been one of Capra's most important innovations in the popular presentation of science during this period—his trademark.[63]

Like the Moody science films, Capra's endeavors self-consciously tried to span the gap between modern science and traditional religious culture—in this case Catholicism.[64] That he succeeded in the face of hesitations and objections from the scientific community represented on the advisory board suggests the power of religion in popular culture. The scientists as well as the advertising agency sponsoring the series conceded to Capra the right to mix science and religion in an overt way because they recognized that the mixture already existed in American culture. In a way, that was Capra's strongest argument. That these films made their way into millions of homes and thousands of public school classrooms for several decades is testimony to the unobtrusiveness of his message in a society where its premises were not generally contested. Few outside the scientific community objected to merging religion and science. For this reason Frank Capra's sermons were largely invisible and inaudible to most of the viewers unless they were looking for them. Only a few in this audience appeared discomforted by his grounding the scientific endeavor in common sense, intuition, and practical observation; no one objected to the implicit bias against expertise and complexity. In the end Capra did not have to build bridges between science and religion; they were already there, and he had only to walk his films across them.

Have you ever read the first 26 verses of Ezekiel? There are many passages in the Bible that seem to suggest the presence of what we now call flying saucers.

Letter to Donald Menzel
(1 March 1964)

Chapter 10

Transgressing the Heavens

In the popular religious imagination, the heavens have been both a tangible world beyond the earth and a passageway of communication between Deity and creation. In recent times, however, the heavens have become reaches populated not just by ethereal souls and angels but by mortals, sailing metal ships in orbit around the earth and to the moon and back. How, in figurative language, could American society conceive of this actual invasion of celestial space by human beings? In the period after World War II, when some of the most breathtaking scientific advances in human history brought space travel close to realization, how could culture describe the scientific appropriation of a realm that had once been the preserve of mystery and religion? What languages and ideas would govern the transformation of the heavens into outer space? And why, as humans prepared to visit other planets, did the world suddenly receive so many purported visits from aliens? Why did "they" decide to visit us on the eve of our first penetration of God's domain? This chapter discusses the struggle during the 1950s to find that appropriate language and symbolic context in two developing elements of popular culture: UFO sightings and science fiction films.

Until humans achieved flight in the twentieth century, earthbound as the species seemed, the upper reaches of the world and the void beyond were peopled only by nonhumans: birds and bats in the lower limits and, beyond, inanimate planets, suns, stars, comets, dust, and gas, as well as heaven and angels and God. Human aspirations to explore this realm had once been either spiritual or fictional. To ascend required a weightless soul that had jettisoned its mortal coil or else some sort of technological magic. Space beyond earth could be inhabited by spirits, gods, and demons, or by angels and other divine messengers, but never by the mundane.

The 1950s altered this age-old separation of heaven and earth as human beings legitimately began to speculate about actual travel into space. But to dream of space flight disrupted and reversed the most basic opposition that defined the human species and threatened to alter the geography of spiritual identities. To live beyond the earth's gravity meant to profane the oldest, perhaps the final, realm of human imagination—a place where to mismeasure God's distances and designs—to presume knowledge of the ultimate—had once been to risk mortal danger from religious persecution. But the postwar period suddenly demanded a new fashion of conceptualizing the meaning of that beyond. It seemed to pose a stark choice. Was this place heaven or space? Could it still be understood in terms of religion and mystery? Did science or did religion provide the relevant vocabulary to portray this new frontier of human experience?

To examine this debate, I have concentrated on two areas where science and religion converged and conflicted within popular culture. First is the appearance of a brilliant subgenre of science fiction films in the mid-1950s. In the best of these the plot inevitably devolved to the question of scientific arrogance and human hubris. They asked: Isn't it dangerous to extend science too far beyond the gravity of human weakness and depravity? Does God approve travel into outer space? The second area I explore reverses the question and the interlopers. Beginning in 1947 with the first modern sighting of a UFO (unidentified flying object), the United States appeared to be under siege from hundreds of ships from outer space. Repeated and believable sightings inspired a huge journal and book literature exploring the possibility that extraterrestrials were landing on American soil even as American rockets aimed for a shot into space. This almost immediately raised a problem that had once concerned only science fiction writers: If there were inhabitants of other planets, where did they fit in the evolutionary scale? Were they superior to human beings? Did they challenge our universal centrality? The growing fear and conflicted feelings about atomic warfare at this time intensified reaction to both films and sightings, threatening a nuclear Armageddon.

Concerning both UFO sightings and science fiction, scientists labored to shape popular culture. Two men in particular had a significant impact on the way Americans came to view space travel and UFOs, although their approaches remained distinct. They were Wernher von Braun, German rocket scientist and tireless advocate of space exploration, and Donald Menzel, adviser to the Frank Capra film project on the sun, expert on UFOs, and consultant for the air force's extensive investigation of sightings. They and other scientists helped to configure the emerging popular culture of outer space. More than that, they also helped reshape the conflict between religion and science that persisted at its core.

High on the agenda of scientists after World War II was the popularization of scientific ideas and understanding. The reasons were self-evident. Science, during the war, had received a massive infusion of funds for applied research. Technological developments in atomic energy, radar, and computing suggested a vast potential for new industrial and consumer applications. This largesse, directed at technology and stimulated by weapons development, raised a demand for greater attention to pure scientific research. One result was the National Science Foundation. But public funding of science implied public understanding of science, not simply to ease the passage of higher budgets but, in a more general sense, to promote science as a shaper of modern society. Important works like James B. Conant's *Modern Science and Modern Man* (1951) and Vannevar Bush's *Science: The Endless Horizons* (1946) attempted to explain and promote science in this dual fashion.[1]

The responsibility for popularizing science also fell to journals and particularly to such organizations as the National Association of Science Writers and the American Association for the Advancement of Science. Although the *Scientific American* did much to translate new theoretical and technological concepts into the language of general scientific culture, the failure of *Science Illustrated,* founded in 1945, suggested the limits of aiming at a large lay audience. As it had in earlier periods, the AAAS acted as a credentialing organization, lending its prestige to ideas and specialized scientific subgroups by exploring their theories at conventions and granting them affiliate status.[2]

At times this informal system became strident and controversial—for instance, during the Velikovsky dispute, when exotic theory threatened to overwhelm elite control of scientific dissemination. A much larger controversy swirled around the atomic bomb and its use, in which moral and political arguments and loyalty oaths threatened to limit or corrupt the independence of researchers.[3] The UFO controversy of the 1950s—which supposed that the American government through the air force and its scientific experts maintained secret files proving the existence of extraterrestrial visitations—provided another prolonged challenge to the hegemony of scientists over popular perceptions.

Yet the popular, imaginary press could also serve science. During the 1950s, scientists such as Wernher von Braun used science fiction and other popular culture genres to promote research and development programs. Indeed, an important contingent of science fiction writers (Robert Heinlein and Isaac Asimov, for example) worked diligently to make science fiction a respectable form of science popularization. As Asimov wrote, science fiction "deals with a fictitious society, differing from our own chiefly in the nature or extent of its technological development."[4] This mission also attracted Donald Menzel to the ranks of science fiction writers—although his fiction appeared under various pseudonyms. Other figures like von Braun positioned their advocacy of specific science projects within popular fantasy, so that the emphasis—if not the ultimate goal—shifted considerably.

If some scientists themselves explored fiction as a means to explain science, others focused on religious interpretations of their enterprise. What Robert Millikan said in the 1920s in his *Evolution in Science and Religion* remained true, more or less, for a great many other scientists in the burgeoning dialogues with religion following World War II. As Millikan put it, "The World is of course 'incurably religious.' Why? Because everyone who reflects at all *must have* conceptions about the world which go beyond the field of science, that is, beyond the present range of intellectual knowledge."[5] In the enterprise of defining a role for humans in space, all these endeavors and influences played a part. How else could American culture come to terms with this new experience except through an extended conversation based on popularized notions of its scientific and religious implications? How could it redefine that "beyond"?

This fundamental debate lay at the heart of the UFO controversy. As Rev. Franklin Loehr of the Religious Research Foundation put it in 1953, "Religion has always claimed there is intelligent, purposeful life beyond this earth. The 'saucers' offer objective, tangible evidence that religion is right in this claim—although in a way different than most of us had expected." He continued: "As Air Force reports received show, most people who express a 'saucer' theory feel there is a religious significance of one sort or another in them."[6]

This postwar flying saucer phenomenon is one of American history's strangest and most extensive adventures in unorthodox science. It affected tens of thousands of believers, sighters, and contactees and generated a vast and contentious literature divided by a running dispute between amateur and expert science. On occasion it directly confronted the argument about the place of religion and science in modern American society. Certainly not all its interpreters insisted on a religious interpretation of extraterrestrial visitors. There was a strong element of magic, mystery, and even horror in the debate about UFOs and numerous secular interpretations of sightings and contacts. Nonetheless, the larger contours of the religion-science debate helped structure the discussion.

Pilot Kenneth Arnold, a businessman from Boise, Idaho, recorded the first modern sighting of a UFO on 24 June 1947 as he flew near Mount Rainier in the Pacific Northwest.[7] Picked up by the national press, his description of curiosities "like pie plates skipping over the water" became "flying saucers" (a new term) in the inventive jargon of journalists. Saucers became the visual model for the stream of sightings that quickly followed. Hundreds of similar reports from other parts of the country flowed into the press. Sighters appeared on radio and television. In response, three important institutions in American society began to scrutinize the reports: the mass media, the air force, and the scientific community. The first included popular journals of mass circulation such as *Life, Saturday Evening Post, Cosmopolitan,* and *True.* In fact, the article by UFO advocate Donald Keyhoe, "Flying Saucers Are Real," published in *True* (January 1950), was described by one commentator as "one of the most widely read and discussed articles in publishing history." Articles in *Time, Life,* and *U.S. News and World Report* and an Edward R. Murrow television special kept the issue current.[8]

This broad airing of extraterrestrial suspicions also attracted interest from the United States Air Force. At first the air corps focused on the possibility that UFOs might be an advanced form of technology invented by the Soviets to spy on the United States (a possibility made plausible by American discussions of spy planes). Although the service quickly rejected this speculation, the air force continued to be the focus of a growing argument over sightings. During the next twenty years it established three internal working groups to investigate and evaluate sightings. And with every attempt to explain UFOs as natural phenomena the air force found itself embroiled in the larger dispute between established and amateur science.

Of the three investigations, the first two were short-lived and ended abruptly. The first, Project Sign, from 1948 to 1949, explored the possibility that Russian technology might be responsible for the outbreak of strange aerial objects. The second phase of investigation, known as Project Grudge, lasted from 1950 to 1952, through the first high point of sightings. During its apogee in the first six months of 1952, there were 16,000 UFO items mentioned in almost 150 newspapers across the country. Sightings reached a peak in July 1952 with reports of spectacular aerial visitations over Washington, D.C. Out of this activity came the founding of two organizations that championed extraterrestrial UFOs: the Civilian Saucer Investigation and the Aerial Phenomena Research Organization. Despite the huge increase in reports, the air force insisted that all of the 244 cases it investigated could be explained as either natural phenomena or mistaken perception.[9]

Responding to repeated new sightings and accusations of a cover-up, the military service organized a third and more important internal research group called Project Blue Book, a special detail that remained active from 1952 through 1969. During the seventeen years of its contentious existence, it received 13,000 reports of UFOs, although it did not investigate them all. Over the entire course of the UFO scare, from 1947 to 1969 and the final report by Edward U. Condon and a special scientific commission established at the University of Colorado that debunked the whole phenomenon, almost 2,600 items, books, and periodical articles were published on UFOs, most of them in the United States.[10]

The third important group to monitor the UFO controversy was the scientific community. Although most scientists rejected sightings out of hand, several, including Donald Menzel and Carl Sagan, paid careful attention to the controversy. Menzel in particular became a leading interpreter of UFOs and wrote books, articles, and reports arguing that sightings, though genuine experiences, mistook natural occurrences for mysterious events. Despite his best efforts, Menzel failed to confine the discussion to scientists and exclude amateurs from important mainstream institutions. The major breakthrough occurred in the late 1960s when the United States Congress held hearings on the issue in 1967 and 1968. Finally even the AAAS held a session on UFOs in 1969.

Menzel himself sharply criticized the air force for its careless and ambivalent attitude toward drawing strict scientific boundaries around its investigations. Some of his pique had a personal edge, for the astronomer had proposed his services as a special consultant in 1952, but the air force relied on his expertise only intermittently.[11] More damaging, he believed, was the Aerial Phenomena Group of the Air Technical Intelligence Center operating within the Pentagon, led by Edward J. Ruppelt, who, he charged, "believed that flying saucers came from outer space." This early "pro-saucer" group, Menzel continued, leaked hints of suppressed discoveries to outsiders such as Donald Kehoe and James McDonald, who were bent on proving a conspiracy of silence in the American military establishment— aided and abetted by mainline scientists.[12]

From his numerous books, articles, and television and radio appearances, Menzel became known as "the arch Demon of Saucerdom." To some degree this moniker is unfair, for Menzel almost always accepted the visual evidence of sighters and frequently used the term "flying saucers" in his writings. He was himself a prolific science fiction author (under various pseudonyms) and an enthusiastic friend of major science fiction writers such as Robert Heinlein and Isaac Asimov. But he was also, first and foremost, a scientist who believed that natural science, properly understood, could explain what so many Americans thought they observed as flying saucers from alien planets.[13]

Because of his extensive writings and public statements, Menzel also attracted considerable correspondence on the subject, particularly from amateur scientists and sighters who fervently believed in UFOs and attempted to convert him to their interpretation. In these exchanges Menzel struck two attitudes. He sarcastically rejected any offer to debate alongside the luminaries of the UFO movement like Donald Kehoe. As he wrote to Kehoe's organization in 1956, he declined to join the lunatic fringe who believed in

Figure 10.1   Donald Menzel catches a flying saucer. Courtesy of the Harvard University Archives.

visitors from outer space. "I have myself observed thousands of flying saucers, . . . I have succeeded in clarifying the nature of these flying saucers in every instance except one, and that was the case I reported in my book."[14]

To individual sighters and amateurs he extended patient explanation. In many cases he exchanged several letters with a writer—usually until the differences froze up and the correspondent broke off in exasperation. In a number of cases the letters progressed through a regular pattern. A sighter would write to Menzel describing his experience and speculating that he had witnessed an extraterrestrial visitation. Menzel usually responded with a scientific interpretation of what might have occurred. At this point the letter writer might pursue an alternative scientific explanation or in some cases would fall back on the Bible.

This fascinating progression from science to religion occurred frequently enough to persuade Menzel that the search for religious meaning was a powerful inspiration for the UFO movement. In correspondence with Bill Prinz, a sighter in 1964, Menzel challenged Prinz's biblical explanations. "As for Ezekiel," Menzel wrote, "I think I was the first flying saucer researcher, to recognize and point out the similarity between these early reported sightings and the modern version. I had a whole chapter on it in my first book." Advocates of saucers, he continued, had seized on this allusion and offered the Bible as proof of UFOs. But they had failed to understand that what "Ezekiel reported was most clearly a full-blown apparition of parhelia, more commonly known as sundogs."[15]

Prinz refused to retreat before this scientific exegesis of the Bible and offered what he believed was a decisive defense of his position. "I don't see how you or anyone for that matter," he wrote, "can assume to know what happened hundreds or perhaps thousands of miles away from you. . . . It just doesn't make any sense as far as I'm concerned." Three months later he discharged another sling against expertise: "I can understand better now just why Jesus Christ gathered about him relatively unschooled men, instead of trying to convince the 'learned' of his day."[16] Here was a scripturally founded defense of commonsense observation.

Menzel's own position on the dispute between religion and science made him an unenthusiastic disputant over theology, and he generally broke off correspondence with writers who insisted on interpreting natural phenomena in religious terms. In the midst of a lengthy exchange of letters with Charles A. Maney of Defiance College, for example, the conversation increasingly focused on the religious possibilities of UFOs. Menzel finally dismissed Maney with an accusation: "You are apparently among the people, of whom there are many, who use a belief in non-terrestrial UFO's (I accept your nomenclature) as a substitute for religion." Maney fired back the last word: "Frankly, Dr. Menzel, I see no logical basis for such a statement on your part." "Incidentally," he added, "I believe that a scientist without the moral code of a religion is an irresponsible and dangerous member of society."[17]

In his private writings Menzel speculated about the reasons for this religious anxiety, ascribing it to the fatal challenge of scientific culture to historical religions. Religion could still be acceptable if private and useful if comforting. But, as he said bluntly in his unpublished autobiography, "The larger our universe, the more difficult I find it to believe in the existence of a personal God, who can suspend the forces of nature at will or grant special immunity to those who repent for their sins." Religions, he continued, were incorrigibly anthropomorphic, and the more primitive the science the stronger this tendency. "Such views were acceptable," he concluded, "as long as the earth was recognized as the center of the world. But religions have failed to grow with human knowledge."[18]

Menzel had stationed himself as the watchful guardian at the temple of science. Although he wrote science fiction, including an unpublished novel on UFOs, and made countless pencil sketches of "Martians" (some of which he published in 1965), he could not countenance religious speculation as a substitute for hard-headed research. This particularly held true for science popularization. As he wrote to Kenneth Heuer of the Hayden Planetarium in 1950 after a request to endorse Heuer's new book, he had always crusaded against esoteric astronomy. "Your section about the moon illustrates it as well as any. You have given first place to the wildest of speculations.... The quasi-religious references, for example to the sun as a possible 'hell,' were particularly jarring."[19]

Menzel's insistence on the religious roots of the UFO phenomenon was seconded by the Project Blue Book report in 1964. The document concluded that UFO sighters adopted a tone and style of argument that incited "religious, superstitious, and science fiction beliefs." This large and widely read underground literature directly challenged ordinary scientific procedures. Several of these books and articles linked UFOs and Christ's Second Coming. In doing so they invoked the antiexpertise, commonsense science of the premodern dispensation. As Rev. Virginia Brasington wrote in her pamphlet *Flying Saucers and the Bible,* "Although the Bible is not a textbook on science, it is scientifically correct." Therefore the frequent examples of flying saucers in Exodus and Ezekiel, plus other forms of levitation and cloud travel in the Scriptures, proved the continuity between UFOs and biblical testimony. Other commentators found UFOs in biblical exegesis. As Morris Jessup wrote in *UFO and the Bible,* a number of verses in the New Testament suggested space travel; for example: "For the Son of Man is as a man taking a far journey."[20]

One of the most interesting of the works to link saucers and salvation recounted a trip to sighting locales by Bryant and Helen Reeve, guided by

George Adamski, one of the most vocal and respected advocates of extraterrestrial visitation. From their journey around the nation, the Reeves realized that a great many sighters testified to a religious interpretation of UFOs. Space visitors, they concluded, had come to warn the world against its transgressions. Evidence for this prophetic mode had even appeared in a Hollywood film, *The Day the Earth Stood Still* (1951). As the authors explained, "Many saucer students who know something of the history of this film sincerely believe that it was 'inspired' by the space-beings in our midst."[21]

Even if such speculations were published and believed by thousands of Americans, is there any reason to take this literature seriously, to place it in the context of an important and abiding cultural dialogue? In fact, there are several reasons to do so. First, the UFO controversy did not arise in a vacuum. It grew as a variant of the larger discussion about the place of science and religion in the postwar world, and as such it extended these controversies into an important genre of popular culture.[22] It represents one element of the search for the proper language and imaginative framework to reimagine the relation of humans to the universe in a space age. The UFO debate also had important ramifications for mainline science itself, because it reiterated and even deepened the contested nature of science popularization. Donald Menzel and Harlow Shapley (in the Velikovsky controversy) immediately recognized that such controversies could damage science by casting doubt on its methods and conclusions. Mystification and panic, they believed, would shunt public attention into the byways of superstition.

When mainline science appeared to stray into the UFO camp, the peril became even greater. Menzel had no difficulty dismissing amateurs such as Donald Kehoe and George Adamski, who pitched their mixture of science and superstition to a popular audience. He was a dogged and effective critic of their works and demanded equal time, even in the popular, nonacademic journals where they published. But when the culprit was a fellow scientist, Menzel could scarcely contain his amazement and dismay. For a short period during this controversy, the UFO phenomenon threatened to subvert the united front of mainline science and substantiate charges that the air force had organized Project Blue Book to hide what it knew of extraterrestrial visitations. Not surprisingly, this threat coincided with the intensification of American space probes and the Apollo moon program of the mid-1960s.

The first possible breakthrough occurred in proposed hearings before

Congress to investigate charges of an air force cover-up. Donald Kehoe developed this strategy in the late 1950s, but it did not bear fruit until April 1966, when the House Committee on Armed Services held a one-day session to explore the issue (and again in 1968 when new hearings began). The second area of respectability that opened was the AAAS, which discussed UFOs at its meeting in Boston in 1969. Menzel and his allies opposed granting UFOs a hearing in any reputable institution; no matter what was said, serious attention to the issue meant granting stature to its wildest advocates and their amateur science.

The April 1966 hearings in the House of Representatives offered no real comfort to saucerists, however. Harold Brown, secretary of the air force, curtly dismissed the possibility of visitations: "I know of no one of scientific standing or executive standing, or with a detailed knowledge of this, in our organization who believes that they come from extraterrestrial sources."[23] A more serious hearing was planned for 1968 by Rep. J. Edward Roush of Indiana, of the House Science and Astronautics Committee. Roush invited several scientists who either were favorable to UFOs or wanted to continue government funding of research. No one asked Donald Menzel, however, and when he discovered this oversight, he rushed a telegram to Roush: "Am amazed, however, that you could plan so unbalanced a Symposium weighted by persons known to favor government support of continuing, expensive and pointless investigation of UFOs without inviting me the leading exponent of opposing views and author of two major books on the subject."[24]

The most important mainstream scientist to testify before Congress was the Cornell University astronomer Carl Sagan, who also persuaded the AAAS to hold a UFO symposium. Menzel blustered at Sagan's remarks to the congressmen. It seems to me, he wrote, that "as a scientist you have shirked your responsibilities to speak out clearly on this subject." Anticipating the worst, Menzel could not support a continuation of serious public attention to UFOs at the AAAS symposium that Sagan proposed. Menzel granted that Sagan rejected interpreting UFOs as alien visitations, but he feared that the Cornell scientist hedged his skepticism. So when Sagan wrote that he was "following with interest the recent work of James McDonald of the University of Arizona," Menzel shot back: "In my opinion James McDonald is an absolute nut." Sagan insisted that he remained "ambivalent" about the issue. "I think it is logically quite clear that, in many cases, one cannot demonstrate what has been seen is *not* an extraterrestrial spacecraft," he insisted. Menzel expressed amazement and dismay at this piling up of double negatives, which he interpreted as backsliding.[25]

Menzel's uncompromising, hostile attitude toward opening up the AAAS to exotic science led him to organize other scientists in a caucus to oppose the session. Apparently he succeeded in 1968. The following year he promised another attack on the Sagan group: "I shall do my best to throw a monkey-wrench into their machinery as I did last Christmas at the Dallas Meeting." But the president of the AAAS in 1969, Walter Orr Roberts, insisted that airing the issue was appropriate. "The UFO buffs, to be sure," he wrote to Edward U. Condon, "are stirring up all sorts of wild notions, but if we simply ignore them, I fear silence by scientists more than I do the kooks." Furthermore, times had changed. For another thing, Condon's recent report for the air force on the entire history of the UFO phenomenon had appeared to settle the issue against the advocates of visitation and religion.[26]

If amateur scientists hoped to breach the wall of expertise—and initiate a new Scopes trial—they were disappointed by the AAAS hearings when they finally occurred in late 1969. Even Sagan's introduction to the volume of the published papers from the session warned about the "drift away from science" toward religious sectarianism. Belief in visitations paralleled borderline subjects such as "astrology and the writings of Velikovsky," he concluded. None of the other contributors to the discussion offered much encouragement to UFO buffs. There was simply no scientific evidence to bolster their claims.[27]

This intervention of mainline science into the dispute about saucers settled nothing permanently, even if it did shore up its boundaries against amateur speculation. Sightings and reports of UFOs washed like waves over the beaches of popular culture from a seemingly inexhaustible sea of invention. Indeed, at the very time of the AAAS session, UFO sightings reached another height. Frank Edwards's *Flying Saucers—Serious Business* (1966) sold 1,300,000 copies, and the air force recorded 40,000 requests by schoolchildren for data on UFOs from 1966 to 1969.[28] Despite the best efforts of scientists, the language of space travel remained, as it had begun, deeply contested and divided between science and a mixture of religious and imaginative notions. The denials and criticisms of scientists only fertilized the debate.

onald Menzel explained that this pandemonium had been stirred up by modern science and technology. "Man was already contemplating space exploration," he wrote, "so why not space travel in reverse?" Why not UFOs? In fact Menzel set his own imagination free in the world of extraterrestrial visitations and human space travel in his prolific output of science fiction stories. Within this older, widely accepted literary genre, Menzel and other writers charted the heavens and mapped the future exploration of space. By means of this contemplative literature, American popular culture also generated another huge and important discussion about the meaning of extraterrestrial travel; and once again science and religion struggled to define the significance of that potential.[29]

Science fiction literature and films produced during the 1950s constituted a vast and complex genre that contained several distinct tendencies and practices. It has been explained in contradictory ways: as a significant popularizer of science, as the mystifier of science, as an intellectual experiment with utopian social arrangements, as adventure literature, and as apocalyptic vision, among many others. Probably it contains all these elements and more. But during the 1950s the best and most widely watched Hollywood science fiction films dramatized the dual questions that aggravated the UFO controversy. Was science a sufficient explanation and justification for human activity? Did God approve the impending voyage of humans into outer space? Such questions were confusing and difficult to answer, if only because the definition of science was itself hotly contested in the genre. Was it the age-old common sense, the intuitive book of the laws of nature, informed by the words of the book of God? Or was it the study of natural phenomena, unlimited except by the possibilities of experiment and human understanding? Science fiction literature and film explored both alternatives.[30]

Before the 1950s, science fiction literature already had a long and distinguished development in which the issues of accuracy and scientific clarity became increasingly significant.[31] After World War II this genre attracted a significant scientific audience, abetted by other professionals. Scientists enjoyed this literature, as Arthur S. Barron speculated, because it engaged the convictions and consequences of their profession. It glamorized science while often posing questions about the larger moral and ethical meaning of experiment. As he put it, "It is likely that science fiction enables them [scientists] to resolve this tension symbolically, at least, in the direction of faith, without making an actual commitment."[32] Although it is not necessary to accept Barron's insistence on moral questions and religious overtones, scientists openly worried about their portrayal in fiction and film. A study published in 1958 examined the content of science fiction stories and concluded that the depiction of scientists had improved—but at a price. Early renderings of scientists as sorcerers had declined. Now anxiety about science, the enterprise itself, the symbolic embodiment of human hubris, replaced overt malice toward its individual practitioners.[33]

As in the debate about UFOs, science fiction literature frequently revealed a powerful religious motivation. Much of this spirit reflected the transfer of apocalyptic speculation from its traditional place in Christian eschatology to imagination about the future. The sudden, terrible birth of atomic energy and then the anxieties of the Cold War made such plots inevitable and popular. Frequently stories contained prophecy, revelation of things to come, secret knowledge, myths about origins and ends, the paranormal, and salvation imposed from beyond—all of which addressed the sorts of questions that religion traditionally answered. No book better illustrates this tendency than the science fiction best-seller *A Canticle for Leibowitz.* by Walter Miller.[34]

Unlike literature, science fiction films, particularly those of the early and mid-1950s, were honed to a simpler structure and a more direct purpose. As critic Susan Sontag has written, "Science fiction films are not about science. They are about disaster, which is one of the oldest subjects of art." True enough: many of the plots revolve around fear, a fantasy about the unthinkable, or a survey of human depravity. Nothing in this list of calamities is new or peculiar to a scientific worldview. Yet beneath this "imagination of disaster" lies another proposition examined anew by almost every science fiction film of the era: a challenge to the overreach of science; the desire to restore religious margins to human aspirations and behavior.[35]

Nothing illustrates this difference better than the transformation of Harry Bates's story "Farewell to the Master," written in 1942, into the film *The Day the Earth Stood Still* (1951), one of the most memorable examples of this genre. Bates's story invented many of the elements and characters later incorporated into the brilliant 1950s film, but his concern is completely different. His story features a robot and a "man, [Klaatu] godlike in appearance and human in form." The "person" is almost immediately murdered by a madman in the crowd that has gathered around the spaceship bringing the visitors to earth. But the humans fail to recognize that they have confused animate with inanimate. What appears to be a robot is actually a "powerful god of the machine of some undreamed-of scientific civilization." Like much of the science fiction of the 1930s, this story expressed a hyperextended fear of machines' seizing control of human life. But the 1950s film transformed this story into a parable of the Last Judgment and a reenactment of the New Covenant, with a Christlike figure murdered by jealous and suspicious humans. Only a last-minute escape from annihilation is possible.[36]

Science fiction films also became the best dramatic medium for exploring the implications of the human conquest of space. Tinged with overtones of anxiety and suspicion about reaching the limits of science, they often caricatured the misguided and feeble reason of contemporary human civilization. Here was an ideal intersection in popular culture at which to stop and ask the question: Did God approve the human adventure in space? Was this exploration a trespass on the heavens or one more step in human destiny?[37]

A remarkable group of men working through a cluster of institutions produced a significant vision of this encounter that attempted to answer such questions. Working together on a series of projects, the Hollywood producer George Pal, Gordon Atwater of the Hayden Planetarium, Walt Disney, the editors of *Collier's* magazine and illustrator Chesley Bonestell, science writer Willy Ley, and rocket scientist Wernher von Braun produced a considerable and compelling film and print literature promoting space travel. They designed and described in popular terms the technology necessary to accomplish this goal. Finally, they invented a popular visual language that domesticated this encroachment on the heavens and justified the conquest of space. Their story reveals the complex and fascinating background of one of Hollywood's most curious—and characteristic—science fiction films, *The Conquest of Space* (1955).

The most important and indefatigable scientist to promote space travel in America was Wernher von Braun, former administrator and organizer of Germany's World War II rocket development program. Now an immigrant to the United States and appointed to head the Redstone Rocket Development Center, von Braun lobbied Congress and the president and agitated among fellow scientists and in the public media for funds to send men to the moon and Mars. It was, as he said, his life-long ambition.

To achieve this goal he increasingly aimed at shaping public opinion, first through the popular press, then in three Walt Disney films, and finally in a deeply flawed but fascinating film that he made with two science fiction masters: Hollywood producer George Pal and director Bryan Haskin. In

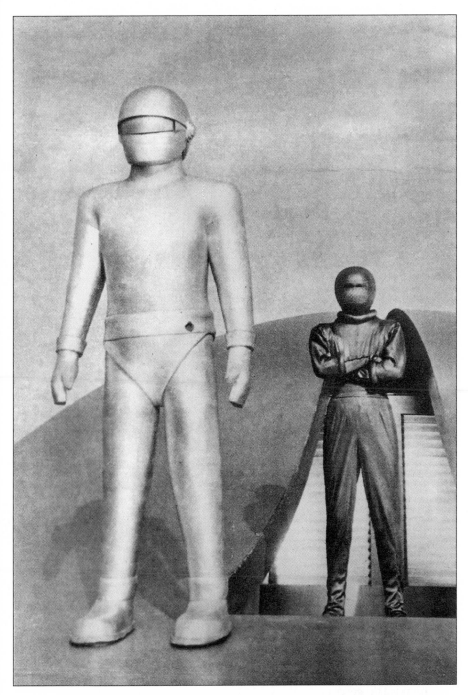

Figure 10.2   Scene from *The Day the Earth Stood Still* (Twentieth Century–Fox, 1951), picturing the robot Gort followed by Klaatu–Mr. Carpenter as they emerge from their spaceship. At this point it is difficult to tell which is the robot. Extraterrestrials invaded the earth to carry a warning not to bring human violence into the cosmos. Courtesy of the Museum of Modern Art, Film Stills Archive.

Figure 10.3   "The Whole World in His Hands," but in fact Wernher von Braun's greatest ambition was travel to other worlds. Courtesy of the Library of Congress.

each of these media, he repeated a lifetime of speculation about the necessary technology for space travel. But the film in particular directly confronted questions that a great many of the best science fiction films of the day considered only obliquely. *The Conquest of Space* specifically asked in what sense travel above and beyond the earth conformed to America's religious expectations. Could earthbound religious language, metaphors, and descriptions of the devotional life and spirituality be extended into space? A positive answer both suited von Braun's own religious sympathies and spoke to hesitations about the arrogance and presumption of science that surrounded the space program.

Von Braun recognized that shooting rockets into the heavens could arouse fear and religious anxiety in an element of the American public. This was potentially an immense problem for realizing his dream of a spaceship to Mars, and he encountered its challenge from the outset. As he wrote, "Since we first began the exploration of space through rocketry, we have regularly received letters expressing concern over what writers call our 'tampering' with God's creation." One letter, he noted, even "revealed an honest fear that a rocket would strike an angel in space high above the earth." To this sort of objection and reluctance von Braun addressed many of his arguments.[38]

From the beginning of his long career in rocketry, von Braun was associated with the science and the science fiction of space travel. In Germany he worked with Herman Oberth, a rocket scientist who had been the technical adviser to the famous fantasy film by Fritz Lang, *Frau im Mond*.[39] During World War II he directed the technical work at Peenemünde, where the Germans developed and launched the V-1 and V-2 rockets, primarily as a terror weapon aimed at the British Isles. Evacuated to the United States in 1945 with other German rocket scientists, he quickly rose to head the Redstone and Jupiter rocket projects for the army in Huntsville, Alabama.

Von Braun shared with his friend and collaborator Willy Ley, another German immigrant, an enthusiasm for space travel and a shrewd understanding of how to shape public opinion to accept the commitment and expense necessary for such projects. Like other scientists and technicians who worked in the world of rocketry, the "Rocket Master," as he was known, used science fiction as a tool of science popularization and, particularly in his case, as a way of promoting space exploration. One of von Braun's first major endeavors in the United States was a manuscript about travel to Mars called the "Marsprojekt." Completed in 1947, the novel was not published, although the technical appendix finally appeared in 1953 as *The Mars Project*.[40] Nonetheless, these writings contained the core of ideas that von Braun promoted through a series of popular culture projects in the 1950s.

Ley and von Braun worked primarily through three institutions to advance their plans for space travel. These included the Hayden Planetarium in New York City, the important mass circulation magazine *Collier's*, and eventually the Hollywood studios of Walt Disney and Paramount Pictures. Their most important collaborator was Chesley Bonestell, one of the leading illustrators of science fiction and an important figure in the artistic imaging of outer space for Hollywood science fiction films.

Willy Ley's association with space travel was even longer than von

Braun's. In Germany he had worked on the film *Frau im Mond*. Besides collaborating with von Braun in the United States, Ley wrote science fiction screenplays and popular books and articles to promote rocketry—one of the reasons Frank Capra recruited him to develop a script for *Our Mr. Sun*. Ley also wrote science and religious speculations, including a fascinating book on theistic evolution called *The Days of Creation* (1941). This dual-entry ledger of parallels between the biblical story of creation and evolutionary theory compared modern scientific concepts with Scripture. Ley wrote that his project relied on no "reasons of high philosophy nor attempts to reconcile ideas that need no reconciling, but the pure joy of comparing two stories, each of them fascinating in itself and doubly so when regarded together."[41]

Von Braun debuted his plans at the space travel conferences held at the Hayden Planetarium in the early 1950s. The Planetarium's seminars on interplanetary space travel originated during the tenure of Gordon Atwater but took place after his resignation in 1950. Atwater's interest in astronomical speculation had become evident in the choice of programs the Planetarium presented in 1949 and 1950. Two of these, "The End of the World" and "Conquest of Space," had "tremendous popular appeal." Their development reflected a change in policy effected under Atwater to shift "presentations in line with topics of current popular interest rather than the more academic type that had predominated the programs of earlier years."[42]

Atwater's openness to speculation about space travel revealed a quality of imagination and enthusiasm that proved fatal to his career when he planned a show to demonstrate Velikovsky's theories. But the space symposium he initiated continued for three years. Largely organized by Willy Ley, the symposium met first on Columbus Day 1951 at the Planetarium. The moment had arrived, announced Ley, "to make the public realize that the problem of space travel is to be regarded as a serious branch of science and technology." Featured speakers included astronomer Fred Whipple of Harvard, Robert Haviland of General Electric, Oscar Schachter of the legal department of the United Nations, and Heinz Haber, another German scientist and an expert on space medicine. The technical specifications about space travel were clearly von Braun's.[43]

The second symposium met a year later and featured many of the same speakers: Ley, Whipple, and von Braun on "The Early Steps in the Realization of the Space Station." The last symposium occurred a year later. By this time the Planetarium had developed a large and expectant following for its symposia, and it received thousands of "reservations" for the first space voyage from an eager public. Such success, however, eventually caused the institution concern about its prestige and scientific credibility. The annual report for 1954, for example, proclaimed that the Planetarium intended to "avoid the questionable and the fantastic, even though their appeal may be highly popular." As Frank Forester of the Planetarium wrote in 1955, "The Planetarium's interest in space travel and rockets is only a supplementary one. Its main function is the popular interpretation of astronomy."[44]

The immediate consequence of the space symposia was a major expedition into journalism—a series of space exploration articles that appeared in *Collier's* magazine beginning in March 1952. An associate editor of *Collier's* had attended the first meeting and convinced his editors to organize a symposium and a series of articles on the potential for space travel. These recognized von Braun as the central figure in rocketry, giving him a chance to describe an earth-orbiting space station and the shuttle that would convey supplies and personnel to and from the earth. Chesley Bonestell did many of the illustrations for the series.[45]

Following the symposia and the *Collier's* series, von Braun and Ley worked actively in shaping films to proselytize for space travel, adapting their ideas to this more visual, dramatic medium. One of the most successful endeavors was consulting with Walt Disney from 1954 to 1956. Together with Disney animator Ward Kimball, they produced three films for the Disney television show: *Man in Space, Man and the Moon,* and *Mars and Beyond,* finally shown in 1957. Part of Disney's strategy to promote the four theme divisions (Adventureland, Frontierland, Fantasyland, and Tomorrowland) at his new Disneyland amusement park, the films provided von Braun with the platform for popularizing ideas about space travel and promoting his own notions about the architecture of the rockets to undertake it.[46]

Disney's fanciful films developed an animated, comic version of the very serious space agenda that von Braun and his associates at Hayden and *Collier's* promoted. Featuring cartoon characters as well as serious interviews with scientists and mock-ups of rockets and space suits, the three films alluded to all the basic elements of the von Braun strategy: space shuttles, an earth-orbiting space laboratory, and—the ultimate goal—an expedition to Mars. This highly successful film venture signaled von Braun's willingness to work within a popular medium. If the only way to present a trip to Mars included "a crazy quilt of cartoon aliens parading around the sands of

Mars," this provoked no second thoughts, for the basic message lay at the dramatic center, and its articulation was von Braun's goal.[47]

Other tactics in von Braun's promotion, of course, suggested the military potential of space exploration. Willy Ley, in the *Collier's* series, fixed on another argument assuring readers that "most astronomers agree that there is primitive plant life, like lichens and algae on Mars." This supposed presence suggested the possibility of animal life too. Beyond the wonder of this potential, Ley intimated there might be economic and commercial exploitation of the planets. But for von Braun and Ley there was also an element of intense ethical and religious speculation to their proposals. Von Braun never hesitated to invoke religious language in justifying his plans to invade the heavens. As he told the International Federation for Space Travel in 1952, "Scientific research is still primarily motivated by divine curiosity. . . . We may be very certain that our star-ward strivings fit somehow into God's plan." An even more explicit confrontation with the religious questions of space travel came in a speech to the American Rocket Society in the same year. "I think it is a fair assumption," he noted, "that the Ten Commandments are entirely adequate, without amendments, to cope with all the problems the technological revolution not only has brought up, but will bring up in the future." The editors of *Missiles and Rockets,* where the speech was reprinted, referred to von Braun's discussion of the relation between God and science as "a matter of vital practicality—a prime consideration in the struggle for survival of the species."[48] A religious person, one might conclude, should welcome expeditions beyond this world.

Von Braun and Ley had a chance to articulate this complex vision of mankind's destiny in outer space, as well as to enter another plea for a space program, in a major Hollywood film, *The Conquest of Space,* released in 1955. Von Braun had already consulted for several science fiction films. In 1950 he and Chesley Bonestell designed an earth satellite for producer George Pal to use in the film *Destination Moon.* Beginning with this film, Pal inaugurated his distinguished series of science fiction films, productions that in many respects represent the best work in this 1950s genre.[49]

Pal's initial Hollywood efforts were based, like his friend Walt Disney's work, on animation. Pal produced cartoons and a complex form of stop-action animation with puppets called the "Puppetoons." Then in the 1950s he suddenly blossomed as Paramount's leading producer of science fiction films. The most important of these were *When Worlds Collide* (1951), a modern Noah's Ark story, and then a brilliant updating of the H. G. Wells novel

The War of the Worlds in 1953. Both of these films radiated a powerful religious vocabulary and symbolism. Aesthetically flawed, *The Conquest of Space* was the last of Pal's trilogy of space odysseys. The most competent in demonstrating the science of space travel, it developed, paradoxically, the most explicit confrontation with the moral and ethical questions surrounding human encroachment on the heavens.[50] Unfortunately the acting and plot were wooden and contrived, as if with this production the genre passed its peak. The plan for what became *Conquest* derived from a book of the same name by Willy Ley and Chesley Bonestell, although many of its ideas about space travel had been urged by von Braun at Hayden, *Collier's*, and Disney. As Bonestell wrote to Ley in 1954, "George Pal who is quite obsessed with 'Conquest of Space' called me a couple of nights ago to say he wanted to be the first to tell me that Paramount is carrying on an investigation with the idea of buying it."[51]

Pal originally intended the project to extend to three films, constituting a scientifically correct trilogy. But the stories were eventually compressed into one that had two distinct and ill-fitting halves. Bryan Haskin, the director for this film as well as *The War of the Worlds*, explained in a long interview that the film was partly a serious explanation of how a space satellite and shuttles to and from the earth would work. Haskin proudly noted two difficult concepts explained through comic relief: weightlessness, and the dead environment of Mars. But he dismissed the film as deeply compromised because of the ending imposed by Paramount. As he noted of the two stories: "The personal story and the technical story—oil and water." "We had Wernher von Braun on the set all the time . . . . as a technical advisor. He kept it straight, but I don't know—it's a mish-mash thing."[52]

The "mishmash" plot that Haskin deplored spliced together two stories, the first depicting life on a space station, construction of an interplanetary ship, and training of a crew, the second narrating a landing on Mars. If the first could boast of technical explanations of weightlessness and other scientific concepts, it also had curious overtones that Haskin apparently did not notice or care to comment on. Space station social relations, for example, recall the "foxhole democracy" films of World War II with their careful stress on good humor and the wisdom of the American character as a means of harmonizing diverse social and ethnic groups. An even more interesting element is the theme of reconciliation with old enemies: Japanese and German characters are both heroes. In other words, the technically correct first half of the film also included a plea for human unity and singularity of purpose despite the recent horrible war and lingering hostility against erst-while enemies.[53]

When a shuttle from the earth brings orders directing the crew to take the new spaceship to Mars, the second plot engages. As the ship blasts out of the earth's orbit, two parallel stories emerge, the first disclosing the troubled relations between a father (Captain Merritt) and his son, a member of the crew. This in turn is gradually absorbed into an overtly religious theme, into answering the question, Does God sanction human invasion of the heavens?

As the ship nears Mars, the captain begins to exhibit bizarre behavior induced by space sickness. In his case its symptoms include an obsession with Bible reading. When the ship finally lands on the surface of the planet, Captain Merritt utters garbled biblical verses to express his wild imaginings. It is blasphemy, he raves, to travel into space. Acting on this perverse inspiration, he begins to jettison the ship's reserve water tanks. Only by shooting him can his son prevent the agonized death of the entire crew.

Now, however, the despondent crew members must wait a year before the positions of Mars and the earth will allow them to return: a year without water, a year without hope. As they begin to languish from thirst and guilt about the captain's death, the calendar reaches Christmas Eve. Their desperation deepens, and one character cries out that only God can make a tree or a flower or bring water. The others begin a tentative Christmas carol, "God Rest Ye Merry, Gentlemen." Looking out through the porthole onto the red desert that surrounds them, one of the crew suddenly sees that a miraculous snow has fallen. The soundtrack swells with the notes of the hymn, and the camera suddenly shifts to a landscape view of the ship in a snow-covered field, looking very much like a New England church steeple. The crew members can collect enough water to last until their return. Later they discover that a seed planted by one of them has begun to sprout. Both of these signs confirm the rightness of their voyage. The question confronted in countless other science fiction films of the day here received a clear and concise symbolic answer: God approved, and he sent a message to confirm his decision.[54]

Although this film represented the least of Pal's efforts and disappointed film critics, it summarized in a very coherent fashion the cultural struggle that gave science fiction its energy and appropriateness for the 1950s. Far from being "oil and water," the plot reconciled science and religion. From the perspective of Wernher von Braun, it focused on technology and the

Figure 10.4   Two crew members, Mahoney and Imoto, toast Christmas Eve with empty water glasses. Moments later the crew members discover their wishes have come true; snow has fallen on Mars, and they will live to return to the earth (with God's blessings). From *Conquest of Space* (1955), Paramount Pictures. Courtesy of the Museum of Modern Art, Film Stills Archive.

possible religious objections to its use in outer space. In a sense it represented the culmination of his arguments for space travel. For a number of years von Braun, Ley, and Bonestell had relied on popular culture to promote space travel. First in books, then in magazines like *Collier's*, at Planetarium exhibits, through the publication of artwork, at Disney's theme park, and in science fiction films, they had reiterated the need to explore the heavens. Along the way they built up a considerable technical literature explaining how this might be accomplished. If the *Marsprojekt* was von Braun's early ambition, *The Conquest of Space* represented the completion of a carefully constructed public relations effort.

As von Braun wrote to Ley in 1955 regarding his forthcoming book *The Conquest of Mars*, "In view of the fact that we have a pretty closely knit audience which collects all literature on space flight I found it necessary to explain in the text why and in what respect the concept presented in

'Conquest of Mars' deviates from 'Across... [*Across the Space Frontier*] and 'Conquest of the Moon,' and also my own 'Mars Project.'" In other words, von Braun recognized science fiction as a crucial part of his very serious efforts to convince the American people and government to initiate a serious program aimed at space travel. Even the "new space man's language and terminology which has been developed in science fiction books or in such television programs as Captain Video or Space Cadet," was useful, he concluded. "This tremendous popularization of the subject has solidly sold the younger generation on the idea of flight through space."[55]

But the appended story of patricide and the religious speculations of *Conquest,* whatever their provenance, resonated with a serious religious tone that also infected von Braun's space fantasies. Later in his life the rocket scientist wrote extensively about his religious views and the relation between religion and science. He did not subscribe to a literal interpretation of the Bible. Certainly he did not agree with Captain Merritt's attempt to derail the trip to Mars. Scientific conquest of space was not blasphemy; it fulfilled part of God's plan. At the same time, however, von Braun emphatically rejected the attempt to separate the book of nature and the book of God. "One of the great tragedies of our times," he wrote in 1969, is "that science and religion have been cast as antagonists." To resolve the conflict by dividing "our experience into two parts," he continued, was equally lethal. The two must be mingled.[56]

Just how this might be done, he wrote elsewhere, was suggested in the religious cosmology of the French Jesuit and paleontologist Pierre Teilhard de Chardin. This work was the "most promising bridge between science and religion and his formulations should be most satisfying to modern man." But von Braun pushed the amalgam even further. When Governor Ronald Reagan and the California superintendent of public schools sought in 1969 to include creation science teachings alongside evolution in public school biology courses, von Braun supported the move.[57]

On the eve of space exploration, the dialogue between science and religion flowed into new and burgeoning forms of American popular culture. The potential for travel into space demanded a fresh look at human scientific endeavors. Did religion countenance this invasion of the heavens? Could religious ideas be extended as far as the imagination could carry humankind? Would American Christianity apply to travel to the moon, to Mars, and beyond? Was the vocabulary of religion adequate to the new ideas and the amazing feats imagined in science fiction and in the purported invasion of the earth by UFOs? There were no clear answers to such speculations, yet the very inquiry gave new energy and shape to the dialogue between science and religion in the 1950s. One conclusion, however, is inescapable. The efforts of scientists like Donald Menzel to control the discussion, to situate it inside a scientific framework, failed to exclude the voices of religion.

Fiction finally became reality in the late 1960s, and all of these cultural messages converged on the first extraterrestrial experiences of Americans. By this time American astronauts had gained the tacit status of sacred adventurers on a celestial mission. Frank Borman made this explicit in 1968 during an Apollo flight around the moon. Experiencing the anxiety and exhilaration of the voyage, he fell back on religious images to articulate his feelings. Looking back at the earth, he said to himself, *"This must be what God sees."* Then on Christmas Eve, as their ship hurtled around the moon, Borman and the other two astronauts took turns reading from Genesis, a message broadcast back to the earth accompanied by television shots panning out of the gray, empty craters and dusty landscape.[58]

The first words Neil Armstrong uttered during America's moon landing extended this continued mixture of responses and dialogues. When he placed his permanent footprint on the moon surface, Armstrong pronounced a short, careful speech: "That's one small step for man, one giant leap for mankind." "One small step" denied the hubris of humans in landing on the moon; a giant step for mankind invoked manifest destiny—a spiritual justification for the conquest of space. But just as obviously, this was a secular statement. One step for man placed Armstrong among a team of scientists and adventurers; one leap for mankind situated the exploit in a long list of human achievements. In American culture both of these interpretations were possible—and that is the point.

Does "objectivity" in religious inquiry differ from "objectivity" in inquiry in the natural sciences human and non-human?

Horace Kallen and
Prentiss Pemberton
(1960)

Chapter 11

The Religious Possibilities
of Social Science

As science and religion engaged each other along the endless boundaries and frontiers of American culture, another major force—social science—entered the fray promising to mediate this spirited dialogue. American social science in particular was a genetic carrier of both science and religion. Born in the Progressive Era crisis of the 1890s, it shared a dual lineage of optimistic Protestantism and secular Germanic and French theory. Its original goals were social reform, social control, and social amelioration, and its methods embraced social inquiry, social experiment, and even "laboratory" schools. At its most creative, it seemed a neutral terrain where science and religion might meet and settle their differences.

This solution seemed particularly apt after World War II. During the 1940s and 1950s social science in its various guises rose to enormous prestige and power in American academic circles, in government, and in business organizations. As Alfred E. Kuenzli, a member of the Society for the Scientific Study of Religion noted in 1957, "Our thesis is the emergence, in American society, of the social sciences as an ideological and ethical force to be contended with."[1] It was no anomaly that the Conference on Science, Philosophy, and Religion hunkered down to discussions of social science and postwar social reform after its champions of science and theology dueled to a bitter stalemate on first principles. Settlement of such ideological disputes in American culture has generally followed this path of practicality. Pluralism was better suited to problem solving than to theoretical uniformity—or so it seemed to the intellectuals, scientists, and theologians who gathered yearly at the Jewish Theological Seminary to explore the deepest difficulties of American society. They redefined these problems as practical questions and set out to offer utilitarian solutions, all the while allowing fundamental disagreements to simmer quietly.

Evidence of the investing of social science with visionary energy during the postwar period is the importance of popular sociological works that redefined American culture. Seminal books such as David Riesman's *The Lonely Crowd*, published in 1950, and Will Herberg's *Protestant, Catholic, Jew*, which appeared in 1956, explored the spiritual history of America using sociological methods and psychological models to plot (and condemn) the developing spiritual vacuum of modern life. Other works purported to demonstrate the human need for spirituality—even in an age of science.[2] But if sociology appeared to underscore the necessity for some essential belief system in every society, what role could sociology as a social science play in relation to established sects—to the ongoing religions in American society?

The immense prestige of social science in the postwar era arose partly from its ability to exclude first principles from the discussion, to solve problems without resolving ideological disputes, without invoking philosophy when philosophy divided and offended. Yet there were difficulties with this position. A great many natural scientists belittled the claims of social scientists to the name and prestige of science. Differences in methodology, training, and outcomes deeply divided those who studied nature from those who studied society. Disputes over funding for the social sciences during the founding and early years of the National Science Foundation suggest how important this controversy became. Furthermore, as Kuenzli continued in his article, the social sciences promised "to challenge nearly every tenet, every maxim, every practice of our traditional morality."[3] In other words, sociology and psychology could also drive a virulent secularization.

Despite this debate over their aspirations, the social sciences seemed to offer a model for achieving practical results in pursuit of moral purpose. Still, from a religious perspective there were problems—even risks—in using social science that had to be faced frankly. Was social science ultimately amenable to religious purposes? Was social science, particularly sociology, a tool that religious organizations could employ to further their aims of proselytization and reform? Or was sociology best devoted to studying religion as a human institution? Was the sociology of religion just another field of academic interest, not engaged with the soul of American culture? Could secular science and religious purposes ever be combined?

Attempts to resolve such questions brought the study of religion to the forefront of American intellectual life, with surprising and mixed results. They opened a way back into the academy for scholars and practitioners of religion who had recently been excluded. But they also sharpened the problems of perspective and orientation. Simply put: Were the social sciences entirely secular, or were they effective only if practiced within a system of religious belief? Such discussions absorbed the founders of the Society for the Scientific Study of Religion (SSSR),[4] created in 1949, and a parallel institution, the Religious Research Association, founded in 1951. Between them these two institutions emphasized distinct sides of sociology's potential impact on religion: scientific study and religious advocacy. Whatever their differences, with many joint members and considerable organizational overlap, they agreed that social science could be a means to recenter religion at the core of the American postwar intellectual conversation. In short, social science was a science that the religiously oriented might live with—even make their own.[5]

Looking back to the earliest days of the SSSR, psychologist Bernard Spilka noted that the sociological study of religion "has always been at the heart of sociology. The heritage of Weber, Durkheim, and Simmel among others encouraged such a development." How to undertake this study and to what purposes, however, preoccupied the earliest proponents of a special organization of religious sociologists. Plans for an organization developed after a talk on psychology and religion at an interfaith meeting at Mount Holyoke College in 1948, what J. Paul Williams of the religion department at Mount Holyoke later characterized as a "campus conference on 'God and the Rat [theology and psychology].'" The speaker, Walter Houston Clark, professor of psychology and education at Middlebury College in Vermont, chatted with Williams after his remarks. "We both agreed," recalled Clark, "that there needed to be more empirical research in the area of religion and that there was no dynamic organization to encourage this." Both committed themselves to organizing a committee for that purpose, to meet the following year.[6]

James Dittes provides a slightly different interpretation of the beginning days of the committee and stresses the activities of Ralph Burhoe of the American Academy of Arts and Sciences in Boston. Burhoe and Clark, he wrote, organized the committee as "a discussion and support group among persons, largely in theological and philosophy faculties, who had an interest in social scientific perspectives usually not shared by colleagues on their own faculties."[7] This account places the emphasis on lending sociological methods to religious practitioners rather than increasing the broad sociological study of religion in the American academy. In fact the committee developed from both purposes.

After several initial organizational meetings, the group quickly gravitated to the Department of Social Relations at Harvard University for annual fall conferences (spring meetings were held in New York City). Walter Clark described the purposes of the organization in letters he wrote to academics and theologians in 1949. He and Williams hoped to stimulate "more concern for the study of religious problems among social scientists and more concern for the use of the methods of social science among students of religious problems, particularly in the fields of religious education, sociology, and psychology."[8] In other words, the group sought to further dual aims: the scientific study of religion and the application of sociology to help religious organizations achieve their goals.

As J. Paul Williams wrote to potential members, he and Clark deplored the lack of interest by social scientists in studying religious problems and "equally the failure of religious workers to make any extended use of scientific procedures." He also outlined the basic aims of the organization. The first was "bringing together the social scientist and the religious person." The Society also pledged to increase attention to the possibilities of studying religious subjects and "creating a critically appreciative audience for reports on religious research."[9]

As a northeastern organization of academics, religious instructors at New England seminaries, and ministers, the Committee on the Social Scientific Study of Religion overlapped with the principal venues of the Conference on Science, Philosophy, and Religion—that is, Harvard, Yale, and Columbia and their associated academic and theological satellites. Some of the membership was also similar, including Professors Pitrim Sorokin and Talcott Parsons of Harvard (Parsons became the first chair of the Society). Nonetheless the purposes remained distinct, for physical scientists were generally not solicited for membership. Nor was the Catholic contingent as prominent in the early stages.[10]

Indeed, the project was dominated from the beginning mostly by Protestant sociologists and psychologists and religious philosophers. The initial absence of Catholic enthusiasm for mainstream sociology, and particularly psychology, grew out of widespread hostility to Freudianism in the church and by Catholic lay leaders. This position tended to soften by the mid-1950s, but for a considerable time Catholic activity remained isolated in such organizations as the American Catholic Psychological Association.[11]

Yet mainstream social sciences indicated some willingness to merge belief and academic inquiry. Why this might be true in the early 1950s is suggested by a survey of teachers at a number of American colleges. The results confirmed that "on the whole, the sociologists show the greatest concern for the integration of their religious beliefs with their subject matter and their teaching practices." At the same time there were fundamental reasons to organize an advocacy group within the profession of sociology. The main body of American sociologists had largely avoided the sociology of religion; few foundations or government groups would regularly fund it. Few churches trusted scientific studies. Even the Census was discreet (to the point of silence) in asking religious questions. The result was an open field of opportunity.[12]

From the very beginning, the Society debated the identity of its membership. Who was the "religious person" named in its original organizing document? Did this include sectarian adherents and ministers or merely educators interested in religion? Then there was the question of advocacy. Was the purpose of the Society to provide a fellowship of researchers engaged in similar work, or should it generate a spiritual union of intellectuals who wished to use science to further the aims of religion? Was it a bit of both?

Most of these issues emerged in a "Review of Research" submitted to the Society by Walter Clark at its April 1950 meeting. There were problems in defining just what the term religious might mean and difficulties in developing objective criteria for talking about religion. Beyond this hurdle lay the risk that the investigator might incur "severe criticism on the part of narrow dogmatists whose sensibilities are offended." Even while aiming for objectivity and scientific standards, the religious researcher was, paradoxically, receiving "a depreciation from his professional brethren who say that he is not objective enough and is therefore not a scientist." Although Clark worried about either extreme of repudiation, he insisted to the group that religion had a profound psychological value that enriched social science. It furthered personal integration and gave meaning and inspiration to human motivation. He accepted no distinction between advocating the necessity and utility of religion and the scientific study of its psychology and sociology. He drew the line only along the borders of sectarianism and next to the boundaries of "narrow dogmatists."[13]

This stance initially suggested that the Society would concentrate on bringing the results of sociological studies to churches and religious movements. This may well account for the early participation of such figures as Prentiss Pemberton of the Student Christian Movement in New England and then two successive directors of the research bureau of the National Council of Churches. But the Society evolved gradually in a more academic, professional direction rather than toward creating a social science bureau of religion.[14]

The prestige of the Society was immensely increased when the distinguished sociologist Talcott Parsons agreed to chair the group. Pemberton became vice-chair and J. Paul Williams its secretary-treasurer. The group also agreed to a list of official aims. These rehearsed the original purpose of bringing together social scientists and (now) "religious scholars." It proposed studying religion by "rigorous social scientific methods." It hoped to stimulate work in this field and direct research by graduate students and "other properly qualified people" by creating a Committee on Research Endorsements. In other words, the group chose to emphasize the professional side of its original commitment to religious research. When its ambitious directed research project fell victim to internal disagreements, the organization maintained an annual bibliography of scientific works on religion.[15]

During the 1950s the SSSR continued its efforts to professionalize itself and the study of American religion. This necessitated moving outside the northeastern intellectual corridor and beyond the heavily Protestant bias in its early membership. It also reconsidered the problem of participants. Was the organization to be composed primarily of academic sociologists and psychologists who were interested in religion? Or was some sort of personal religious commitment an unwritten qualification for admittance? Certainly, in the early days of the organization religious commitment counted. As sociologist Charles Y. Glock found in an early informal study he conducted of speakers in the first six or so meetings of the Society, of forty-six participants, twenty-seven were social scientists, fifteen were religious scholars, one a natural scientist, and three "I was unable to classify." In effect, the early Society succeeded in bringing together religious scholars and professional social scientists. Furthermore, of the first ten presidents of the Society, five could be classified as religious scholars: Prentiss Pemberton, Richard Mc-Cann, James Luther Adams, Horace Kallen, and Horace Friess.[16]

That the scientific study of religion might reinforce spiritual life served as both an assumption and a proposition to debate within the organization. Members staked out several positions around this question. Some clearly recognized the deeper issue: the possible reconciliation between science and religion—a harmony with immense promise for American culture. The accepted wisdom for most academic sociologists was informed skepticism. In an article for the *Journal of Religion* in 1952, Fred Berthold Jr. evaluated this attitude toward studying religion. At a time when the analysis of religious experience "is being carried forward by various empirical sciences, especially psychology," "'science' increasingly regarded it [religion] with suspicion." At the same time theologians increasingly worried that the study of 'religious experience' endangered theology. Both sides should realize, he concluded, that two issues informed the religious experience, one psychological and one philosophical. The philosophical could not be derived from the psychological: "The meaning of religious experience is, therefore, primarily a theological question."[17]

This conclusion might be reassuring to purists on either side, but what role did it leave for social science? What if social scientists could demonstrate the usefulness and confirm the empirical function of religious concepts? Then objectivity and subjectivity might be reconciled. Sociologist William Kolb, in his paper on the Judeo-Christian image of man "As a Tool for the Ordering of Social Data," proposed to demonstrate how sociology could lead to faith. Any sociologist risked the charge of bias by espousing Judeo-Christian presuppositions, he told the SSSR meeting in 1956. "Yet some image of man is necessary to every social science scholar," he continued, "even though he may accept empirical objectivity as necessary in his study." Some image of humanity was necessary for "common societal living." His conclusion surely would have startled a secular social scientist: "The Judaic-Christian image is the only image which satisfactorily orders such data." In other words, science and religion agreed; objectivity and subjective faith coincided in the Christian understanding of human nature.[18]

Werner Wolff, chair of the planning committee of the Society, proposed a slightly different way to achieve the same reconciliation. "As far as a scientific study of religion focuses upon structural processes of thought," he told the 1955 meeting at Columbia University, "it may even come in contact with the natural sciences that focus upon structure of matter and energy." The potential at this juncture for unity of endeavor could be fascinating. He proposed a convergence "in which the three hostile brothers—reason, emotion and action—come together." Through the scientific study of religion in all its guises as theology, psychology, sociology, anthropology, from its relation to art and to the natural sciences, "there may develop a new insight into basic sources of man's motivation, into laws of thought processes and symbolizations." Pushing forward even further, "we may advance toward a new ethic." Sociology, theology, and science could agree on new insights into the spiritual side of human society.[19]

Ralph Burhoe put this proposition squarely before the Society in his capacity as organizer of the 1955 Boston session, which featured Talcott Parsons, anthropologists Clyde Kluckhohn and Henry A. Murray, and the physicist Philipp Frank. Burhoe sent several questions to the speakers for comment. Now that the Society was beginning to grow and attract attention and membership, he proposed, it should be asked: "Does it appear that a scientific approach might constructively modify religious doctrine and practice as it has modified such areas of human concern as agriculture, medicine, transportation, etc? If so, how?"[20]

Horace Kallen, who joined the Society in 1952, played a major role in its establishment, eventually serving as president in 1959. His characterization of the problem was decidedly more secular and hewed to a more widely held manner of reconciling science and religion. In a lecture to the New School in 1959, he revealed how far he shared William James's assumptions about science and faith. He agreed with the philosopher's sermon to scientists: they should take faith seriously. The scientist should welcome every species of religious discussion "so long as he is willing to allow that some religious hypothesis may be true." This open-minded pluralism offered a way to reconcile science and religion by entertaining the option that religion "may be true" as a consequence of test, experiment, or life experience. But Kallen insisted that the organization maintain professional standards in its explorations of religion. This demanded unusual precision in defining both science and religion.[21]

A strikingly different approach within the Society was represented by Ralph Burhoe, an important figure in its establishment and ongoing activities but, in his sociology of religion, a faction of one. Burhoe's interest in reconciling religion and science extended beyond the social sciences. He proposed integrating biology and the physical sciences with religion. So he tried to convince the organization to explore the philosophy of science and relinquish the study of religious behavior. This approach to religion rejected the behavioral, pragmatic approach followed by other members such as Kallen and Wolff. In his first paper to the group in 1950, titled, "A Scientific Theory of Soul," he called for a union of science and religion in a grand scheme of evolutionary cosmology.

Burhoe's disagreements with his colleagues came to a head in 1963 when he submitted a paper to the new *Journal for the Scientific Study of Religion,* which he had been instrumental in founding. The editors rejected his piece, and Burhoe fired off an angry critique of the journal and the Society. The study of religious behavior could never emerge from superficiality, he contended, although that seemed to be the only method the organization entertained. "It is my observation that most of the papers at the meetings of the Society and published in the *Journal* have been social-psychological studies of these various social or psychological parameters which are religious only nominally." His own work, on the other hand, asserted the validity of religion: "I suggest, therefore, that the *Journal* is unscientific in its strong overrepresentation of studies of the trivia of religion as compared with some of the depths from a scientific point of view." Unfortunately, the *Journal* had the "effect of denigrating or ridiculing religion."[22]

Editor Pemberton shot back: "Our basic problem is one which goes far back in our interpretation of religion." He disagreed that the *Journal* insulted religion. The dispute was all in the word "religion." "I cannot conclude that your intellectual and aesthetic approach," he wrote, "constitutes the full gamut of religious experience." Pemberton, like other members, rejected Burhoe's attempt to convert the organization into a society to study cosmology.[23]

Small but significant signs of change in the direction of the SSSR began to appear during the later 1950s and early 1960s. Toward the end of the 1950s, the SSSR considered changing its name to the Society for the Study of Religion, dropping the science reference. But this step was impossible, if only because the proposed name had already been claimed by a group of historians. A more important step changed the prospectus of the organization and its commitment to "bringing together the social scientist and the religious person." By the end of the 1950s a revised statement read: "Stimulating intercommunication between students of religion and social scientists," a slight change in wording (and an accumulation of jargon) but with considerable significance. Students of religion were, after all, not necessarily religious persons. This linguistic turn confirmed a further step in professionalization.[24] As Charles Glock wrote in his reminiscence of the organization, "I have the impression that in more recent years, religious scholars have come to play less of a role in the Society's affairs." Even if emphasis had shifted somewhat, in 1970 a survey of membership revealed that about half the members had earned advanced degrees in the social sciences and that the rest had some degree in religious higher education.[25]

By the mid-1960s the organization had also begun to attract a larger contingent from the Catholic academic world. Given an initial membership that was almost exclusively Protestant, this represented a considerable transition. By then it also had thriving branches on the Pacific coast and in the Midwest as well as the Northeast. Its membership was drawn from the most urbanized (and academically strong regions): California, New York, Illinois, Pennsylvania, Massachusetts, and Ohio. It had also maintained a distinct identity alongside similar and competitive groups such as the Religious Research Association. Most important, it finally managed to founded a professional journal.[26]

Proposals for the journal appeared early in the history of the Society, with preliminary discussions in 1953 between Walter Clark and Werner Wolff at Bard College. Another, more serious effort began in 1956 following a suggestion by Burhoe for a publication. An alternative strategy envisioned affiliation with other organizations or ongoing journals. Burhoe wrote to Walter Clark in May suggesting that the Society might combine with the Institute on Religion in an Age of Science (another Burhoe project) for the joint publication of papers. Just a few months later Burhoe tried another tack, suggesting an affiliation with *Pastoral Psychology*, published by Princeton Theological Seminary, an existing publication that was "an excellent vehicle" with a general perspective "quite close to that of the SSSR" and an offer from the editor that "is very heartening." But nothing came of either suggestion. The Institute did not proceed with its publication plans because several members opposed the project. *Pastoral Psychology* was too practically oriented and not academic enough to suit the Society.[27] Another possible affiliation was with the *Review of Religion*, which offered space to publish

Society papers, but this opportunity faded after inconclusive negotiations.[28]

Creating a healthy journal depended on the enthusiasm of the members, the prospects for an audience, funding, and strong leadership in the SSSR. These finally came together under the presidency of Horace Kallen in 1960. Kallen successfully applied to the J. M. Kaplan Fund for a grant to publish the *Journal for the Scientific Study of Religion.* Although he asked for about $17,000, Kallen received only the first year's grant of $5,000, but it was enough to begin publication in 1961.[29]

The "Proposal for Establishing a Journal for the SSSR" described the dual purpose of the organization and its commitment to professionalism and to furthering religion. "The membership," the document reported, included representatives from "all the social sciences, from theology, philosophy and history, and from the churches themselves." The Society was nonsectarian in the sense of including all religious faiths. The purpose of the journal would be to publicize the work being done in and around the Society. And "in a small way, a journal focused on presenting the results of research on religion would inevitably contribute to more general understanding of the relevancy of religion in meeting the crises of our times."[30]

Prentiss Pemberton, the first editor of the journal, wrote a justification for it in 1960 titled "Historical Timeliness and the Scientific Study of Religion" that elaborated what had now become the watchword of the organization. The Society aspired to be both a scientific and religious champion, a missionary devoted to exploring and interpreting religion through social science. Pemberton's position left no doubt; social science was the ally of religion, and religion the companion of science.

This position, he noted, contradicted the contemporary notion that science and religion glowered at each other across a divide of hostility. Recently both disciplines had achieved a higher sophistication that encouraged discussion and mutual respect. The "philosophy of science and scientific methodologies have now attained a sophisticated maturity where both religionists and scientists can join in the scientific study of religion" without compromising their disciplines. "The believer," he continued, "is eager to ascertain every possible fact concerning his own and other religious systems. The scientist disciplines himself to examine objectively all data, including that of religious devotion."

So far Pemberton merely established that social scientists and believers had a common interest in studying religious experience. But beyond this practical reason, science and religion needed each other—for reasons that the *Journal* intended to investigate. Beyond the simple facts of religion lay important philosophic concepts. Which of these, he asked, would become "more empirically productive for work in religion?" "Which combinations of religious and/or scientific motivation will generate that quality of objectivity best fitted for the investigation of religion?"[31] This last question—really an assumption of the *Journal* and the Society—was most significant, for it implicitly argued that a combination of religious and scientific motivations could be objective. Perhaps not quite as explicit as Ralph Burhoe's hope that "solid religious *belief and motivation* could be brought about within the context of science," it still articulated a similar expectation.[32]

The bumpy reality behind such optimistic plans quickly surfaced in the first issues of the *Journal*. Sociologist William Kolb, in the very first article, revisited his argument that secular sociology languished under the domination of positivist determinism. Only a Judeo-Christian image of humans with free will, he argued, could generate a rich and fruitful scientific sociology. In his rejoinder Talcott Parsons dismissed the notion, defending traditional secular sociology. After a second turn of responses, Parsons emphatically summed up his position: "It would be undesirable and unduly restrictive, in any way to suggest that the 'Judeo-Christian' image of man was the 'chosen image' for the future of Sociology."[33]

Parsons could not settle the issue so handily, however, and it returned, both explicitly and in less contentious forms. If the *Journal* frequently declared a cease-fire in the warfare between science and religion, such repetitions probably expressed hope rather than fact. Authors seemed drawn again and again to the fundamental questions that inspired the organization. Did religion matter? Did faith deepen the possibilities of sociology? Looking secularism squarely in its neutral eye, in 1967 Peter Berger declared what many members still believed: a religious reality existed "out there." Despite the progress of secularism, religion mattered, and sociology provided a means to explore and amplify it.[34]

When it appeared in 1961, the *Journal* joined a field of quickening interest in the academic study of religion in the United States and a growing consciousness of religious revivalism. The Society took partial credit for this surge. In 1958, writing to the Lilly Endowment to request support for the organization, Walter Clark declared: "Our society was a factor in stimulating the formation of a committee on relations between psychology and religion in the American Psychological Association." He hoped this influence would "stimulate further work in the area of religion by social scientists."[35]

Clark's claim of a major impact on the American psychological profession is surely overstated. The relations of psychology, religion, and science extend backward to William James's works and beyond and forward through a variety of groups organized to bring religion and psychology together. Nor did the SSSR seriously intervene in the burgeoning field of psychotherapy and psychiatry.[36] One of the most important early groups that sought to reconcile science and religion was Norman Vincent Peale's American Foundation of Religion and Psychiatry, organized in 1937 at the Marble Collegiate Church in New York City. Eventually growing into a large clinic and research program, in 1963 the Foundation began publishing a journal, *Pastoral Counselor*. But its energies were invested just where the attention of the SSSR ebbed: in practical treatment.[37]

Because of the existence of such other established groups, the Society had been very jealous of its associations, especially in its initial years. The leaders carefully followed a middle way in making religious affiliations. At the same time, it encouraged new research into religious behavior, partly in hopes of stimulating and directing such projects. Consequently the organization established ties with other religious research organizations in the early 1950s—for example, with the National Council of Churches of Christ through their department of research and survey. In 1954 the Society considered, but did not accept, a merger with the Fellowship of Church Research Workers, a group at the Chicago Theological Seminary.[38]

Many of the new religious research organizations could be identified with one or another specific sect or tendency in American religion. In 1958 Walter R. Hearn, who was "a member of the SSSR and also of the American Scientific Affiliation," unsuccessfully tried to engineer a formal link between the two groups. The Society also rejected ties with the Board of National Missions of the Evangelical and Reformed Church. Another somewhat similar organization of Christian scholars, the Faculty Christian Fellowship, was also interested in the "basic presuppositions or philosophical assumptions" of various academic disciplines as they related to "the Christian faith." The Fellowship had active groups in literature, sociology, history, and philosophy. In 1960, for example, the Fellowship organized a psychology research committee to parallel an older group in sociology.[39] But this organization remained too specifically religious to satisfy the SSSR.

The Society was just as cautious about liberalism. In 1958 the West Coast Conference on Science and Religion proposed affiliation. But Walter Clark wrote to Ralph Burhoe warning him that the group was "too sectarian." He had heard that "some of their members are so liberal as to approach the crackpot category." Shortly thereafter the Society refused any formal ties. Although sympathetic to the aims of the organization, they believed themselves more empirically oriented. Furthermore, "some of the theologically more conservative members of our Society might object." In effect the organization was identified with "the liberal movement," and the Society could not afford such a commitment.[40]

While the Society carefully picked its way through affiliations with religiously identified scholars, it enthusiastically pursued mainstream professional organizations in sociology and psychology. This was not always easy, for there was considerable resistance to its aims among other academics. After unsuccessful negotiations in 1960 with the executive committee of the American Sociological Association on behalf of the Society, Arnold S. Nash explained to James Dittes that genuine confusion erupted when it became clear that "philosophical issues were involved in the assumptions of the Society." "Underneath this confusion," he continued, "was a certain 'anxiety' about anything affecting religion (which in this case was not even mentioned but which seemed to be implied)." Affiliation with the American Association for the Advancement of Science proved somewhat easier. The Society applied for affiliation with the AAAS in 1962, a request that was granted in early 1964.[41]

The organization achieved this recognition in part because it had transformed itself in the late 1950s and early 1960s. The publication of a successful journal and a sudden influx of new members in the early 1960s gave the group increased visibility and prestige. Probably the most significant reason for the spurt in attention to the Society came from growing academic interest in the sociology of religion. This tendency in the United States paralleled a similar movement in Europe dedicated to the study of modern religion. SSSR correspondent Norman Birnbaum, writing from Europe in 1961, explained three contemporary impulses that inspired the European study of religion. The first simply continued the rich traditions of Emile Durkheim and Max Weber. A second reflected new interest by both Catholics and Protestants who believed sociology and psychology might open up the modern world to their message. The final reason was the attention paid to non-Western religions as the world decolonized. Casting his eye around Europe, Birnbaum pointed to new professional groups in France, Germany, Belgium, the Netherlands, and Poland. In recognition of this activity, the International Sociological Association had just convened a subcommittee on the sociology of religion, with Birnbaum as secretary. Plans were set for a session on the sociology of religion at the World Congress of Sociology, to be held in 1962 in Washington, D.C.[42]

The most interesting relationship of the SSSR, and in some respects the crucial one, was with its closely related affiliate the Religious Research Association (RRA). Existing in parallel, each with its own journal, the two organizations helped to define each other. Both groups stressed their separate identities, but their positions fell near each other on the continuum of views that asserted the compatibility of the social sciences and religion. There was also a significant overlap in their membership, particularly after the 1950s, when one survey estimated that two-thirds of the members of the RRA also belonged to the Society.[43]

The Religious Research Association (originally the Religious Research Fellowship) was organized in June 1951. Its origins reach back to the activities of the Committee for Cooperative Field Research, created in 1944 by the Home Missions Council and the Federal Council of Churches. Much of the activity of this group had been directed by the clergyman-sociologist H. Paul Douglass, who had long been conducting research for denominational agencies and local church bodies. His purpose, and the intention of the new Fellowship, was to utilize sociological research as a tool of modern evangelism. The RRA revived this commitment. The president of the RRA (and director of the Bureau of Research and Survey of the National Council of Churches of Christ), Lauris Whitman, summarized its purposes: "As an organization we are committed to the task of [making] the theory, the insights and methods of the social sciences helpful and meaningful to the institution of religion. We do not hesitate to admit that we have a favorable bias toward religious institutions." "We do not study religion" he continued, out of academic interest, but because "we believe that the effective functioning of religion in society is dependent upon an application of the knowledge and insights of social science."[44]

If the SSSR wanted its principal constituency to be the sociological profession, the Religious Research Association desired close ties with religious organizations like the National Council of Churches. Most of the early members were Protestant clergy or members of other religious institutions. None was a professional academic with a university position. Charles Glock, also a member of the SSSR, was the first academic sociologist to be recruited.[45]

With a small membership, the group met yearly to discuss projects like the National Christian Teaching Missions in St. Louis and Wichita in 1952.

Although separate organizations, the Teaching Mission and the Fellowship cooperated in several communities. The purpose of the Mission was evangelism—research was only a means to that end. For the Mission, sociological study of the local community permitted more effective recruitment drives. This impressed the fellows of the Religious Research organization. They hoped that a study of the Mission project might "provide us with standards for development of a church program; we might eventually get a 'standard' profile of churches." Here was an instance where sociology could invigorate the churches.[46]

But what manner of sociology and how should it be used? In the early years of the RRA, the issue of professionalization dogged the organization—far more than it did the SSSR. Since none of the original members had academic sociology credentials, there was open tension with the secular profession. A reputation for amateurism continued to threaten the organization. Finally, in 1955 a Committee on Professional Standards was established and the organization began its evolution toward a more respectable academic status. Still, the continuing commitment of the RRA to religious service prevented the complete adoption of professional culture. As the minutes of a meeting in 1964 indicate, this made the organization self-consciously unique: "[The] RRA is interested in bringing the theory and methods and empirical approach of social science research to the service of organized religion. We have assumed that the bias of the person interested in religion is no more dangerous than [that of] the person who is anti-religious."[47]

This position placed the RRA close to the camp of evangelism. Its attitude toward science was far less a question of reconciling methods and philosophies than of exploiting social science techniques to further religious institutions. This commitment clearly differentiated it from the Society for the Scientific Study of Religion, which chose to emphasize theoretical as well as the practical problems of social science and religion. A membership questionnaire undertaken in the mid-1950s by the RRA revealed that among the forty-five persons who responded, thirty-five were ordained ministers—half of them Methodist or Congregational.[48] No wonder the organization was reluctant to move too close to the sociological profession.

Yet the forces of professionalization still spurred the RRA, and by the mid-1950s it began to plan for publication of a journal. A professional journal emerged as one of crucial commitments in its revised constitution of 1958. Other professionalizing tendencies convinced the RRA to promote higher standards in religious research and the establishment of research training centers. The group also intended to cultivate relationships with "other professional societies having similar concerns." Finally, the RRA committed itself to fostering "a climate favorable to research within organized religious bodies and other related institutions." It rejected a purely academic interest in religious research, and its goals remained practical and applied. To recognize and promote this form of religious sociology, it established the H. Paul Douglass Religious Research Lectureship, with which it honored such important figures as Will Herberg.[49]

The initial decision in publishing a journal meant going it alone. After discussions with the SSSR, the Religious Research Association decided not to affiliate in a publishing venture. "It was generally expressed by the membership," the 1959 meeting reported "that considering basic differences between this organization and the SSSR (emphasis on religion here; emphasis on science there), it would not be feasible to enter into a cooperative venture at this time." Like other organizations and individuals, the RRA used the science/religion dichotomy in American culture to construct an identity. Nonetheless, as the organization moved toward publishing a journal, it (like the Society) responded to the power of professionalism. This evoked comment in 1960 from some of the older members, who objected to the narrowing of interests and to the growing importance of academic standards.[50]

When the *Review of Religious Research* appeared in the summer of 1959, it focused, as President Whitman described it, on the "reawakening concern of the social sciences for the serious study of religion" and on the "current 'religious revival,'" about which popular magazines, the press, and the intellectual community in general desired more information and research. Whitman believed that an American religious awakening led by Billy Graham and the renewal of academic interest in religious faith coincided to favor the launching of a new journal devoted to religious research.[51] But the slow growth of the *Journal* belied his optimism; circulation reached only about eight hundred in 1965, including two hundred library subscriptions. Its position remained marginal because the *Journal* was unfocused. When the editor, W. Widick Schroeder, resigned in 1967, he noted this confusion in the organization. "My own view," he asserted, "is that it should self-consciously set out to focus on explorations of the relationship between theology, social ethics and the policy sciences," because of the importance of these issues to the churches and in order to "to distinguish it from the S.S.S.R." He explained further: "Our major problem over the past years has been the problem of obtaining sufficient high quality manuscripts."[52]

Schroeder's lament only restated contradictions that had plagued the RRA from the beginning. He demanded a stronger commitment to the practical problems of the church—more applied sociology—but he also sought more professional articles for the *Journal*. Given the position of the Religious Research Association, the two goals were probably contradictory. As for relations with the SSSR, these ranged from friendly cooperation to competition to considerable duplication of effort. The two organizations oriented themselves differently toward the promise and threat of social science. The Society for the Scientific Study of Religion took a far more professional approach, whereas the Religious Research Association always aimed at serving established religious organizations and denominations. Both benefited from the burst of interest in religious studies toward the end of the 1950s. Both absorbed a far more ecumenical membership after the beginning of the 1960s, with increasing membership of Jews and Catholics buoyed by the liberalism of Vatican II. Both seized on social science as a way of moderating the claims of a scientific culture.[53]

But did either or both succeed in moving science and religion closer together through the medium of social science? Did they cure social science of its secular biases? Neither could claim to have resolved such enormous problems, but each in its way increased the visibility of religious research, in both the religious and academic communities. Furthermore, their efforts normalized an important place within professional sociology for religiously oriented social criticism. This important legacy can be found in the works of the sociologist Peter L. Berger, a second-generation member of the SSSR and later its president. Berger became an influential thinker not just in the sociological profession, but among a wider range of similar intellectuals such as Robert Bellah, who also pursued religious sociology—a group that employed sociology in the pursuit of a more spiritual society. In their works sociology became a site for prophetic social criticism.

In two important books in the 1960s, Berger astutely measured the contradictory effects of sociology on American religion. In his explanation he focused on the different roles of the RRA and the SSSR. The Religious Research Association, he noted, emerged from the wish to use market research, to employ the techniques of sociology to study potential sources of membership and conduct opinion surveys that might influence the growth of churches. On the other hand, groups like the SSSR engaged religion at a more philosophical level. Both bodies, he continued, responded to a larger trend toward secularization in Western culture, and especially the United

States. In itself, striving to reconcile sociology and religion resulted from having internalized the methods and principles of social science.

Berger argued that sociology had become the new dismal science of modern life, replacing Darwinism as the primary aggressor against religion. Listening to its indifferent heart, it completed the revolution of relativism that Darwinism had begun. History and sociology countenanced a pluralism that pillaged sacred society. Yet Berger maintained a faith that turned the tables on these human sciences. He insisted that empirical reality would reveal "signals of transcendence." This "theological empiricism" would disclose intimations of religion in human experience and sources of spirituality confirmed by history.[54]

Although Berger's "empirical theology" remained only a theoretical possibility for reconciling religion and social science, he understood the effects of sociology on the structures of religion in American culture; he recognized the seductions of professionalization. But the efforts of the SSSR and his own writings contradicted this bleak appraisal. The important academic discussion of religion provoked by the SSSR and the RRA did not simply constitute further secularization. These religiously oriented academics used the prestige of social science to promote a variety of conciliatory gestures between secularism and religion. Yet two fundamental problems remained unsettled. Did the promised reconciliation between social science and religion still threaten the integrity of both approaches to human society? And was it enough to reconcile with social science? What about physical science?

One of the most active members of both the SSSR and the RRA remained deeply distressed by these divisions and unconvinced by either approach. Ralph Burhoe concluded that neither group could resolve the inherent dispute between science and religion that distorted modern culture. Looking back to his activities on behalf of both organizations, he retained his "confidence in the potential compatibility of sacred religious belief in the context of most scientific theories or beliefs. At the same time, I believed that religion could be enhanced, not only by social science, but by viewing religion in the light of the sciences."[55] The final resolution, he urged, could be achieved through cosmological theory, with both scientific theory and religious culture evolving toward consummation of a grand, universal scheme for all human and natural history. Sociology was not enough.

A task which requires
some new Emersons for
the modern age.

Letter to Ralph Burhoe
(1957)

Chapter 12

The Religion of Science

The awareness of crisis as well as opportunity
that washed in tandem waves across so many endeavors of scientists and
theologians in the 1950s reached a high-water mark in a new organization,
the Institute on Religion in an Age of Science (IRAS), founded in 1954. The
work of Ralph Burhoe and Harlow Shapley, among others, the Institute
grew from a Harvard-based discussion club to become an important center
for cosmological speculation. Unlike the Society for the Scientific Study of
Religion or the Religious Research Association, this organization experienced none of the undertow of professionalism. Instead its tide rose elsewhere, as both Burhoe and Shapley speculated about creating a new
religiousness derived from modern science. Their accomplishment was a

religious conviction in which system—form and process, "the austerity of a rational religion"—produced a spiritual interpretation of universal evolution.[1]

Although Burhoe and Shapley both participated in a number of organizations designed to bridge the gap between modern science and religion, none of the others spoke so directly to the deep sense of general crisis that both men felt after the end of World War II. The Conference on Science, Philosophy, and Religion had waned, as a history of the Institute noted in 1972, just as the Institute was being formed. Although there was considerable overlap in membership, the Conference failed to "keep a sharp focus on the problem of integrating religion and science."[2] Shapley, who appeared frequently at the conference, also spent considerable time working with Louis Finkelstein in planning meetings and discussions at the Jewish Theological Seminary that had the same general purpose. Burhoe worked closely with the SSSR. But only in the Institute did scientists exercise the primary inspiration—not just a veto, not just a limit—and not just a hesitation.

The Institute squarely confronted the problem that inspired so many of the individuals and animated so many of the organizations thus far considered in this book. But in almost every other case the results had proved inconclusive and members turned in frustration from their original purpose. Only the Institute articulated a scientific theology, a unity of theory and purpose integrating religion and science. This development became possible, finally, only because its adherents embraced a form of scientific cosmology—religion informed and defined by science.

If the problems modern science presented for religious thinkers and theologians deepened around World War II and in its atomic aftermath, scientists too expressed anxiety about the impact of their theories and discoveries on society. Often they sought to cast their endeavors, beliefs, and practices into some form of ultimate religious culture or spiritualism. In much-noted remarks, Albert Einstein simply refused to relinquish religious thinking. "Science without religion is lame," he wrote; "religion without science is blind." As the greatest revolutionary in cosmological thinking and the scientist who called forth the grand speculative theories of the twentieth century, Einstein still could not give up on God. But this was not the anthropomorphic God of the principal historical religions of the world; Einstein depicted God as the creator of order, nature, and the universe, more as did the Deists of the eighteenth century than the Fundamentalists of the twentieth. As he wrote, "The further the spiritual evolution of mankind advances, the more certain it seems to me that the path to genuine religiosity does not lie through the fear of life, and the fear of death, and blind faith, but through striving after rational knowledge."[3]

Scientists' concern about the cultural status of religion came from an understanding of the revolutionary impact of science on society. Some even called for a retreat. The philosopher of science Ernest Nagel wrote in 1949 that he was "dismayed by the slowly rising tide of cynical irrationalism that has engulfed so many influential writers, and not less dismayed because of the peculiar views they appear to hold concerning the nature of scientific reason." This tendency, he continued, had been encouraged by scientists themselves, who put "current scientific doctrine in support of some questionable metaphysics, *Lebensphilosophie,* or political program, or through contrasting in disparaging but dubious manner the allegedly limited competence of scientific method with the satisfying fullness of some other form of human experience."[4] A clear danger lay in compromise with established faith, concessions to historical religions, and even the transformation of ideology into belief—with what Einstein would have called the religions of fear.

The problem, then, was simple to state but terribly difficult to resolve. How could a scientific society, founded on rationality and buttressed by the experimental mode of thought, still entertain religious thinking without being overwhelmed by tradition and dogma? Conversely, how could religion be updated and opened to the achievements of scientific thinking without the evaporation of all meaningful faith and spiritualism? The questions themselves suggested the need for a new form of modernism. That, in many respects, was the reasoning with which the Institute came to guide itself.

The origins of the Institute on Religion in an Age of Science are deeply rooted in the careers and interests of Ralph Burhoe and Harlow Shapley and took place within the general evolution of American Unitarianism. Ralph Burhoe was born in Massachusetts in 1911. His father was a lawyer, a banker, and a self-educated man, deeply interested in classical literature. Burhoe grew up in a family steeped in religion and religious tradition. His grandfather had been a Baptist minister, and his father was a lay leader in the church. As he retells his childhood, Burhoe was always deeply interested in religion and science and treasured a kind of spiritual vision of science that frequently came to him in dreams. As he recalled, when he could not finish his physics homework he would go to bed and dream the answer: "During my sleep, I would have quite clear dreams about the problems that I had not solved when awake. The dream rehearsed the whole problem and provided a solution that seemed correct." This imaginative process continued through his life, giving even his scientific thinking an aura of spirituality.[5]

Burhoe's education was hesitant, interrupted, and incomplete, partly for financial reasons and because of his impatience with academics. In 1928 he enrolled in Harvard College to pursue a liberal arts curriculum including philosophy, physics, and anthropology. As he recounts it, he was moved by certain similar philosophies: the ideas of William James and Alfred North Whitehead in philosophy and the notions of Earnest Albert Hooton in anthropology. (Hooton posited a science of design and a teleological evolutionary theory in which nature and God coincided.) Burhoe also joined the Baptist campus ministry. But the Great Crash of 1929 and the subsequent depression intervened, and without money, Burhoe left school to find employment. In 1932 Burhoe, with the help and encouragement of his father, made another stab at formal education, this time to train for the ministry at Andover Newton Theological School. Burhoe was accepted without a college degree (provided he eventually completed his Harvard A.B.). But this too proved a false start, and Burhoe left, discouraged with the required course of study and its lack of relevance to his interests. Shortly afterward Burhoe and his new wife retreated to the White Mountains of New Hampshire, where, together, as he says, they developed a "vision and actual practice together of a credible religion in the context of science for reforming and saving civilization." Returning to Boston, Burhoe continued his self-directed education, finding considerable inspiration in Julian Huxley's *What Dare I Think?* and the author's scientific approach to religion.[6] What Burhoe demanded from his theological education was a new form of science-relevant modernism, something highly unlikely to exist in a theological school.

Nonetheless, in 1935–36 he resumed his work at Andover Newton, spending considerable time with the Protestant revival movement Moral Rearmament, until its intense discipline and demanding spirituality proved unsatisfying. He left school again. After briefly considering an appointment as minister to the Congregational-Universalist church in Enfield, Massachusetts, Burhoe found permanent employment at the Blue Hill Observatory of Harvard University in Milton, Massachusetts. This was his first real scientific employment and gave him the occasion to meet Harlow Shapley, who served on the academic visitation committee for the observatory in the 1930s. At the same time he joined the Unitarian Church. Burhoe remained at the observatory until 1947, when he resigned to become the executive officer of the Boston-based American Academy of Arts and Sciences.[7]

Burhoe's search for education and profession was increasingly tinged with a sense of intellectual and spiritual anxiety. The competition between science and religion, he believed, had wounded both endeavors. The solution, he concluded, lay in applying science to religion. Science offered techniques "to make it possible to think about religion more clearly than the religious people knew." In fact, sociologists and anthropologists had already made considerable advances in this direction. So perhaps natural science itself offered the ultimate way to explore religious questions, to restore the wholeness of society and the completeness of faith.[8]

The American Academy, which had very close ties to Harvard, was a venerable institution that begged for rejuvenation. It received that stimulus from two presidents, Harlow Shapley (1939–44) and Howard Mumford Jones (1944–51). Under their leadership it undertook a broad program of discussions and conferences on a variety of problems associated with modern science and culture. In some respects it occupied the same intellectual space as the ongoing Conference on Science, Philosophy, and Religion, but without the piety of Finkelstein or the disagreements over neo-Thomism that forced the conference to suppress its first purposes. By 1955–56 the American Academy had founded the journal *Daedalus,* one of the most distinguished intellectual periodicals of the day.[9]

At the Academy Burhoe found a willing audience for his program to unite science and religion and an able mentor in Harlow Shapley. Besides helping to establish the Conference on Science, Philosophy, and Religion, Shapley, together with the neurophysiologist Hudson Hoagland (secretary of the Academy) organized an early discussion group housed at the Academy, called the Committee on Science and Values, which initiated discussions on the place of science in modern culture. As Shapley explained to Louis Finkelstein in September 1940, he had dined at the Harvard Faculty Club with a "local group of scientists, philosophers, and theologians . . . to consider the possibilities of a small group of conferences on this general subject under the auspices of the American Academy of Arts and Sciences during the coming season."[10]

After this, and once Burhoe assumed the executive directorship, the Academy council approved a new Committee on Science and Values in 1948, and in 1954 this group in turn helped to organize the Institute on Religion in an Age of Science. Another of Burhoe's contemporary interests was the unity of science movement, housed at the Academy in the Institute for the Unity of Science. Led by Philipp Frank, Percy W. Bridgman, and Horace S. Ford, the group pursued the fusion of natural science, social science, and the humanities under the general aegis of science. Burhoe was especially close to Frank and keenly approved his notion that some of the links between science and humanism could be discovered in the philosophy of science.[11]

If this flurry of organizational activity, with new committees and frequent discussion groups springing up in Boston and New York, is in some ways redundant and overlapping, it can be explained in two ways. First, there was the fundamental interest in reconciling modern science and religion expressed by a substantial element of America's intellectual and academic community, although the community was deeply divided about where the emphasis should lie. Hence the varieties of associations. Second, men like Burhoe, Harlow Shapley, and others bent on finding a solution to the immense cultural problems that had been fostered by the impact of modern science appeared to have almost boundless organizational energy.

As an organizer, participant, and gadfly at religious-scientific conferences, Shapley played a role that expressed his intense interest in the problems of science and religion as well as his profound ambivalence about them. Donning his Copernican guise, he frequently addressed religious groups about the need to make the "Fourth Adjustment" (in cosmology). As he wrote in his autobiography, "After my findings about our peripheral position in our galaxy began to be talked about considerably, the ideas reached the preachers and theologians and worried them a bit." They wanted me, he said, "to come and talk in their churches."[12] He obliged them.

Shapley's role in this debate is difficult to fathom if only his words and writings are seriously considered. Almost always he presented them in a bantering tone of mock seriousness. For example, in a speech he delivered in December 1953 called "A Cosmographer Talks to the Clergy," he said: "The Universe, it seems to me (who am, by the way, a religious man) (On my definition of religion), is much more glorious than the prophets of old reported." "We are actors in a greater show than the old billing led us to expect."[13] Beneath such intentionally flippant and slangy phrasing lay a persistent and serious craving for inclusion in the conversation. Shapley's presence at so many religious occasions revealed his deep interest in religion, perhaps even a hope that science might discover a new spiritual design. Nothing else could explain the immense energy he poured into the variety of organizations that he organized and participated in—and also disrupted with his insistence on the primacy of scientific knowledge and thinking. This led an admiring Burhoe to say more than half-seriously: "I find Harlow to be a good theologian."[14]

Beyond Shapley's specific contributions to astronomy, his belief in the abundance of life elsewhere in the cosmos attracted considerable comment. This idea also formed a cornerstone of his religious orientation, for it denied the anthropomorphism of established religions and pushed speculation toward the largest possible considerations. "We see," he wrote in 1929, "in the new astronomical revelations the stuff that philosophic dreams are made of. We see the stars as providers of human interest of the deepest kind—as feeders of the inherent religious hunger."[15] If the meaning of this judgment is cryptic and vague—if it proposes a religion yet to be encountered or discovered or developed—it nonetheless provided Shapley with a way of spiritualizing science and no doubt of satisfying his own pursuit of ultimate meaning. It also forged a link of sympathy to Burhoe's much more detailed, ambitious, and concrete evolutionary cosmology. Shapley delighted in repeating that he had shoved humankind out of the center of the universe, out of the last possible focal point of the physical universe. Humans were "peripheral"—for neither the earth, the sun, nor the galaxy, he concluded, occupied the center of any celestial map. But the glee with which the astronomer pronounced this somber verdict never successfully hid his fascination with its religious implications and the mystery he found in contemplating the whole of existence.[16]

The organizational host for the Institute and its cosmological speculations was the Unitarian Church, then in the process of moving toward amalgamation with the Universalists. For decades the Unitarians had been acolytes of modernism, hospitable to the ideas of twentieth-century science and earnestly searching for a new unity of theology and spiritualism. One local Boston group went so far in 1936 as to organize the Cosmotheist Society, dedicated to the belief that "we are a part of the cosmos which is characterized by life, intelligence, and moral and physical laws." The group insisted that the universe was identical to God, making their beliefs practically indistinguishable from pantheism. "We are organized," they asserted, "to study and investigate the evolutionary processes and our relation to them, to the cosmos in general, and to humanity in particular."[17]

Representatives of more orthodox Unitarianism provided institutional hospitality for Burhoe and Shapley. Dana McLean Greeley, minister of the Arlington Street Church in Boston and president of the American Unitarian Association, the Unitarian minister, Lyman V. Rutledge, and Edwin Prince Booth, professor of historical theology at Boston University School of Theology, were leaders of a group that in the summer of 1950 initiated annual meetings at the Unitarian conference center on Star Island off Portsmouth, New Hampshire. This group constituted itself first as the "Coming Great Church," a title to indicate its aspiration to create a new basis for church unity and universal religion. Burhoe attended several of these gatherings, and for the 1954 meeting he persuaded the conferees to invite a group of scientists to explore the relation between modern religion and science.[18]

As Burhoe wrote to publicize the anticipated conference, "It is the conviction of the Program Committee that the coming great church will arise out of a new and universally valid synthesis of religious doctrine in which the universally acceptable approach to truth established in the sciences will be a crucial source of inspiration and insight." The scientists invited would include those who had notably "given considerable thought to the relationship between science and religion."[19] The special science-religion session of the Great Church Conference met during the first week of August 1954 at Star Island resort. Among the two hundred or so members attending the meeting were twenty-two persons invited to join the board of directors of a new group. They included the religious founders of the Coming Great Church meetings, several other churchmen, and ten scientists, among them psychologist B. F. Skinner, physicist Paul E. Sabine, anthropologist M. F. Ashley Montagu, psychologist Henry Murray, physicist Philipp Frank, and of course Harlow Shapley. After several days of deliberation the group decided to constitute itself the Institute on Religion in an Age of Science and hold an annual summer convocation on the island to discuss ways to reconcile religion and science. As the official program described its purpose and expectations: "The program of the Institute proceeds in the faith that there is no wall isolating any department of human understanding, and that, therefore, any doctrine of human salvation cannot successfully be separated from the realities pictured by science."[20] In a sense the new group had picked up the original purpose of the Conference on Science, Philosophy, and Religion, but aiming to reform religion rather than discipline science.

After the meetings Burhoe and Shapley pushed the organization to explore science and scientific thinking. This was no easy task, wrote Shapley to Burhoe in a letter commenting on the progress toward creating a permanent organization. It looked as if "after the fights on Star Island we may need two or three organizations."[21]

Despite his hesitations, however, Shapley wrote a long, thoughtful explanation to Burhoe after the Star Island meeting to outline his thinking about the religious-scientific crisis and suggest what might be done to resolve it. The questions he raised were obviously rhetorical, for to answer them positively (which he intended) argued the need for a permanent organization. "Assuming that the alleged emptiness of religion in these days is responsible for the aversion to church and creed on the part of intelligent and educated people, is there something we can do about it?" he asked. Might a "great contribution be made by science to the activity and growth of non-animal man"? Would it be possible to examine the potential of a "rational religion"? And most interesting, what sort of new evangelism could the group develop to spread these ideas?

The second part of his query focused on the idea of creating a special generic lecture to summarize the "best current views on religion in an age of science." This might include "a psychological survey of the nature of man and his emotions" and an outline of the place of man in the cosmos, with a review of evolution from the "primeval ooze" to the present. Shapley concluded on a personal note: he had grown tired of popular shock treatments of the subject (some of which he had personally administered). He wanted instead a "quiet propaganda for rationality" that might take the form of "sermons, articles, books"—all of which aimed at presenting "Cosmic Facts in Relation to Human Destinies."[22]

In his final section of advice Shapley speculated about the organizational character of the Institute. Above all else it should be an elite brotherhood of intellectuals and philosophers dedicated to the principles of a rational religion and devoted to the pursuit of science. The model organization Shapley had in mind was not, however, any existing church, but something more akin to the university. This solution is not surprising, for Shapley was already situated at the nucleus of the very intellectual network he imagined; he understood clearly how it operated. As a formal organization, he suggested, such a center could turn out "quiet propaganda for rationality . . . in the form of sermons, articles, books, which could contribute to the intelligent consideration of our religious situation."[23]

If these were tentative but potentially grand ambitions, Burhoe invested in even greater expectations. In a document prepared for the 1954 conference, he explained to the board of the Coming Great Church that the proper, if controversial, response to the contemporary irrelevance and alienation of religion in America must be to enlist religion in the modern scientific enterprise. "Most people," he exulted, "see this direction only as that of the death of the Christian tradition. In my own mind I am perfectly clear that the program outlined leads directly to the greatest reformation in centuries and to the general acceptance of the reality of the spiritual ideas of the Sermon on the Mount."[24]

Inspired by the desire for progress in reconciling science and religion, the Institute met annually on Star Island. During the remainder of the 1950s (five years), two of its meetings were explicitly devoted to the subject, but all its endeavors aimed in this general direction. For the rest of the decade Burhoe and Shapley continued to exert a force on the direction of the organization, both hoping it could become a major center for intellectual discussions and perhaps the publisher of a scholarly journal. Shapley (elected its first president in 1961) in particular played an important, if quixotic, public role. Taking over the "owl sessions" (late-night gatherings), Shapley, "supported by an ad hoc selection of minstrels, end men, and any wit present, makes light and dark thrusts at anything and anybody associated with the Conference." Sometimes the tone was humorous; at other times "the spirits move in to provide us with gifts of prophecy, vision, and peak experiences." Shapley also made his peculiar religious attitude obvious to everyone on Star Island. As the mimeographed newspaper published during the conference noted, "A familiar image for those who have been with us during the past few years is the figure of Harlow Shapley at Chapel, stretched out on the grass, an old hat on his head, a cigar in his mouth." He was both communing with nature and listening—from a distance—to the daily chapel sermon of Chaplain Booth.[25]

Many of the Institute's activities during the 1950s followed the cosmic yearnings of Burhoe and Shapley. As Edwin Booth, head of the board of IRAS, said in 1958, the purpose of the organization was "to work on a major restatement to resolve the conflict between religious and scientific thinking and ideas; to seek a common denominator for the various religions through science, in the belief that the truth is one." This scientific ecumenism formed one of the bases for the modernism that IRAS and the Unitarian Church advocated at this time. Although it would still require more careful exposition, the groundwork had also been laid for the cosmology that Burhoe and others began to affirm in the 1960s.[26] During this period, Shapley's pantheism remained close enough to Burhoe's more elaborate cosmology to present a united theoretical position. As Shapley put it at a meeting in Boston in 1958, religious ideas probably evolved alongside atoms, the metagalaxy, social insects, and mammals.[27]

During the late 1950s, Burhoe and Shapley exchanged correspondence and ideas that cemented their unity behind new cosmological thinking. At a luncheon meeting at Harvard they discussed with other members of the Institute "religions as cultural products whose evolutionary selection guaranteed values in them." They talked of "the revision of ancient scriptures"—in other words, the creation of a new religion. At one point Burhoe wrote to the astronomer: "We ought to get together a modern bible." And as Burhoe commented to Shapley after one long conversation (penning the salutation "Dear Moses"), "As I walked back to the office this afternoon I meditated on your revised and enlarged edition of the first chapter of genesis," which they had been discussing. "It has seemed to me quite clear for some time," he continued "that we need to publish a completely revised library or handbook of human salvation." Burhoe, in his enthusiasm, proposed nothing less than to rewrite the Bible in cosmological terms. As Burhoe told Henry Margenau of IRAS, "I believe that we have in store for us in the last half of the 20th century AD the rise of a powerful new leap of religious belief, based on our new science."[28]

Despite the optimism Burhoe and Shapley expressed, both were somewhat hesitant to expose their arguments to the general public yet. As Burhoe wrote to Shapley, he was reluctant to flirt with popularization, "for we have a lot of hard thinking to do before we come up with a reformulation of religion that can be expressed in the language of the scientists' conceptions of the cosmos." As the call for the conference of 1956 warned, "We recognize that this faith in the relevance of science for religion is a minority faith today and is not shared by many scientists, clergymen, nor in general by the population of the United States or of the world."[29]

Their position on evolutionary cosmology naturally aligned Shapley and Burhoe with the famous British intellectual Julian Huxley. The 1959 centennial commemoration of Darwin's *Origin of Species* brought Shapley and Huxley face-to-face on the same speakers' platform at the University of Chicago. Plans to celebrate the publication of Darwinian theory naturally included the contemporary scion of the Huxley family, which had long defended the theory. Julian Huxley was the featured speaker among other celebrants of the works of Darwin. Organized by anthropologist Sol Tax of the university, the conference included several days of talks about evolution and a (comic) play, "Time Will Tell: A Musical Reconstruction of Darwin's Discovery and Life." Only during the last meeting of the last day, sponsored by the Federated Theological Faculty of the university, did the conference get around to noticing the theological implications of evolutionary theory.[30]

The celebration was an important intellectual event in 1959 (as the leaders of the American Scientific Affiliation predicted it would be), and one result was the publication of a volume of papers by the University of Chicago Press examining the implications of Darwinism. The Encyclopaedia Britannica Film Company (also located at Chicago) recorded all the events. The National Science Foundation provided a grant to finance the conference. During the festivities, the university awarded honorary doctorates of philosophy to distinguished scientists such as the anthropologist Alfred Kroeber.

Julian Huxley's address to the conference was perhaps its highlight, and it certainly provoked the most commentary. He took the occasion to recast the theory of evolution and to explore its cosmological implications. Ever since the appearance of human beings, the course of evolution had changed as "major steps in the human phase of evolution are achieved by breakthroughs to new dominant patterns of mental organization, of knowledge, ideas and beliefs, ideological instead of physiological or biological organization." Successive waves of "idea-systems" replaced each other, and with them religions evolved too. The contemporary period, like all others before it, demanded a new religion to express its new idea systems. Such a modern religion should "take advantage of the vast amounts of new knowledge produced by the knowledge explosion of the last few centuries in constructing what we may call its theology." Modern spiritualism would leap beyond historical religions to a higher worship, to a new rational religion. Once understood as a function of man's brain and body, religion could be seen for what it was: a form of advanced adjustment to the environment. To some observers this sounded like the tolling in of atheism, but Shapley reassured the

Figure 12.1   Panelists at the final session of the University of Chicago's 1959 Darwin centennial, including Julian Huxley, consider the impact of Darwin's theory of evolution. Courtesy of Special Collections, University of Chicago Libraries.

press that "Huxley's not really an atheist even if he says he is. He's a pantheist" (like Shapley himself).[31]

Shapley's own paper at Chicago, titled "Evidences of Inorganic Evolution," raised the discussion of evolution to a galactic level. It would be better to grope toward some evolutionary truth, he noted, "than to remain ignorantly idle and offer false panaceas, such as the claim that all and every [question] can be answered through reliance on supernatural deity." Sol Tax, summing up the conference, paraphrased the remarks of Huxley and some of the other speakers, saying he hoped "that in the next hundred years our religious leaders may come to quote the Gospel as saying, 'Render unto science that which belongs to science.'" Still, Tax urged caution based on the remarkable reluctance of contemporary Americans to come to terms with Darwinism. Evolutionary theory had not yet even entered the American public-school classroom, he noted. This presented an enormous problem, for it would not be possible "to deal with the difficult problems of the world unless our education takes account of the demonstrated empirical facts."[32]

This sort of soul searching and audacious religious speculation rarely surfaced beyond the membership of the Institute and a few related organizations. When the group did attempt to proselytize, it dispatched missionaries to speak about science only to fellow intellectuals and theologians. It almost always avoided other audiences. Its solution to the cultural problems of the United States was to undertake an elite conversation around science and religion and then spread the results among other intellectuals. Tax's warning about the fundamental division in American culture justified what was already a cautious strategy.[33]

Nothing could be more controversial than a restatement of religion affirming a theory of cosmic evolution. The Institute group hoped to generate a rational religion out of the very scientific theories considered anathema in the Fundamentalist and creationist circles that were growing rapidly in American society. It is no small irony that evolutionary theory once again reinforced and widened the profound gap between elite scientists and liberal theologians and evangelical Protestant groups on the issue of how to reconcile religion and science.

The members of the Institute were certainly not naive about the unpopularity of their religious-science faith. It is "a minority faith today and is not shared by many scientists, clergymen, nor in general by the population of the United States or of the world," noted the 1956 call for the summer conference. Unfortunately, many Americans insisted on a clean separation between science and religion, with each the master of its own realm. If conceded, this schism would cut science off from speculating about values and consign it to describing the physical processes of the natural world.[34]

Beginning in the mid-1950s, during meetings of the Committee on Science and Values of the American Academy, members of the Institute, including theologian Paul Tillich, decided they should first try to convince schools of theology to pay closer attention to science. Under the aegis of IRAS they planned a conference and then outreach work and applied to the Danforth Foundation for funds. Their strategy was part Emersonian, part Chautauquan—old and tried strategies of American self-education. As early as 1956, the IRAS board outlined a program of lectures and "missionary" work to intellectual institutions such as universities and theological schools that could begin to popularize their insights. This strategy would involve "the participation of scientists as true scientists" speaking for the conviction that religion should be interpreted in the light of modern science.

The educational program drawn up by the Institute established "missionary teams of members of our Advisory Board to speak at meetings or conferences in various universities and scientific and scholarly centers." These science proselytes met first in Boston at the American Academy of Arts and Sciences. Funded by a small Danforth grant, the inaugural outreach colloquium took place at Hartford Seminary Foundation in the fall of 1957. In 1958 the Institute sent out letters to a dozen theological schools including an eight-page proposal describing a program on science and religion.[35]

Shapley was enthusiastic about the possibilities. "The richest prospect," he wrote to Burhoe in 1958, "could be the solid development of the Visitations—the group visits of IRASites to theological seminaries and departments of religion." "I would be happy to join a group once or twice," he noted, "if nothing easier and better turns up." Burhoe responded: "Yes, a committee on missionary work in the theological hinterland." But few of the schools solicited responded with anything more than polite indifference. Three more colloquiums were held: at Hartford (again) in 1959 and at St. Lawrence University and Colgate Rochester Divinity School in 1960. But even this program of modest evangelism failed to reach much beyond Ivy League schools and the network of friends that Shapley and other members of IRAS could command.[36]

Other means to expand the influence of IRAS entailed the hard work— and disappointments—of fund-raising, for the organization needed to establish a headquarters, a newsletter, and paid employees.[37] It proposed these goals in an application to the Rockefeller Foundation for $100,000 to provide a center for "advanced study of religion in the light of science," a publication program, a permanent staff, mailings, and meetings. Rockefeller declined to grant the sum and instead offered a modest donation of $5,000 to support the summer meetings at Star Island.[38] This pattern of ambitious plans, large applications, and small successes typified the Institute. It had intellectual backing with considerable prestige, plus important contacts at Rockefeller and Danforth. But it could not transform these advantages into funds for a major expansion. One reason was the difficult and complex purpose the Institute had set for itself. As Ralph Burhoe wrote to an acquaintance at the Rockefeller Foundation, she was badly mistaken in thinking that his organization was only trying to save religion through science. "None of us," he wrote, "accepts or would try to preserve any fossilized form of religion that cannot stand up rationally in the light of modern knowledge." This argument might have been honest, but Burhoe's ambitions were unrestrained, asking Rockefeller in effect to underwrite the invention of a new American religion.[39]

Another route to influence lay in acquiring credentials and recognition. Like many of the other religious-science academic institutions of this age, the IRAS proposed affiliation with like-minded groups. Although Burhoe suggested links to the SSSR, nothing came of this attempt. There were also efforts to set up auxiliary groups in other locations. A West Coast branch at Cal Tech began to hold monthly meetings in 1958.[40] Despite such outreach efforts, the organization remained centered on Boston, Harvard, and the American Academy.

Even with the development of IRAS and its acceptance of grand plans, by the late 1950s Burhoe became discouraged about the direction of the organization. In 1958, in a report to the Society for the Scientific Study of Religion, of which he was also a member, Burhoe defined "A Step toward a Scientific Theology: Notes on Certain Aspects of the 1957 Conference on Religion in an Age of Science." He noted that IRAS seemed to be divided between those who wished to spread the ideas of a scientific, modern religion and those who held back. As for his own plans, Burhoe once had high hopes for the organization, for at least in this group science was master. Yet, he lamented, most members were not as enthusiastic as he was about becoming a public advocate of rational religion or pushing into the arena of public opinion with a journal.[41]

This reluctance to found a journal was particularly troubling to Burhoe, since this had been one of his aims even before the organization of the Institute itself. As he wrote in 1953 to Roy Hoskins, "I have several times mulled over your hint of a year or so ago that I might do something on the side, independent of the [American] Academy." He had reached a conclusion: now was "an opportune time to launch a journal on cosmos and man to serve as a communications channel for those interested in developing a view of life in accord with [the] world view of science." As Burhoe wrote to Sophia Fahs of the Rockefeller Foundation, "The fundamentalist and neo-orthodox are hopelessly out of the picture." Consequently only a newly defined religious faith could solve modern problems, and that would require a serious publication.[42]

Burhoe urged a somewhat reluctant organization toward publication of a journal in the late 1950s. He proceeded on two fronts. In 1957 he proposed publishing a bulletin of the Institute in a bimonthly format (to be called *BIRAS*). Burhoe and a publications committee got the council's go-ahead to design a "bulletin or news sheet to carry ideas pertinent to the Institute's interests." Burhoe's suggestion lay somewhere between a newsletter and a journal. This initiative in turn evolved into a design for a quarterly journal.[43]

Planning for a quarterly journal continued, but Burhoe reported his discouragement to the council in 1959. His report chided the organization for its lack of a coherent sense of what a journal could do. More important, he concluded that few members of the Institute wanted "to associate themselves with the kind of program I have been advocating—a program of reformulation of religion in the light of science." Feeling the intense isolation forced on him by this commitment, he offered to resign from the publication committee.[44]

Although a journal did not appear for several more years (1966), the Institute published several books, including two edited collections of chapel talks by Rev. Edwin P. Booth delivered at the Star Island summer conferences and two collections of papers, also from the conferences. The first, titled *Science Ponders Religion* (1960), edited by Harlow Shapley, and the rejoinder, *Religion Ponders Science,* edited by Booth (1964), concluded the most ambitious early efforts of Shapley and other scientists and the theologians to find a meeting point for science and religion. Both books displayed the best of the Star Island intellectual efforts of the 1950s.

Shapley and his fellow scientists who wrote in his volume agreed, almost unanimously, with his definition of the problem facing science and religion. As the astronomer wrote in his introduction, some form of religion seemed inevitable, if only because anthropologists had discovered belief in spiritual matters to be universal in advanced cultures as well as primitive societies. To accommodate this very human motive force in modern life, he concluded, "effective religions must now pay closer attention to reasonableness and salute more diligently our expanding knowledge of a myriad-starred universe with its probably very rich spread of organic life." But, he warned, the "anthropomorphic one-planet Deity" had lost its appeal.[45]

The science model of religion certainly appealed to one longtime IRAS member, the psychologist Hudson Hoagland. Hoagland expressed sympathy for with those who claimed that religion suffered from the advent of a scientific culture, but he found personal consolation in the conclusion that science as a universal human endeavor had rejuvenated the notion of the brotherhood of man. In an argument that revived the position of the atomic scientists group, he declared international sharing and interchange to be a model for the democratic life. Yale physicist Henry Margenau also agreed that to rejoin the separate paths of science and religion modern theologians had to welcome the insights of science into religion. This meant, he concluded, finding a common method—a unified approach to link the two.[46]

Other scientists like R. W. Gerard (a neurophysiologist) remained less optimistic about joining religion and science. "I fear I'm pessimistic about all this," Gerard wrote. "I do not think the great bulk of people will accept the austerity of a rational religion any more than they will accept the austerity of science." This was indeed a discouraging voice, for he would not even agree that the contemporary age was the age of science; instead, he called it the era of technique and "scientific results, but not of scientific attitudes." The public neither accepted nor understood science as theory and method. How then could science (thus misunderstood) and religion (still dogmatic) ever illuminate each other?[47]

Ralph Burhoe, as ever, carried the torch of scientific optimism. Despite popular philosophies of impending doom and cyclical historical theories espoused by the likes of Spengler, Toynbee, and Sorokin, he remained positive that social evolution had a purposeful direction. Even his definition of religion was sociological and instrumental: religion meant those attitudes that "allow men to adapt to total environment so as to realize values." Religion, in other words, was the institution of culture providing "the most all-embracing and fundamental integration of ideas and attitudes that move man to behavior that makes life possible." If this sounded like a remote paraphrase of John Dewey, it was probably unintended. What linked the two thinkers was their keen acceptance of the structure of scientific thinking and the importance of process rather than outcomes. However, Burhoe aimed his evolution not toward more and more democracy, but toward a fuller realization of cosmological evolution in which culture increasingly carried the chromosomes of salvation. A creator God existed, he asserted; in the vastness of the universe, orderly design and inevitable law ruled. Only science could discover the reality and teach this lesson.[48]

Taken together, these articles provided a comprehensive sample of rational religious thinking and suggested the outlines of a theological cosmology. But their pallor is visible. Lacking the color and emotion of the anthropocentric bias, they placed humans on a continuum of such enormousness and within an evolution of such remarkable comprehensiveness as to lose those questions (and answers) that have always animated religious people: How am I different from and superior to all other creatures? What is my special place in the universe? How does religion teach me to act now?

In some respects Edwin Booth's edited response to the Shapley collection began with the same note of abstract compromise, for these authors relied on the same vague geography of modernism. Booth, for example, suggested rewriting the Ten Commandments to fit the ideas of modern evolution. After changing them from a list of prohibitions and perils into a polite catalog of recommendations, Booth suggested that all modern, practicing religions transform themselves. "All creeds, all dogmas, all affirmations of eternal validity," he declared, "must moderate themselves." "Quiet, gentle humility must possess us all," he continued, "as we face the universality and the majesty and the intricacy of the works of nature to which we belong."[49]

"Science" in the hands of some of these clerical authors ranged over a surprisingly broad terrain. In a discussion recalling some of William James's earlier writings, Walter Houston Clark, dean of the Hartford School of Religious Education, discussed the religious experience of taking LSD and his work with psychedelic drug advocate Timothy Leary. Drugs were, he concluded, a window opened by modern science "into oneself as well as onto the vastness of history." The church, he continued, should proceed cautiously with chemical spiritualism, but, he concluded, "it can hardly turn its face completely away from the religious implications of these awesome and astounding substances."[50]

This piece could hardly have been more different from the traditionalism espoused by Methodist bishop Francis Gerald Ensley. Ensley wrote disparagingly of the efforts to construct rational religions, "An artificial religion is about as consequential as Esperanto." To be a living, breathing religious faith, a creed must "be continuous with a historical tradition and be embodied in a cult and a community."[51]

Between these two positions lay several articles exploring religious cosmology, and here the Booth volume corresponded most closely with Shapley's edition of papers. Lyman Rutledge, a founder of the Institute, rejoiced in the instructive history of the organization. Its burden had been to bring science and religion together, but most of all to persuade the churches to include science and advancing knowledge in their continuing spiritual mission. "Thus religion and science together," he wrote, "would create a cultural climate wherein the Law and the Prophets would be fulfilled and all mankind would have a life, and have it more abundantly." Sophia Fahs, now associated with the Council of Liberal Churches, expressed the same thought more cosmologically: contemporary humans dwelt in a "surpassingly great organic, living body that seems to be guided or controlled from within by something akin to Mind or Spirit."[52]

Despite the efforts of this volume to sound scientific, to incorporate the scientific spirit of inquiry, and to pose religious questions at the cosmological level, like Shapley's effort it fell far short of providing a convincing analysis of a new religion. In fact the whole IRAS endeavor was perhaps more important for its attempt than for any successful resolution of problems. As the facilitator of dialogue in bringing together liberal churchmen, usually associated with the Unitarian-Universalist movement, with distinguished scientists like Harlow Shapley, commitment to the process ultimately mattered most.

Undeterred by their slim achievement, Ralph Burhoe and Harlow Shapley pushed ahead with their search. Finally it was Burhoe who put together the most convincing brief for a union of science and religion. During the early 1960s, Burhoe established an institutional presence in theology that ultimately led to his appointment to a major theological seminary and the foundation of the journal *Zygon* at the University of Chicago, creating an important American publication devoted to the exploration of religious cosmology.

Burhoe's unique position as a scientist teaching in a theological seminary (he was in fact neither a trained scientist nor a trained theologian) came in part from the coincidence of developments in the Unitarian movement and as a result of the activities of IRAS. Taking advantage of plans to unite the Universalist and Unitarian churches in 1958, Dana Greeley, one of the founders of IRAS, convinced the two churches to establish a Commission on Theology and the Frontiers of Learning. When this commission was appointed in 1959, over half of its members were scientists. When it reported in 1963, the author of the section on science and religion was Burhoe.[53]

That same year Malcolm R. Sutherland Jr., a vice president of the American Unitarian Association, became president of the Meadville Theological School, a seminary affiliated with the University of Chicago. Sutherland, who had became active in IRAS, invited the organization to help redesign theological training at Meadville. Ralph Burhoe responded with a long memorandum proposing a "new design." The program suggested scientific training for students and proposed hiring Julian Huxley as director. Sutherland asked Burhoe to take the position instead. He accepted, and from 1964 to 1974 he served as professor and chair of Theology and the Frontiers of Learning. As Burhoe enthusiastically put in, "I think Meadville may be the first theological school to set up a systematic effort to build and teach theology in the light of 20th century sciences." "What bowled me over was that an old theological school—President, Faculty, and Trustees—should unanimously vote for this radical experiment."[54]

Burhoe's grand scheme included teaching "scientific" theology to students—enlisting the scientific faculty to help "form the religious and philosophical thought of the coming generations." Although this ambition proved both controversial and only moderately successful, Burhoe made substantial progress on his plans to found a professional publication dedicated to the unity of science and religion. The journal *Zygon* appeared in 1966, jointly sponsored by IRAS and Meadville and published by the University of Chicago Press, with Burhoe as editor. The Greek word *zygon* means "yoke," and in this case it signified linking science and religion.

To help in his mission, Burhoe asked Shapley to consult on the publishing endeavor. Shapley did more. He both helped persuade Meadville to undertake *Zygon* and served on its editorial board. In recognition of this and his other contributions on behalf of religion, Meadville awarded the astronomer an honorary doctor of divinity degree in 1969. The theological school noted in its citation: "Through his missionary journeys across the country and around the world . . . [he] has pointed to the need for and the possibility of religious and ethical views growing out of the scientific picture of man and the reality in which he lives." Shapley knew better than others how apt this was. Without any irony, he described his life since retirement as "twenty five years as an active Christian Scientist educator."[55]

For Burhoe the founding of *Zygon* represented a vision made concrete, although his assessment of its early years was not sanguine. Even Shapley was puzzled "as to why the Unitarians and other liberals have not swept the world." *Zygon* did not revitalize the world's social institutions as Burhoe had once hoped it might—but then no institution had fared well, he explained, in the "antiscience revival of primitive forms of religion and 'countercultures'" of the 1960s. It had not, as he and others hoped, narrowed the "chasm in twentieth-century culture"—or closed the fault lines between C. P. Snow's "two cultures."[56] On the other hand, it did accomplish the different mission of energizing the discussion of the relation between science

Figure 12.2   Ralph Burhoe and Ralph Fuchs, president of the Meadville-Lombard School of Theology at the University of Chcago, celebrate the first issue of *Zygon*. The sign was later corrected to read "Institute on Religion in an Age of Science, Established in 1954." Courtesy of *Zygon*, Chicago Center for Religion and Science.

and religion; it offered a place to publish papers given at IRAS summer conferences; and perhaps most important, it created a venue for airing ideas in the burgeoning field of religious cosmology. The pages of *Zygon* opened to the writings of Teilhard de Chardin, Burhoe, Ian Barbour, Eric J. Chaisson, Theodosius Dobzhansky, and other philosophers, theologians, and scientists who explored varieties of this important topic. It helped open the way for considerable subsequent attention to theories of evolutionary cosmology such as the "anthropic principle" developed by physicists to suggest that the laws of nature either predicted or made inevitable human life in the universe.[57]

For his lifelong labor to unite religion and science, Ralph Burhoe received the Templeton Award in 1980, a citation funded by the mutual fund investment financier John Templeton and designed to supplement the Nobel Prize, which failed to recognize achievement in religious thinking. This reward at the end of a long pilgrimage to the twin peaks of religion and science by Burhoe, Shapley, and the others who founded IRAS and maintained its discussions for several decades never did resolve the contradictions of religion and science. Despite efforts to engage the intimate, personal questions of religious experience, *Zygon* emphasized a cosmology that lacked the immediacy and spiritualism of contemporary American religious culture. The comfort it lent to the problems of life was distant, even cold. Yet IRAS and *Zygon* maintained the conversation between liberal theologians and an important wing of the scientific community. They staked out space for the claims of religion for relevance in a scientific society and provided a way for religion and science to engage each other as equal partners in an age when the pressures to choose one side or the other were growing rapidly. But a meeting of science and religion, like the ever-receding goal of religious ecumenism, evaded Burhoe and Shapley even as they succeeded in making small conquests and conversions.

It is a cold world, this divided world in which mystery and wonder has little place. If we must think of science and God separately, then more and more of a true sense of wonder is lost.

Stephen F. Bayne, *Space Age Christianity* (1963)

Chapter 13

SPACE GOTHIC IN SEATTLE

A world's fair is an emporium of ideas. In the twentieth century these displays have made periodic reports on the progress of science and technology. They have measured the intensity of international rivalries. They have been the marketplace for new products and old entertainments. They display the racial and ethnic prejudices of their conceivers. They have served as projects for urban renewal. They are the destination of tourists; sometimes they are so important that they even confer status on celebrity itself.

Although the ostensible purpose of the Seattle World's Fair of 1962—"Century 21"—was to celebrate science and technology in American culture (America's Space Age World's Fair), it too had multiple purposes. The fair opened during a significant and harsh stage in the international rivalry of the United States and the Soviet Union. Its buildings constituted a significant urban renewal project for Seattle. Science popularization became its official theme, but it displayed the popular clichés of other fairs: games of chance, ethnic eateries, games, rides, "Girls of the Galaxie" (and for a brief, controversial moment Fantasia, an "authentic" Egyptian belly dancer). Visitors, including the royalty of popular culture, politicians, foreign dignitaries, and itinerant ministers like Billy Graham, flocked to savor the new Northwest. Toward the end of its season it even served Hollywood as the backdrop for the Elvis Presley film, *Take Me to the Fair*.

In this chapter I employ a selective focus on the fair, to explore its presentation of science and religion, and in particular to follow the development of two important exhibits: the Spacearium, featuring a ten-minute film called *Journey to the Stars*, and the Christian Witness pavilion, with its controversial film *Reclaimed*. The stressful evolution of these two exhibits, their reception, and what I believe can be learned from their juxtaposition suggests the status of the science-religion dialogue in the early 1960s. I will also follow the appearance of several of the important figures of the postwar science-religion dialogue who attended Century 21 and brought this dialogue onto the fairgrounds. As the topics range from American and Russian astronauts arguing over angels in space, to the display of Moody Institute of Science films and paintings and illustrations by space illustrator and Hollywood studio artist Chesley Bonestell, to a religious symposium featuring William Pollard, the atomic science and Episcopal priest, to the omnipresence of Donald Menzel as science adviser, many of the persons discussed earlier reappear for a reprise of established positions and arguments.

This chapter also brings my narrative to a close at a moment when the relations between science and religion had begun to change significantly from their pre–World War II configuration. In larger sense, however, this can only be the penultimate chapter in a never-ending account. The interaction between science and religion has not ceased, nor has the pace of change declined. The books of God and nature in American culture continue to be rewritten after this period, but in new ways.

The era of science triumphalism, if it had ever existed for more than a brief moment, began to close by the early 1960s. John W. Campbell Jr., the editor of *Astounding Science-Fiction*, described the declining prestige of science in terms that would certainly have astounded an earlier

Figure 13.1   Donald Menzel
as a young astronomer, with
Albert Einstein. Courtesy of the
Harvard University Archives.

generation—and maybe even some of his contemporary colleagues. Responding to a query from Donald Menzel, one of the chief advisers to the Seattle fair, Campbell warned of terrible problems planners would face in convincing the nation to support the enterprise of general science. "The American people have been thoroughly scared witless by the accomplishments of science," he cautioned. Contemporary science had all the appeal of "the mortician's trade." The atomic bomb and the bleeping and blinking of *Sputnik* III in the night skies terrified the public. "Americans do *not* want scientists, they want *anti*-scientists. They do *not* want young men trained to *do* science—but to *combat* science—Russian science," he concluded. Science fiction author Robert Heinlein, responding to a similar solicitation from Menzel, wrote with the same dark ink of pessimism. "Most unfortunately," he concluded, "We are in an anti-intellectual era and the scientific fraternity are blamed by the ignorant for all the woes of the world, especially those associated with weapons—instead of being credited, as they should indeed be, with having saved the world from destruction and/or slavery up to now."[1]

Although unusually well placed to gauge popular attitudes to science, these two science fiction writers did not stand alone in their worry about the reputation of science in America. Since the successful tests of atomic and hydrogen weapons by the Soviet Union and its surprise launch of *Sputnik* in 1957, federal science planners, universities, and other American research institutions had published worried assessments of science training and of science's low public esteem in the United States. In taking the pulse of excitement about science, they discovered it was feeble at best. The science fair in Seattle, then, offered a place for educators, the federal government, and scientists themselves to communicate to the public their enthusiasm about the enterprise of science. So important was this purpose that for the first time in the history of American fairs the federal government made a significant investment in an official display within the United States.[2] But what sort of science? How should it be presented? What about its context (a question quite as relevant to the architecture of its pavilions as to the intellectual design of its exhibits)? What about culture? How should religion be represented, if at all? Asking such questions meant delving into the foundations of modern society. As it turned out, even in an age of science it would be unthinkable to avoid a major gesture toward religion.

The Seattle Exposition of 1962 took place because of a fortuitous combination of local and national events that brought city boosters together with the highest echelons of federal science and economic planning agencies. The origins of the fair lie in the mid-1950s with the idea of commemorating the fiftieth anniversary of the Alaskan-Yukon-Pacific Exposition (held in Seattle in 1909). The Seattle city council asked the state for funds to study the project. By 1957, they had received $7.5 million for a fair to celebrate the "New Science and the Pan-Pacific World." Edward E. Carlson, president of Western Hotels and later chairman of the board of the World's Fair Commission, suggested the landmark that became the centerpiece of the exposition. During a trip to West Germany, he had been deeply impressed by a revolving restaurant in Stuttgart. He wanted to build something similar for Seattle. Eventually this became the "Space Needle," a revolving restaurant on top of a tower—a flying saucer pinned to the Seattle skyline like a mounted butterfly.[3]

The theme of a modern science fair attracted Seattle boosters as well as the Washington state congressional delegation, and eventually they convinced the federal government to participate. Seattle had become a major site of the defense industry with Boeing Aircraft as its centerpiece. Given the huge government investment in military research and development during the 1950s, much of it on the West Coast, the federal government wanted to justify its expenditures. But beyond this direct linkage to the Cold War, many members of the scientific community believed that in science education and general understanding America lagged dangerously behind other nations. As Francis D. Miller, deputy commissioner of Century 21, explained to the House of Representatives, "This might be considered a report to the American stockholders of this Government's determined efforts to make science work as man's servant and not his destroyer. It is hoped that such an event can . . . provide the germination for a new crop of young scientists devoted to that same end."[4]

The launch of the first Russian space satellite in October 1957 transformed a good idea into a compelling one. Just a few days after the launch, several scientists and science administrators, including Dr. Orr Reynolds, chief of the Office of Science, Department of Defense, and James Mitchell, associate director of the National Science Foundation, met in Washington, D.C., to discuss the impact of the Russian achievement. They agreed that an international science fair was badly needed "to demonstrate the main areas in which U.S. science was preeminent and to awaken the U.S. public to the significance of the general scientific effort and the importance of supporting it."[5]

Although the justification of the Cold War and defense spending certainly motivated federal participation in the fair, it remained mostly a silent reason. President Dwight Eisenhower supported the project but warned against "undue competition" with the Soviet Union such as had broken out at the 1958 Brussels World's Fair. This purpose could be muted by billing the exposition as an international celebration of science—with science depicted as a universal discourse. As a confidential telegram from Phil Evans, the federal commissioner of Century 21, explained in 1959, the theme should be "American philosophy expressed internationally at [the] Exposition which shows that the productive energies of 1 man work most abundantly in law." The anticipated audience was Americans who were skeptical about science or indifferent to the profession of science and yet worried over competition with the Russians. As C. T. Lloyd wrote in a paper outlining the reasons for federal participation in the fair: "The Century 21 Exposition forum offers the first opportunity within the borders of the United States for this country to affirmatively illustrate our attitude of moral responsibility in international relations that go along with scientific progress." The international character of the exposition would demonstrate that "no one nation can have a monopoly on scientific ability and achievement." Only faintly evident through this scrim of bureaucratic language was the crisis of confidence that inspired federal participation and worried American scientists.[6]

Nonetheless, there was considerable opposition to federal funding of any aspect of a domestic project of this sort. It took the combined efforts of the Washington State delegation, James Killian, president of MIT and the new special assistant for science and technology, the Departments of Defense, Commerce, and State, and the National Science Foundation, plus endorsement by the AAAS and other science organizations, to marshall the necessary support. Leadership in this effort fell to the Commerce Department, which set up a special National Science Planning Board, made up largely of scientists, to recommend the extent and character of United States participation in the fair. Congress finally agreed to the concept in the late summer of 1958, and the president designated the secretary of commerce to continue officiating over federal participation in the exposition.[7]

If the federal government had distinct purposes in funding this science fair project, the intentions of scientists were somewhat different. Out of earshot of congressional hearings, they tended to emphasize the need for a kind of national science literacy exhibit designed to awaken public interest, recruit students for university laboratories and advanced degrees, and fend off critics of spending on pure science. Over and over, scientists on the advisory panel stressed the opportunity to propagandize for pure science and sort out its differences from applied science. Following this reasoning, the second meeting of the National Science Planning Board suggested as a theme: "A demonstration of what basic science *is* and how in its modern emerging and energizing forms it is laying the groundwork for the transformation of human life."[8]

This distinction between pure and applied science—between science and technology—ran through the preparations of the board and the local Century 21 commission in Seattle like a fluorescent element. Its purpose was manifold: to direct public attention to the more difficult aspects of science, to recruit students for careers in science, and to bolster funding for pure research, among other things. But it also had another purpose: to dissuade the public from the distracting assumption that technology could engineer solutions to all the most difficult problems facing the nation. Disease, overpopulation, and resource exhaustion might be conquered, the argument went, but not without the initial critical work of pure scientific research.

Achieving this balance between pure and practical would be difficult enough by itself; but scientists traveling the road of popularization unfortunately looked over more than one precipice. As Froelich Rainey, an anthropologist and director of the University of Pennsylvania Museum, wrote to Donald Menzel in 1959, "Somewhere in this exhibition there should be a serious consideration of the probable effects of fall-out from any all-out war, grim as that may be." This problem plus the "population explosion" would be very "sticky" and, he concluded, "for the life of me [I] can't see how to present the [over]population business, except as a simple statement of fact."[9] So science would have to tread warily around the political and cultural pitfalls that troubled this discussion.

Another persistent and nagging problem of science presentation at the fair emerged in the suggestions made by a project development report the Seattle fair committee solicited from the Stanford Research Institute in 1957. The report warned that fairs had become difficult to finance. Crowds were too sophisticated to be attracted to "perispheres, skyrides, and Ziegfield Follies." Perhaps something to appeal to the American "spiritual and physical restlessness" would be more appropriate. A follow-up report in early 1958 suggested the Disney solution: combining something novel, a firm story line, and a special atmosphere. In fact the proposals suggested asking Disney to help design the enterprise.[10] And so scientists faced all the usual difficulties associated with popularization: the temptation to describe science as magic or, conversely, as a destructive force aimed at demolishing the structures of culture and society; the confusion between technology and pure research; and the loss of integrity through popular presentation.

Despite President Eisenhower's reluctance to make overt competition with the Soviet Union the theme of the fair, space science—where that competition most visibly intruded into public discussion—came to play the largest role in defining the focus of Century 21. Not only did the celebration of the West and its relations with Pacific nations take second place, but science was redefined to emphasize space travel and rocketry, with whatever on-earth displays could be tricked up as "space age." Even the planning board endorsed this overall theme.[11]

Although the board eventually defined the general areas to be covered by the United States exhibit, its work did not go smoothly, and frequent disagreements erupted between the scientists and Commissioner Evans and his staff at the Commerce Department. A typical dispute broke out over what Dael Wolfle of the AAAS worried would be the "dishonest" conclusion a visitor would inevitably receive "that science solves all." Such tensions between a serious science message and the aesthetics of display divided the board from beginning to end. As a result of the inevitable indecision and argument, Evans appointed a special new scientific advisory committee called the Committee on Scientific Theme, Content, and Presentation of the United States Science Exhibit. In effect there would now be two groups planning the fair, but with the Commerce Department making the final decisions.[12]

Donald Menzel played an important role in both groups, and he became the principal adviser to Area III, designated to house the space exhibit. Menzel had very firm ideas about the nature of the whole exhibit as well as the special part to which he was assigned. From the first he hoped to make space travel the central focus of the fair. Consulting with science fiction writers Robert Heinlein and Isaac Asimov, who together with Chesley Bonestell formed his subcommittee of experts, Menzel proposed a "full-scale model of a rocket designed for a round-trip exploration to the moon." It should be large enough to accommodate exhibits and restaurants. Next to this the fair would erect a hemispherical model of the moon designed by Bonestell on which scientists would be "doing work and experiments." A special advantage was that the exhibit provided a place to demonstrate cooperation with the Soviet Union in joint explorations. Here the benefits of international science could be visualized.[13]

Menzel formally submitted his plan to the Science Planning Board on 15 November 1958. He mentioned that he had already spoken to several Soviet scientists about participating in the project. Not only did his plan identify the sort of science to be exhibited in the rocket and moonscape, but he had even worked out details of crowd movement and exhibit design. The 15 November meeting of the scientists' board approved his outline. But for several reasons, Menzel lost control of the exhibit. His grandiose scheme for a rocket and moon hemisphere (which Isaac Asimov reminded him looked like the Trylon and Perisphere of the 1939 World's Fair), disturbed the State Department because he proposed cooperating with Soviet scientists.[14] Commerce Department members also voiced strenuous objections to his overall design.

By April 1960, when the new advisory committee began to meet, the plan remained very much in doubt. The State Department rejected the lunar colony on the grounds that it was "very impracticable and difficult to accomplish and that it will not meet with Congress's approval." Eliminated from the United States exhibit, the colony proposal moved over to a new, temporary home as part of the exhibit in a site controlled by the city of Seattle for a "City of the Future." Still optimistic, during a second trip to the Soviet Union Menzel broached the modified scheme with Soviet scientists. But once again the federal government intervened, advising the Seattle committee that no one could negotiate with the Soviet government about any exhibit without permission from the State Department.[15]

As for Area III and its concentration on space flight, Menzel had lost more than his model spaceship and lunar landscape, even though he remained the principal adviser. Commissioner Evans decided that instead the centerpiece should be an imaginative film trip to outer space, to be shown in a special theater named the "Spacearium." Menzel was furious. At a board meeting in 1960, his mock praise for the proposal dripped with sarcasm. "How beautiful it sounds and what does it mean? Nothing. A moving picture into space has been done again and again; it is 'old hat.' You can see it anywhere." His own plan, he contended, was distinctly superior. Nor did he give up the fight. Two days later at another board meeting, he chided Evans and his staff for designing exhibits that depicted the "magic of science." That terrible canard, he recalled, had been the substance over which he fought with Frank Capra several years earlier in making *Our Mr. Sun*. The theme of Area III must remain the pure science of space travel. An exhibit of the moon "would attract people much more than would a movie." Finally, he added that it was disturbing and wrong to exclude Soviet scientists.[16]

But Evans remained adamant about the film, which he proudly claimed to be his own original contribution to Area III. As he explained in November 1960, "The original concept of a spacearium show, from the Federal Government standpoint, originated with me and was considered a fundamental part of preliminary planning for the United States Science Exhibit." Perhaps most important, Evans succeeded in securing a financial partnership with Boeing Aircraft Corportion. On 19 October the Commerce Department announced that Boeing and the federal government would cooperate to create "the first production of an outer space voyage among the moving heavens in the world's first spacearium."[17]

Defeated on his general scheme for a "scientific" exploration of the moon and now concentrating on the film, Menzel suffered the further indignity of losing out to Hollywood writers. Menzel wanted a hand in designing the script of the film as well as the accompanying material for the whole exhibit on space. After the film project had been accepted, he offered an outline of how a simulated voyage into space might be accomplished. In June he volunteered to cooperate with two science fiction writers (Heinlein and Asimov) to carry out the project. Once again he ran into a veto. The Commerce Department engaged Walter Dorwin Teague Associates as the general United States science exhibit designers. Teague strongly objected to Menzel's suggestion to bring in science fiction writers. "Mr. Conrad," representing the company, "expressed his doubts about the type of story that Dr. Menzel would write and felt strongly against his participation in this Area." Working with Isaac Asimov, Menzel submitted a script anyway.[18]

Deputy Commissioner Miller and Commissioner Evans both believed that Hollywood was the best place to find writers and producers for the film on a space voyage. Miller visited Disneyland in early 1960 and reported that the film *Trip to the Moon,* featured in Tomorrowland, exemplified the studio's impressive work. Asked if the firm could produce a "Circarama" (a 360-degree movie), Disney replied that the company was overcommitted at the moment and could not undertake the project. Consequently John Wilson, president of Fine Arts Productions, was hired to prepare a script for the Spacearium. Thus by early 1961 most of Menzel's plans had been discarded. But the clumsy advising and sponsorship structure remained, with both the Commerce Department and Menzel claiming paternity for ideas in the film and with at least four separate groups fiddling with the script: Menzel and other members of the science advisory board, the Boeing Corporation, the Commerce Department acting through the fair commissioner, and Fine Arts Productions in Hollywood.[19]

As various scripts came to Menzel for comment, he discovered his worst fears in print. *Journey to the Stars* looked like an unscientific Hollywood trifle complete with blastoff countdown and three perilous encounters with asteroids and other dangers designed to sustain audience attention. Science, he believed, had been sacrificed to showmanship. By early 1961 Menzel could scarcely contain his anger at the distortions of science that seemed to infest the Fine Arts scripts. As he wrote to Ewen Dingwall, general manager of Century 21, the scripts gradually improved, but he wondered if he would eventually be tossed out "because of my insistence on scientific integrity of the production." To a colleague in Minnesota he confided an even bleaker appraisal. The show could be important, he wrote, but its present format made him "feel desperate." The previous commissioner did not back him. "And," he finished, "if I do not receive a vote of confidence from here on, so that we can control this Hollywood presentation, I am, very frankly, resigning."[20]

Meetings between Menzel, the Boeing Corporation, John Wilson of Fine Arts Productions, and federal representatives in 1961 continued to be tense and argumentative. In May Menzel voiced his extreme dislike of the script. He found "too much poetic license, inaccuracies as to celestial bodies, too much violent shifting and reversing of course." The film "should be presented as a scientific show rather than a poetic one." But even on these counts he could not prevail, for the Boeing representative disagreed with his conclusions and the board rejected his revisions. Further acrimony broke out during a discussion "as to whether God should be brought into the script." Some scientists desired a fuller quotation of religion in the displays, while others, like oceanographer Athelstan Spilhaus, commissioner of the United States science pavilion, who wrote a general overview of the displays for the board, argued that science had become a new universal language and human cohesive force.[21]

Menzel finally scored a late success. He won over Craig Colgate, the new Commerce Department commissioner, appointed in February 1961, with the change in presidential administration from Eisenhower to Kennedy.[22] In early May Colgate wrote a long critique to Orr Reynolds of the Department of Defense blasting the Hollywood film script. As written, it lacked "dignity and is on a much lower intellectual plane than any of the other presentations that we are intending to have in the Pavilion." The mock rocketship trip was "undignified and unnecessary." The "Hollywood touches" degraded the show.

Nonetheless, the final script and show retained many quotations from the genre of science fiction films as well as other Hollywood flourishes. The Boeing Spacearium, with a standing audience of 750, featured a brief imaginary space trip. Projected onto a seventy-five-foot dome through a 770-millimeter lens, the rapid trip took the viewer to the far reaches of the universe and back in ten minutes. After Menzel visited the fair in late summer of 1962, he sent a reluctant word of praise to Colgate. "The exhibits were all most impressive." Even though the "Spacearium did not quite come up to my expectations, it was nevertheless good enough to satisfy most of the general public. I have recovered from my sense of disappointment at it."[23]

This effort to pass science through the sieve of differing purposes resulted in a confection of mixed messages and meanings. Compromise with the desires of the State Department, the aesthetics and established genres of Hollywood, and the corporate purposes of Boeing resulted in a film that escaped the scientists' control. No doubt this happened partly because of the impolitic actions of Menzel in pushing his own rather impractical ideas for an exhibit. More fundamentally, however, scientists, even at this science fair, could not control how their theories and their profession would be popularized, nor did the federal government ever intend to concede them this power. As Commissioner Evans wrote, no one but the government could have the final say: "Single minded, single direction has, therefore, been necessary and justified." No more than the atomic scientists fifteen years before could Menzel and his allies disentangle their message of the scientific ethos of experimentation and internationalism from the demands of government, the exigencies of the Cold War, and the power of popular culture.[24]

To be sure, the fair did encourage a very positive view of science. It even brought a group of journalists together in August to discuss a better presentation of science issues to the public. Perhaps the high point was a July celebration dinner for Wernher von Braun, proclaiming him the space chairman for Century 21 in recognition of his life of promoting space travel as well as the "Man in the Space Age" theme of the fair. But the complex ideas that Menzel supported never quite emerged in the prominent displays of Area III.[25]

But what of the religious presence in Seattle? Where did it fit? *Journey to the Stars* made no explicit reference to religion except through the vague use of the open-ended language of awe: words like destiny, for example. The script to narrate other parts of Area III resonated with sentences such as: "humbled in our search for truth and by our new discoveries, we can look outward to the planets, to the stars, and to space itself." The opening of narrative for the whole exhibit in Area I, "The Threat and the Threshold," pictured a small girl being guided through the science of the twentieth century.

"In the mystery of the universe," intoned the guide's voice, "our earth . . . our single star is less than infinitesimal—and the miracle of man, microscopic. And yet man looms important . . . at least the affairs of man. Man alone reasons, hopes and has faith." One observer, writing for *Christian Century*, noticed the religious overtones to several films in the pavilions and detected their presence in much of the narrative of the other science exhibits. Even the official description of science written for the United States exhibit reached for a broad, nonthreatening definition of science. It was "essentially an artistic or philosophical enterprise, carried on for its own sake." It was "more akin to play than to work." But none of these narratives developed the explicit syncretic combination that characterized Frank Capra's productions, nor did they ever quite pass over from the implication of mystery into religion. Instead religion found a different, although prominent, place at the fair, set off from the center but still in a position to challenge the hegemony of the science motif.[26]

An early decision of the Seattle World's Fair Commission included religion as a major aspect of the fair but in a decidedly anthropological guise. This idea seemed to have multiple origins. In 1957 an Olympic College instructor, Romaine Nicholson, wrote to Dingwall suggesting a "Shrine for All Faiths." This commemoration of many religions would, the writer noted, recognize the "root values" of people from all around the world.

The Episcopal bishop of Olympia, Washington, Rev. Stephen F. Bayne, also wanted something to display spiritual unity. The Pacific Ocean, he noted, could be imagined as a seaway that linked all of the great religions of the world together. This conjunction should become a part of the fair. A second theme could be the special need for religion in the contemporary period. "Part of the tragedy of our predicament is that we have so far separated the worlds of physics and God that we do not often think of them together." The World's Fair might serve to "reclaim that lost unity." Edward Carlson of the Seattle commission wrote back approvingly. This feeling "with respect to the scientific and nuclear age and their relationship to religion to some extent is shared by many of the scientists that Ewen Dingwall and I met with in Washington, D.C. recently."[27]

Specific plans to construct an anthropological Hall of Religions or a Temple of Religions (the proposal went by two names) came primarily from the local architectural firm of Johnston, Campanella, and Associates, but it quickly gained support inside the Seattle commission. It provided a prompt and workable response to the desire of many of the planners to represent the great religions of the world in one ecumenical exhibit. Such a building would surely allow the balance "between science and culture" that many of the scientists on the board desired.[28]

The commission staff took up the project and approached a local committee of churches, the "Christian Witness," which had united to create a Protestant presence at the fair. The Century 21 commission promised to construct a building and then offer space to the five major religions of the world. In plans to depict Christianity, for example, it proposed to solicit the participation of the Eastern Orthodox Churches, the Vatican, and the World Council of Churches. As Georgia Gellert, assistant to the exhibits director of the commission, explained to the group, "We are thinking . . . in terms of a single building within which all these faiths (and their many subdivisions) might find equal space in which to display their histories, beliefs and sacred objects." Tape-recorded music "of all kinds played over a hi-fi system" would embellish the religious center.[29]

The Christian Witness group detected the brimstone of sociology and felt the heat of an unwelcome ecumenism in this proposal. After their board meeting in early March 1961, the group decided not to endorse the Hall of Religions. In fact the proposal appeared "an embarrassment and source of confusion to us as Protestant Christians at this time." The group decided instead to construct their own building to celebrate a Christian presence at the fair.

This abrupt refusal ended plans for a World of Religion display, partly because the proposal had never been universally accepted by members of the Seattle commission and partly because local support had always been a crucial factor in planning. Now the commission grew wary of Christian Witness, fearing that it might "end up being *the* religious thing on the grounds." On the other hand, the organization had to be included in any large plan for religious display. The best solution allowed Christian Witness as well as several other religious groups to erect their own pavilions.[30]

The leaders of Christian Witness developed grandiose plans that eventually fell through, but their ambitious reach revealed their belief in mounting a challenge to science. Originally their plan foresaw appointing a national board of theologians to deliberate, on the model of the National Science Planning Board, over how best to present religion to millions of visitors. They planned a series of discussions among clergy, physical and social scientists, laypersons, and exposition officials about the aims and purposes of the Witness group. Among events proposed for the fair was a "Mission to

Scientists" living in the Seattle area. This huge evangelical effort would result in a "world-wide inventory of our scientific, technological and cultural assets and from these strike a balance sheet for the era ahead in which man will come of age—Century 21."[31] In this initial, optimistic stage, Christian Witness could imagine itself facing science as an equal power.

Relinquishing its Hall of Religion proposal, the Seattle commission made two important gestures that helped impart an unmistakable religious tone to the fair and had an impact on the plans of the Witness group. The first was to hire Minoru Yamasaki as chief architect of the United States pavilion. A Seattle resident, Yamasaki created a brilliant unity of spiritual—even religious—symbolism to encase the federal science exhibits. He designed five buildings with exteriors adorned by rising concrete arches pressed up against the sides of the buildings. These buildings were connected by five arched colonnades grouped around a pool. Finally, at the center, soaring above the other structures, he placed five freestanding Gothic arches, positioned as if to support the vault of the sky. Almost immediately this style earned the name "space Gothic," in recognition of the link the architect made between ancient cathedral symbolism and the limitless human aspirations of the future.[32]

The second decision made by the Seattle commission located the Christian Witness pavilion. As Lemuel Petersen, executive vice president of Christian Witness and a member of the Council of Churches of Greater Seattle, said, "Our building is directly across from the Federal Science Pavilion, and although our building is modest in comparison to the magnificent science pavilion, the very fact that we are directly across from it is a reminder to man that God was and is and ever shall be."[33]

Having decided to go it alone, Christian Witness planned to build an impressive pavilion across from the entrance to the federal science buildings, which would house an exhibit to exhort visitors to make a more spiritual interpretation of the future. Designing this exhibit then became the preoccupation of the group. Christian Witness had been organized in 1959 by nineteen local Protestant organizations and twenty-three participating denominations. One of its purposes was evangelical; a survey taken for the group revealed that only about 30 percent of the population of the Northwest belonged to any church. Consequently, the founders remarked, "we have an enormous missionary and evangelistic task." The fair, they concluded, would bring tourists who might never attend church in their own communities to the Christian Witness pavilion. Here churches could com-

Figure 13.2   Space Gothic in Seattle: the graceful arches of the United States Science Pavilion, designed by Minoru Yamasaki. Courtesy of the United States Archives—Pacific Northwest Branch.

pete "in the marketplace of ideas and entertainment." They planned a building and an exhibit to facilitate this.[34]

The founding documents of Christian Witness made it clear that its purpose combined this evangelism with a more subtle notion of spiritual presence. They also proposed to "witness," to provoke a different interpretation of the future than that promised in the displays of scientific theories and technological marvels of the federal buildings. As a news release explained, the building "will be a witness in its very location that God's image, and that of Jesus Christ, stands before man's technological and scientific achievements."[35] The Witness group believed it had received special encouragement for this role from the Seattle commission. "The scientists who have participated in the National Science Planning board for the Fair, as well as the top management of the Exposition, have encouraged a strong religious emphasis with moral and spiritual values right from the beginning of the planning for the fair," wrote Lemuel Petersen.[36]

Robert Durham, the architect hired to design the Witness chapel, proposed a building of "simple Northwest native materials . . . done in a way that would contrast with the uncertainties and confusion of the space age." The resulting structure revealed a one-story pavilion, crowned by exposed wooden arches topped by a cross. Although not as striking as Yamasaki's integrated space Gothic structures and patterned landscape, the chapel echoed the design of the science segment but translated its vague spiritual motif into a specific religious content. Its wooden arches and cross were unmistakably Christian.[37] Groundbreaking ceremonies held in late November 1961 featured two young children, a boy dressed in a space suit and a girl in a Pilgrim costume, symbolizing the confidence that "we are venturing in faith and that no matter what tomorrow brings, God in Jesus Christ is with us just the same as he was yesterday and is today and will be forever."[38]

Like the science exhibits, the Christian Witness employed film as the nucleus of its display. The group hired Rev. Paul Keller of Minneapolis to prepare a documentary. Unfortunately his production proved controversial, distressing, and often baffling to the hundreds of thousands of visitors who saw it. Keller shot his film, which he called *Son and Lumière* (also called *Redeemed*) in stark black-and-white images. After numerous complaints, the Christian pavilion issued a pamphlet, handed out by ushers before the film, to explain its bleak symbolism. Keller advanced the message of his production through montage and image rather than spoken narrative, beginning with a countdown that had come to symbolize modern science in American popular culture. Keller intended his work to be a retelling of the Christian message in modern images. As the pamphlet explained, "After the visitors are seated in the theater, it becomes dark. They are surrounded by sound. Then it is silent. A sweet voice and the excitement of life are heard. Then, death. All seems quite hopeless; it is swift and final. We die by the count of a

Figure 13.3 The arches and cross of the nearby Christian Witness pavilion interact visually with the arches of the United States science pavilion. Photo by Roy Scully, copyright © 1962 by the *Seattle Times*.

nuclear age. We view creation and relish its beauty. We hear a stern warning but heed a slick temptation; then, eat of the fruit."[39]

The problem lay in translating these symbols into understandable impressions. The outlines of the Christian message were unmistakable, but the images that conveyed it were often obscure. To Keller it was clear enough: "The only optimism for a world living with a cobalt bomb is in God. The Church's message is hope." But for many visitors the film failed to enact the allegory it referred to. Thus the handbook had to lead the tourist carefully through each sequence of the film, including the interesting beginning that in fact pictured Century 21 itself as a sort of "Vanity Fair." "A carousel, 3/4 shot, with wild music, people going round and round. The idea of this is to symbolize the Gayway [amusement section of Century 21] or the entire fair."[40]

Criticism of the film became so intense that despite efforts to unscramble its message, the Christian Witness considered reshooting or replacing it. But the actual solution was the easiest at hand. "When controversy developed," wrote Lemuel Petersen, recalling the events of 1962, "much of the bitterness spilled over and had to be handled by Council staff." This meant explaining the content of the film to puzzled visitors and reaffirming its basic Christian message. But Petersen defended the film. The Christian Witness declared that most protests came from ministers and church members, whereas "outsiders" were often moved by the production.[41]

Christian Witness also took part in the numerous religious conferences and commemorations that punctuated the schedule of the fair over the summer of 1962. Principal among these were Bible Week (14–20 May), pro claimed by Mayor Gordon Clinton, Liturgical Week, 20–23 August, and rousing visit in midsummer by evangelist Billy Graham, who pronounced the Witness film a fine success. Religious observations at the fair came so thick and fast that an internal memo of the commission in early 1962 warned of a spiritual surfeit. "It now far exceeds science and all other . . . [events] in terms of scheduled events and will be curtailed to be brought into focus with a balanced program." For a fair that celebrated the preeminence of science, this was an astounding situation.[42]

By far the most striking religious symposium of the year occurred in August. Held at the New Playhouse on the fairgrounds, it was headed by Rev. Stephen Bayne, former navy chaplain and Episcopal bishop of Olympia. Gathered under the title "Space Age Christianity," several speakers, including Bayne, explored the modern relevance of Christianity. Their common theme implored inclusion in the scientific endeavors to come. Rev. William Pollard (former director of Oak Ridge Institute of Nuclear Studies) warned that the rise of science had brought on "imprisonment of the mind and spirit of man in space, time, and matter." J. Milton Yinger of the Religious Research Association questioned the sufficiency of social science. Despite its usefulness, he warned, it could never substitute for religion. Other speakers included Edward C. Wells, a vice president of the Boeing Corporation, and Paul Dudley White, personal physician of former president Dwight Eisenhower. If together these men offered no precise definition of space age Christianity and merely argued for its spiritual relevance, their ideas reflected and reproduced the multiple discussions of religion and science over the past twenty-five years—and that alone made their appearance significant. By 1962 these notions had become so much the common language of American culture that they were an obvious resource to be drawn on in discussing the profoundest values of society.[43]

In the end, even by its own estimate, the Christian Witness movement failed. The pavilion attracted only about 900,000 visitors out of a possible 10 million entries, and as late as 1964 the group was still attempting to retire a large debt. Controversy over its film did not translate into excitement about Protestant Christianity, nor did the alliance of churches accomplish any serious recruitment or conversion. Part of this feeling of letdown came from the spirited competition of the Moody Sermons from Science pavilion, erected by the evangelical Seattle Christian Business Men's Committee. Here George Speake presented two daily performances of Sermons from Science interspersed with showings of MIS science films. The modest Moody pavilion attracted a smaller audience than the Witness building but inspired very vocal enthusiasm. After viewing both displays, several visitors wrote in disappointment to the Christian Witness while praising the simplicity, clarity, and beauty of the Moody productions. One author denounced the Witness film as "a profound disappointment." By contrast, "'Sermons in Science' were wonderful!" This and several other letters chided the Witness film for want of a sufficient counterweight to the lure of science. To view religion abstractly as the Witness film did, several writers concluded, translated the Christian message into the very language of abstraction that science had mastered.[44]

If religion ultimately failed to provoke a notable challenge to the positive presentation of science with its universal claims, the divisiveness and squabbling of local religious organizations could be blamed. Neither main-

Figure 13.4 Sermons from Science pavilion at the Seattle World's Fair. At the conclusion of the fair, the Moody Institute of Science presented the building to the United States Air Force for use as a chapel at nearby Paine Air Force Base, a gesture that underscored the relationship that brought MIS films to thousands of members of the service. Courtesy of the Moody Institute of Science.

line Christian groups nor Fundamentalists nor Catholics could unite in a common front to pursue a collective goal at the fair. Their weakness diluted the message or, better, split it into competing messages. The audience traveled to Seattle primarily to see the science exhibits and rarely anticipated anything more than a side excursion to visit a religious pavilion. Almost 7 million people entered the science pavilion, more than 7 million rode the monorail, and about 2.5 million entered the Washington State exhibit, "World of Tomorrow."[45]

A follow-up opinion survey of visitors to the fair confirmed the impression formed by the Christian Witness group. Most visitors traveled to the fair to see the Space Needle, the federal science exhibit, or the monorail; significantly fewer intended to visit the religious exhibits. In a ranking of exhibits from most to least interesting, the federal science display placed first and "Sermons from Science" ranked fourteenth; the Witness film placed not at all.

Yet the science exhibits did not effectively teach the lessons that Donald Menzel and the science board had intended either. A survey of attitudes by visitors to the science pavilions captured their continuing ambivalence about questions in science that the board had intended to resolve. Going into the exhibits, visitors tended to hold science and scientists in high esteem, although many mentioned reservations. After seeing the introductory film to the exhibit, they changed their minds slightly, but surely not in the direction intended. "The film's general effect," continued the report, "was to make scientists seem more academic and more eccentric. Science came to be seen as warmer and more feminine, but the public's conception of science became more vague." The problem, it summarized, related to attention span: "Relative to its complexity the typical visitor spent little time at the Pavilion." Another independent survey of the audiences arrived at the same discouraging conclusion: "It appeared that most visitors to the Science Pavilion at the Seattle fair did not fully understand any of the complicated exhibits which were there displayed. However most visitors learned something from almost every exhibit at which they stopped."[46]

Neither science nor religion had quite discovered the most effective way to present itself in this important arena of the World's Fair. Nor had either come to terms with the other. Overtones of spirituality crept into the architecture and the language of the science pavilions. Religious displays presented themselves as commentary, at the fringes of the science endeavor. The major religious presence on the grounds, the Christian Witness, had more success as a day care center and Sunday school for the children of visitors than it could claim in converting contemporary worry about the huge social and international problems into a renewed Christian commitment.

Only once did the continuing touchiness of Americans about such complex issues explode—around the contest between astronaut and cosmonaut. Soviet cosmonaut Gherman Titov, touring the fairgrounds on 6 May, declared that while in space he had seen "no God or angels." He believed in "toil and labor and the reason of man." Asked to reply in a television interview, Lt. Comm. M. Scott Carpenter replied: "Well I feel that faith in God has helped me in preparation for life in general. It couldn't help but have some effect on the preparation for the flight." Or citizens could recall the bumbling but comforting words of American astronaut John Glenn before the United States Senate Aeronautical and Space Science Committee just a few months before. Fielding repeated entreaties to make a theological pronouncement about space travel, Glenn finally blurted out: "I cannot say that while I was in orbit I sat there and prayed. I was pretty busy. People . . . have tried to put words in my mouth on this. . . . My religion is not of the fire-engine type . . . to be called on only in emergency and then put God back in the woodwork. . . . My peace has been made with my Maker for a number of years." Even in July, Billy Graham commented sarcastically on Titov's offensive remarks.[47]

As a measure of American culture, the whole thrust of the fair—in its inclusiveness, its desire to juxtapose science and religion, to encourage Christianity to witness at the celebration of science—made a profound statement. At this grand festival of science, religion was as a privileged guest, seated at the head table and the host's right hand. It was simply unimaginable that the federal government or scientists themselves could present a great public scientific spectacle without including religion in some prominent position. There could be no more profound comment on the place of religion and science in American culture.[48]

Even if in 1962 no one could reconcile science and religion to the satisfaction of scientists or religious groups, if neither orientation to the world and its problems could prevail in public discussion, if the federal government, scientists, and the business community believed they needed to bring religion inside this grand American commemoration of scientific achievement, the lesson then and now is that science and religion cannot be reconciled, nor can either be conquered or contained. The accommodation at Seattle continued the dialectic, extended a running exchange, and signaled the continuing revision of relationships. Extraordinary changes had occurred in American culture since the Scopes trial of 1925 and the foundation of the Conference on Science, Philosophy, and Religion fifteen years later. But nothing had been settled, and that in itself was the only settlement possible.

For God doth know that in
the day ye eat thereof, then
your eyes shall be opened,
and ye shall be as gods,
knowing good and evil.

Gen. 3:4

Chapter 14

Conclusion

Several years ago, while preparing a paper for an international conference on contemporary religions, and having in mind some of the ideas explored in this book, I tried to find a symbol both universally recognizable and uniquely American with which to open my discussion. I chose the Apple Computer logo: the red apple with a bite taken out. This trademark seemed to me to be one of those witty images, based on double meanings, that if taken halfway seriously leads right over the edge of superficiality into the cultural deep. To inquire about its possible significance is to begin to fathom the way multiple ideas in a culture can be held simultaneously. The computer is a machine that works with symbolic logic and electrical impulses, that produces virtual reality, a machine for creating

Figure 14.1   Apple Computer logo.

new forms of knowledge. What a brilliant idea to market this product as the genesis of a second temptation, another tree bearing the fruit of secular knowledge! In our culture, what a powerful example of the continuing dialogue—available even to the commercial world—between science and religion.

Of course the symbol has an equally powerful alternative meaning, largely innocent of any religious connotation. When Steve Jobs and Stephen Wozniak developed their earliest computer board and planned to market it, they chose the name Apple, perhaps because of Jobs's earlier employment in orchards. The first logo design depicted Sir Isaac Newton, a potent scientific figure to whom the falling apple reputedly suggested the theory of gravity. This evolved into the contemporary symbol of the apple minus a bite—or byte—referring to the measure of electronic memory. One of the earliest slogans of the young company was "Byte into an Apple," suggesting the further reference to the Byte shops that sold computers.[1]

In this manner the logo resonated with multiple cultural overtones. A single symbol compressed a world of arguments; it contained the opposing polarities of culture. The apple conjured up two forms of knowledge: science and religion, Newton and the Garden of Eden, the liberating spirit of science shadowed by the temptations of hubris.

I hope it is now apparent that the dialogue between science and religion in America expresses essential ideas and deep-seated structures of culture. It reveals a theological problem and a profound concern of philosophy; it also shapes a significant portion of everyday popular culture. It provides categories for thinking about modern existence: to structure that world as divided between science and religion, or to imagine it united with their convergence.

The importance of this continuing conversation for American religion—

and to some extent even for science—should not be underestimated. That significance lies not in any final success or failure, but in the repetition of encounters and the energy these spark in the cultural atmosphere. Even if words like science and religion are at once hazy and overcharged with meaning, they supply the cultural stuff of the imagination. In the end religion and science probably cannot be reconciled, if only because we do not really desire any such closure. Too much has been gained by maintaining their differences; too much would be lost in ending the struggle. I am persuaded that the constant interchange between these two supposed polarities constitutes a powerful element in mastering the challenges of cultural and social change. From this conclusion, it is difficult not to suppose that one of the most creative impulses of American culture is the continuing presence of religion at the heart of scientific civilization.

Notes

CHAPTER ONE

1. John C. Pollock et al., *Connecticut Mutual Life Report on American Values: The Impact of Belief* (Hartford: Mutual Life Insurance, 1981), 217. At this sounding, 74 percent of Americans professed being religious persons. In answer to a variety of other questions, scientists consistently demonstrated the lowest level of religiousness compared with others.

2. Daniel Kevles, *The Physicists: The History of a Scientific Community in America* (New York: Alfred A. Knopf, 1978). Kevles notes this framework as the period when "big science" predominated in the United States.

3. Kevles, *Physicists*, 391. Physicist was third in prestigious reputation behind Supreme Court justice and physician. See Charles Percy Snow, *The Two Cultures and the Scientific Revolution* (Cambridge: Cambridge University Press, 1959), and idem, *The Physicists* (Boston: Little, Brown, 1981). In the latter book Snow argues that scientists represent a higher type of personality: "I think on a whole the scientists make slightly better husbands and fathers than most of us and I admire them for it" (180). Note his

masculinization of scientists. Changes in the reputation and definition of science are reflected in the history of the National Science Foundation. See Milton Lomask, *A Minor Miracle: An Informal History of the National Science Foundation* (Washington, D.C.: National Science Foundation, 1976), 202–9.

4. Thomas S. Kuhn, *The Structure of Scientific Revolutions* (Chicago: University of Chicago Press, 1962); Rachel Carson, *Silent Spring* (Boston: Houghton Mifflin, 1994); Theodore Roszak, *The Making of the Counter Culture: Reflections on the Technocratic Society and Its Youthful Opposition* (Garden City, N.Y.: Doubleday, 1969); and John C. Whitcomb Jr. and Henry M. Morris, *The Genesis Flood: The Bible Record and Its Scientific Implications* (Philadelphia: Presbyterian and Reformed Publishing Co., 1961). See also Ronald L. Numbers, *The Creationists* (New York: Alfred A. Knopf, 1992), 191ff.

5. A very large and interesting literature discussing women scientists and offering a variety of feminist critiques of the structures and ideas of the male scientific establishment appeared beginning in the 1980s. There are three fundamental issues that preoccupy this scholarship: reclaiming the lost and underestimated contribution of women throughout the history of science; reviewing the history of science and its contemporary structures to explain the exclusion or underrepresentation of women; and exploring the history of scientific activity and its present theoretical assumptions to determine ways a feminist science would change perspectives on the past and reorder research and theorizing in the present. A few examples of this literature include Margaret Wertheim, *Pythagoras' Trousers: God, Physics, and the Gender Wars* (New York: Random House, 1994), which stresses the ideological similarities of religion and physics; Cecilia Payne-Gopschkin, an astronomer at Harvard and protégée of Harlow Shapley enlightens Wertheim's point when she says, "Someone who knows me will say that science, to me, has been a religious experience. He is probably right. If my religious passion had been turned toward the Catholic church I should have wanted to be a priest." Gaposchkin, Celilia Helena Payne, *Cecilia Payne-Gaposchkin: An Autobiography and Other Recollections*, ed. Katherine Haramundanis (New York: Cambridge University Press, 1984), 221. See also David Noble, *A World without Women: The Christian Clerical Culture of Western Science* (New York: Alfred A. Knopf, 1992); Evelyn Fox Keller, *Reflections on Gender and Science* (New Haven: Yale University Press, 1985); Sandra Harding, *Whose Science? Whose Knowledge? Thinking from Women's Lives* (Ithaca: Cornell University Press, 1991).

6. Mott Greene, *Geology in the Nineteenth Century* (Ithaca: Cornell University Press, 1982), 13ff.

7. On the dispute over Einstein's theories see Ronald C. Tobey, *The American Ideology of National Science, 1919–1930* (Pittsburgh: University of Pittsburgh Press, 1971). See also Susan Faye Cannon, *Science in Culture: The Early Victorian Period* (New York: Dawson and Science History Publications, 1978), 276ff.

8. For an astute discussion of postwar American science, see Nathan Reingold, *Science, American Style* (New Brunswick, N.J.: Rutgers University Press, 1991).

9. A version of the doubts raised by Kuhn and others can be found at the turn of the century in what has been described as the "probabalistic" revolution, by which scientists acknowledged that chance and other forces played a significant role in scientific prediction. See Paul Jerome Croce, *Science and Religion in the Era of William James,* vol. 1, *Eclipse of Certainty, 1820–1880* (Chapel Hill: University of North Carolina Press,

1995). Despite increasing hesitation about what could or could not be known through science, the prestige of science in American culture rose and fell throughout the twentieth century for other historical reasons.

10. For another chilling account of suspect scientists, see Jessica Wang, "Science, Security, and the Cold War: The Case of E. U. Condon," *Isis* 83 (June 1992): 238–69. On Soviet and Nazi science, see Loren R. Graham, *Science in Russia and the Soviet Union* (Cambridge: Cambridge University Press, 1993), and Michael J. Neufield, *The Rocket and the Reich* (New York: Free Press, 1995).

11. See José Casanova, *Public Religions in the Modern World* (Chicago: University of Chicago Press, 1994). In this fascinating book, Casanova argues that secularization has generally proceeded in modernizing societies with many of the expected results. At the same time he discovers significant countermovements of deprivatization that have moved Protestant and Catholic sects back into the secular world of civil society. My book is not an exploration of the deep structures of society that have been transformed during the secularization of religious traditions. Such a study would yield other ways religion and science relate, compete, and define each other. For a very important discussion of the persistence of religion in this era, see Paul Boyer, *When Time Shall Be No More* (Cambridge: Harvard University Press, 1992).

12. These characteristics of what might be called an ideal type were assembled from comprehensive definitions in the *Encyclopedia of Religion* and the *Encyclopedia of Philosophy*. They are not intended to be definitive or complete, but rather suggest the difficulty of defining religion precisely. See Mircea Eliade, ed., *The Encyclopedia of Religion*, vol. 12 (New York: Macmillan, 1987), and Paul Edwards, ed., *Encyclopedia of Philosophy*, vols. 7 and 8 (New York: Macmillan and Free Press, 1967).

13. In most cases scientific activity does not concern itself with the metaphysics of its own endeavor. In this book, however, such ultimate speculations play an important role in determining the relative place of religion and science in culture.

14. For an excellent introduction to the shifting role of religion in American culture, see Charles H. Lippy, ed., *Twentieth-Century Shapers of American Popular Religion* (New York: Greenwood Press, 1989).

15. Albert E. Moyer has an interesting discussion of public science. See *A Scientist's Voice in American Culture: Simon Newcomb and the Rhetoric of Scientific Method* (Berkeley: University of California Press, 1992), introduction.

16. Obviously the relationship between the three levels of religious expression I have defined is a complex one in which each and all levels interact and create each other.

17. Robert Bellah, "Civil Religion in America," in *Beyond Belief: Essays on Religion in a Post-traditional World* (New York: Harper and Row, 1970): 168–92.

18. See Walter Wilkins, *Science and Religious Thought: A Darwinian Case Study* (Ann Arbor: UMI Research Press, 1985), 5.

19. A number of very important books on nineteenth-century American Protestantism suggest that this reaction is characteristic, not unusual, for American culture. See Nathan Hatch, *The Democratization of American Christianity* (New Haven: Yale University Press, 1989); Jon Butler, *Awash in a Sea of Faith: Christianizing the American People* (Cambridge: Harvard University Press, 1990); and R. Laurence Moore, *Selling God: American Religion in the Marketplace of Culture* (New York: Oxford University Press, 1994).

CHAPTER TWO

1. William Jennings Bryan to Philip Troup, 3 July 1925, box 47, file 1925, 1–9 July in William Jennings Bryan Manuscripts, Library of Congress, Washington, D.C. Hereafter cited as Bryan MSS.

2. Bryan to Samuel Untermeyer, 11 June 1925, box 47, file: 1925, 18–23 June, Dayton trial, Bryan MSS.

3. Joel Carpenter, introduction to *Enterprising Fundamentalism: Two Second-Generation Leaders* (New York: Garland, 1988). Thomas Gieryn, George M. Bevins, and Stephen C. Zehr argue that both the Scopes trial and the McLean creation-science trial of 1981–82 were examples of professionalization in science. Specifically, both trials represented examples of what the authors call "boundary work," or the establishment of impassable distinctions between scientific expertise and public opinion. See "Professionalization of American Scientists: Public Science in the Creation/Evolution Trials," *American Sociological Review* 50 (June 1985): 392–409.

4. In 1922 John Dewey wrote that Bryan was a symptom of "the forces which are most powerful in holding down the intellectual level of American life." See "American Intellectual Frontier," in Dewey, *Characters and Events: Popular Essays in Social and Political Philosophy* (1929), ed. Joseph Ratner, 2 vols. (New York: Octagon Books, 1970), 2:451. See also Hugh R. Slotten, "The Dilemmas of Science in the United States," in *The Scientific Enterprise in America*, ed. Ronald L. Numbers and Charles E. Rosenberg (Chicago: University of Chicago Press, 1996), 38.

5. Robert Bruce, *The Launching of American Science, 1846–1878* (New York: Alfred A. Knopf, 1987), 256ff.

6. *Washington Post*, 2 January 1925, and *New York Times*, 2 January 1925, 4. Bryan apparently sent in his inquiry about AAAS membership in September, during the heated presidential campaign. "Application Form for AAAS Membership," dated 29 September 1924, box 40, file: September 1924, Bryan MSS.

Paolo E. Coletta in his biography of Bryan has a good discussion of Bryan's motives at the trial and mentions in a footnote the AAAS affiliation. See *William Jennings Bryan*, vol. 3, *Political Puritan* (Lincoln: University of Nebraska Press, 1969), 228ff.

See "Directory of Fellows and Other Members of the American Association for the Advancement of Science," *Proceedings of the AAAS* 79 (1925). Other members of the AAAS include such nonscientists as sculptor Lorado Taft, W. E. B. DuBois, and the reformer Rufus Weeks.

7. Herbert W. Rand, "Report of AAAS Meeting, *Science* 61 (6 February 1925): 148.

8. *Washington Post*, 4 January 1925. The *Post*, in a revealing piece of layout, placed a story of the discovery of ten-million-year-old dinosaur bones next to its AAAS story about the threat of evolution.

9. Lawrence W. Levine, *Defender of the Faith: William Jennings Bryan, the Last Decade, 1915–1925* (New York: Oxford University Press, 1965), 326ff. This early book on Bryan has a spirited and intelligent account of the trial.

10. William Jennings Bryan, "Testimony," in Bryan, *Orthodox Christianity* (New York: Fleming Revell, 1923), 39, 4. See also Cannon, *Science in Culture*, 266ff.

11. The classical steps to knowledge in the scientific procedure developed by Francis Bacon include:

1. A description of the facts.
2. A tabulation or classification of these facts according to three degrees.
   a. The presence of a characteristic
   b. The absence of a characteristic
   c. Its presence in varying degrees
3. The rejection of what is not connected to the phenomenon under investigation and the determination of what is connected.

Bryan's formulation of scientific method, insofar as it can be determined, follows this description.

Nathan Reingold has an interesting discussion of American science in the nineteenth century in which he stresses the importance of geography and natural history as a part of nation building. See Nathan Reingold, ed., *Science in Nineteenth-Century America: A Documentary History* (New York: Hill and Wang, 1964), 29–30, 162.

12. Theodore Dwight Bozeman, *Protestants in an Age of Science: The Baconian Ideal and Antebellum American Religious Thought* (Chapel Hill: University of North Carolina Press, 1977), 4–11; M. L. Righini Bonelli and William R. Shea, eds., *Reason, Experiment, and Mysticism in the Scientific Revolution* (London: Macmillan, 1975), 5–11. See also Charles Whitney, *Francis Bacon and Modernity* (New Haven: Yale University Press, 1986), 28–29. Whitney argues that science was based on reason and knowledge and religion based on faith and belief. Their separation strengthened their common glorification of God's universe.

Bryan's caricature of modern science is fascinating: "Evolution is an imaginary development which cannot be proven and therefore requires no thought. All one needs to do is to lie on his back in the shade, shut his eyes, and allow his imagination free reign. He can spend every moment of every precious day during his life imagining, without finding one solid thing upon which to base a logical conclusion." Bryan to W. B. Riley, 27 March 1925, p. 2, box 40, file: March 1925, Bryan MSS.

13. John C. Greene, *American Science in the Age of Jefferson* (Ames: Iowa State University Press, 1988), esp. 413–15. Martin Marty discusses the role of Scottish realism in the philosophy of Fundamentalists. See Martin E. Marty, *Modern American Religion*, vol. 2, *The Noise of Conflict* (Chicago: University of Chicago Press, 1991), 176–78.

14. William Paley, *Natural Theology* (Boston: Gould, Kindall and Lincoln, 1838). See also Bruce, *Launching of American Science*, passim. Of course not all scientists subscribed to Paley in the nineteenth century, particularly as the era waned. But the religiousness of American scientists remains noteworthy.

15. What is common sense to one culture or group may appear to an outsider as religion, ideology, or superstition. This is merely another way of recognizing that common sense has meaning only in a specific cultural setting.

16. See the very interesting discussion of some of these issues as they pertained to the career of the nineteenth-century scientist Simon Newcomb. Moyer, *Scientist's Voice in American Culture*, passim. Science, in its public guise, adopted the scientific method as a means of achieving unity. This is precisely what Bryan tried to challenge. Christopher P. Toumey, *God's Own Scientists: Creationists in a Secular World* (New Brunswick, N.J.: Rutgers University Press, 1994), 13–17. Toumey traces the history and growth of creation science.

17. Much of the interpretative literature about Bryan emphasizes his opposition to Darwinism as a reaction to World War I. I do not disagree, but I believe that Bryan also took the issues of science and religion just as seriously, if not more so. Edward J. Larson, *Trial and Error: The American Controversy over Creation and Evolution* (New York: Oxford University Press, 1985), 41–46; Stephen Jay Gould, "William Jennings Bryan's Last Campaign," *Natural History* 96, no. 11 (1987): 16–22, 26.

18. This is not quite certain, for on occasion Bryan did discuss compulsory Bible reading in schools. See, for example, Bryan to John A. Taylor, 17 April 1925, box 40, file: 1925: 16–30 April 1925, Bryan MSS. See also Levine, *Defender,* 334.

19. See George E. Webb, *The Evolution Controversy in America* (Lexington: University Press of Kentucky, 1994), 66ff. Webb's is an excellent account of the Darwinian controversy in America.

20. Robert Millikan, *Evolution in Science and Religion* (New Haven: Yale University Press, 1927). See also Tobey, *American Ideology of Science,* for a more complex accounting of post–World War I science.

21. William Jennings Bryan, "Who Shall Control?" June 1925, box 47, file: June 1925, Bryan MSS.

22. Bryan to S. K. Hicks, 10 June 1925, box 47, file: June 1925, Bryan MSS. See also George Washburn to Bryan, 24 July 1925, box 47, file: 20–25 July, Bryan MSS.

23. James M. Gray to Bryan, July 1925, p. 1, box 47, file: July 1925, Bryan MSS.

24. James M. Gray to William Jennings Bryan, 2 July 1925, pp. 1–2, box 47, file: July 1925, Bryan MSS.

25. Guy T. Viskniskki to Bryan, 31 December 1924, box 40, file: December 1924, Bryan MSS.

26. William Jennings Bryan, "Mr. Darrow's Charge of Ignorance," 21 or 22 July 1925, pp. 1–3, box 47, file: July 1925, Bryan MSS. Parts of this document are reproduced in Leslie H. Allen's *Bryan and Darrow at Dayton.* Allen describes this as a press release. By not quoting the document in full, however, he represses some of its poignancy and anguish. See Allen, *Bryan and Darrow at Dayton: The Record and Documents of the Bible-Evolution Trial* (1925) (New York: Russell and Russell, 1967).

Willard B. Gatewood Jr. has an interesting discussion of the ramifications of the anti-Darwin trial and the rise of Fundamentalism in the 1920s, which he links with a variety of other general anti-intellectual developments and a reaction against change. Willard B. Gatewood Jr., *Controversy in the Twenties: Fundamentalism, Modernism, and Evolution* (Nashville: Vanderbilt University Press, 1969).

CHAPTER THREE

1. Kevles, *Physicists,* 334. Kevles also explores the diminished support for science in the 1930s.

2. Kirtley Mather, "The Problem of Anti-scientific Trends Today," *Science* 115 (16 May 1952): 533–36. In his address to the AAAS in December 1951, Mather was also reacting to loyalty oaths demanded from scientists and attacks on their (and his) patriotism. See also Kennard Baker Bork, *Cracking Rocks and Defending Democracy: Kirtley Fletcher Mather, Scientist, Teacher, Social Activist, 1888–1978* (San Francisco: Pacific Division AAAS, 1994), passim.

3. "Testimony of Harold C. Urey," in U.S. Congress, Senate, Committee on Atomic

Energy, *Hearings before the Special Committee on Atomic Energy,* 79th Cong., 1st sess., 29 November 1945 (Washington, D.C.: Government Printing Office, 1945), 94.

4. David Hollinger discusses the de-Christianization of American culture in the postwar period, based on the universalism of science and the cosmopolitanism of the scientific ethic. Hollinger, *Science, Jews, and Secular Culture* (Princeton: Princeton University Press, 1996).

5. "Testimony of Harold C. Urey," 28 November 1945, 163. At the same time, Bush was engaged in administration of defense research and development that was certainly not bound by these principles.

6. "Testimony of Harlow Shapley," U.S. Congress, Senate, Special Committee on Atomic Energy, 29 January, 1946, *Typescript Record* (Washington, D.C.: Ward and Paul, Official Reporters, 1946), 328ff.

7. An example of this use of portents is found in Shakespeare's *Julius Caesar,* act 1, scene 3:

CASCA: When these prodigies
    Do so conjointly meet, let not men say
    "These are their reasons, they are natural";
    For, I believe, they are portentous things
    Unto the climate that they point upon.
CICERO: Indeed, it is a strange-disposed time;
    But men may construe things after their fashion,
    Clean from the purpose of the things themselves.

"Portentous" things in Shakespeare are generally unnatural forms of behavior, in this case a wandering lion that does not accost humans.

8. "Testimony of Mrs. Harper Sibley," in *Hearings before the Special Committee on Atomic Energy,* 19 February 1946, 1218–20. In an interesting essay in 1954, Reinhold Niebuhr raised the question of the superiority of the common sense "of a man in the street" to esoteric methods of science. Niebuhr, "The Tyranny of Science," *Theology Today* 10 (January 1954): 466.

9. Quoted in Paul S. Boyer, *By the Bomb's Early Light: American Thought and Culture at the Dawn of the Atomic Age* (New York: Pantheon, 1985), 51.

10. Arthur Holly Compton, *Atomic Quest: A Personal Narrative* (Cambridge: Cambridge University Press, 1965), 334. The notion of scientific internationalism is certainly not unique to the 1940s, but it was nonetheless a powerful argument for the independence of science.

11. Jerome Nathanson, *The Scientific Spirit and Democratic Faith* (Freeport, N.Y.: Books for Libraries Press, 1944), 40ff.

12. James B. Conant, *On Understanding Science: A Historical Approach* (New Haven: Yale University Press, 1947), 1–24, 101. See also James G. Hershberg, *James B. Conant: Harvard to Hiroshima and the Making of the Nuclear Age* (New York: Alfred A. Knopf, 1993). Peter J. Kuznick argues that in the late 1930s scientists also offered their services to reorganize American society. See *Beyond the Laboratory: Scientists as Political Activists in 1930s America* (Chicago: University of Chicago Press, 1987).

13. Robert Friedel and Paul Israel, with Bernard S. Finn, *Edison's Electric Light: Biography of an Invention* (New Brunswick, N.J.: Rutgers University Press, 1986), ix–xi;

Lewis Wolpert, *The Unnatural Nature of Science* (Cambridge: Harvard University Press, 1993). Wolpert is blunt about this: "I would almost contend that if something fits in with common sense it almost certainly isn't science" (11). See also James Bryant Conant, with Leonard K. Nash, *Harvard Case Histories in Experimental Science*, 2 vols. (Cambridge: Harvard University Press, 1957), 1:vii–xiv, and Ernest Nagel, *The Structure of Science: Problems in the Logic of Scientific Explanation* (New York: Harcourt, Brace and World, 1961), 13 and passim.

14. Joseph Ben-David, *The Scientist's Role in Society: A Comparative Study* (Chicago: University of Chicago Press, 1984), xii–xv.

15. Michael Polanyi, *Knowing and Being: Essays of Michael Polanyi*, ed. Marjorie Grene (London: Routledge and Paul, 1969), 81. See also P. W. Bridgman, "Scientists and Social Responsibility," *Scientific Monthly* 65 (August 1947): 151; George H. Daniels, "The Pure Science Ideal and Democratic Culture," *Science* 156 (30 June 1967): 1699–1705.

16. Margaret Mead and Rhoda Métraux, "The Image of the Scientist among High-School Students—a Pilot Study." in *The Sociology of Science*, ed. Bernard Barber and Walter Hirsch (New York: Free Press, 1962), 236–38. See also in ibid., Richard Harrison Shryock, "American Indifference to Basic Science during the Nineteenth Century," 98–110.

17. "Appeal Letter," 1942, p. 1, box 12a, file: National Science Fund, Harlow Shapley Papers, HUG 4773.10, Harvard University Archives, Harvard University, Cambridge. Hereafter cited as Shapley MSS. See also Harlow Shapley to Frank B. Jewett, 14 May 1945, p. 1, box 12b, file: National Science Foundation, Shapley MSS.

18. J. Merton England, *A Patron for Pure Science: The National Science Foundation's Formative Years, 1945–1957* (Washington, D.C.: National Science Foundation, 1983), passim. This excellent account of the very complex history of the National Science Foundation is an indispensable source for anyone interested in this subject. See also Michael D. Reagan, *Science and the Federal Patron* (New York: Oxford, 1969), 33. Reagan argues that this is the age of public science in which science has become an establishment free from most of the vicissitudes of politics. See also Daniel J. Kevles, "The National Science Foundation and the Debate over Postwar Research Policy, 1942–1945," in Numbers and Rosenberg, *Scientific Enterprise in America*, 297–319.

19. Robert K. Merton, "Science and Social Order," in Barber and Hirsch, *Sociology of Science*, 22.

20. National Patent Council Release, 26 April 1949, box 12c, file: National Science Foundation, Shapley MSS.

21. Martin Gardner, *Science: Good, Bad and Bogus* (Buffalo, N.Y.: Prometheus Books, 1981), 4–5. See Martin Gardner, *In the Name of Science* (New York: G. P. Putnam's, 1952), 143–52 on Lysenko and Nazi science. See also "What Happened to the Dreamworld?" *Fortune* 35 (February 1947): 90–93ff.

22. Spencer R. Weart, *Nuclear Fear: A History of Images* (Cambridge: Harvard University Press, 1988); John C. Burnham, *How Superstition Won and Science Lost: Popularizing Science and Health in the United States* (New Brunswick, N.J.: Rutgers University Press, 1987), passim. Although somewhat exaggerated, Burnham's point is important. See also Hillier Krieghbaum, *Science and the Mass Media* (New York: New York Univer-

sity Press, 1967), passim. Krieghbaum explores the nature of science writing in American journalism and the response to it.

23. *The Public Impact of Science in the Mass Media*, Report of the National Association of Science Writers (Ann Arbor: Survey Research Center, 1958), 179–98. This very interesting survey suggests that attitudes to science also depended on economic status.

24. Edward Shils, "Freedom and influence: Observations on the Scientists' Movement in the United States," *Bulletin of the Atomic Scientists* 13 (January 1957): 15. See also Ron Doel, "International Science in the Cold War: The Politics of U.S.–Soviet Astronomy, 1950–1961," 1–16, forthcoming in *Diplomatic History*, for an interesting discussion of the comparison of science with other elements of culture in resisting control and censorship from the U.S. State Department in its international contacts.

25. Elizabeth Crawford, *Nationalism and Internationalism in Science, 1880–1939: Four Studies of the Nobel Population* (Cambridge: Cambridge University Press, 1992), 12ff. Crawford argues that these issues were all apparent during the nineteenth century.

26. See Alice Kimball Smith, *A Peril and a Hope* (Chicago: University of Chicago Press, 1965), for a very extensive and skillful discussion of the atomic scientists movement.

27. See Harry S. Hall, "Scientists and Politicians," in Barber and Hirsch, *Sociology of Science*, 280ff. Paul Boyer has an excellent discussion of the atomic scientists movement and the world government movement in *By the Bomb's Early Light*, 60ff.

28. Boyer, *By the Bomb's Early Light*, 29ff.

29. Leo Szilard, "The Need for a Crusade," typescript of discussion draft, December 1946, box 15, file 8, Papers of the Emergency Committee of Atomic Scientists, Special Collections, Joseph Regenstein Library, University of Chicago, Chicago, Illinois. Hereafter cited as ECAS MSS.

30. "Scientists and World Government," reprint of an editorial from *Bulletin of the Atomic Scientists* 3, no. 12 (1947): 4. Bulletin of the Atomic Scientists Papers, box 24, file 8: Princeton Conference, Special Collections, Joseph Regenstein Library, University of Chicago, Chicago, Illinois. Hereafter cited as BAS MSS.

31. Selig Hecht, "History of the Emergency Committee of Atomic Scientists," p. 9, box 7, file 2, ECAS MSS. The papers have other citations depicting the widespread activities of the atomic scientists.

32. David Inglis, "Should the FA [Federation of American Scientists] Promote International Federation?" p. 1, box 30, folder 5, Papers of the Federation of American Scientists, Special Collections, Joseph Regenstein Library, University of Chicago, Chicago, Illinois. Hereafter cited as FAS MSS.

33. "Statements" re: Sen. Cong., Res. 56 supporting the efforts of the United World Federalists, 3 February 1950, pp. 2–5, box 30, file 5, FAS MSS. "Background Facts for an Editorial Good for March–April, 1948," box 51, file 4, FAS MSS. See also "World Federation Called for by Rally," *New York Herald Tribune*, 6 December 1949.

34. Robert M. Hutchins, "Higher Education Today," typescript of a speech to the Inland Empire Association, 6 April 1949, p. 2, box 29, folder 8, BAS MSS. Hutchins goes on to support world government and world law, though recognizing that the support of the atomic scientists has by this date become less important.

35. Bernard Iddings Bell to Katherine Chamberlain, 17 July 1946, Joint Committee

[of religious persons and atomic scientists], p. 1, box 4, file 3, in Papers of the Atomic Scientists of Chicago, Special Collections, Joseph Regenstein Library, University of Chicago, Chicago, Illinois. Hereafter cited as ASC MSS.

36. Fred Eastman, Special Educational Representative for the Atomic Scientists of Chicago and the Federation of American Scientists to Theodore Smith of the Motion Picture Association, 22 August 1946, pp. 1–2. Skinner to [John?] regarding the conference on a proposed conference with radio men, 11 June 1946: "It is important, according to Chicago network men, to 'scare the living hell' out of the radio men during the morning sessions and at the luncheon talk. It also is important to give them some off-the-record inside dope or at [least?] what seems to be information of this nature," box 3, file 11, ASC MSS.

37. Nathan Reingold, "Metro-Goldwyn-Mayer Meets the Atom Bomb," in *Expository Science: Forms and Functions of Popularization*, ed. Terry Shinn and Richard Whitley, Sociology of the Sciences (Boston: D. Reidel, 1985), 230–45. This excellent article recounts the making of the film and points out its scientific errors and fantasy plot inventions.

38. Walter Lippmann to Frank Aydelotte, 28 October 1946, box 12, file 14, ECAS MSS.

39. Sam Max to Norman Cousins, 10 January 1946, copy of a letter, box 14, file 1, ECAS MSS. Apparently Cousins had something to do with promoting the Manhattan scientists' cooperation with MGM.

40. "Facts about the Making of M-G-M's remarkable motion picture, THE BEGINNING OR THE END?" pp. 4, 8, box 14, folder 12, ECAS MSS.

41. MGM, *The Beginning or the End?* 21 January 1947, screenplay by Frank Wead and starring Robert Walker, Bryan Donlevy, Tom Drake, Beverly Tyler, Audry Totter, and Hume Cronyn. Matt's last words were, of course, quoted in the publicity booklet.

42. The atomic scientists tried on other occasions to have films made about atomic energy and cooperated as advisers with several of these. One film the scientists were enthusiastic about was *The Church in the Atomic Age*. Another was *The Way of Peace*, made by East-West Films. In 1947 Blanding Sloan of East-West films planned to make a scientist's film called *What to do about It*. This would favor achieving world government. As Sloan wrote to Einstein, "The religious angle limits 'The Way of Peace' primarily to religious audiences. The world government film would have the greater and farther reaching effectiveness." Another film, produced by Pare Lorentz and based on David Bradley's book *No Place to Hide*, about the Bikini Atoll atomic tests, attracted considerable attention from the United World Federalists as well as Common Cause, the University of Chicago administration, and a number of atomic scientists including Einstein, Szilard, and Franck. Blanding Sloan to Albert Einstein, 24 July 1947, box 14, file 13, ECAS MSS. Lorentz wrote to Harrison Brown at Chicago of the script: "I could not be more excited about the movie. Within the confines of the motion picture form, I believe finally we have evolved a script which will tell the movie audiences in dramatic form all the main points your committee has worked so diligently to get across to the public these last three years." Pare Lorentz to Harrison Brown of the Emergency Committee, [no date], p. 2, box 15, file 1, ECAS MSS. The Emergency Committee, the United World Federalists, and the Committee to Frame a World Constitution were the original three producers of the film. The film was apparently not made.

43. Michael Amrine, "The Purpose of the Bulletin," 1951, typescript, 1951, p. 1, box 33, file 25, BAS MSS. Paul Boyer rightly argues that the atomic scientists had lost much of their prestige by 1951 and that this decline began even earlier; see *By the Bomb's Early Light*, 93–99.

44. Ernest Nagel, "Malicious Philosophies of Science" [1954], in Barber and Hirsch, *Sociology of Science*, 636, and Ernest Nagel, "Methods of Science: What Are They? Can They Be Taught?" *Scientific Monthly* 70 (January 1950): 22.

45. Yaron Ezahi, "Science and the Problem of Authority in Democracy," in "Science and Social Structure: A Festschrift for Robert K. Merton," ed. Thomas F. Gieryn, *Transactions of the New York Academy of Sciences*, ser. 2, 39 (24 April 1980): 45–46.

46. "The Scientist's Responsibility," *Christian Century* 65 (28 April 1948): 376–77; "Scientists—Our Modern Mercenaries," *Christian Century* 65 (16 June 1948): 597.

47. James B. Conant, *Science and Common Sense* (New Haven: Yale University Press, 1951), 15, 262.

48. Vannevar Bush, *Science Is Not Enough* (New York: William Morrow, 1967), 29–33.

49. See Boyer, *By the Bomb's Early Light*, 199–240, for an excellent discussion of this.

50. William Pollard, *Transcendence and Providence: Reflections of a Physicist and Priest* (Edinburgh: Scottish Academic Press, 1987), 2–4; Daniel Lang, *Man in the Thick Lead Suit* (New York: Oxford University Press, 1954), 198.

51. Jacques Maritain, comments on an article by Cuthbert Daniel and Arthur M. Squires regarding "Responsibility of Scientists," p. 1, submitted to the *Bulletin*, box 32, folder 5, BAS MSS.

52. Richard J. Cushing [archbishop of Boston], "A Spiritual Approach to the Atomic Age," *Bulletin of the Atomic Scientists* 3 (July 1948): 224.

53. Albert Einstein, "On the Moral Obligation of the Scientist," *Bulletin of the Atomic Scientists* 7 (February 1952): 34–35. This was clearly a question that concerned Einstein. In his earlier essay "Science and Religion" (1939) he stated the question very clearly. "Science can only ascertain what *is*, but not what *should be*," reprinted in *Out of My Later Years* (New York: Philosophic Library, 1950), 25.

54. "Science and the Catholic Church," two documents with commentary: "Humani Generis," papal encyclical, 12 August 1950, and "Theology and Modern Science," by Pope Pius XII, 28 November 1951 address, *Bulletin of the Atomic Scientists* 7 (June 1952): 142–46, 165. This article inspired other commentaries on the degree of reconciliation between Catholicism and science. Looking at the number of articles on religion and science, it appears that the *Bulletin* was most interested in the attitudes of the Catholic Church.

55. Pierre Auger, "Who? Why? How?" *Bulletin of the Atomic Scientists* 10 (March 1955): 76.

56. Reinhold Niebuhr, "Limitations of the Scientific Method: An Answer to Pierre Auger," *Bulletin of the Atomic Scientists* 10 (March 1955): 87. This debate reproduces something akin to the "two cultures" problem enunciated by C. P. Snow in 1959. See Snow, *The Two Cultures and a Second Look* (Cambridge: Cambridge University Press, 1965): 8–14. See also Nora Calhoun Graves, *The Two Culture Theory in C. P. Snow's Novels* (Hattiesburg: University of Mississippi Press, 1971), 1–7.

57. Beginning with the publication of Thomas Kuhn's *The Structure of Scientific Revolutions* (Chicago: University of Chicago Press, 1962) and the later elaboration of the strong and weak programs of the sociology of scientific knowledge, the science community has undergone extensive scrutiny for its procedures of experimentation and verification. The feminist critique is an even further development of this sort of exploration. See Andrew Pickering, ed., *Science as Practice and Culture* (Chicago: University of Chicago Press, 1992).

58. A fine collection of essays edited by Ruth Anshen in 1942 raises many of the issues that atomic scientists would later face. In particular the essays by Reinhold Niebuhr, Jacques Maritain, and Lewis Mumford suggest that the objections to atomic science were only extensions of earlier objections to science in general. See Ruth Nanda Anshen, ed., *Science and Man* (Westport, Conn.: Greenwood Press, 1968).

59. Robert K. Merton, "Puritanism, Pietism, and Science," in Barber and Hirsch, *Sociology of Science*, 35–66.

60. Kenneth R. Hardy, "Social Origins of American Scientists," *Science* 185 (9 August 1974): 498–503; Walter Hirsch, *Scientists in American Society* (New York: Random House, 1962), 14–16; Robert H. Knapp and Hubert B. Goodrich, "The Origins of American Scientists," *Science* 113 (11 May 1951): 543–44; A. W. Astin, "Productivity of Undergraduate Institutions," *Science* 136 (13 April 1962): 133.

61. Lewis Mumford, "Looking Forward," in Anshen, *Science and Man*, 355.

CHAPTER FOUR

1. Robert B. Westbrook, *John Dewey and American Democracy* (Ithaca: Cornell University Press, 1991), 537. Westbrook contends that Dewey was at the nadir of his influence by the 1950s. Dewey was not, of course, a logical positivist.

2. John Dewey, "Religion, Science, and Philosophy," in *Problems of Men* (New York: Philosophic Library, 1946).

3. Ibid.

4. Quoted from John Dewey, "The Supreme Intellectual Obligation," *Science*, 16 March 1934, 241, reprinted in *In Honor of John Dewey on His Ninetieth Birthday*, ed. Max C. Otto et al. (Madison: University of Wisconsin, 1951), 17.

5. See his remarks at the conference, 1937, p. 8, box 7, file 95, in Horace M. Kallen Archives, Yivo Institute for Jewish Research, New York, New York. Hereafter cited as Kallen Yivo MSS.

6. Otto Neurath, "Unified Science as Encyclopedic Integration" in *International Encyclopedia of Unified Science*, vol. 1 (Chicago: University of Chicago, 1938), 20; Gerald Holton, *Science and Anti-science* (Cambridge: Harvard University Press, 1993), 14–33.

7. John Dewey, "Unity of Science as a Social Problem," in *International Encyclopedia of Unified Science*, vol. 1, passim.

8. Bruce Kuklick, "John Dewey, American Theology, and Scientific Politics," in *Religion and Twentieth-Century American Intellectual Life*, ed. Michael Lacey (Cambridge: Cambridge University Press, 1989), 78ff. See also David Hollinger, "Justification by Verification: The Scientific Challenge to the Moral Authority of Christianity in Modern America," in ibid., 116–35.

9. See Westbrook's interesting discussion of this in *John Dewey*, 19ff., 35–36. See

also John Patrick Diggins, *The Promise of Pragmatism: Modernism and the Crisis of Knowledge and Authority* (Chicago: University of Chicago Press, 1994). Diggins agrees about the importance of Dewey's interest in reconciling religion and science. He is less sure that he succeeded; see 7–14, 121–214, and his criticisms, 227ff. The theologian Reinhold Niebuhr was especially critical of Dewey's Enlightenment leanings.

10. Mortimer J. Adler, *Philosopher at Large: An Intellectual Autobiography* (New York: Macmillan, 1977), 161, 163. For other criticisms of Dewey see Francis Pickens Miller, *The Church against the World* (Chicago: Willett, Clark, 1935).

11. Joan Shelley Rubin, *The Making of Middlebrow Culture* (Chapel Hill: University of North Carolina Press, 1992), 191ff. Adler sponsored great books seminars across the country beginning in 1943. In 1952 the *Encyclopaedia Britannica* published the fifty-four-volume Great Books of the Western World series. Adler also prepared its two-volume index of great ideas, the *Syntopicon*. Adler remained close to the Van Doren family. Charles, Geraldine, and John Van Doren became executives of the Institute for Philosophical Research, of which Adler was director.

12. John Dewey, "President Hutchins' Proposals to Remake Higher Education," *Social Frontier* 3 (January 1937): 103-4.

13. In his book *The Crisis of Democratic Theory*, Edward Purcell discusses the neo-Thomist dispute of the 1930s as well as the Conference on Science, Philosophy, and Religion and Dewey's Conference on the Scientific Spirit and the Democratic Faith. His primary interest in this book is defining the nature of postwar democratic theory. See Edward A. Purcell Jr., *The Crisis of Democratic Theory: Scientific Naturalism and the Problem of Value* (Lexington: University of Kentucky Press, 1973).

14. Mortimer J. Adler, *Hierarchy: Commencement Address, 1940* (St. Paul, Minn.: College of St. Thomas, 1940), 5. In the 1930s the University of Chicago was characterized as a "place where Protestant students were taught Roman Catholic philosophy by Jewish professors."

15. Ibid., 9.

16. Mortimer J. Adler, *Problems for Thomists: The Problem of Species* (New York: Sheed and Ward, 1940), 239–41. In this book Adler attacks Dewey for confusing the meaning of evolution and the nature of species.

17. William H. McNeill, *Hutchins' University: A Memoir of the University of Chicago, 1929–1958* (Chicago: University of Chicago Press, 1991), 3ff.

18. Adler, *Philosopher at Large*, 186–87.

19. For an alternative and very interesting view of the conference, see Fred W. Beuttler, "Organizing an American Conscience: The Conference on Science, Philosophy and Religion" (Ph.D. diss., University of Chicago, 1995). Beuttler looks back on the conference in terms of the culture wars of the 1990s. It was, he concludes, an effort to resolve the central problem of American culture—its lack of moral unity—a task, he contends, that pragmatism (as a secular philosophy) failed to accomplish.

20. "Statement by Louis Finkelstein, 1940," Conference on Science, Philosophy, and Religion, box 3, file: Conference—statement on origins, 1940, in Papers of the Conference on Science, Philosophy, and Religion, Record Group (hereafter RG) 5, Joseph and Miriam Ratern Center for the Study of Conservative Judaism, Jewish Theological Seminary, New York. Hereafter cited as JTS Conference MSS. "Report on Institute of Interdenominational Studies as of February 20, 1940," p. 9, ibid. Louis Finkelstein was

an adherent of the "Science of Judaism"—a version of the higher criticism of theology. But he was ambivalent about how far to push this sociological analysis. See Marshall Sklar, *Conservative Judaism: An American Religious Movement* (New York: Schocken, 1972), 171–73.

21. Pamela S. Nadell, "Finkelstein," in *Encyclopedia of World Biography: Twentieth Century Supplement* (Palatine, Ill.: Jack Heraty, 1987), 471. Finkelstein to Harlow Shapley, 6 April 1944, box 13b, file: Rabbi Louis Finkelstein, 1942–45, Shapley MSS. See also "Draft" describing the origins of the Conference on Science, Philosophy, and Religion, p. 6, box 1, file: Confidential Memoranda, JTS Conference MSS.

22. William Albright, "Remarks" to the Conference on Science, Philosophy, and Religion, Wednesday Afternoon, Eighth Conference, box 37, file: Transcripts, Eighth Conference, pp. 603–4, JTS Conference MSS. Paul Weiss, "Remarks" to the Conference on Science, Philosophy, and Religion, Wednesday Afternoon, 11 September 1940, p. 271, box 36, file: Transcripts, JTS Conference MSS. See also Michael B. Greenbaum, "Mission Conflict in Religiously Affiliated Institutions of Higher Education: The Jewish Theological Seminary of America during the Presidency of Louis Finkelstein, 1940–1955" (Ph.D. diss.: Columbia Teachers College, 1994), 11. Greenbaum argues that Finkelstein succeeded where no other religious leader had in bringing Jews and Christians together for "the purpose of searching for solutions to society's moral and ethical dilemmas."

23. Mark Silk, "Notes on the Judeo-Christian Tradition in America," *American Quarterly* 36 (spring 1984): 65–85. Silk explores this ambiguous tradition, which becomes important only in the late 1930s and which culminated in discussions during the 1950s. He finds it to be the basis of Will Herberg's Hebraism as well as the watered-down versions of American religion supported by Dwight Eisenhower. See also several articles in the first two volumes of *Judaism* (1952–53) in which authors Paul Tillich, Bernard Heller, and Robert Gordis debate the limits of the Judeo-Christian tradition as a theological concept. See also John Murray Cuddihy, *No Offense: Civil Religion and Protestant Taste* (New York: Seabury Press, 1978), 33–38.

24. While in Chicago, Compton taught Sunday school at a local church. He also wrote an unpublished manuscript titled "Immortality from the Point of View of the Sciences." See James A. Simpson, "Arthur Holly Compton," in *Remembering the University of Chicago: Teachers, Scientists, and Scholars*, ed. Edward Shils (Chicago: University of Chicago Press, 1991), 82.

25. Louis Finkelstein to Harlow Shapley, 8 September 1939, series A, box 24, file: Harlow Shapley, General Files of the Seminary, RG 1, Joseph and Miriam Ratner Center for the Study of Conservative Judaism, Jewish Theological Seminary, New York, New York. Hereafter cited as JTS General MSS. Finkelstein also wrote to Henry Sloane Coffin about enlarging and changing the Institute. Coffin responded, 11 August 1939, "As I told you I am thoroughly behind you in any effort to make both your people and my own more thoroughly believing." But he disagreed with Finkelstein's analysis: "I am not aware that our people are at the moment troubled by Science." Coffin to Finkelstein, 11 August 1939, series A, box 5, file: Henry Sloane Coffin, JTS General MSS.

26. Louis Finkelstein, "Institute," p. 1, box 1, file: Confidential Memoranda, JTS Conference MSS.

27. "Transcript of Luncheon Meeting, 3 November 1939," p. 53, box 2, file: Transcripts, JTS Conference MSS.

28. "Comments of Arthur Compton and Harlow Shapley," 3 November 1939, pp. 3–4, 8, box 2, file: Meeting—Transcript, 1940, JTS Conference MSS.

29. "Transcript for November 3, 1939," p. 57, box 39, file: Meeting—Transcript, 1940, JTS Conference MSS.

30. "Draft" memorandum, 1940, passim, box 2, file: Memoranda, "Draft, 1949," JTS Conference MSS. Fred Beuttler notes that Catholics rarely participated in ecumenical discussions at this time. Beuttler, "Organizing," 60.

31. Harlow Shapley, "Remarks" and rewritten "Call for the Conference," ibid., 63.

32. Harlow Shapley, "Remarks," 3 November 1939, p. 14, box 2, file: Meeting—Transcript, 1940, JTS Conference MSS.

33. Harlow Shapley, *Through Rugged Ways to the Stars* (New York: Scribner's Sons, 1969), 59–60, 168.

34. Harlow Shapley, "The Center of the Universe," *Forum* 81 (June 1929): 371, 375.

35. "Transcript of the Meeting 3 November 1939," p. 63, box 36, file: Transcript, 3 November 1939, JTS Conference MSS.

36. Louis Finkelstein to Mortimer J. Adler, 13 February 1940, series A, box 1, file: Adler, JTS General MSS. At this early stage Finkelstein mentions that the board included Charles Beard, Arthur Compton, Albert Einstein, Theodore Green, and Shapley. Beard and Einstein apparently dropped out early.

37. Mortimer J. Adler to Louis Finkelstein, 2 April 1940, and Mortimer J. Adler to Louis Finkelstein, 30 May 1940, series A, box 1, file: Adler, JTS General MSS.

38. Mortimer J. Adler to Louis Finkelstein, "On the Fundamental Position of the Conference on Science, Philosophy and Religion," pp. 1, 2, 4, ibid.

39. Louis Finkelstein to Mortimer J. Adler, 20 July 1940, pp. 2, 4, 5, ibid.

40. "Preliminary Meeting, August 9, 1940," box 36, file: Transcripts, JTS Conference MSS. In 1947 Robert MacIver published a book, *The Web of Government*, that linked assimilation and pluralism.

41. Press Releases: 1 June 1940, by Louis Finkelstein; 4 August 1940 by Pitirim Sorokin; 2 July 1940 by William Albright, p. 2; by Louis Finkelstein to the Jewish Telegraphic Agency, 1940; by Arthur H. Compton, n.d., p. 3; by Harlow Shapley, 26 August 1940, p. 2, box 3, file: Press Releases, Articles, 1940, JTS Conference MSS.

42. Harlow Shapley, "Remarks," 9 September 1940, p. 14, box 36, file: First Conference, Monday Morning Session, 9 September 1940, JTS Conference MSS. Harlow Shapley to Louis Finkelstein, 31 August 1940, box 24, series A, file: Harlow Shapley, JTS General MSS.

43. Sidney Hook, "Remarks," 9 September 1940, p. 67, box 36, file: 9 September 1940, Afternoon Session, JTS Conference MSS. Hook later appealed to intellectuals to quit the conference.

44. Van Wyck Brooks, "Opening Remarks," pp. 1–4, box 36, file: Opening Session, JTS Conference MSS.

45. Van Wyck Brooks, "Conference on Science, Philosophy in Their Relation to the Democratic Way of Life," in *Science, Philosophy and Religion: A Symposium* (New York: Conference on Science Philosophy, and Religion, 1941), 1–2.

46. Mortimer J. Adler, "God and the Professors," in *Science, Philosophy, and Religion*, 121–38. Adler's speech was reprinted in the University of Chicago student newspaper, the *Maroon*, and after considerable outcry so was Sidney Hook's caustic reply. Adler considered himself a pagan until he joined the Catholic Church in 1984. See Mortimer J. Adler, *A Second Look in the Rearview Mirror: Further Autobiographical Reflections of a Philosopher at Large* (New York: Macmillan, 1992), 3ff.

47. Sidney Hook, *Out of Step: An Unquiet Life in the Twentieth Century* (New York: Harper and Row, 1987), 337. Hook interprets much of this event as a vendetta by Finkelstein against him because he had "stolen" some of his best students. There are, of course, other reasons. Hook wrote to Kallen that "the way that Conference was run was *scandalous.*" Sidney Hook to Horace Kallen, [no date], box 40, file 720, Kallen Yivo MSS.

48. "Remarks of Sidney Hook," following Adler's speech, Session Transcript, p. 143, box 36, file: 1st conference, 9–11 September 1940, Tuesday Morning and Afternoon, JTS Conference MSS.

49. "Paper by Pitirim Sorokin" and "Response by Lyman Bryson," p. 36, box 36, file: First Conference, 9–11 September 1940, JTS Conference MSS. Bryson became director of education at the Columbia Broadcasting System.

50. Sorokin, ibid., p. 64.

51. Jacques Maritain to Louis Finkelstein, 21 July 1940, pp. 1–2, box 17, file: Jacques Maritain, JTS General MSS. Maritain was a converted Protestant; his wife was a converted Jew. In 1938 Hutchins tried without success to convince the Chicago philosophy department to hire him. See also Brand Blandshard to Louis Finkelstein, 1945, Response to Questionnaire, box 13, file: Questionnaire, Replies, JTS Conference MSS.

52. "Remarks of Harry Overstreet," Session Transcript, p. 206, box 36, file: First Conference, JTS Conference MSS.

53. "Remarks of Philipp Frank," 11 September 1940, Morning Session, Session Transcript, p. 172, box 36, file: First Conference, JTS Conference MSS. Shapley is responsible for Frank's being invited. Shapley says, "He himself is a 'Dissident' but undoubtedly sympathetic with problems of religion." Harlow Shapley to Louis Finkelstein, 8 December 1939, box 24, series A, file: Harlow Shapley, JTS General MSS.

54. "Remarks of Louis Finkelstein," Session Transcript, pp. 221–22, box 36, file: First Conference, JTS Conference MSS. Finkelstein used the analogy of Maimonides' portrayal of knowledge, divided between an inner courtyard and shrine and those places distant from it—in effect, he seconded the notion of hierarchy (p. 234).

55. "Remarks by Van Wyck Brooks," Session Transcript, pp. 314ff., box 36, file: First Conference, JTS Conference MSS.

56. Box 2, file: General Material, 1940, JTS Conference MSS. The most successful group was organized by Shapley and psychologist Hudson Hoagland at Harvard and included Ernest Hocking, Walter B. Cannon, and Stanley Cobb.

57. Finkelstein published articles for the Catholic publications *Thought*, in 1940, and the *Thomist*, in 1943. The editor of *Thought*, Father Gerald Walsh, was an active member of the conference. Finkelstein's friendship with the Catholic Church continued throughout the postwar period. In 1963 President John F. Kennedy appointed him to the delegation to attend the coronation of Pope Paul VI. The other three members were Supreme Court Justice Earl Warren (head), Senator Mike Mansfield, and Charles

W. Engelhart, an important Catholic benefactor of the Democratic Party. In 1941 the conference set up a subcommittee to study the Judeo-Christian tradition. See "Report to Founding Members," February 1941, p. 5, box 1, file: Founding members, JTS Conference MSS.

58. Press Release, 11 September 1940, p. 2, box 11, file: Executive Committee Press Releases, Conference Papers, JTS Conference MSS.

59. "Conference on Science, Philosophy and Religion, " 13 October 1940, box 2, file: Memoranda and Letters, 1940, JTS Conference MSS. The publicity files are fascinating because they show Finkelstein's considerable success in achieving broad notice for the conference. Although the press was most interested in the Adler-Hook dispute, more positive outcomes of the conference were also broadcast.

60. A count of identifiable university affiliations at an early conference discloses twenty-nine participants from eastern schools, nine from midwestern schools, three from western schools, and two from southern schools. In the late 1930s Chicago, Columbia, and Harvard were among the largest universities in the nation. Throughout the 1930s they vied to produce the most leading scientists in the nation. See McNeill, *Hutchins' University,* 43. Of course the University of California at Berkeley challenged this eastern hegemony and by the early 1940s had moved the intellectual center of gravity.

61. Stephen Vincent Benét, "The Stake of Art and Literature in the Preservation of the Democratic Way of Life," Session Transcript, p. 297, and Van Wyck Brooks, "Primary Literature and Coterie Literature," Session Transcript, p. 240, box 36, file: Second Conference, Transcript, JTS Conference MSS.

62. "Remarks of Charles W. Morris," Session Transcript, p. 163, box 36, file: Second Conference, Tuesday, 9 September 1941, JTS Conference MSS. This remark incited considerable discussion.

63. William O'Meara, "The Religious Background of Democratic Ideas," Session Transcript, p. 446, box 36, file: Second Conference, Morning, 11 September, JTS Conference MSS.

64. "Remarks of Margaret Mead," Session Transcript, p. 104, box 36, file: Second Conference, 8 September, Morning Session, JTS Conference MSS.

65. "Transcript of Remarks," Session Transcript, pp. 502–13, box 36, file: Second Conference, Afternoon, 11 September, JTS Conference MSS.

66. "Remarks of Harold Urey," Session Transcript, p. 37, box 36, file: Second Conference, 8 September, Morning, JTS Conference MSS.

67. John Dewey to Sidney Hook, 30 April 1941, box 38, file 671, Kallen Yivo MSS. Fred Beuttler maintains that Dewey's group misunderstood the conference and its commitment to openness; see Beuttler, "Organizing," 271.

68. Louis Finkelstein to Horace Kallen, 22 May 1941, and Horace Kallen to Louis Finkelstein, 20 May 1941, box 38, file 671, Kallen Yivo MSS. Milton R. Konvitz, "Kallen and the Hebraic Idea," in *The Legacy of Horace M. Kallen,* ed. Milton R. Konvitz (Rutherford, N.J.: Fairleigh Dickinson University Press, 1987), 72.

69. "Remarks by John Dewey to the Conference on Methods in Philosophy and the Sciences," 1937, and Sidney Hook's rejoinder, pp. 8ff., 24, box 7, file 95, Kallen Yivo MSS. Hook, Kallen, and Dewey worked on numerous projects like this, including organizing a League against Totalitarianism in 1939. The Conference on Methods ran occasionally until about 1952.

70. Gary Gerstle, "American Liberals and the Quest for Cultural Pluralism, 1915–1970," paper presented to the Washington Seminar on American History and Culture, 19 October 1994, 10ff. Horace M. Kallen to Henry Smith Leiper of the Federal Council of Churches, 25 July 1940, box 5, file 71, Kallen Yivo MSS.

71. Everett R. Clinchy to Horace Kallen, 3 June 1940, box 6, file 90; Horace Kallen to Ferdinand Lundberg, 2 December 1939, and Horace Kallen to Harry Elmer Barnes, 8 December 1939, box 6, file 89; Horace Kallen to Charles Morrison of the *Christian Century*, 11 July 1940, box 5, file 71, Kallen Yivo MSS. Kallen's reference to the assault on schools had to do with New York State's McLaughlin bill, passed in 1940 to release children for religious instruction during public school hours.

72. "Clerics Fight Science as Threat to Religious Ideas," *New Leader* 24 (1 March 1941): 5. See also Ronald Kronish, "Horace M. Kallen and John Dewey on Cultural Pluralism and Jewish Education," in Konvitz, *Legacy of Horace Kallen*, 93ff. Russell was eventually hired by the Barnes Foundation, organized by Albert C. Barnes in the 1920s to promote Dewey's educational theories.

73. Horace Kallen, "Behind the Bertrand Russell Case," in *The Bertrand Russell Case*, ed. John Dewey and Horace M. Kallen (New York: Viking Press, 1941), 30.

74. Sidney Hook, "The General Pattern," in Dewey and Kallen, *Bertrand Russell Case*, 203–5. Hook also carried this argument into his piece for the *Partisan Review* in early 1943; see Hook, "The New Failure of Nerve," *Partisan Review* 10 (January–February 1943): 2–23.

75. Edwin Wilson to Horace Kallen, 15 January 1943, 18 January 1943, and Minutes of the Committee Meeting, 24 March 1943, box 7, file 99, Kallen Yivo MSS.

76. "Announcement," box 7, file 99, Kallen Yivo MSS. The planning committee included Kallen, Hook, Corliss Lamont, Jerome Nathanson, Edwin H. Wilson, and others; Horace Kallen to Abraham Flexner, 16 April 1943, box 7, file 99, Kallen Yivo MSS.

77. Mark May, "The Moral Code of Scientists," Jerome Nathanson, "The Democratic Responsibility of Religious Leadership," and Herbert Schneider, "The Power of Free Religion," all in *The Scientific Spirit and Democratic Faith* (Freeport, N.Y.: Books for Libraries Press, 1944), 40ff. and passim. Richard Fox in his biography of Reinhold Niebuhr has a lengthy and interesting discussion of Niebuhr's relationship with Dewey. Despite their long and vocal contention, Fox finds certain parallels in their concern for problems of human power. Richard Wightman Fox, *Reinhold Niebuhr: A Biography* (New York: Pantheon, 1985), 164ff.

78. Horace M. Kallen, "Freedom and Authoritarianism in Religion," in *Scientific Spirit*, 3–11.

79. Edwin Wilson to Horace Kallen, 24 November 1943, and Horace Kallen to Edwin Wilson, 26 November 1943, box 7, file 99, Kallen Yivo MSS.

80. See *The Authoritarian Attempt to Capture Education: Papers from the Second Conference on the Scientific Spirit and Democratic Faith* (Freeport, N.Y.: Books for Libraries Press, 1945, 1970), and Jerome Nathanson, ed., *Science for Democracy: Conference on the Scientific Spirit and Democratic Faith* (Freeport, N.Y.: Books for Libraries Press, 1970, 1946), 4. The *Authoritarian Attempt* volume rehearsed the attack on neo-Thomism and the "neo-Reformation" theology of Protestants. Dewey, in his speech, expressed his surprise and dismay that his expectations of fifty years ago had suddenly moved in the opposite direction. He worried deeply about the "organized attack now being made

against science." The *Humanist* continued to survey the Catholic educational effort for the next decade, although it also began to express serious worries about attacks on academic freedom in the name of security. The journal remained vocally hostile to Finkelstein's conference only until 1943.

81. "Remarks of Harry A. Overstreet," Session Transcript, p. 477; at the session on history, Chairman Lyman Bryson disagreed with Overstreet's optimistic appraisal. See also "Remarks by F. Ernest Johnson," p. 29, box 36, file: Third Conference, JTS Conference MSS.

82. James T. Farrell to Van Wyck Brooks, 29 July 1943, series B, box 31, file: Van Wyck Brooks, and Van Wyck Brooks to Louis Finkelstein, 11 August 1943, series A, box 31, file: Van Wyck Brooks, JTS General MSS.

83. Louis Finkelstein to Van Wyck Brooks, 25 July 1947, series D, box 56, file: Van Wyck Brooks, JTS General MSS.

84. Louis Finkelstein to Robert MacIver, 23 June 1947, series D, box 60, file: Robert MacIver, JTS General MSS.

85. "Memorandum of Harold Lasswell," p. 1, box 12, file: Meeting—New York Group, JTS Conference MSS. In fact Finkelstein, Shapley, and MacIver had gone to Washington in 1942 to meet with Vice President Henry Wallace to discuss the conference and its ideas. See box 13b, file: Rabbi Louis Finkelstein, 1942–45, Shapley MSS.

86. Ibid., and Anton Pegis to Louis Finkelstein, 24 October 1945, box 13, file: Questionnaire, Replies, 1945, JTS Conference MSS.

87. See Beuttler, "Organizing," 486ff., for the later history of the conference and in particular its efforts to influence social policy in its contribution to the 1950s Special Studies Project of the Rockefeller Fund.

88. Those attending the 1949 conference included Shapley, Lasswell, Finkelstein, Mead, Adler, Van Wyck Brooks, Norman Cousins, Lewis Mumford, Reinhold Niebuhr, Talcott Parsons, Linus Pauling, Ordway Tead, Paul Tillich, Robert Hutchins, and others. David Hollinger has a number of insights into the role of Jews in creating the modern secular public intellectual. See his essay in the forthcoming Harry S. Stout and D. G. Hart, eds., *New Directions in American Religious History* (New York: Oxford University Press, 1997).

89. "Remarks," in "Notes on the Background and Development of the Institute on Ethics [of the Conference]," p. 12, box 13c, file: IRAS for 1959, Shapley MSS.

90. One of the most interesting results of Finkelstein's efforts were his edited volumes, *American Spiritual Autobiographies*, published by Harper (New York, 1948), containing the inspirational biographies of some of America's leading intellectuals. See Silk, "Notes on the Judeo-Christian Tradition," 65.

CHAPTER FIVE

1. Wayne A. Hebert to Robert Constable, 22 September 1949, p. 1, Papers of the Moody Institute of Science, Moody Bible Institute, Chicago, Illinois. Hereafter cited as MIS MSS.

2. I am using the term creationist science here to designate the general theology of natural design, not specific interpretations such as creation science or theistic evolution.

3. C. T. Lanham, "The Moral Core of Military Strength," speech to the National Small Business Men's Association, 16 February 1949, p. 4, in President's Committee on

Religion and Welfare in the Armed Forces, box 23, file: Information and Education, Papers of Harry S. Truman, Harry S. Truman Library, Independence, Missouri. Hereafter cited as President's Committee MSS.

4. Rabbi Solomon B. Freehof, testimony to the President's Committee on Religion and Welfare in the Armed Forces, pp. 10–11, box 1, file: Stenographic Report of the Conference, 25 May 1949, in President's Committee MSS.

5. Curtis Lemay, "Multiple Address Message," 17 December 1947, box 92, file: Morale and Welfare, in Records of the Office of the Chief of Chaplains, RG 341, National Record Center, Washington, D.C. Hereafter cited as Chaplain's Records.

6. Quoted in Thomas H. Bodie, "A Sociological Analysis of the Conceptual Framework and Operation of the U.S. Air Force Character Guidance Program" (Ph.D. diss., St. John's University, 1953); notes in box 1, Loose Leaf Notebook, Chaplain's Records. Bodie was a naval chaplain. The historian of the United States chaplains movement remarks that World War II found American men morally deficient and unfit. The occupation of Japan and Germany, he concluded, had been a terrible moral debacle because the United States assumed soldiers understood democracy, whereas the communists and the Nazis used indoctrination into their own system. The result was venereal disease, prisoner of war defections, and rising juvenile delinquency. See Daniel B. Jorgensen et al., *Air Force Chaplains, 1947–1960,* 4 vols. (Washington, D.C.: Office, Chief of the Air Force Chaplains, 1961–86), 2:251.

7. President's Committee on Religion and Welfare in the Armed Forces, *A Report on the Military Chaplaincy,* 1 October 1950 (Washington, D.C.: Government Printing Office, 1950), 7–8.

8. The impetus for the new Information and Education Department came partly from Arthur Sulzberger of the *New York Times* in 1941.

9. Jorgensen et al., *Air Force Chaplains,* 2:252ff.

10. Bodie, "Character Guidance," xiiff. Bodie argues that the initial Character Guidance programs were used for rehabilitating soldiers in 1945–46. The other origin of Character Guidance may be found in the Citizenship Lectures of the Civilian Conservation Corps during the 1930s. Daniel B. Jorgensen to the author, 1 June 1992.

11. Some observers saw the moral and patriotic instruction as purely a persuasive tactic. See "Washington Calling," *Progressive and LaFollette's Magazine* 11 (12 May 1947): 1ff. "Last January Patterson [Robert P., secretary of war] and his aides recognized they were whipped in their head-on campaign for conscription, so they worked out a back-door strategy."

12. Colonel Croker to Committee, testimony, "Transcripts of Committee Meeting," 22 June 1950, p. 1, box 6, file: Transcripts of Committee Meetings, 1950–51, President's Committee MSS.

13. John F. Bantell, "Search for Military Preparedness in the Postwar Era," *Social Studies* 63 (November 1972): 262ff.

14. Frank Cunningham, "The Army and Universal Military Training" (Ph.D. diss., University of Texas, 1976), 323ff., 385–88. See also Pearl G. Spindler, "A Brief Historical Summary of Universal Military Training," 1 May 1947, prepared for the President's Commission on Universal Military Training in Universal Military Training Papers, box 4, file: UMT Commission Hearings, Harry S. Truman Papers, Harry S. Truman Library, Independence, Missouri. Hereafter cited as UMT MSS.

15. When universal military training failed immediately after World War II, Congress adopted a year's renewal of the draft. This lapsed in 1947 and the draft was renewed; it was renewed again in June 1948 and June 1950. See John M. Swomley Jr., "A Study of the Universal Military Training Campaign, 1944–1952" (Ph.D. diss., University of Colorado, 1959), passim, and David R. Segal, *Recruiting for Uncle Sam: Citizenship and Military Manpower Policy* (Lawrence: University Press of Kansas, 1989), 31. In 1951 Congress passed the Universal Military Training and Service Act. Under its rubric, Truman appointed a National Security Training Commission, which proposed universal military training in 1951. Congress never approved this plan, but it retained and renewed the Selective Service aspects of the act in 1955. At a later stage, James B. Conant and Vannevar Bush proposed another universal military training plan known as the "Conant Plan." See Harry A. Marmion, "Historical Background of Selective Service in the United States," in *Selective Service and American Society*, ed. Roger W. Little (New York: Russell Sage Foundation, 1969), passim. An excellent overview of the complex negotiations over UMT and the draft can be found in George Q. Flynn, *The Draft, 1940–1973* (Lawrence: University Press of Kansas, 1993).

16. Compton wrote to Truman on 26 November 1946 accepting his appointment, reassuring the president that he had supported universal military training during World War II and continued to do so. Compton to Harry S. Truman, 29 December 1946, box 2, file: File Resolutions of Final Report, UMT MSS. *Current Biography* of 1954, in its sketch of Compton, concluded that the scientist "held that science and religion are in accord." In numerous speeches Compton returned to the issue of science and religion, attempting to work out a modern accommodation between the two. See Karl T. Compton, *A Scientist Speaks* (Cambridge: MIT Press, 1955).

17. Harry S. Truman, "Informal Remarks of the President to His Advisory Commission on Universal Training," 20 December 1946, pp. 1–2, box 1, file: Press Releases, UMT MSS.

18. Testimony of Vannevar Bush to the President's Advisory Commission on Universal Training, 20 December 1946, p. 54, box 10, file: PACUT—Minutes of the First Meeting, UMT MSS. "Scientific Research and Development in Relation to National Security" draft, 15 May 1947, box 1, file: Correspondence, General, UMT MSS. These papers have frequent references to the possible institution of a national science foundation and its (positive) relationship with UMT. The final report of the commission stressed the importance of education in science and mathematics—and the uncertainty of the new scientific age. "Report to the President's Advisory Commission on Universal Training," p. III-4, box 41, file 2, President's Committee MSS.

19. "Report to the President's Advisory Commission on Universal Training Prepared by the Federal Security Agency," Office of Education, April 1947, pp. III-3–4, box 41, file 2, President's Committee MSS.

20. Testimony of Father Edmund A. Walsh, "Minutes of the Fourth Meeting, 10–11 January, 1947," p. 286, box 11, file: PACUT: Minutes of Fourth Meeting, 1-10–11-47, UMT MSS.

21. William C. Hodgson to the President, 21 January 1947, box 1, file: Correspondence, General, UMT MSS.

22. Gen. George C. Marshall, "General Principles of National Military Policy to

Govern Preparation of Post-war Plans," War Department Circular, 347, 25 August 1944, p. 11, box 3, file: Commissions Kit, Ninth Meeting, UMT MSS.

23. Testimony of Gen. C. T. Lanham, Chief, I&E Division of the War Department Special Staff, 31 January 1947, box 11, file: PACUT, "Minutes of 7th Meeting," 31 January–1 February 1947, p. 919, and Father Edmund A. Walsh, "Statement," p. 1324, box 11, file: PACUT "Minutes of 10th Meeting," 22 February 1947, UMT MSS.

24. Karl T. Compton, "Statement," Minutes of the 15th Meeting, 16 May 1947, p. 2049, box 11, file: PACUT, "Minutes of 15th Meeting," 5-16–17-1947, UMT MSS.

25. David Landman, "Can Soldiers Be Gentlemen?" *Colliers'* 64 (28 May 1947): 19, 86, and Cunningham, "Army and Universal Military Training," 436.

26. Cunningham, "Universal Military Training," 436–38; U.S. Congress, House, Subcommittee on Publicity and Propaganda, Committee on Expenditures in the Executive Department, "Investigation of War Department Publicity and Propaganda in Relation to Universal Military Training," 80th Cong., 1st sess., 20 June and 16 July 1947 (Washington, D.C.: Government Printing Office, 1947), 3, 51.

27. Gilbert Bailey, "UMTees—First Soldiers of the New Army," *New York Times Magazine,* 23 February 1947, 58.

28. "Report on the Activities and Program of the Protestant Chaplain, UMT Experimental Unit," 18 March 1947, p. 2, box 8, file: Fort Knox, Kentucky, UMT MSS.

29. M. June Boeckman, "The AGF UMT Experimental Unit," 5 June 1947, box 8, file: Fort Knox, Kentucky, UMT MSS. The lectures given to Fort Knox recruits were written by the chaplain school at Carlisle barracks and planned for general use in the armed forces. Based on their success during the experiment, they were later incorporated into the "Chaplain's Hour" program.

30. Jim G. Lucas, "Teen-agers and Parents Are Enthusiastic about New United States Military Training Program," *San Francisco News,* 2 May 1947. "Report on Activities of Protestant Chaplain," p. 2, UMT MSS. Of course these figures about conversions and baptisms do not suggest that the 20 percent that were unchurched at the beginning were the soldiers who in fact received special instruction, although clearly some were.

31. "Report of the Sub-committee of the Louisville Army Advisory Committee on Universal Military Training Experiment," [February 1947?], pp. 1–3, box 8, file: Fort Knox, Kentucky, UMT MSS.

32. The influence the commission had on the army is suggested by Truman Gibson in remarks before the President's Committee on Religion and Welfare in the Armed Forces, 3 December 1948, p. 27, box 3, file: Committee Meeting, President's Committee MSS. See also Poling, "Notes on Universal Military Training," p. 1, box 9, file: Staff Studies—"Universal Military Training," UMT MSS.

33. U.S. Congress, "UMT Hearings," passim, and Cunningham, "Army and Universal Military Training," 442.

34. U.S. Congress, "UMT Hearings," 75ff. Kenneth C. Royall, secretary of the army, testified that a recruit in universal military training had "an equal or perhaps a little better chance to be a good boy than if he is not" (p. 17).

35. U.S. Congress, "UMT Hearings," 19. In 1963 the Church-State Committee of the American Civil Liberties Union began a study of the military chaplaincy because of

its implications for constitutional issues. Indeed, the chaplaincy itself was in ferment during the early 1960s. See Jorgensen et al., *Air Force Chaplains*, 3:17–18.

36. U.S. Congress, House, "Supplemental Report to the Fourth Intermediate Report," 4 March 1948, 80th Cong., 2d sess. (Washington, D.C.: Government Printing Office, 1948), 1–3.

37. Harry S. Truman to Daniel Poling, 1 April 1949, p. 5, box 4, file: Proceedings of the 7th Meeting, President's Committee MSS. See also Statement of Frank L. Weil, box 3, file: Meeting, 3 December 1948, p. 6, ibid. The Compton Commission sent the president a supplementary report, "On Moral Safeguards for Trainees to Be Inducted under the Selective Service Act," on 13 September 1948. This report stressed the very striking reality that at least 50 percent of inductees in the current draft would be under twenty-one. See "Background Material: The President's Committee on Religion and Welfare in the Armed Forces," box 1653, file 1285-P, Truman Official Files, Harry S. Truman Papers, Harry S. Truman Library, Independence, Missouri. Hereafter cited as Truman Official Files. In December 1948 the Synagogue Council of America wrote to Truman that it was deeply gratified that he had appointed Weil, a Jew, as chairman of the committee. But, they added, because there were also a distinguished Protestant minister and a distinguished Catholic priest, it would be appropriate to add a rabbi to the group. Dr. Robert Gordis to Harry S. Truman, 17 December 1948, box 1653, file: 1285-P, Truman Official Files.

38. "Transcript of a Meeting, 3 December 1948," pp. 1–6, box 3, file: Meeting of the President and the Four Service Secretaries," President's Committee MSS. Maj. Gen. Parker told the committee in late December 1948 that the armed forces were even trying to "control the type of comic books that go on armed forces' reservations." "Testimony," p. 46, box 3, file: Notes of Meeting, Monday, 20 December 1948, President's Committee MSS. At the same meeting, Brig. Gen. Lanham told the committee that the continued need for Information and Education was one of the "great reasons why this Committee has been convened" (p. 33, ibid.). Forrestal told the committee that he hoped it would highlight such problems as poor housing for servicemen. See "Memorandum for the Secretaries of the Army, Navy, and Air Force," 1 December 1948, box 17, file 1-a, Departments and Agencies, President's Committee MSS. The USO was organized in 1940 and continued through World War II. It suffered numerous financial problems after the war, and despite encouragement from Secretary Forrestal, it had to struggle to remain in existence.

39. "Executive Order, 27 October, 1948," box 1652, file 1285-P, Truman Official Files.

40. "First Report of the President's Committee on Religion and Welfare in the Armed Forces," 24 March 1949, pp. 26ff., box 1652, file 1285-P, Truman Official Files. Note that the committee name was changed from the original "Religion and Moral Welfare and Character Guidance in the Armed Forces" to an abbreviated designation.

41. "Statement by the President's Committee on Religion and Welfare in the Armed Forces," 25 May 1949, p. 8, box 36, file: Press Releases, President's Committee MSS; and "Remarks of Weil," p. 69, box 1, file: Proceedings of Conference on Community Responsibility," President's Committee MSS.

42. "Remarks" of Tuttle to the Conference, 25 May 1949, pp. 1–2, box 1, file: Pro-

ceedings: National Conference on Community Responsibility to Our Peacetime Servicemen and Women," President's Committee MSS. It is noteworthy that this ecumenism was approximately the same as the Conference on Science, Philosophy, and Religion had developed as a compromise doctrine. See chapter 13 for a different outcome and the rejection of religious pluralism at the Seattle World's Fair in 1962.

43. Rev. G. H. Whiting, p. 59, box 1, file: Stenographic Account of the Conference, President's Committee MSS.

44. Daniel A. Poling, "Report," May 1949, pp. 2, 10, box 97, file: 21 September 1949, Chaplain's Records.

45. "Final Report on Information and Education, 1 December 1949," pp. 2, 4, 15, box 2, file: Reports, President's Committee MSS.

46. "Chaplains in the Army," p. 3, box 9, file: Chaplains in the Army, President's Committee MSS.

47. "Statement by the President's Committee on Religion and Welfare in the Armed Forces," 24 August 1950, pp. 1–2, box 1652, file 1285-P, Truman Official Files. "Truman Meets Committee on Religion in Armed Forces," *New York Times*, 11 October 1950, 14.

48. Poling, "Statement to the Committee," 26 October 1950, p. 115, box 6, file: Transcripts of Committee Meetings, 1950–51, President's Committee MSS. The Selective Service was renewed in June 1948, June 1950, and June 1951. Advocates of UMT did not disappear during the Korean War. In fact the Committee on the Present Danger, organized in 1950 by such figures as James B. Conant, continued to advocate UMT. Swomley, "Universal Military Training," 252.

49. "Committee Urges Chaplain's School," *New York Times*, 2 December 1950, 13. The committee also investigated and advocated the importance of ideological instruction through the "Chaplain's Hour" and Character Guidance. This activity was almost always controversial. In 1951 Benjamin Fine published a highly critical study in the *New York Times*, disparaging the efforts of military information programs. See, for example, "Unanswered Whys Hurt Army Morale," 16 May 1951, 14. This suggests that the problem of morale and morals was not solved by the extensive efforts in the 1940s to upgrade the chaplains' role.

50. Interview with Charles I. Carpenter, 24 August 1992, Medford, Delaware. Carpenter, a Methodist in his civilian career, played semiprofessional baseball and when ordained was active in church youth groups. Picturing himself as a renegade, he was particularly critical of the army chaplaincy and worked after 1941 to create a separate air force corps.

51. Wallace I. Wolverton, "Ethical Judgments of a Group of Air Force Officers," p. 2, box 9, file 3-e, Chaplaincy, President's Committee MSS. See also Charles I. Carpenter, "Testimony," pp. 69, 71, box 6, file: Transcripts of Committee Meetings, 1950–51, President's Committee MSS.

52. Charles I. Carpenter, "Testimony," 13 January 1950, pp. 76, 82, 90, box 6, file: Transcripts of Committee Meetings, 13 January 1950, President's Committee MSS. When he was chaplain at the Air Force Academy from 1958 to 1960, Carpenter opposed several regulations including mandatory chapel. He also fought to have the modernistic chapel built. A number of evangelical groups opposed him, including the present-day

evangelist Pat Robertson's father. The chapel apparently was "too ornate." Carpenter interview.

53. "The Military Chaplaincy: A Report to the President, October 1, 1950," pp. 2, 37–42, box 10, file: Chaplaincy—Publications—Report, President's Committee MSS. The President's Committee reported in 1951 that there were 1,690 chaplains in the armed services: 787 in the army, 456 in the air force, and 447 in the navy. Salaries, travel, construction, and training of chaplains were part of the general military budget. On top of this were appropriated funds for each service for ecclesiastical supplies, altar equipment, communion sets, religious films, and so on. Finally, there were unappropriated funds supplied by base commanders. "Chaplaincy Budget," box 8, file: Budget—Fiscal Years, 1951–52, President's Committee MSS.

54. Charles I. Carpenter, "Morale in the Military," *Virginia Methodist Advocate*, n.d., from clipping file of Charles I. Carpenter. In February 1952 Carpenter joined in with the American Legion to promote its new "Back to God" program, established in 1951. See Carpenter Clipping File. See also Statement by Gen. C. T. Lanham to the assembled committee, p. [40?], box 4, file: Proceedings, President's Committee MSS.

CHAPTER SIX

1. Ormonde S. Brown, "Group Program—First Phase," p. 2, box 107, file: Air University CMD, 1950, Chaplain's Records. There is evidence that the conference occurred in some form. The Brotherhood was active at Maxwell, Tyndall, and other bases. Charles Carpenter says that the group was primarily conservative evangelicals—"storefront" Christians, as he called them. Charles I. Carpenter, Interview.

2. Ray Ginger, *Six Days or Forever? Tennessee v. John Thomas Scopes* (New York: Oxford University Press, 1958), 213–16.

3. Quoted in Don Carlos Ellis and Laura Thornborough, *Motion Pictures in Education* (New York: Thomas Crowell, 1923), 65.

4. "Publicity Statement," 30 October 1950, p. 2, MIS MSS.

5. "Evangelist in Scientist's Role Refutes Old Ideas of Conflict," 19 October 1938, *Buffalo Courier Express*, Clipping File in MIS MSS. Moon was echoing Bryan's distinction between true and false science, although he did not inject political democracy into the mix.

6. James Gilbert, *Perfect Cities: Chicago's Utopias of 1893* (Chicago: University of Chicago Press, 1991). Historian Joel Carpenter credits Houghton with founding the Moody Institute of Science and the American Scientific Affiliation. During World War II, he continues, Houghton pushed the Extension Department to evangelize the armed services. Joel A. Carpenter, introduction to *Enterprising Fundamentalism: Two Second-Generation Leaders* (New York: Garland, 1988).

7. J. W. Hass Jr., "Irwin A. Moon, F. Alton Everest, and Will H. Houghton: Early Links between the Moody Bible Institute and the American Scientific Affiliation," *Perspectives on Science and Christian Faith* 43 (December 1991): 250–51.

8. F. Alton Everest to Carl F. H. Henry, editor of *Christianity Today*, 13 April 1962, MIS MSS. Wilbur M. Smith, *A Watchman on the Wall: The Life Story of Will H. Houghton* (Grand Rapids, Mich.: Eerdman's, 1951), 145ff.

9. "News Release," [no date but probably early in World War II], pp. 1–2, Press Office, 38th Division, 139th Field Artillery, Camp Shelby, Mississippi, MIS MSS.

10. Typescript of Publicity Handout, n.d., MIS MSS.

11. Werner C. Graendorf, "'Sermons from Science' among the Armed Forces," *Sunday School Times*, 5 December 1943, 935, Clipping File, MIS MSS.

12. Smith, *Watchman on the Wall*, 148.

13. "Publicity Statement," 1949, p. 2, MIS MSS. Even the *Moody Monthly* made occasional efforts at popularizing modern science. In 1945, for example, Irving A. Cowperthwaite wrote an article, "The Marvels of God's Atom," stressing that God's glory in putting atoms together was greater than man's ability to split them.

14. "Spiritual Application," memorandum, n.d. [1949–50?], pp. 2–3, MIS MSS.

15. F. Alton Everest, "Address to the A.S.A.," typescript, 1954, p. 3, MIS MSS.

16. Irwin A. Moon, "Technical Specialists for the Mission Field," *Moody Monthly* 48 (December 1947): 262.

17. [Irwin A. Moon?] to John Raymond, 2 May 1950, MIS MSS. The MIS was, in fact, making a film about the mechanic-missionary called *The Eleventh Hour*—eleventh because of the critical work to be done "in these last days."

18. Moody Institute of Science, *God of Creation*, 1946, MIS MSS.

19. [Writer unknown] to Russell T. Hitt, [1947?], MIS MSS.

20. [Dick?] to Russell T. Hitt, 30 July 1947, interoffice memo, p. 2, MIS MSS. Lawrence Johnston was at Berkeley from 1945 to 1950. He worked on the atomic bomb and had been a research assistant at MIT. In 1950, after he received his Ph.D. in physics, he went on to teach at the University of Minnesota. Eventually he taught at the University of Idaho.

21. Ibid., p. 1.

22. "Sermons from Science," typescript of publicity statement, n.d., p. 4, MIS MSS. "Analysis, 'Voice of the Deep,'" publicity release, n.d., Moody Institute of Science, MIS MSS. The Moody Institute of Science received a grant from the Kresge Foundation to help finance their filmmaking. See Wayne Crew, "Our Laboratory Is a Pulpit," *Moody Monthly* 57 (February 1957): 27. Kresge's contribution was one of the largest the foundation made. Crew noted that the MIS had more than sixty persons on the staff.

23. F. Alton Everest, "Can Christians Be Scientific?" *Moody Monthly*, 47, suppl. (May 1947): 663ff.; F. Alton Everest, *Dust or Destiny* (Chicago: Moody Press, 1949), passim. "'Dust or Destiny' in New Release Form," 30 October 1950, MIS MSS.

24. F. Alton Everest, *Hidden Treasures* (Chicago: Moody Press, 1951), passim. The book publication was "Approved by the American Scientific Affiliation."

25. John C. Whitcomb Jr. to Noel O. Lyons, 21 May 1947, MIS MSS.

26. "Film Showings, January 1947 through October 1948," n.d., n.a., p. 1, MIS MSS. See also Jack Houston, "News about the Moody Bible Institute, Moody Science Films on Television," news release, [1959?], p. 1, MIS MSS. Houston reported in another release that since 1954 thirty films had been produced for the public school curriculum and that they were being used in more than nine hundred school systems throughout the United States. The Kiwanis International in March 1951 published an article urging the use of MIS films for assembly-line workers.

27. In its ten years of existence, the MIS produced eight more science films, about a hundred shorter films, and sixty-nine filmstrips on religion and science. See Crew, "Our

Laboratory Is a pulpit," 24. There were Moody pavilions at the Seattle World's Fair and at the New York World's Fair in the 1960s. See chapter 13.

28. Carpenter interview. The ratio of air force chaplains by faith was the following: Jews, 5 percent; Catholics, 33 percent; and Protestants, 62 percent.

29. Charles I. Carpenter to Chaplain Foster B. Perry, Randolph Air Force Base, Texas, 17 September 1948, box 93, file: Protestant Missions, 1948, Chaplain's Records.

30. Wayne A. Hebert to Robert Constable, 4 February 1949, MIS MSS. Apparently Witherspoon traveled with him on this early trip to observe the effects of the films.

31. Ibid. Carpenter interview.

32. Faith Coxe Bailey, "Reel Science... Wins the Airmen," *Moody Monthly* 49 (July 1949): 774. Hebert to Constable, 4 February 1949, p. 2. MIS MSS.

33. Hebert to Robert Constable, 22 September 1949, pp. 1–4, MIS MSS.

34. Wentworth Goss, Colonel, USAF, to Wayne A. Hebert, 28 November 1949, MIS MSS.

35. Copy of article, "Films Show at Air Base," in *Reading Eagle*, 9 April 1949, and Floyd S. Smith, Chaplain USAF, "Film Presentation, Ninth Air Force Information-Education and Chaplain Program," 3 May 1949, MIS MSS.

36. J. R. Propst to Commanding General, First Air Force, 22 March 1949, box 2, file: Correspondence, Chaplain's Records. The official history of the air force chaplains suggests that the Moody films were the most popular films used by the chaplains. Jorgensen et al., *Air Force Chaplains*, 2:255.

37. Harry A. Johnson, Brig. Gen. USAF, 10th Air Force, to William Culbertson, 29 June 1949, MIS MSS. Character Guidance Council Meeting, "Minutes," 27 June 1949, pp. 1–2, box 96, file: Character Guidance, Chaplain's Records.

38. Anthony Czarnecki, "Air Chaplains in Parley Here," *Chicago Daily News*, 2 July 1949.

39. Carpenter to Director of Public Relations, Moody Bible Institute, 22 December 1949, box 103, file: Society and Organization, Chaplain's Records.

40. Charles Carpenter to E. A. Scott, Moody Bible Institute, 2 March 1950, box 103, file: Society and Organization, Chaplain's Records.

41. Carpenter to R. L. Constable, 5 December 1950, box 103, file: Society and Organization, Chaplain's Records. Carpenter recalled that he took Culbertson, head of the Moody Institute, to Lackland Air Force Base to show him how they employed the Moody science films. Carpenter interview. In fact, it was R. L. Constable, vice president of Moody, and the trip was in early 1951. Charles Carpenter to R. L. Constable, 13 December 1950, box 106, file: Films, Chaplain's Records.

42. Bailey, "Reel Science," 813. Apparently in 1953 Chaplain Glenn Witherspoon worried that the programs might be unacceptable to other religions. Based on a survey he made, he discovered that they were not objectionable. Jorgensen et al., *Air Force Chaplains*, 2:255.

43. Ken Hughes, "Religion and Science Join Forces," *Chaplain* 7 (May–June 1950): 11, 14.

44. *Air Chaplains' Monthly News Letter*, Headquarters, Air Training Command, 1 February 1950, box 2, and J. A. Bruner to Irwin A. Moon, 22 June 1950, box 106, file: Transportation of Persons, Chaplain's Records. That this was more or less an exclusive arrangement is revealed by a general letter sent by Charles Carpenter to various com-

manding generals in the field. Carpenter wrote that "certain religious groups have sought access to Air Force bases and have stated such access has the approval of Headquarters, USAF." The chief chaplain continued that all such approval would be in writing from his headquarters. Each commander should ask to see this permission. Charles I. Carpenter to Commanding General Air Materiel Command, Wright-Patterson Air Force Base, 30 August 1950 (sample letter), box 103, file: Air Force Chaplain Policy, Chaplain's Records.

45. *Air Chaplains' Monthly News Letter,* pp. 26–27, Headquarters, Air Training Command, 1 October 1950, box 2, Chaplain's Records.

46. *Air Chaplains' Monthly News Letter,* pp. 1–3, 1 December 1950, box 2, Chaplain's Records.

47. *Air Chaplains' Monthly News Letter,* Headquarters, Air Training Command, 1 February 1951, p. 2, and 1 October 1951, p. 12, box 2, Chaplain's Records.

48. Ibid., 1 October 1951, p. 12.

49. James A. DeMarco, Colonel, USAF Command, to Chaplain Almus B. Polsgrove, 29 May 1951 (copy), MIS MSS.

50. *Air Chaplains' Monthly News Letter,* Headquarters, Air Training Command, 1 June 1952, box 2, Chaplain's Records.

51. "News from Moody Bible Institute," n.d. [internal evidence indicates 1963], p. 30, MIS MSS. It may be true that the Moody films continued to be used in the military and in particular in the air force, but there is little discussion of their use in the Chaplains' Quarterly Reports after the late 1950s, although there is significant mention before that time. In 1953 F. Alton Everest wrote: "In New Zealand each of these films has been shown to every secondary school student. In England, pioneer work was done in showing the films in military groups and industrial factories; both areas being large users of the films in this country today. In the U.S. military, there are about 1,000 prints of these films in active use in character guidance and other programs." F. Alton Everest, "The Moody Institute of Science," *Journal of the American Scientific Affiliation* 5 (September 1953): 10.

52. Jorgensen et al., *Air Force Chaplains,* 2:255.

53. S. E. McGregor to Jack Houston, 6 March 1965, MIS MSS. McGregor was apparently not an official representative of the Moody Bible Institute but a volunteer who had wanted to show the film. About 1960 the Moody Press Service issued a release on MIS films in the public schools. The report commented that since 1954, thirty films had been produced especially for the science curriculum. These were in active use in nine hundred school systems in the United States. The release concluded that the films had been specially prepared to circumvent suspicions of church-state interference. Jack Houston, "News about Moody Bible Institute," [1960?], p. 1, MIS MSS. The verdict on this film was certainly not all discouraging. In March 1964 the film won a Freedom Foundation award, and the *National Geographic* expressed interest. The idea for the film came in 1954 when Irwin Moon was watching a report on a Russian interpretation of bee behavior that was "anti-Christian and communistic." He decided to make a film that would be an answer. S. E. McGregor to Jack Houston, 6 March [1965?], MIS MSS.

CHAPTER SEVEN

1. Smith, *Watchman,* 34. See also William Clark Duke Jr., "The American Scientific Affiliation and the Creation Research Society: The Creation-Evolution Issue" (Ph.D.

diss., Southern Baptist Theological Seminary, 1982). This interesting work explores the history of the ASA and its move from recent creationism to progressive creationism to theistic evolution, an evolution toward an increasingly modernist position. This position, which he also calls macroevolutionism, posits that God created natural law and that this guides evolution. Hence the Bible is literally true only from a philosophic and moral position. This chapter will discuss the history of the ASA only up through the early 1960s and the serious splits with creation science that propelled it toward a more modernist position. Numbers, *Creationists*, has a superb discussion of various streams of creationist thought and activities. Two very different but interesting books make the strong point that the mass media had a very large impact on the direction of religious and science dialogues. See Moore, *Selling God*, and Burnham, *How Superstition Won and Science Lost*.

2. Duke, "American Scientific Affiliation," pp. 142–43. Everest earned his bachelor of science degree in 1932 from Oregon and his electrical engineering degree in 1936 from Stanford. He wrote several papers on television and other phases of electronics. He also belonged to a number of mainstream professional organizations, the Acoustical Society of America, the American Association for the Advancement of Science, and the Institute of Radio Engineers. See F. Alton Everest, ed., *Modern Science and Christian Faith: Eleven Essays on the Relationship of the Bible to Modern Science by Members of the American Scientific Affiliation* (Wheaton, Ill.: Van Kampen Press, 1948).

3. F. Alton Everest, "The American Scientific Affiliation—the First Decade," address to the sixth annual convention, 30 August 1951, reprinted in *Journal of the American Scientific Affiliation* 3 (September 1951): 36–37. F. Alton Everest, "The American Scientific Affiliation: Its Growth and Early Development," typescript, 1986, box 2, American Scientific Affiliation Papers, Buswell Memorial Library, Wheaton College, Wheaton, Illinois. Hereafter cited as ASA MSS. Several of the original members had previously attempted to found such organizations; for example, John Van Haitsma organized the Nature and Scripture Study Club of Grand Rapids in 1935. George Marsden in his interesting essay "A Case of the Excluded Middle: Creation versus Evolution in America," writes that a high percentage of literalist biblical scientists are engineers by training; in Robert N. Bellah and Frederick E. Greenspahn, *Uncivil Religion: Interreligious Hostility in America* (New York: Crossroad, 1987), 139. This essay is significant for other reasons because it attempts to place modern creation science into a larger history of biblical science. See also George M. Marsden, *Understanding Fundamentalism and Evangelicalism* (Grand Rapids, Mich.: Eerdmans, 1991), for a general discussion of the origins and history of Fundamentalism.

4. Everest to Herbert Butt, 16 October 1941 in box 5, file: Correspondence, March 1941, ASA MSS. For an important history of the relations between science and American Protestantism, see Bozeman, *Protestants in an Age of Science*. Mark Kalthoff has a brief but very imformative history of the ASA up to the early 1960s in his introduction to *Creation and Evolution in the Early American Scientific Affiliation*, xi–xxxix, Creationism in Twentieth-Century America, vol. 10, ed. Ronald L. Numbers (New York: Garland, 1995).

5. Everest, "American Scientific Affiliation—the First Decade," 36. Whatever organizational similarities there might have been, the ASA was concerned not with popularizing the very latest scientific discoveries but with translating a select group of

discoveries into established belief. To a degree, this matches Thomas Kuhn's notion of the function of paradigm work; in other respects it is a caricature of it. See Kuhn, *Structure of Scientific Revolutions.*

6. "Constitution, May 1942," in F. Alton Everest, "The American Scientific Affiliation: Its Growth and Early Development," Appendix 2, ASA MSS.

7. Everest, "American Scientific Affiliation—the First Decade," 27–28. See also Mark A. Kalthoff, "The Harmonious Dissonance of Evangelical Scientists: Rhetoric and Reality in the Early Decades of the American Scientific Affiliation," *Perspectives on Science and Christian Faith* 43 (December 1991): 259–60, on the origins of the ASA.

8. D. G. Hart, "The Fundamentalist Origins of the American Scientific Affiliation," *Perspectives on Science and Christian Faith* 43 (December 1991): 238–48.

9. In a description of deluge geology, Ben F. Allen wrote to F. Alton Everest describing the basic propositions of the philosophy. They include the premises that creation took place within a literal twenty-four-hour-day week of activity; there was no preexisting matter on earth; the deluge should be studied as the "geological cause for the main geological changes since Creation." Ben F. Allen to F. Alton Everest, October 1942, p. 1, box 1, file: Contemporary Organizations—Creation-Deluge Society, Correspondence, ASA MSS. In 1947 Laurence Kulp wrote to Everest that he was distressed by the editorial policy of the *Moody Monthly,* which had just featured two very strident attacks on evolutionary science. Kulp to Everest, 27 October 1947, box 8, file: October 1947, ASA MSS. (An example of such an article came in 1951 in "Science's Shifting Frontiers," *Moody Monthly* 51 (January 1951): 304–5, which argued that a rat's bone structure could be altered in the laboratory: hence an argument against evolution. Joel Carpenter assesses the postwar era as one in which serious splits occurred among evangelicals, particularly during the 1940s and 1950s. Carpenter, introduction to *Enterprising Fundamentalism.*

10. Everest to John Bunyan Smith, 25 August 1945, box 7, file: Correspondence, August 1945, ASA MSS. In one respect the ASA followed in Bryan's footsteps by emphasizing the importance of teaching biblical science to students. A recent article about the ASA suggests that the organization occasionally suffered from financial problems and disputes over amateurism: "The American Scientific Affiliation at 50," *Perspectives on Science and Christian Faith* 43 (June 1991): 73–74.

11. Arthur I. Brown, *Miracles of Science* (Finlay, Ohio: Fundamental Truth Publishers, 1945). These talks used familiar arguments from design and urged scientists to recognize, finally, that their work demonstrated the necessity of a "Supreme Creator" (254). Will Houghton had himself been a popular radio evangelist. Hart, "Fundamentalist Origins of the American Scientific Affiliation," 239.

12. Everest, *Hidden Treasures,* 86. In this same book Everest referred to Harlow Shapley's estimate that man was midway in size between the cosmos and the microscopic universe. See also Everest to Russell D. Sturgis, November 1945, box 7, file: Correspondence, November 1945, ASA MSS.

13. Everest letters, January 1946, box 6, file: February 1946, ASA MSS.

14. Moody did a promotional pamphlet for them in 1942, and in the same year Everest forwarded a number of papers from the Deluge Society to the ASA membership. See box 5, file: Correspondence, October 1941, ASA MSS.

15. Everest to Dr. Chalmers W. Sherwin, 6 May 1944, p. 2, box 6, file: Correspondence, May 1944, ASA MSS.

16. George McCready Price, *The Modern Flood Theory of Geology* (New York: Fleming Revell, 1935). Price organized the Natural Science Foundation in 1946.

17. F. Alton Everest to Peter W. Stoner, 23 February 1944, box 6, file: Correspondence, February 1944, ASA MSS; Everest to Dudley Joseph Whitney, 21 March 1944; Dudley J. Whitney to Everest, 24 March 1944, box 6, file: Correspondence, March 1944, ASA MSS. In the early years of the organization there were frequent acrimonious letters from Whitney as well as public disagreements with him.

18. "Summary of the Annual Convention," [1946], pp. 1, 10, 19, box 3, file: Convention—1946 Reports and Summary, ASA MSS. The original ASA had an executive council that could vote and guide the organization and a general membership without such privileges.

19. Everest, "American Scientific Affiliation," pp. 39–44, ASA MSS.

20. F. Alton Everest to J. Wright Baylor, 24 February 1946, box 6, file: February 1946, ASA MSS.

21. F. Alton Everest to C. Stacey Woods, 22 November 1943, box 5, file: Correspondence, November 1943, ASA MSS.

22. Everest, *Modern Science and Christian Faith*, v. See Kalthoff, "Harmonious Dissonance," passim. The ASA hired an editor from McGraw-Hill to help with revisions and the correction of errors discovered by Laurence Kulp.

23. Edwin K. Gedney, "Geology and the Bible," in Everest, *Modern Science and Christian Faith*, 23ff., 40, 47.

24. Peter W. Stoner, "Astronomy and the First Chapter of Genesis," in Everest, *Modern Science and Christian Faith*, 10–21.

25. Harold Hartzler to Jean Pierre Pressan, 27 November 1953, box 12, file: November 1953, ASA MSS.

26. Chester Stock and John M. Harris, *Rancho La Brea: A Record of Pleistocene Life in California*, 7th ed. (Los Angeles: Natural History Museum, 1992), 1–23ff. Extinct animals found in the tar pits include mammoths, saber-toothed tigers, giant sloths, bison, and several species of large birds.

27. At the time the geological and biological community generally subscribed to one version or another of the nineteenth-century uniformitarian theory of evolution. More recent amendments to evolution (associated with Stephen Jay Gould) have stressed "punctuated equilibria," or long periods of stability marked by times of rapid geological and organic development.

28. F. Alton Everest to Dr. J. Z. Gilbert, 8 November 1944, box 6, file: Correspondence, November 1944, ASA MSS.

29. Everest, "American Scientific Affiliation," 85; J. Laurence Kulp, "Deluge Geology," *Journal of the American Scientific Affiliation* 2, 1 (1949): 1–15. Ronald L. Numbers credits Kulp with a strong early influence on the ASA; see "The Creationists," in *God and Nature: Historical Essays on the Encounter between Christianity and Science*, ed. David C. Lindberg and Ronald L. Numbers (Berkeley: University of California Press, 1986), 405.

30. F. Alton Everest to J. Laurence Kulp, 20 September 1947, pp. 2–3, box 8, file: Correspondence, September 1947, ASA MSS.

31. F. Alton Everest to Executive Council Members, 21 September 1947, pp. 1, 3, box 8, file: Correspondence, September 1947, ASA MSS.

32. F. Alton Everest to Council, 30 March 1948, p. 2, box 8, file: Correspondence, March 1948, ASA MSS. Everest, for one, accepted what he called "radioactive dating."

33. Marion Cordelia Erdman, "Fossil Sequence in Clearly Superimposed Rock Strata," *Journal of the American Scientific Affiliation* 2 (June 1950): 17; Marion Erdman-Barber, "Fossils and Their Occurrence," *Journal of the American Scientific Affiliation* 9 (March 1957): 10.

34. See Marion Cordelia Erdman, "The Paleontology of the Horse," *Journal of the American Scientific Affiliation* 2 (December 1950), passim, and Roy M. Allen, "Eye Witness," *Journal of the American Scientific Affiliation* 2 (June 1950): 18–25.

35. Harold Hartzler to William J. Tinkle, 13 February 1957, box 13, file: Correspondence, February 1957, ASA MSS.

36. F. Alton Everest to J. Frank Cassel, 31 July 1951, box 11, file: Correspondence, July 1951, ASA MSS, and Cassel to Everest, 4 August 1951, box 11, file: Correspondence, August 1951, ASA MSS. A 1955 letter from Irving W. Knobloch, professor at Michigan State, to Everest said it was impossible to find a middle ground: "We cannot write one [a book] frankly endorsing organic evolution or one damning evolution." Knobloch to Everest, 8 March 1955, box 12, file: Correspondence, March 1955, ASA MSS. These were prophetic words for the organization.

37. Russell L. Mixter, ed., *Evolution and Christian Thought Today* (Grand Rapids, Mich.: William B. Eerdmans, 1959), 221. A number of the authors either had earned bachelor of science degrees at Wheaton College or were currently teaching there. The most common place for them to have received Ph.D.s was the University of Illinois.

38. Irving A. Cowperthwaite, "Some Implications of Evolution for A.S.A." *Journal of the American Scientific Affiliation* 12 (June 1960): 12–13; J. Frank Cassel, "The Origin of Man and the Bible," *Journal of the American Scientific Affiliation* 12 (June 1960): 13–16. See also Willard Gatewood Jr., "From Scopes to Creation Science," *Proceedings and Papers of the Georgia Association of Historians*, 1983, 7–9. Gates suggests that the centennial ultimately touched off a very large reaction to Darwinism and the teaching of Darwin in schools. This culminated in a dispute in 1962 in the California State School Board about including creation science in the curriculum.

39. David O. Moberg, "Christian Beliefs and Personal Adjustment in Old Age," *Journal of the American Scientific Affiliation* 10 (March 1958): 11. Moberg joined in 1955; he eventually became editor of the *Journal*. In 1956 he had told the annual convention that sociology could be very valuable in exploring sexual mores; it could be used or misused to support conservative values. See David O. Moberg, "Christian Sexual Mores and Contemporary Social Science," *Journal of the American Scientific Affiliation* 8 (September 1956): 5–9. Increasingly, the *Journal* devoted space to social science considerations. Harold Hartzler to David O. Moberg, 5 February 1961, box 3, file: Correspondence, January–June 1962, ASA MSS.

40. Everest, "American Scientific Affiliation," 144; Walter R. Hearn to S. A. Witmer, 12 February 1960, box 14, file: Correspondence, February 1960, ASA MSS.

41. Letter to the ASA Council," 28 August 1953, pp. 1–3, box 1, file: Constitution, 1953, 1954, ASA MSS. Members of the group included James O. Buswell as well as sev-

eral scientists from Lamont Observatory, Lever Brothers, American Cyanamid Company, and Vitro Corporation.

42. Harold Hartzler to Arthur C. Custance, 17 March 1954, box 12, file: Correspondence, August 1954, ASA MSS.

43. Eugene Nida to [Harold Hartzler?] and John R. Howitt to Harold Hartzler, 9 November 1956, box 13, file: Correspondence, November 1956, ASA MSS.

44. "Proposed Constitution of the ASA," 4 August 1950, pp. 1–2, box 1, file: Constitution, 1949, 1950, 1951, ASA MSS. This was announced in the *Journal of the American Scientific Affiliation* in March 1952.

45. "Proposed Revision," box 1, file: Constitution, 1953, 1954; B. Sutherland to D. Johnson, 17 March 1955, box 12, file: Correspondence, March 1955, ASA MSS.

46. "Summary of Information from the Constitution and By-Laws, 1959," box 1, file: Constitution, 1959, 1961, 1963, 1968, ASA MSS. Walter R. Hearn to Ralph T. Overman, 27 August 1959, box 13, file: Correspondence, 1959, ASA MSS. See Duke, "American Scientific Affiliation," 55.

47. F. Alton Everest to the Executive Council, "Minutes," 31 August 1950, box 23, file: 1941–51, ASA MSS. The Society was mostly made up of ordained ministers and confined its studies to biblical interpretations of theology, church history, and philosophy.

48. Reports of meeting, 25 June 1955, box 2, file: Evangelical Theological Society; "Report by James O. Buswell III, on the 1957 ASA-ETS Joint Meeting," p. 1, box 2, file: Evangelical Theological Society, 1 June–31 December 1957; James O. Buswell to the ASA Liaison Committee, 24 July 1958, box 2, file: Evangelical Theological Society, 1958, ASA MSS.

49. Marion Barnes to F. Alton Everest, March 1945, box 6, file: Correspondence, March 1945, ASA MSS.

50. Everest, "American Scientific Affiliation," p. 126, ASA MSS; Harold Hartzler to L. V. Cleveland, 15 November 1955, box 12, file: Correspondence, November 1955, ASA MSS.

51. John R. Howitt, "The Crisis in the A.S.A.," October 1956, pp. 2, 4, 23, box 12, file: Correspondence, October 1956, ASA MSS. Hartzler responded that the problem was not "a very severe one." Harold Hartzler to John R. Howitt, 30 October 1956, p. 1, ibid.

52. Walter Hearn to Colin Brackenridge, 11 August 1960, box 14, file: Correspondence, August 1960, ASA MSS.

53. Everest, "American Scientific Affiliation," pp. 126–28, ASA MSS. Everest estimated that the losses to the ASA in terms of membership were minimal. However, they included a number of familiar names: Morris, Frank Marsh, William J. Tinkle, John W. Klotz, R. Laird Harris, Edwin Y. Monsma, and Walter E. Lammerts. See also "Report to the Executive Council," 14 May 1964, on relations with the Evangelical Theological Society, box 14, file: Correspondence, 1960, ASA MSS. The anniversary article on the "ASA at 50" in *Perspectives on Science and Christian Faith* argued that the organization had a troubled history with financial problems. It spoke of a "major split" in the early 1960s. The importance of manuscripts denouncing evolutionism is based on an impressionistic reading of the ASA correspondence.

54. Duke in his dissertation on the ASA and creation research sees the evolution of the ASA from antievolution to what he calls macroevolutionism, or those who believe that God, operating through natural laws, guides evolution. This position also tends to separate the Bible from science. See Duke, "American Scientific Affiliation," 43, 63.

55. William J. Tinkle, "The A.S.A. In Retrospect," *Journal of the American Scientific Affiliation* 11 (June 1959): 9.

56. Howard A. Meyerhoff to Russell L. Mixter, 1 June 1951, and John A. Behnke to Harold Hartzler, 24 March 1954, box 1, file: Contemporary Organizations, ASA MSS; Walter R. Hearn to ASA Council, 18 July 1958, box 13, file: Correspondence, July 1958, ASA MSS.

57. F. Alton Everest to Marion Barnes, 11 August 1946, box 7, file: Correspondence, August 1946; F. Alton Everest to Macmillan Publishers, 22 September 1946, box 7, file: Correspondence, September 1946; R. L. De Wilton to F. Alton Everest, 15 October 1946, box 7, file: Correspondence, October 1946, ASA MSS. Hartzler wrote to Mixter in 1956 that the organization wanted a secular press to do the Darwin book, but he feared, after Everest's experience with Macmillan, that they would not succeed. Harold Hartzler to Russell L. Mixter, 3 May 1956, box 12, file: Correspondence, May 1956, ASA MSS.

58. Harold Hartzler to Karl Turekian, 19 April 1955, box 12, file: Correspondence, April 1955, ASA MSS. Hartzler did admit that a number of the ASA members might be considered neoorthodox.

59. Russell L. Mixter to Edward J. Carnell, 9 October 1950, box 10, file: Correspondence, 1950, ASA MSS. Hartzler led a discussion of Velikovsky at the Theology and Science Forum in Los Angeles on 25 March 1950.

60. Harold Hartzler to David O. Moberg, 5 February 1961, box 3, file: Correspondence, January–June 1961, ASA MSS; see also box 1, file: Contemporary Organizations, Christian Association for Psychological Studies, ASA MSS.

61. There were initially plans to publish an attack on Dewey in the second edition of the *Handbook*. Laurence Kulp to F. Alton Everest, 3 September 1949, box 9, file: Correspondence, September 1949, ASA MSS.

CHAPTER EIGHT

1. Humphrey Doermann, "Shapley Brands 'Worlds in Collision' a Hoax," *Harvard Crimson*, 25 September 1950.

2. Horace Kallen, "Dr. Freud Says It's Compensation," *Humanist*, no. 2 (1950): 54–57. The resemblances between this poem and Matthew Arnold's "Dover Beach" are striking, although Kallen's point is different.

3. Horace Kallen, "What I Believe and Why," in *What I Believe and Why—Maybe*, ed. Alfred J. Marrow (New York: Horizon Press, 1971), 173. See Konvitz, *Legacy of Horace M. Kallen*, passim. This is an excellent exploration of Kallen's ideas about Judaism and pluralism. For a much more recent discussion of the broader issue of Jews (and especially Kallen) in American culture, see David A. Hollinger, *Science, Jews and Secular Culture: Studies in Mid-century American Intellectual History* (Princeton: Princeton University Press, 1996).

4. Horace Kallen, *Culture and Democracy in the United States* (1924) (New York: Arno Press, 1970), 84.

5. Kallen, *Judaism at Bay* (1932), quoted in Konvitz, *Legacy of Horace Kallen*, 28. Kallen's view of the importance of Jewish tradition in the origins of science parallels Finkelstein's ascription of democracy to the same tradition.

6. Horace Kallen, "The Meanings of 'Unity' among the Sciences," talk to the Conference on the Unity of Science, Harvard University, 3–9 September 1939, reprinted in *Educational Administration and Supervision* 26 (February 1940): 89, 96, Horace Kallen Papers, 1902–75, box 74, file 5, American Jewish Archives, Hebrew Union College, Cincinnati, Ohio. Hereafter cited as Kallen Archives. Horace Kallen, "Democracy's True Religion," *Saturday Review of Literature* 34 (28 July 1951): 7, 29; Kallen, "What I Believe and Why," 144–45. In this article published after World War II, Kallen argued that dogmatism had destroyed Soviet science by suppressing genetics, relativity theory, and quantum mechanics (159).

7. Horace Kallen to Mrs. L. Schiller, [1941?], box 46, file 840, Horace Kallen Manuscripts, RG 317, Yivo Institute, New York, New York. Hereafter cited as Kallen MSS. Kallen to Laura Dale, 29 November 1941, box 3: file 33, Kallen MSS.

8. Kallen, "Democracy's True Religion," 29.

9. For this correspondence, see box 15, file 225, Kallen MSS.

10. "Curriculum Vitae," Immanuel Velikovsky, 23 June 1941, box 47: file 867, Kallen MSS. In his curriculum vitae Velikovsky notes that he brought a manuscript with him from Palestine titled, "A New Interpretation of Dreams Dreamed by Freud" (elsewhere titled "Freud and His Heroes"), and in 1941 he wrote "Chaos and Genesis" and "The Historical Oedipus" while in New York. The manuscript "Freud and His Heroes" was eventually published in part in 1960 as *Oedipus and Akhnaton*.

11. This original manuscript concerned Freud, psychoanalysis, and Freud's interest in Judaism.

12. Immanual Velikovsky to Horace Kallen, 11 December 1964, p. 2, box 30, file 9, and Velikovsky to Kallen, 22 November 1955, p. 2, box 30, file: 9, Kallen Archives. This second letter was in response to a note from Kallen suggesting that Velikovsky engage in "less controversial fields."

13. Kallen to Oxford University Press, 7 August 1944, pp. 1–2, box 47, file 867, Kallen MSS.

14. Horace Kallen, "Shapley, Velikovsky and the Scientific Spirit," June 1970, p. 5, box 73, file 1, Kallen MSS.

15. Ibid., p. 9.

16. Harlow Shapley to James Putnam, 25 January 1950, box 221C, file: Macmillan, Shapley MSS.

17. Horace Kallen to Harlow Shapley, 23 May 1946, box 30, file 1, Kallen Archives, and Immanuel Velikovsky to Harlow Shapley, 31 March 1947, box 22e, file: Immanuel Velikovsky, Shapley MSS.

18. Horace Kallen to Immanuel Velikovsky, 31 May 1946, box 47, file 867, Kallen MSS. Elsewhere Kallen recounted that they had approached Shapley because he was a "known libertarian." Yet Kallen repeated Sydney Hook's accusation that Shapley really supported liberty only for "the communist variety of totalitarianism." In effect Kallen was attempting to explain what he believed was an irrational reaction on Shapley's part, a totalitarian closing off of discussion of a theory he believed might be true. See Kallen, "Shapley, Velikovsky, and the Scientific Spirit," p. 8, Kallen MSS.

19. Immanuel Velikovsky to Harlow Shapley, 31 March 1947, box 22e, file: Immanuel Velikovsky, Shapley MSS.

20. Duane Leroy Vorhees, "The 'Jewish Science' of Immanuel Velikovsky: Culture and Biography as Ideational Determinants" (Ph.D. diss., Bowling Green University, 1990), 454, 458. This is an interesting and informed dissertation about Velikovsky by an admirer.

21. Kallen, "Shapley, Velikovsky and the Scientific Spirit," p. 2, Kallen MSS.

22. Hook, *Out of Step*, 389ff., and unpublished paper by Barbara L. Welther, "Political Activity at Harvard College Observatory in the Shapley Era (1921–1952): Controversy and Consequences," 1994. A good brief sketch of Shapley's career is contained in Bart J. Bok, "Harlow Shapley, November 2, 1885–October 20, 1972," *Biographical Memoirs* (National Academy of Science) 49 (1978): 241–91. That Hook injected anticommunism into this dispute suggests that the earlier split between the Conference on Science, Philosophy, and Religion and the Committee on Cultural Freedom may have been motivated partly by politics. There is no direct evidence for this conclusion, although members of the conference during the 1950s tended to be somewhat less anticommunist than Hook and his allies.

23. Bok, "Harlow Shapley," 257. Shapley worked to bring refugee scientists from Nazi-occupied countries to the United States during the war. He also helped to found UNESCO. See Owen Gingerich, "Harlow Shapley," manuscript of entry in the *American National Biography*, forthcoming.

24. Harvey Breit, "Talk with Mr. Velikovsky," *New York Times Book Review Section*, 2 April 1950, 12. This article was published after the controversy began.

25. Immanuel Velikovsky, *Worlds in Collision* (New York: Macmillan and Doubleday, 1950). Velikovsky did not appear to be acquainted with a similarly titled science fiction story by Edwin Balmer, *When Worlds Collide*, published in 1933. Letter, James Putnam to Immanuel Velikovsky, 16 May 1950, quoted in Vorhees, "Velikovsky," 664. In some respects this science fiction story parallels Velikovsky's work. Two planets invade the solar system; one will smash into Earth and the other offers a haven for a new human history. In other words, God destroys and recreates. There are Adam and Eve characters and a spaceship called "the Ark," designed to carry a few humans to the new world. This fantastic retelling of the Bible story from Genesis through Joshua in effect reverses the story, placing Eden in the future. It thus conflates end time with beginning time and substitutes planetary collision for Noah's flood. See Edwin Balmer and Philip Wylie, *When Worlds Collide* (New York: Frederich A. Stokes, 1933). Hollywood science fiction producer George Pal made a film of this story in 1952.

26. Fulton Oursler, "Why the Sun Stood Still," *Reader's Digest* 56 (March 1950): 148.

27. Ibid., 140–48.

28. Harlow Shapley to Macmillan Publishers, 18 January 1950, box 21c, file: Macmillan, Shapley MSS.

29. James Putnam to Harlow Shapley, 24 January 1950, box 21c: file: Macmillan, Shapley MSS.

30. Vorhees, "Velikovsky," 615, 125.

31. Harlow Shapley to George Brett, 9 February 1950, p. 1, box 21c, file: Immanuel Velikovsky, Shapley MSS. Vorhees, "Velikovsky," 590, 596. Shapley was Payne-

Gaposchkin's mentor at Harvard. Of him she wrote, "A generous supporter, a stimulating companion, he could also be an implacable enemy." See Gaposchkin, *Cecilia Payne-Gaposchkin*, 156.

32. Donald Menzel, "Manuscript Autobiography," p. 591, Donald Menzel Papers, RUG4567.3, Harvard University, Cambridge, Massachusetts. Hereafter cited as Menzel Autobiography MSS. Menzel published a very unkind review of the book in *Physics Today* titled "In the Daze of the Comet."

33. Alfred de Grazia, *The Velikovsky Affair: The Warfare of Science and Scientism* (New Hyde Park, N.Y.: University Books, 1966), 26. Harlow Shapley to T. O. Thackrey, 6 June 1950, p. 1, box 21c, file: Immanuel Velikovsky, Shapley MSS.

34. Gordon Atwater, "Explosion in Science," *Herald Tribune Magazine*, 2 April 1950, 10–11ff. Atwater was instrumental in originating the series of conferences on space travel held at the Planetarium in the early 1950s by Willy Ley and Wernher von Braun.

35. Ibid., 10. The distinction between Velikovsky's religion-science analogy and religious holiday commemorations may not be immediately apparent, but the Russian author had attempted to alter scientific theories, whereas shows on the Christmas star and the Easter sky were attempts to use accepted theories to explain visual anomalies in the Bible.

36. Memoranda to Gordon Atwater from Wayne M. Faunce, 9 March 1950 and 10 March 1950. Charles H. Smiley to Wayne M. Faunce, 4 March 1950, RG 5:4, box 28, file 6, Manuscripts of the Hayden Planetarium, Richard S. Perkin Reference Library, Hayden Planetarium, Museum of Natural History, New York, New York.

37. Gordon Atwater never did find another position in science.

38. Breit, "Talk with Velikovsky," 12.

39. Immanuel Velikovsky, "Answer to My Critics," 51ff.; James Q. Stewart, "Disciplines in Collision," 59ff.; and Immanuel Velikovsky, "Answer to Professor Stewart," 66, all in *Harpers* 202 (June 1951): 51–66.

40. Horace Kallen to Immanuel Velikovsky, 14 June 1951, Velikovsky to Kallen, 27 July 1951, and Kallen to Velikovsky, 17 September 1951, box 56, file 1025, Kallen MSS. Kallen responded that he did not control the curriculum and advised Velikovsky to apply through the regular channels. Velikovsky did not actually teach a course at the New School until 1964. The correspondence during the early 1950s between Kallen and Velikovsky is extensive. Clearly Velikovsky relied on Kallen's advice and paid close attention to his suggestions in publishing subsequent works.

41. Horace Kallen to Immanuel Velikovsky, 2 August 1951, and Kallen to Velikovsky, 17 September 1951, box 56, file 1025, Kallen MSS.

42. Kallen, "Shapley, Velikovsky and the Scientific Spirit," p. 3, Kallen MSS. Sagan's treatment of Velikovsky so infuriated Velikovsky loyalists that one of them, Charles Ginenthal, published a book attacking Sagan. See *Carl Sagan and Immanuel Velikovsky* (New York: Ivy Books, 1990).

43. Immanuel Velikovsky to Horace Kallen, 26 August 1952, and Velikovsky to Kallen, 4 November 1953, box 30, file 8, Kallen Archives.

44. Immanuel Velikovsky to Bernard Cohen, 18 July 1955, Immanuel Velikovsky to Horace Kallen, 1 September 1955, and Velikovsky to Kallen, 22 November, 1955, box 30, file 8, Kallen Archives.

45. Immanuel Velikovsky to Horace Kallen, 30 October 1962, box 30, file 8, Kallen Archives.

46. Horace Kallen to Immanuel Velikovsky, 4 November 1962, box 30, file 8, Kallen Archives; Horace Kallen, "'Jew' and 'Judaist,'" *Jewish Spectator* 28 (November 1962): 7–8.

47. Henry H. Bauer, *Beyond Velikovsky: The History of a Public Controversy* (Urbana: University of Illinois Press, 1984). Bauer provides the basic chronology of Velikovsky interest as well as many of the details of his later reputation. This book itself is an attempt to come to terms with Velikovsky's scientific theories by an author who once viewed them with some sympathy. Immanuel Velikovsky to Horace Kallen, 9 September 1965, box 30, file 9, Kallen Archives. See also de Grazia, *Velikovsky Affair,* passim.

48. Horace Kallen, "Shapley, Velikovsky, and the Scientific Spirit," in *Velikovsky Reconsidered,* by the editors of *Pensée* (Garden City, N.Y.: Doubleday, 1976), 21–30.

49. Horace M. Kallen, *Creativity, Imagination, Logic: Meditations for the Eleventh Hour* (New York: Gordon and Breach, 1973), 97.

50. Immanuel Velikovsky to Horace Kallen, 12 July 1959, 10 September 1959, 4 March 1963, p. 2, box 30, file 8, Kallen Archives. Kallen apparently never again wrote to Shapley directly.

51. Horace Kallen to Immanuel Velikovsky, 9 April 1970, box 30, file 10, Kallen Archives. The precise occasion for this optimism is unknown, although Velikovsky's works attracted considerable attention during this period. Still, Shapley did continue to protest the publication of Velikovsky's writings and their serious consideration. During this time Kallen served on the board of the Foundation for Studies of Modern Science at Princeton, devoted to publishing on Velikovsky's theories; box 55, file 3, Kallen Archives.

52. Carl Sagan, "An Analysis of 'Worlds in Collision,'" in *Scientists Confront Velikovsky,* ed. Donald Goldsmith (Ithaca: Cornell University Press, 1977), 43–93. Several of the articles in this book were based on papers presented to the AAAS in 1974.

53. Immanuel Velikovsky, *Stargazers and Gravediggers: Memoirs to "Worlds in Collision"* (New York: William Morrow, 1983). In this work Velikovsky cedes nothing to his critics, claiming they were, to a person, completely wrong in their science.

54. Velikovsky, *Stargazers,* 202. In thinking about a lawsuit against Shapley, Velikovsky consulted Arthur Garfield Hays, the lawyer for Sacco and Vanzetti. It is very possible that Kallen suggested him.

55. Kallen, "Democracy's True Religion," passim.

56. Horace Kallen, "Lecture Notes: On the Role of Religion in Society," at Cornell, 13 November 1967, pp. 15ff., box 69, file 12, Kallen Archives.

57. "Interview of Dr. Immanuel Velikovsky," WHRB, Cambridge, Mass, 18 February 1972, p. 4, box 30, file 10, Kallen Archives.

58. Fulton Oursler, *Lights along the Shore* (Garden City, N.Y.: Hanover House, 1954), 178–79. See also Velikovsky's account of the hostility of German churches on exactly these grounds, in *Stargazers and Gravediggers,* 281–82. See Robert McAulay's important piece "Velikovsky and the Infra-structure of Science: The Metaphysics of a Close Encounter," *Theory and Society* 6 (November 1978): 313–42. In this excellent article, McAulay makes the point that catastrophism has been much more important to Fundamentalism, with its short, violent history of the world as related in the Bible, than

uniformitarianism, which is compatible with liberal Christianity and the gradual progress of the world toward the kingdom of God on Earth.

59. See, for example, Kenneth L. Feder, "The Challenge of Pseudo Science," *Journal of College Science Teaching* 15 (December 1985–January 1986): 180–86; Burnham, *How Superstition Won and Science Lost;* Michael Polyani, "The Republic of Science: Its Political and Economic Theory," in *Criteria for Scientific Development: Public Policy and National Goals,* ed. Edward Shils (Cambridge: MIT Press, 1968); Nachman Ben-Yehuda, *Deviance and Moral Boundaries: Witchcraft, the Occult, Science Fiction, Deviant Sciences, and Scientists* (Chicago: University of Chicago Press, 1985); Gardner, *In the Name of Science;* and Holton, *Science and Anti-science.* In 1969 Erich von Daniken published a work that drew heavily on Velikovsky and cited the Bible for traces of extraterrestrial visitors. See his *Chariots of the Gods? Unsolved Mysteries of the Past,* trans. Michael Heron (London: Souvenir Press, 1969).

CHAPTER NINE

1. I am indebted to Douglas Gomery for pointing out the existence of these films at an early stage in my research. These productions also contain vague elements of some of Capra's serious film characters—in particular the practical, commonsense character played by Richard Carlson in *The Strange Case of Cosmic Rays.*

2. Paul Giles, *American Catholic Arts and Fictions: Culture, Ideology and Aesthetics* (Cambridge: Cambridge University Press, 1992). Giles has an interesting discussion of the Catholic influence on the American arts and its artists. His discussion of Capra, however, is very brief.

3. Frank Capra, "Manuscript Autobiography," p. 23, Frank Capra Collection, Cinema Archives, Wesleyan University, Middletown, Connecticut. Hereafter cited as Capra MSS.

4. Joseph McBride, *Frank Capra: The Catastrophe of Success* (New York: Simon and Schuster, 1992), 561ff.

5. Frank Capra, "Chronology of 'The Trial,'" box 35, file: "The Trial," Capra MSS.

6. Frank Capra, "The Strange Case of the Cosmic Rays: A Scientific Detective Story," p. 1, box 24, file: Film Projects Series, Strange Case of Cosmic Rays, 1950. See also Charles Newton to Frank Capra, 29 September 1950, in which the Cal Tech official talks about continuing efforts to organize finances for the film on cosmic rays; box 19, file: Film Projects, Careers for Youth, Correspondence, 1950–51, Capra MSS. Capra eventually prepared several scripts promoting the university as a place to learn physical, moral, and spiritual values.

7. McBride, *Frank Capra,* 612. See also Charlie Stearns to Capra, 9 June 1950, box 24, file: Film Projects Series, "The Strange Case of the Cosmic Rays," Capra MSS.

8. Neal Gabler, *An Empire of Their Own: How the Jews Invented Hollywood* (New York: Crown, 1988). For a different interpretation see Jeffrey Richards, "Frank Capra and the Cinema of Populism," *Film Society Review* 7 (February and March–May 1972): 38–46, 61–71. Richards stresses the commonsense, antielitist and anti-intellectual aspects of Capra's 1930s heroes. McBride calls Capra a "Born Again Catholic" in this period. McBride, *Frank Capra,* 618. See also James Terence Fisher, *The Catholic Counterculture in America, 1933–1962* (Chapel Hill: University of North Carolina Press, 1989).

9. "N. W. Ayer Television History," box 2898, N. W. Ayer Company records, New York, New York. Hereafter cited as Ayer MSS. McBride, *Frank Capra*, 617. Capra had returned to the Catholic Church in the 1950s.

10. Frank Capra, *The Name above the Title: An Autobiography* (New York: Macmillan, 1971), 440.

11. Interview with Don Jones, 25 March 1994, New York, New York. Jones relates that he more or less fell into the position of Ayer's in-house producer because he was enthusiastic about the project. See also William E. Haesche Jr., "Our New Science TV Series Performs a Public Service," *Bell Telephone Magazine* 36 (spring 1957): 5–16. Haesche relates that Harry Batten, chairman of the Ayer agency, and Bartlett T. Miller, of the AT&T public relations department, drew up guidelines for the series in October 1951. These included a stress on authenticity, interest, universality, and quality, and "they must not risk offending the normal viewer." This might be translated as trying to avoid offending the normal religious views of the audience.

12. Capra, "Manuscript Autobiography," p. 1425, Capra MSS. Somewhat later Capra had difficulty getting releases from scientists associated with the films. Apparently "they are concerned about possible criticism from educators that they have sold their souls to the business world. "Mabel Walker Willebrandt to Frank Capra, 17 May 1957, box 16a, file: Correspondence, 16–17 May, Capra MSS.

13. "Transcript of interview with James Hanna," former head of Radio and Television Department, N. W. Ayer, 2 May 1988, Ayer MSS.

14. Capra, "Manuscript Autobiography," p. 1433, Capra MSS. Capra recounts his speech in slightly different words in his autobiography *Name above the Title*, 442.

15. Haesche, "Our New Science TV Series," 9. At the same time Capra was negotiating with the State Department to make an "anticommunist film," as well as attempting to get the foreign service to adopt Bishop Fulton J. Sheen's telecasts for broadcast abroad. Frank Capra to Bishop Fulton J. Sheen, 23 August 1942, box 36, file: "Peace with Freedom," Capra MSS.

16. Donald King Dunaway, *Huxley in Hollywood* (New York: Harper and Row, 1989), 274, 199. See contracts of Ley and Huxley, box ATT-4, files: Writers: Willy Ley and Aldous Huxley, Ayer MSS.

17. Aldous Huxley to Julian Huxley, 25 January 1953, in *Letters of Aldous Huxley*, ed. Grover Smith (New York: Harper and Row, 1969), 663.

18. "Our Mr. Sun," script by Aldous Huxley, 1953, passim, box 18, Capra MSS.

19. Donald H. Menzel, *Our Sun*, Harvard Books on Astronomy (Philadelphia: Blakiston, 1949), 315.

20. Donald Menzel, "Manuscript Autobiography," pp. 661ff., Menzel Autobiography MSS.

21. Donald Jones to Donald Menzel, 21 February 1953, box: "Our Mr. Sun," file: "Our Mr. Sun": Correspondence with Donald Jones, papers of Donald H. Menzel, RUG 4567.17, Harvard University Archives, Harvard University, Cambridge, Massachusetts. Hereafter cited as Harvard Menzel MSS.

22. Summary of comments [by Don Jones] by Warren Weaver, 25 February 1953 and 7 March 1953, and Warren Weaver to Don Jones, 27 February 1953, p. 5, box 18, file: "Our Mr. Sun," Comments on Script, March 1953, Capra MSS.

23. Otto Struve to Don Jones, 9 March 1953, and "Summary of Meeting with

Struve, 16 March 1953," box 18, file: "Our Mr. Sun," Comments on Script, March 1953, Capra MSS.

24. Frank Capra, "Our Mr. Sun," second draft, 4 February 1953, pp. 83–84, box 18, file: Film Projects Series, "Our Mr. Sun" Scripts, Capra MSS.

25. Don Jones, "Memo of Conversation with Walter Roberts, 22 February 1953, 4 March 1953," p. 7, and "Comments of Walter O. Roberts, 28 February on Second Draft of the Script," p. 6, box 18, file: Film Projects Series, "Our Mr. Sun," Comments on Script, February, 1953, Capra MSS.

26. Capra, "Our Mr. Sun," second script, p. 15, and Donald H. Menzel, "Criticism of 'Our Mr. Sun,' Second Draft," 27 February 1953, p. 1, and 4 March 1953, p. 7, box, "Our Mr. Sun," file: "Our Mr. Sun" Correspondence, Harvard Menzel MSS.

27. "The Canticle of the Creatures," in *St. Francis at Prayer* (New York: New York City Press, 1990), 42–43.

28. Capra, "Our Mr. Sun," second draft, pp. 102–3, box 18, file: Film Projects Series, "Our Mr. Sun" Scripts, Second Draft, 4 February 1953, Capra MSS.

29. Menzel, "Criticism of 'Our Mr. Sun,' Second Draft," 4 March 1953, pp. 23–24, box: "Our Mr. Sun," file: "Our Mr. Sun" Correspondence, Harvard Menzel MSS.

30. Frank Capra to Don Jones, teletype, 10 March 1953, box 18, file: Film Projects Series, "Our Mr. Sun," Comments on Script, April–June 1953, Capra MSS.

31. Undated fragmentary statement about objections to religious content, n.d., [never sent?], pp. 12–13, box 19, file: "Our Mr. Sun," Fan Mail, 1956–65, December–March, Capra MSS.

32. Don Jones to Menzel, 15 March 1956, and Don Jones to Menzel, 6 February 1946, box: "Our Mr. Sun," file: Donald Jones, Harvard Menzel MSS.

33. Donald Jones interview.

34. Frank C. Baxter was an English professor at the University of Southern California. He conducted a televised course on Shakespeare as well as a series on literature in 1954 called "Then and Now."

35. "Our Mr. Sun" shooting script, box ATT-2, file: Scene-by-Scene Breakdown, "Our Mr. Sun," Ayer MSS. "Continuity for 'Our Mr. Sun,'" pp. 97–98, box ATT-6, Ayer MSS.

36. Frank Capra, "'Our Mr. Sun,' Continuity," passim, box ATT-6, Ayer MSS.

37. N. W. Ayer to Frank Capra Productions, 20 August 1954, p. 3, box ATT-5, file: Contracts—Production Firm—"Hemo," Ayer MSS.

38. "'Our Mr. Sun,'Viewer Survey," box 19, file: Viewer Surveys, pp. 1–3, Capra MSS.

39. William Haesche Jr. to Frank Capra, 23 December 1957, regarding results of Nielsen survey, box 17, file: Correspondence, Capra MSS. "Our Mr. Sun," viewer surveys, box 19, file: Viewer Surveys, 1956–58, Capra MSS. "Ayer News File," 17 December 1956, p. 8, Ayer MSS.

40. Irwin A. Moon to Frank Capra, 23 November 1956, and Capra to Moon, November [1956?], box 19, file: "Our Mr. Sun," Correspondence, August–November 1956, Capra MSS.

41. Award materials in box 17, file: July 1957, Capra MSS. Capra also received the award for *Hemo the Magnificent,* the second work in the series.

42. Ralph Bowen to Frank Capra, 3 October 1956, box 26, file: "The Strange Case of the Cosmic Rays," Correspondence, 1954–62, Capra MSS.

43. "Hemo the Magnificent," Comments by Science Board, summarized 3 October 1956, box 22, file: Film Projects Series, "Hemo the Magnificent," Comments, Capra MSS.

44. Frank Capra Productions, *Hemo the Magnificent*.

45. "Hemo the Magnificent," Continuities, Reel Four, Part A, 27 January 1957, pp. 84–85, box ATT-6, file: Loose Continuities, Ayer MSS.

46. Father James Keller to Capra, 1 May 1957, and Capra to Keller, 8 May 1957, box 19, file: Fan Mail, Capra MSS. Keller's relationship to other figures in this book is fascinating. He was a good friend of Fulton Oursler's, for example. His organization gave a Christopher award to Jacques Maritain. Unlike the movie censorship board in Hollywood, which generally tried to excise flagrant attacks on standard morality and religion from movies, the Christophers attempted to promote popular culture that was sensitive to Christian (and Catholic) ideals. See Richard Armstrong, *Out to Change the World: A Life of Father James Keller of the Christophers* (New York: Crossroad, 1984). The inscription on the medallion read: "Better to Light One Candle Than to Curse the Dark."

47. Jeanne Curtis Webber, "Science Enlists the Capra Genius," *Sign: National Catholic Magazine* 36 (June 1957): 19. Webber wrote other articles for Catholic periodicals including *Catholic Digest* and *Columbia*.

48. Rev. P. H. Yancey, S.J., to Capra, 10 June 1957, and Capra to Yancey, [10?] June 1957, box 16a, Correspondence, 1–15 June 1957, Capra MSS. The Albertus Magnus Guild was named after the Catholic saint who the teacher of Thomas Aquinas. The Guild met annually during the AAAS meetings and published a Guild journal with eight issues a year. The Guild held a conference in 1947 at the College of St. Thomas in St. Paul to dedicate a new science building. Papers given at the conference and published later suggest that Catholics as well as Protestants had their problems of reconciliation. The published account speaks of the neutrality of science—its nonintrusion into religious questions. A 1953 conference sponsored by the group was deeply concerned about the relationship of traditional Aristotelian philosophy and modern science. Were they compatible, asked the scientists? The answer was decidedly yes. Hugh Stott Taylor, *Science in the Modern World*, Aquinas Papers no. 9 (St. Paul: College of St. Thomas, 1948), passim, and William H. Kane, *Science in Synthesis: A Dialectical Approach to the Integration of the Physical and Natural Sciences*, Albertus Magnus Lyceum for Natural Science (Saint Paul, Minn.: Aquinas Library, Dominican College of St. Thomas Aquinas, 1953), passim.

49. Patrick Yancey, S.J., to Frank Capra, 10 June 1957, box 16a, file: Film Projects Series, 1–15 June 1957, Capra MSS; Pope Pius XII, "Humani Generis," in Claudia Carlen, ed., *The Papal Encyclicals, 1939–1958*, vol. 4 (Raleigh, N.C.: McGrath, 1981), 181. In 1956 and 1957 only about 2 percent of National Science Foundation fellowships went to Catholic college graduate students—a measure of the problem that the Albertus Magnus Guild hoped to overcome. See Rodney Stark, "On the Incompatibility of Religion and Science: A Survey of American Graduate Students," *Journal of the Society for the Scientific Study of Religion* 3 (fall 1963): 5.

50. Ed Gannon to Frank Capra, 2 June 1957, box 16a: file: Correspondence, 1957, 1–15 June 1957, Capra MSS. Gannon apparently lived in Vista, California, and had been inspired to write to Capra after reading the Webber piece in the *Sign*. The reference to "candle lighting" in the letter is probably an allusion to the Christophers' motto.

51. Frater Irvin Tye, OFM, to Frank Capra, 8 November 1957, box 19, file: "Our

Mr. Sun," Correspondence, Capra MSS. In the Capra manuscripts, the correspondence about religion is almost entirely from and to Catholics. Whether this is because Capra saved only this correspondence or whether primarily Catholics responded to the messages of the films is impossible to determine. It is undoubtedly true that Webber's piece stimulated interest in the science series among Catholics, however.

52. Richard Carlson also starred in the 1953 television production *I Led Three Lives* as the anticommunist FBI informer.

53. "The Strange Case of Cosmic Rays," revised script, 25 February 1955, 22 March 1955, 4 May 1955, 11 May 1955, October, 1955, passim, box 24, file: Film Projects Series: "Strange Case of the Cosmic Rays," Scripts, Capra MSS.

54. "Comments on 'The Strange Case of the Cosmic Rays' from the Scientific Standpoint," pp. 1–2, box 25, file: Scientific Comments, 3 October 1956, Capra MSS.

55. Frank Capra to Ralph Bowen, 15 October 1956, p. 6, box 25, file: Scientific Comments, 3 October 1956, Capra MSS. The beginning used the scientists' formulation: "The Bell Telephone System brings you one of a series of programs on science . . . man's effort to understand Nature's Laws."

56. "The Strange Case of Cosmic Rays," continuity script, pp. 93–94, box ATT-6, Ayer MSS.

57. Press releases, box 26, file: Press Reviews, 11 November 1957, Capra MSS.

58. Frank Capra to Janet Tyler, 14 April 1958, box 27, file: Correspondence, 1958, April–December, Capra MSS. "The Unchained Goddess," continuity script, pp. 92–93, box ATT-7, Ayer MSS.

59. Ralph Bowen to Capra, 3 March 1958, box 27, file: Correspondence, 1958, January–March, Capra MSS.

60. Frank Capra to Bert Allenberg, 12 November 1954, p. 4, box 16, file: Correspondence, 1954, September–November, Ayer MSS. Frank Capra to Harry A. Batten, n.d. [March, 1957?], box 23, file: Fan Mail, Capra MSS.

61. Frank Capra, "Manuscript Autobiography," p. 1442, Capra MSS. Sanford B. Cousins to Frank Capra, 19 March 1958, box 17, file: Correspondence, Film Projects Series, 1958, 10–31 March. See also Harry Batten to Frank Capra, 7 May 1954, box 16, file: Correspondence, 1954, January–June, Capra MSS. Ayer retained substantially the same structure, including the science advisory board, for its later productions. Later Capra was hired to be a consultant on twenty-minute science films for high schools by the Physical Science Study Committee. See Charles Wolfe, *Frank Capra: A Guide to References and Resources* (Boston: G. K. Hall, 1987), 419.

62. Frank Capra, "Manuscript Autobiography," p. 1464, Capra MSS. An estimate of the numbers of students in United States schools who saw at least one of the science series films follows:

	Elementary	Secondary	College
Number	1,895,000	2,970,000	540,000
Percentage	7.3	37.3	22.7

"Estimated Number of Students . . . ," box: "'Our Mr. Sun' Correspondence," file: 1956–63, Harvard Menzel MSS.

63. Frank Capra to Frank Baxter, 30 November 1961, box 19, file: Correspondence, "Our Mr. Sun," 1957–62, Capra MSS.

64. In notes for the proposed Martin-Marietta science film for the New York World's Fair, Capra remained an unrepentant apostle of religious interpretations of science. His proposal repeated many of the elements of the Bell series, from the skeptic questioning science to the notion that research was a form of prayer. Frank Capra, "Notes on Martin-Marietta Science Film for New York World's Fair," 14 January 1964, box 36, file: "Rendezvous in Space," Capra MSS.

CHAPTER TEN

1. Bruce Levenstein, "Public Understanding of Science in America, 1945–1965" (Ph.D. diss., University of Pennsylvania, 1987), passim. Besides Vannevar Bush's and Conant's works, there were extensive public discussions of the role of science, particularly in respect to public funding. See, for example, President's Scientific Research Board, *Science and Public Policy,* a report to the president by John R. Steelman, 5 vols. (Washington, D.C.: Government Printing Office, 1947).

2. Levenstein, "Public Understanding of Science," 90–111, 142–50.

3. Boyer, *By the Bomb's Early Light,* 229–40. Boyer discusses the rise of apocalyptic thinking around development of atomic weaponry.

4. Quoted by Donald Menzel in a draft of a lecture, n.d., box 1, file: Paul Blanchard, · Donald Menzel UFO Papers, American Philosophical Society, Philadelphia, Pennsylvania. Hereafter cited as UFO MSS. Menzel argued that this form of sociological science fiction blossomed after World War II.

5. Millikan, *Evolution in Science and Religion,* 86.

6. Franklin Loehr, Pamphlet of the Religious Research Foundation, passim, box: Meeting—O, file: Religious Research Foundation, papers of the Institute on Religion in an Age of Science, Chicago Center for Religion and Science, Chicago, Illinois. Hereafter cited as IRAS MSS. See also Ted Peters, *UFO's—God's Chariots? Flying Saucers in Politics, Science, and Religion* (Atlanta: John Knox Press, 1977).

7. Earlier UFOs had been seen in the 1890s in the Midwest and California. These were generally seen to be slow-moving airships. The modern versions moved much more quickly. David Michael Jacobs, *The UFO Controversy in America* (Bloomington: Indiana University Press, 1975), 5.

8. Jacobs, *UFO Controversy,* 57. Keyhoe's tactic in writing of the flying saucer issue was to dwell on the potentially hostile purposes of saucers. At the same time, he frequently implied that the air force knew much more than it released to the public but withheld the knowledge for fear of causing panic. Donald E. Keyhoe, *Flying Saucers from Outer Space* (New York: Henry Holt, 1953).

9. Jacobs, *UFO Controversy,* 52. James E. McDonald, "Science in Default: Twenty-one Years of Inadequate UFO Investigations," in *UFO's—a Scientific Debate,* ed. Carl Sagan and Thornton Page (Ithaca: Cornell University Press, 1972), 53ff.

10. Lynn E. Catoe, *UFO's and Related Subjects: An Annotated Bibliography* (Washington, D.C.: Library of Congress, 1969), iii. The contemporary television series *The X-Files* is quite clearly a continuation of the accusation that government has been covering up what it knows about the invasion of extraterrestrials. See Edward U. Condon, *Scientific Study of Unidentified Flying Objects* (London: Vision Press, 1969). Condon's study has an excellent historical summary of the saucer phenomenon.

11. Menzel was working as a consultant for a company called Salisbury Engineer-

ing. It offered to undertake the study for about $80,000 and "to make the saucers come to us." "We expect," they proposed, "to make extensive use of expert consultants under the supervision of Dr. Menzel." Salisbury Engineering Co. to John A. O'Hara, USAF, at Wright Patterson, 31 July 1952, p. 3, box 13, file: Winfield W. Salisbury, UFO MSS. In 1953 Menzel wrote a popular book debunking saucers. Donald Menzel, *Flying Saucers* (Cambridge: Harvard University Press, 1958).

12. Donald Menzel to Lyle G. Boyd, 13 June 1961, pp. 12–14, box 2, file: Lyle Boyd, UFO MSS. Ruppelt wrote a book published in 1956 recommending the expansion of Project Blue Book, not its termination, as Menzel often suggested. Edward Ruppelt, *The Report on Unidentified Flying Objects* (Garden City, N.Y.: Doubleday, 1956). Ruppelt was head of Project Grudge and Project Blue Book. Boyd was a coauthor with Menzel of one of his UFO publications. He worked at the Smithsonian Astrophysical Observatory. McDonald, a meteorologist at the University of Arizona, was one of Menzel's chief antagonists.

13. Donald Menzel, "Manuscript Autobiography," Menzel Autobiography MS; "Bibliography of Donald Menzel," box: Biography and Bibliography, file: DHM Bibliography, 1976, Harvard Menzel MSS.

14. Donald Menzel to T. Townsend Brown, 26 October 1956, box 2, file: Brown, T. Townsend, UFO MSS. Brown was vice president of the new National Investigations Committee on Aerial Phenomena, located in Washington, D.C., and headed by Keyhoe.

15. Donald Menzel to Bill Prinz, 9 March 1964, p. 2, box 12, file: Bill Prinz, UFO MSS.

16. Bill Prinz to Donald H. Menzel, 8 September 1964, p. 2, and 23 December 1964, p. 2, box 12, file: Bill Prinz, UFO MSS.

17. Donald Menzel to Charles A. Maney, 14 February 1962, p. 1, and Maney to Menzel, 28 February 1962, p. 1, box 8, file: M, UFO MSS.

18. Donald Menzel, "Manuscript Autobiography," pp. 670ff., 680–81, Menzel Autobiography MSS.

19. Donald Menzel to Kenneth Heuer, 8 November 1950, box a–i, 1950, file: H, Harvard Menzel MSS. Menzel referred to his sketches as "My Martians." Menzel was only one among a number of science popularizers who battled pseudoscience. Radio station WEVD in New York, for example, broadcast a weekly half-hour show in the early 1950s devoted to debunking such ideas as extraterrestrial UFOs. Edith L. Hamburg to Robert Cole [of the Hayden Planetarium], 1 April 1952, RG 3:2, box 1, file 1, Records of the Hayden Planetarium, Richard S. Perkins Library, American Museum of Natural History, New York, New York. Hereafter cited as Hayden MSS.

20. Virginia Brasington, *Flying Saucers and the Bible* (Clarksburg, W.V.: Saucerian Books, 1963), 14, 53; Morris K. Jessup, *UFO and the Bible* (New York: Citadel Press, 1956), 59. See also Norman W. Pittenger, "Christianity and the Man on Mars," *Christianity Today* 73 (20 June 1956): 747–48. Brasington was a minister from North Carolina in the Church of the Nazarene. Pittenger was professor of Christian apologetics at the General Theological Seminary in New York. Ted Peters, in "UFO's: The Religious Dimension," *Cross Currents* 27 (fall 1977): 261ff., writes that UFOs released the "psychic tension" caused by the modern need for religious vision and its frustration by science. Carl G. Jung argued that people believed in UFOs because they represented psychic fantasies that related to profound archetypical human symbols of order. Jung, *Flying*

Saucers: A Modern Myth of Things Seen in the Skies (London: Routledge and Kegan Paul, 1959), passim. Although much of the speculation about flying saucers focused on secular terror of extraterrestrials or an interest in space travel, much of it had religious overtones. See Condon, *Scientific Study*, 14, and Peters, *UFO's—God's Chariots?* passim.

21. Bryant Reeve and Helen Reeve, *Flying Saucer Pilgrimage* (Amherst, Wis.: Amherst Press, 1957), 158–59. In *Chariots of the Gods?* (1969) Erich von Daniken made a case for the visitation of flying saucers before contemporary times. They were, he claimed, the progenitors of *Homo sapiens.* It is also noteworthy that L. Ron Hubbard, the science fiction writer, organized the religion of Scientology in 1950 around a combination of religion and science fiction. See Leslie Shepard, ed., *Encyclopedia of Occultism and Parapsychology*, 3d ed., 2 vols. (Detroit: Gale Research, 1991), vol. 1, passim.

22. A Gallup poll of 1973 indicated that 51 percent of Americans thought UFOs were real. Eleven percent of respondents claimed to have seen them. Jacobs, *UFO Controversy*, 295.

23. Harold Brown, "Statement," in House Committee on Armed Services, *Unidentified Flying Objects*, 99th Cong., 2d sess., 5 April 1966 (Washington, D.C.: Government Printing Office, 1966), 6004–5. Representative Gerald Ford was one of those congressmen pushing for this hearing.

24. Those invited included J. Allen Hynek, Northwestern University Astronomy Department, James E. Mcdonald, Institute of Atmospheric Physics, University of Arizona, Robert L. Hall, Department of Sociology, University of Illinois at Chicago, Robert M. L. Baker Jr., senior scientist, Systems Sciences Corporation, James A. Harder, associate professor of civil engineering, University of California at Berkeley, and Carl Sagan, Cornell. Donald Menzel to Congressman J. Edward Roush, 24 July 1968, box 13, file: Roush, UFO MSS. The hearings occurred on 29 July 1968.

25. Donald Menzel to Carl Sagan, 11 September 1968, Sagan to Menzel, 5 May 1967, and Menzel to Sagan, 16 June 1967, box 13, file: Carl Sagan, UFO MSS. Carl Sagan to Donald Menzel, 28 October 1968, and Menzel to Sagan, 4 November 1968, p. 2, box 13, file: Carl Sagan, UFO MSS. Sagan did note that he had no good evidence that "strongly" pointed to extraterrestrial spacecraft.

26. Donald Menzel to Edward U. Condon, 19 August 1969, box 3, file: Edward U. Condon, UFO MSS. William Markowitz of the physics department at Marquette University organized a petition against the proposed UFO session in 1968. Walter Orr Roberts to Edward U. Condon, 16 September 1969, box 13, file: Walter Orr Roberts, UFO MSS. The title of Condon's study was *Final Report on the Scientific Study of Unidentified Flying Objects* (New York: Dutton, 1969).

27. Sagan and Page, *UFO's*, xiii, passim.

28. Donald Menzel to Edward U. Condon, 8 February 1967, box 3, file: Edward U. Condon, UFO MSS. Edwards was a newscaster.

29. Donald Menzel, "UFOs—the Modern Myth," manuscript, box 9, file: Menzel, "UFOs—the Modern Myth," UFO MSS. The science fiction literature in the 1950s was very extensive. In 1953, for example, sixteen publishers put out thirty science fiction magazines. Walter Hirsch, "Image of the Scientist in Science Fiction: A Content Analysis," *American Journal of Sociology* 63 (March 1958): 507.

30. For an important discussion of the religiousness of science fiction writing in

America see Robert Reilly, ed., *The Transcendent Adventure* (Westport, Conn.: Greenwood Press, 1985).

31. Peter Nicholls, ed., *The Science in Science Fiction* (New York: Crescent, 1982), 7, passim.

32. Arthur S. Barron, "Why Do Scientists Read Science Fiction?" *Bulletin of Atomic Scientists* 13 (February 1957): 62–65. In a 1948 study, the author relates research done by science fiction publishers indicating that from 30 to 40 percent of readers were professional men; 15 percent were housewives, and the rest were mostly college students, with a sprinkling of high-school students. See Barron, "Growth of Science Fiction and Fantasy Publishing in Book Form," *Publishers Weekly* 154 (25 December 1948): 2466–67.

33. Walter Hirsch, "Image of the Scientist," 506–7.

34. Frederick A. Kreuziger, *Religion of Science Fiction* (Bowling Green, Ohio: Bowling Green State University Popular Press, 1986), 111ff. This book carefully examines science fiction literature and suggests a complex pattern of similarities with religious apocalyptic thought. See also Walter M. Miller, *A Canticle for Leibowitz* (Philadelphia: Lippincott, 1960).

35. Susan Sontag, "The Imagination of Disaster," in *Against Interpretation and Other Essays* (New York: Farrar, Straus, Giroux, 1966), 209–23. This essay explores the recurrent patterns of low-budget science fiction films. As the author concludes, the interest of these films "consists in the intersection between a naive and largely debased commercial art product and the most profound dilemmas of the contemporary situation" (224). See also John Baxter, *Science Fiction in the Cinema* (New York: A. S. Barnes, 1970), 10–11. My own emphasis is somewhat different from that of these two works.

36. Harry Bates, "Farewell to the Master," in *Adventures in Time and Space*, ed. Raymond J. Healy and J. Francis McComas (New York: Random House, 1946).

37. The idea of a "step of destiny," of course, recalls the carefully scripted words spoken by the first human to land on the moon. In George Pal's 1950 film *Destination Moon*, for which von Braun consulted, the first words spoken by a human landing on the moon were: "By the grace of God and in the name of the United States, I take possession of this moon for the benefit of all mankind." Gail Morgan Hickman, *The Films of George Pal* (South Brunswick, N.J.: A. S. Barnes, 1977), passim.

38. Wernher von Braun, "My Faith," *American Weekly*, 10 February 1963, 1.

39. According to Willy Ley, Oberth was the first scientist to speak seriously of developing a space station (1923). The notion had appeared somewhat earlier in the science fiction story of Edward Everett Hale, "The Birch Moon." Willy Ley, *Rockets, Missiles, and Space Travel*, rev. ed. (New York: Viking Press, 1956), 366.

40. Erik Berganst, *Wernher von Braun* (Washington, D.C.: National Space Institute, 1976), 20ff. See also Wernher von Braun, *The Mars Project* (Urbana: University of Illinois Press, 1953). This book worked out the details of a massive expedition to Mars by ten ships and seventy men. In 1960 von Braun's philosophical speculations from the original novel were published.

41. Willy Ley, *The Days of Creation* (New York: Modern Age Books, 1941), 8. In addition to his notoriety as a science popularizer, Ley's religious sympathies may well have recommended him to Frank Capra as a potential writer for his science series. See also biographical material in box 6, file: "Space Travel," Willy Ley Papers, Smithsonian Insti-

tution, National Air and Space Archives, Suitland, Maryland. Hereafter cited as Ley MSS. Chesley Bonestell was a major figure in the visual design of space and planetary exploration. He worked not only for *Collier's* but also for *Life* magazine. See David Houston, "Chesley Bonestell: Space Painter," *Future* 1 (April 1978): 66–75, and Frederick C. Durant, *Worlds Beyond: The Art of Chesley Bonestell* (Norfolk, Va.: Downing, 1983).

42. "General Statement," *Annual Report of the Hayden Planetarium, July 1, 1949–June 30, 1950,* n.p., RG 2:5, box 1, file 3, Hayden MSS. The Planetarium also developed a program called "A Trip to the Moon," shown during the summer of 1950.

43. Willy Ley to Robert P. Haviland, 13 June 1951, RG 1:2, box 1, file 10, Hayden MSS.

44. Hayden Planetarium, *Annual Report, July 1, 1953–June 30, 1954,* p. 1, RG 2:5, box 1, file 3, Hayden MSS. The last symposium occurred in May 1954, before these cautious words were written. None of the speakers at this last meeting appeared to be close to the Ley–von Braun group. Frank H. Forrester to Ann M. Russell, 30 November 1955, RG 1:2, box 1, file 11, Hayden MSS. The Planetarium began to take "reservations" for space travel as a result of these symposia and its display of Chesley Bonestell paintings for the book by Chesley Bonestell and Willy Ley, *Conquest of Space* (New York: Viking Press, 1949).

45. Randy Liebermann, "*Collier's* and Disney Series," in *Blueprint for Space: Science Fiction to Science Fact,* ed. Frederick I. Ordway III and Randy Liebermann (Washington, D.C.: Smithsonian Institution Press, 1992), 137ff. In effect the series was a record of the *Collier's* symposium. See Ernest Stuhlinger and Frederick I. Ordway III, *Wernher von Braun: Crusader for Space* (Malabar, Fla.: Krieger, 1994), 113. Two books resulted from the series, Cornelius Ryan, ed., *Across the Space Frontier* (New York: Viking Press, 1952), and Wernher von Braun, *Conquest of the Moon* (New York: Viking, 1953).

46. Liebermann, "*Collier's* and Disney Series," 144ff. When Disney approached Ward Kimball about films for Tomorrowland, Kimball mentioned the *Collier's* series and the important work of von Braun and Ley. See David R. Smith, "Walt Disney's Trip to Tomorrowland," *Future,* 1 (May 1978): 54–63. Apparently the Disney showing of *Man in Space* came somewhat before President Eisenhower committed the United States to building a space satellite. Disney intended to claim that their show had persuaded the president. Von Braun wrote Disney a quick note asking to "try to have the pitch changed." Otherwise this would undercut the "preparatory work that finally led up to this announcement" and unfairly slight those who had worked so long toward that goal. Wernher von Braun to Ward Kimball, 30 August 1955, box 45, file: Publicity, Wernher von Braun Manuscripts, Library of Congress, Washington, D.C. Hereafter cited as von Braun MSS.

47. David K. Smith, "Walt Disney's Conquest of Space," *Starlog* 3 (May 1978): 32.

48. Wernher von Braun, "Speech to the International Federation for Space Travel," 1952, box 61, file: Speeches and Writings, 1950–53, von Braun MSS. Wernher von Braun, "Space Travel and Our Technological Revolution," *Missiles and Rockets* 2 (July 1957): 75–78. Stuhlinger and Ordway in *Wernher von Braun* comment on the rocket scientist's religiousness.

49. Leibovit Productions, "The Fantasy World of George Pal," PBS video broadcast, 16 September 1989. Bonestell worked on *Destination Moon,* as well as *War of the Worlds, When Worlds Collide,* and *Conquest of Space.*

50. Hickman, *Films of George Pal*, 36ff. Hickman argues that Pal's *Destination Moon* created a whole new science fiction genre that treated the subject intelligently.

51. Bonestell and Ley, *Conquest of Space*. It is difficult to sort out the origin of the various ideas in this film because Ley and von Braun collaborated on a number of projects and shared many of the same ideas. For example, in a letter to Bonestell in 1952, von Braun spoke of "George Pal's project," perhaps alluding to a planned film on his ideas for a Mars launch. Wernher von Braun to Chesley Bonestell, 8 October 1952, box 1, file: 1952, A–Z, von Braun MSS. Chesley Bonestell to Willy Ley, 15 April 1954, box 19, file: Space Travel, Space Station, WVB, Ley MSS. In early 1955 Willy Ley wrote to Bonestell about his assessment of this film and various Disney efforts: "I told George Pal this film is what he should have done but of course he could not without the Disney cartoon talent." Ley to Chesley Bonestell, 21 February 1955, box 45, file: Publications, von Braun MSS. Donald Keyhoe also had some success in turning his work into science fiction film. In 1956 Columbia Pictures released "Earth versus Flying Saucers," based on Keyhoe's book *Flying Saucers from Outer Space* (New York: Holt, 1953); see Jacobs, *UFO Controversy*, 130. Keyhoe founded the National Investigating Committee for Aerial Phenomena in 1956.

52. Joe Adamson, *Bryan Haskin* (Metuchen, N.J.: Directors Guild of America and Scarecrow Press, 1984), 230–31. Haskin dismissed the film as sentimental and accused Pete Freeman of Paramount of imposing the end on it because of "a maudlin relationship with his father." Freeman was coproducer of the film and the son of Y. Frank Freeman, head of the studio.

53. It might be possible to interpret this reconciliation theme as an expression of the willingness of the United States to accept Germans such as Wernher von Braun as heroes.

54. See Hickman, *Films of George Pal*, 87ff., for a description of the production of the film and Paramount's efforts to transform *Conquest* into a television series. In an apparent attempt to capitalize on the film, Willy Ley published a book, *Exploration of Mars*, in June 1956 following the release of the film. In it he notes the split between the two stories of the film and stresses the importance of the technical explanations. Willy Ley, *Exploration of Mars* (New York: Viking Press, 1956), 138ff. Despite the aesthetic failure of *Conquest of Space*, Willy Ley and Albert Hecht organized a new company called Kineo–Graphics to produce special effects, stop-motion action, and various forms of filmed puppets for "science and technical films." Albert Hecht to George Pal, 28 January 1957, box 24, file: Correspondence, Ley MSS.

55. Wernher von Braun to Willy Ley, 11 June 1955, box 45, file: Publications; Wernher von Braun, "Notes for a Speech," Chicago, 9 September 1952, p. 2, box 46, file: Speeches and Writings 1951–55, von Braun MSS. Von Braun was not above popular and speculative statements. As he wrote for inclusion of his *Conquest of the Moon*, "Maybe our expedition will discover a marvelous underground civilization on Mars, far superior or at least strangely different from ours, living completely independent of the enmical [*sic*] conditions on Mars's surface." Von Braun to Connie Ryan, 24 September 1953, box 50, file: "Conquest of the Moon," von Braun MSS.

56. Wernher von Braun, "Science as Religious Activity," in *All Believers Are Brothers*, ed. Roland Gammon (New York: Doubleday, 1969), 256.

57. Wernher von Braun, "Responsible Scientific Investigation," in *The Nature of a*

Humane Society, ed. H. Ober Hess (Philadelphia: Fortress Press, 1976–77), 146. In this same work, see his discussion of the theistic evolution of the eye. In the controversy over creationism, Vernon L. Grose persuaded the California School Board to consider the idea. Of Grose Nicholas Wade wrote: "His views seem to be shared in part by aerospace acquaintances of his such as Wernher von Braun and Apollo astronauts Jim Irwin and Edgar D. Mitchell." See Nicholas Wade, "Creationists and Evolutionists: Confrontation in California," *Science* 178 (17 November 1972): 727.

58. Frank Borman with Robert J. Sterling, *Countdown: An Autobiography* (New York: William Morrow, 1988), 204, 214.

CHAPTER ELEVEN

1. Alfred E. Kuenzli, "Ethical Implications of the Social Sciences," *Educational Theory* 8 (January 1957): 72, copy in box 1, file: Secretary/Treasurer, General Correspondence, 1957, in Papers of the Society for the Scientific Study of Religion, Memorial Library, Marquette University, Milwaukee, Wisconsin. Hereafter cited as SSSR MSS.

2. Andrew M. Greeley, *Unsecular Man: The Persistence of Religion* (New York: Schocken, 1985), passim. Greeley discusses Martin Marty, Peter Berger, Robert Bellah, Robert Nisbet, Langdon Gilkey, Claude Lévi-Strauss, Clifford Geertz, and so on. Each of these thinkers, he concludes, stresses the need for spirit and myth in social construction.

3. Kuenzli, "Ethical Implications of the Social Sciences," 72, box 1, file: Secretary/Treasurer, General Correspondence, 1957, SSSR MSS. England, *Patron for Pure Science,* 258–68. By 1966 the National Science Foundation was beginning to fund projects in all of the social sciences, although grants to the social sciences began in the early 1950s. Sociology was a field that received support later than such areas as economics. See Reagan, *Science and the Federal Patron,* 121.

4. The Society was originally called the Committee for the Social Scientific Study of Religion, then the Committee for the Scientific Study of Religion, and then, in 1956, the Society for the Scientific Study of Religion. In this chapter I will refer to it, despite these various title changes, as the Society.

5. A parallel development of the sociology of science in the 1950s had very different results. Although considerable sociological study of religion pointed to the importance of the spiritual and mythical life of every society, the sociological study of science tended to contradict many of its claims to uniqueness. As the works of Thomas Kuhn, Robert Merton, Michael Polanyi, and many others indicated, science was very much a historical, human endeavor. In this sense sociology leveled the playing field between science and religion. See Robert Merton, *Sociology of Science: Theoretical and Empirical Investigations* (Chicago: University of Chicago Press, 1973), especially the introduction by Norman W. Storer.

6. Bernard Spilka, "Psychologists and Psychology in the Society for the Scientific Study of Religion: An 'Old-Timers' View," unpublished manuscripts supplied by Armand L. Mauss, editor of the *Journal of the Society for the Scientific Study of Religion.* Hereafter cited as Mauss MSS. Walter H. Clark to Benson Y. Landis, 5 January 1963, box 3, file: January–August 1963, SSSR MSS. J. Paul Williams, "This We Intended: A Brief History of the Society," Summary of Proceedings of the SSSR Meeting, 10–11

April 1956, box 42, file: Society for the Scientific Study of Religion, Kallen Archives.

7. James E. Dittes to Charles Y. Glock, "My Recollections," 7 November 1992, p. 7, Mauss MSS. Dittes also suggests that the organization developed because religion was "absent from public campuses" and not treated professionally by private colleges.

8. Walter H. Clark to Rev. Joseph Fletcher, 30 April 1949, box 1, file: General Correspondence on Founding of Society, 1949, SSSR MSS.

9. J. Paul Williams to Dr. and Mrs. Howard Spoerl, 26 April 1949, box 1, file: General Correspondence on Founding of the Society, 1949, SSSR MSS.

10. Samuel Z. Klausner, "Presentation on History of the Society for the Scientific Study of Religion," 7 November 1992, p. 1, Mauss MSS. The Harvard anthropologist Clyde Kluckhohn was also active in these early years. Kluckhohn was at the same time a general adviser on the Frank Capra science film project.

11. Miles Bradbury, "Biodivinity: The Encounters of Religion and Medicine," in *Transforming Faith: The Sacred and Secular in Modern American History*, ed. M. L. Bradbury and James Gilbert (New York: Greenwood Press, 1989), 170–71.

12. R. H. Edwin Espy, *The Religion of College Teachers* (New York: Association Press, 1951), 167. Even as late as 1974, Myer S. Reed Jr. noted that there were strong forces that retarded the study of religion. See Reed, "The Sociology of the Sociology of Religion: A Report on Research in Progress," *Review of Religious Research* 15 (spring 1974). See also Murray G. Murphy, "On the Scientific Study of Religion in the United States, 1870–1980," in Lacey, *Religion and Twentieth-Century American Intellectual Life*, 146. Murphy argues that it was Talcott Parsons's 1937 *Structure of Social Action* that placed the study of religion as well as the theories of Emile Durkheim and Max Weber at the foreground of American sociology.

13. Walter Clark, "Review of Research in the Field of Religious Value and Motivation," April 1950, p. 1, box 1, file: Correspondence on Founding of the Society, 1950, SSSR MSS.

14. Charles Y. Glock, "Remembrances of Things Past; SSSR's Formative Years," p. 8, Mauss MSS.

15. "Report of the 'Business Session' of the 3rd Meeting of the Committee for the Scientific Study of Religion," 21 April 1951, box 1, file: Walter Clark, 1951, and "Memo by James E. Dittes," 15 March 1963, box 3, file: Administrative: Secretary/Treasurer, General Correspondence, January–August 1963, SSSR MSS. This penchant for professionalism is suggested in a letter by Walter Clark regarding the proposal of a paper for the 1953 meeting, "The Place of Discipline in Christian Ethics." Clark wrote, "This sounds like an intriguing subject, my question, however, being whether it might not be rephrased in order to sound more pertinent to Social Science. In our Committee we try to make one of our functions the liaison between religious scholars and social scientists." Walter Clark to [James Adams?], 13 March 1953, box 1, file: Administrative: Secretary/Treasurer, General Correspondence, 1954, SSSR MSS. Prentiss Pemberton was a Baptist clergyman and a close acquaintance of Ralph Burhoe.

16. Glock, "Remembrances of Things Past," p. 7, Mauss MSS. Although Kallen was an active member of the Society almost from its inception, he did not push for sociological studies of religion (Catholicism and Protestant Fundamentalism) that might reveal their pernicious effects—as he had during the acrimony surrounding the Bertrand Russell case during World War II.

17. Fred Berthold Jr., "The Meaning of Religious Experience," *Journal of Religion* 32 (October 1952): 263–64, 270.

18. William Kolb, "The Judaic-Christian Image of Man as a Tool for the Ordering of Social Data," in "Summary of Proceedings of the SSSR Meeting," Chicago, 10–11 April, p. 1, box 42, file: Society for the Scientific Study of Religion, Kallen MSS.

19. Werner Wolff, "Introductory Remarks" to "Minutes of the 10th Meeting of the Committee (Society), box 1, file: Administrative: 16 April 1955, SSSR MSS. From notes at the same meeting, it is clear that other members of the Society had different aims than reconciling science and religion (in favor of religion). For example, at the third session on defining religion, there was considerable disagreement about broadening the concept. Horace Kallen even argued that communism was the manifestation of religious belief. Ibid.

20. Ralph Burhoe to Richard V. McCann, 21 September 1955, p. 2, box 1, file: Administrative: Secretary/Treasurer, General Correspondence, 1955, SSSR MSS.

21. Horace Kallen, "The Modern World, the Intellectual and William James," to New School (mimeograph), 16 December 1959, pp. 16–18, box 73, file 5, Kallen Archives. Kallen was much less enthusiastic about using the organization to further religion. In 1971 he wrote to Allan Eister of the Department of Sociology and Anthropology at Wellesley that he was deeply distressed by the tone of a questionnaire sent to members that seemed to imply a special commitment to religion. "In short," he wrote, "I am *not* interested in delivering the SSR over to non-scientists or to ideas and individuals not controlled by scientific discipline of the most sophisticated sort." In the same letter he criticized H. Richard Niebuhr for the hidden agenda implied in his study of American Protestantism. Kallen to Allan Eister, 29 January 1971, box 42, file 9, Kallen Archives. Kallen wrote to Prentiss Pemberton asking the organization to come up with a better concept of science; heretofore the group had been sloppy and imprecise. Kallen to Pemberton, n.d., box 24, file 26, Kallen MSS.

22. Ralph Burhoe to Prentiss Pemberton, 18 November 1963, box 3, file: September–December 1963, SSSR MSS.

23. Prentiss Pemberton to Ralph Burhoe, 2 December 1963, box 3, file: Correspondence, September–December 1963, SSSR MSS. That Burhoe's push for cosmology was unpopular in the organization is revealed by an angry letter from James E. Dittes to James Adams following the 1963 meeting of the Society. "I frankly thought," he wrote, "that Burhoe's proposals were fantastic and resembled nothing so much as a paranoid system built in air out of forty-year old notions." James E. Dittes to James Adams, 31 October 1963, box 3, file: Correspondence, September–December 1963, SSSR MSS.

24. "Circular," 1959, box 1, file: Administrative: Secretary/Treasurer, General Correspondence, 1959, SSSR MSS.

25. Glock, "Remembrances," p. 7, Mauss MSS. William M. Newman, "The Society for the Scientific Study of Religion: The Development of an Academic Society," 16 October 1973, pp. 25ff., box 7, file: Publications, 1973, SSSR MSS.

26. "Membership list, 1963," etc., in *Newsletter,* vols. 1–4, box 7, file: Publications, Newsletter, SSSR MSS. There was some discussion in 1958 about Erik Erikson's proposal to present a paper on Luther at the upcoming SSSR meeting. James Luther Adams assured Walter Clark that this would not offend Roman Catholics in the organization. But the discussion itself suggests the recognition that the Society was primarily a

Protestant organization. James Luther Adams to Walter Clark, 28 July 1958, box 1, file: Administrative: Secretary/Treasurer, General Correspondence, July–December 1958, SSSR MSS.

27. Walter H. Clark to Werner Wolff, 8 June 1953, box 1, file: Administrative: Secretary/Treasurer, General Correspondence, 1954. Clark suggested approaching the Ford Foundation for funds. Ralph W. Burhoe to Walter H. Clark, 2 May 1956, and Ralph W. Burhoe to James Luther Adams, 5 June 1956, box 1, file: Administrative: Secretary/Treasurer, General Correspondence, 1956. James Luther Adams appears to have opposed a joint publication; Adams to Walter Clark, 28 July 1958, box 1, file: Administrative: Secretary/Treasurer, General Correspondence, July–December 1958, SSSR MSS.

28. Box 1, file: Administrative: Secretary/Treasurer, General Correspondence, 1956, SSSR MSS. An informal ballot was sent out by the group in 1957 to solicit opinions about a journal.

29. "Minutes of Special Meeting of the Council," 10 June 1960, box 2, file: Administrative, January–June 1960, SSSR MSS. James Dittes recalls that the Kaplan Foundation was a controversial group because it was presumed to be "a CIA front." James Dittes, "Untitled Manuscript," 7 November 1992, p. 2, Mauss MSS. Original applications to the Lilly and Danforth Foundations in 1958 had failed. The committee set up to pursue publishing a journal originally wanted Charles Glock as editor. Walter Clark to Ralph Burhoe, 6 October 1958, box 1, file: Administrative: General Correspondence, July–December 1958, SSSR MSS.

30. "Proposal for Establishing a Journal for the SSSR," pp. 1–2, box 1, file: Annual Meeting, 1960, SSSR MSS.

31. Prentiss Pemberton, "Historical Timeliness and the Scientific Study of Religion," 27 October 1960, p. 1, box 2, file: Administrative, January–June 1960, SSSR MSS.

32. Ralph Burhoe, "Ralph Burhoe's Recollections on the Origins of the Society for the Scientific Study of Religion" (typescript), 24 October 1992, p. 3, Mauss MSS.

33. William Kolb, "Images of Man and the Sociology of Religion," *Journal of the Scientific Study of Religion* 1 (October 1961): passim, and Talcott Parsons, "Comment on Professor Kolb's Reply," *Journal of the Scientific Study of Religion* 2 (April 1962): 219.

34. Peter Berger, "A Sociological View of the Secularization of Theology," *Journal of the Scientific Study of Religion* 6 (spring 1967): 16.

35. Walter Clark to G. Harold Duling, 12 May 1958, box 1, file: Administrative: Secretary/Treasurer, General Correspondence, January–June 1958, SSSR MSS.

36. See Croce, *Science and Religion in the Era of William James.*

37. Carol V. C. George, *God's Salesman: Norman Vincent Peale and the Power of Positive Thinking* (New York: Oxford University Press, 1993), 88–93, and Smiley Blanton, "New Venture: An Editorial," *Pastoral Counselor* 1 (spring 1963): 1–2. Blanton's words are revealing. First, he denied a conflict between religion and science. After tracing the great contributions of psychiatry to human understanding, he concluded: "The pastor has the same function as the psychiatrist, but each needs to understand the other's discipline with greater clarity. It has been found that by combining religious and psychiatric insights, a type of healing power more effective than any we have had can be developed." Neil Warren argues that practical psychology is completely intertwined with religion.

For example: "Much of the language, assumptions, and procedures of the human potential movement today [a pop psychology movement of the early 1960s] are unselfconsciously rooted in religious traditions from which that movement ordinarily considers itself to be estranged, particularly Protestant and Jewish pietism." See Warren, *After Therapy What?* (Springfield, Ill.: Charles C. Thomas, 1973), 12.

38. James L. Adams to Walter Clark, 5 February 1954. This proposal had to do with establishing a Midwest branch of the Society; box 1, file: Administrative: Secretary/Treasurer, General Correspondence, 1954, SSSR MSS.

39. Description of Organizations, 1960, box 2, file: Administrative, July–December 1960, SSSR MSS. There were other parallel groups organized at this time, including the American Society for the Scientific Study of Religion, organized in 1959 by the American Council of Learned Societies. Professor Joseph Havens of Carleton College wrote to Walter H. Clark in 1958 recommending the Faculty Christian Fellowship. Havens to Clark, 21 August 1958, box 1, file: Administrative: Secretary/Treasurer, General Correspondence, July–December 1958, SSSR MSS.

40. Walter Clark to Ralph Burhoe, 6 October 1958, box 1, file: Administrative: General Correspondence, July–December 1958, and Walter Clark to Rev. Leland Stewart, 25 November 1958, box 1, file: Administrative: Secretary/Treasurer, General Correspondence, January–June 1958, SSSR MSS.

41. Arnold S. Nash to James Dittes, 8 April 1960, box 3, file: Administrative: Secretary/Treasurer, Literature regarding Affiliations, 1959–60, SSSR MSS. In 1970 the membership of the SSSR continued to be about half professional social scientists, with sociologists leading at 29 percent. Articles in the *Journal* were predominantly from academic professionals, including 38 percent from sociology, 22 percent psychology, 12 percent social anthropology, and only 5 percent theology and 4 percent philosophy. Newman, "Society for the Scientific Study of Religion," pp. 25ff., SSSR MSS.

42. Memo from Norman Birnbaum, September 1961, p. 1, box 2, file: Administrative, July–December 1961, SSSR MSS. Murray Murphy notes the establishment of publications such as the *Journal of Religion and Health* (1961) and the activities of Charles Glock at Berkeley as two important signs of the growth of religious sociology; he also points out the appearance of works by Robert Bellah, Clifford Geertz, and Gerhard Lenski as symbols of this burgeoning interest. Murphy, "Scientific Study of Religion," 154–62.

43. Jeffrey Hadden, "A Brief Social History of the Religious Research Association," 26 October 1973, p. 7, series 1, box 1, file: "A Brief Social History of the RRA," in Papers of the Religious Research Association, Memorial Library, Marquette University, Milwaukee, Wisconsin. Hereafter cited as RRA MSS.

44. Hadden, "Brief History of the Religious Research Association," p. 1, and Lauris Whitman, "Report of the President," p. 1, series 2, box 1, file: Annual Meeting, Indianapolis, 16–17 June 1961, RRA MSS. H. Paul Douglass, the inspiration of much of the work of the RRA, studied at the University of Chicago but never acquired a Ph.D. He wrote several books on the changing demography and membership of churches in urban, suburban, and rural areas. Douglass, like so many other religious men and women in American society, was deeply distressed by the Scopes trial and had to make his peace with Darwinism. Indeed, Douglass also reconciled science and religion, writing that "the scientific method strengthens the conviction that the inner and outer aspects of religion are but two sides of a single whole." Edmund de S. Brunner, "Harlan Paul Dou-

glass: Pioneer Researcher in the Sociology of Religion," p. 12, series 2, box 1, file: Harlan Paul Douglass, RRA MSS.

45. Hadden, "Brief History of the Religious Research Association," pp. 1–2, RRA MSS. Another much earlier organization pledged itself to some of the same purposes. Resulting from conversations among John R. Mott, Charles R. Watson, Ernest DeWitt Benton, and John D. Rockefeller Jr., the Institute of Social and Religious Research was founded in 1921 and existed through 1934. Its purpose was to "increase the effectiveness for good of the social and religious forces of the world, especially those of Protestant Christianity" by bringing in "scientific inquiry, accurate knowledge, and broad horizons." Galen M. Fisher, *The Institute of Social and Religious Research, 1921–1934* (n.p., 1934), 8.

46. "Minutes," p. 1, series 2, box 1, file: RRF Meeting, 14–15 June 1952, RRA MSS. The Fellowship also worked with other church outreach groups: for example, Research and Church Planning, Detroit Council of Churches, Protestant Council of the City of New York, Presbyterian Board of National Missions, and Bureau of Research and Planning of the Church Federation of Greater Chicago. Religious Research Fellowship Conference at Williams Bay, Wisconsin, 17–19 June 1955, series 1, box 2, file: Secretary's File, Religious Research Fellowship, 1951–55, RRA MSS.

47. The organization decided not to affiliate with the American Sociological Society, for example. Hadden, "Brief History of the Religious Research Association," pp. 4–6, RRA MSS.

48. "Tabulation of Selected Questions on the Religious Research Fellowship Membership," [1957?], pp. 1–2, series 1, box 1, file: Religious Research Fellowships, General Subject File, 1953–57. RRA MSS. David O. Moberg, an active member of the RRA, tried to interest the organization in the American Scientific Affiliation, of which he was also a member.

49. "Proposed Constitution, 1958," p. 1, series 1, box 2, file: Secretary's File: Religious Research Fellowship, 1958, RRA MSS. Several other groups supported the lectureship, including the Board of Home Missions, Congregational and Christian Churches, the United Christian Missionary Society, the Chicago Theological Seminary, and the National Council of Churches.

50. "Minutes of the Annual Meeting," p. 2, series 2, box 1, file: RRA Annual Meeting, Chicago, 10–12 June 1959, and "Minutes of the Board of the RRA," 11 February 1960, p. 1, series 2, box 1, file: Board Meeting, 11 February 1960, RRA MSS.

51. "Statement of Lauris B. Whitman," *Review of Religious Research* 1 (summer 1959): 1. Perhaps the model of this was the religio-psychiatric movement, as Samuel Z. Klausner called it. This movement among psychiatrists blended modern psychology and religious insight into a major "encounter between religion and science." To Klausner this amounted to a proposal to create a Protestant rather than a Jewish therapy. See Samuel Z. Klausner, "The Religio-Psychiatric Movement," *Review of Religious Research* 6 (fall 1964): 22.

52. W. Widick Schroeder to David O. Moberg, 28 November 1967, pp. 2–3, series 5, box 1, file: Review of RRA, General Correspondence, 1965–68, RRA MSS.

53. There were occasional difficulties between the two organizations. For example, in 1963, after a jointly sponsored conference following the World Congress of Sociology held in Washington in 1962, the National Council of Churches of Christ published the

official report of the conference. Alan Eister, book review editor of the Society's *Journal*, wrote an angry note to Lauris Whitman. The issue was one of "institutional integrity" and not about religiously inspired scientific research. Eister was particularly upset because Lauris implied that the SSSR and the Council of Churches were affiliated. Alan Eister to Lauris Whitman, 23 November 1963, box 3, file: Administrative: Secretary/Treasurer, General Correspondence, September–December 1963, SSSR MSS. Several academic organizations eventually organized their own divisions to study religion. For example, the Psychologists Interested in Religious Issues was organized in 1976. The SSSR experimented with a consortium of religious associations in the early 1970s but ended this when the relationships began to pose serious questions about the scientific orientation of the Society. William V. D'Antonio to Armand L. Mauss, 19 November 1992, p. 5, Mauss MSS.

54. Peter L. Berger, *A Rumor of Angels: Modern Society and the Rediscovery of the Supernatural* (Garden City, N.Y.: Doubleday, 1969; reprinted New York: Anchor, 1990), and Peter L. Berger, *The Sacred Canopy: Elements of a Sociological Theory of Religion* (Garden City, N.Y.: Doubleday, 1967).

55. Ralph Burhoe, "Recollections on the Origins of the SSSR," 29 October 1992, p. 3, Mauss MSS. Burhoe also commented on the tension between the two organizations.

CHAPTER TWELVE

1. R. W. Gerard, "Comments on Religion in an Age of Science," in *Science Ponders Religion*, ed. Harlow Shapley (New York: Appleton-Century-Crofts, 1960), 98.

2. "The Sources of the Institute" (typescript), October 1972, p. 15, box 10, file: IRAS COD, IRAS MSS.

3. Einstein, *Out of My Later Years*, 26, 29–30.

4. Nagel, "Methods of Science," 22.

5. "Meadville Lombard Interviews on Professor Burhoe's Career," conducted by Dr. Wallace Rusterholtz, 23 June 1993, Ralph Burhoe private papers, Chicago, Illinois. Hereafter cited as Burhoe MSS.

6. Rusterholtz, "Burhoe Interview," p. 10, Burhoe MSS. See also Earnest Albert Hooton, *Up from the Ape* (New York: Macmillan, 1931).

7. Much of this biographical material is drawn from David R. Breed, "Ralph Wendell Burhoe: His Life and His Thought," *Zygon* 25 (September 1990): 323–51. For the time of his conversion to Unitarianism, see Rusterholtz, "Burhoe Interview," Burhoe MSS.

8. Rusterholtz, "Burhoe Interview," Burhoe MSS.

9. Rusterholtz, "Burhoe Interview," pp. 21–22, Burhoe MSS. Burhoe credits Shapley with being the main force behind the foundation of the journal, even to the extent of choosing its name. Ralph Burhoe, "Memoir of Harlow Shapley," p. 5, box S, file: Shapley, IRAS MSS.

10. Harlow Shapley to Louis Finkelstein, 24 September 1940, p. 1, box 13a, file: Finkelstein, Louis, Shapley MSS. Many of the participants in these discussions joined in other organizations such as the Conference on Science, Philosophy, and Religion. Others were members of the SSSR or were well known to the public as intellectuals in the field of science, social science, or letters: for example, Philipp Frank, Kirtley Mather,

J. Robert Oppenheimer, Michael Polanyi, Leo Szilard, Gordon Allport, Erik Erikson, Clyde Kluckhohn, Margaret Mead, Robert K. Merton, Talcott Parsons, B. F. Skinner, and I. A. Richards. See David Breed, "Toward a Credible Faith in an Age of Science: The Life and Work of Ralph W. Burhoe" (Ph.D. diss., Lutheran School of Theology, Chicago, 1988), appendix 2. This work is an excellent source for the details of Burhoe's life and evolving beliefs.

11. Breed, "Ralph Wendell Burhoe," 340–41.

12. Shapley, *Through Rugged Ways*, 61, 115.

13. Harlow Shapley, "Ideals Needed for New Horizons, or A Cosmographer Talks to the Clergy," December 1953, p. 6, box S, file: Shapley, IRAS MSS.

14. Ralph Burhoe, "Memo" to Edwin Booth and Harlow Shapley, 15 November 1957, box 13c, file: IRAS, 1959, Shapley MSS.

15. Shapley, "Center of the Universe," 375.

16. In a memorial to the astronomer, Burhoe recalls Shapley's astute observations on "human values and religion." That this spirit appealed to others is revealed in a fascinating recollection. Burhoe was present when Norman Thomas was to address an audience at the Unitarian church in Princeton. "Thomas wanted to look up a quotation in the Book of Job and was scratching around for a Bible in the shelves behind the pulpit, when he exclaimed, 'Don't you have a Bible here; all I can find is a couple of magazines and a copy of Shapley's *Of Stars and Men!*'" Burhoe, "Shapley Memoir," pp. 7–8, box [?], file: Shapley, IRAS MSS.

17. "Untitled notice," May 1936, box IRAS—CASIRAS—ZYGON, file: Cosmotheist Society, IRAS MSS. Shapley addressed the Society in 1955. Peter Bentley proposed a formal relationship between the Cosmotheist Society and the Institute, which the Institute rejected.

18. See "Early Members of IRAS as of September 28, 1958," appendix A, "History of IRAS," p. 16, box 10, file: COD, IRAS MSS. See also Breed, "Ralph Wendell Burhoe," 344ff. Edwin Booth was a liberal Methodist.

19. "Ralph Burhoe," publicity, 17 January 1954, p. 1, box 5: file: Publicity, 1954, IRAS MSS. Burhoe recounts that the conference center had a week's hiatus between Unitarian meetings and Congregational meetings during the summer: an ideal time to host IRAS. Rusterholtz, "Burhoe Interview," Burhoe MSS.

20. Ralph Burhoe, "Religion in the Age of Science," "Scientific Meetings," *Science* 122 (30 December 1955): 1277–78.

21. "Minutes of the Executive Committee of the Institute on Religion and Science, 9 November 1954," p. 1, box 13, file: 1954 IRAS, IRAS MSS; Harlow Shapley to Ralph Burhoe, 25 June 1954, p. 1, box 18a, file: Miscellaneous Correspondence, Shapley MSS.

22. Burhoe, "Shapley Memoir," pp. 6–7, IRAS MSS.

23. Harlow Shapley, "After-thoughts of the Star Island Conference," 1955, pp. 1–2, box 13d, file: Miscellaneous Papers, Shapley MSS. Shapley was also interested in creating a world academy of ethics as part of the ongoing meetings and conferences that were held during the summer at Mohonk resort in New York. These summer meetings and the proposed academy were all outgrowths of the Jewish Theological Seminary and its sponsorship of the Conference on Science, Philosophy, and Religion, the Institute for Religious and Social Studies, and the Institute on Ethics. C. I. Barnard, "Toward a World Academy of Ethics," passim, box 13c, file: IRAS for 1959, Shapley MSS.

24. Ralph Burhoe to the Program Committee, n.d., box 13, file: IRAS Documents, 1954, IRAS MSS.

25. Announcement, "Science, Religion, and the Human Potential," 8th Star Island Conference of IRAS, 22–29 July 1961, p. 2, box 13c, file: IRAS, Shapley MSS; *Star and Beacon*, 18 August 1958, p. 2, in box 12, file: 1958, IRAS MSS. Some participants in the Star Island conferences were obviously offended by the tone Shapley set. Rev. George W. Walker of the Presbyterian church in Buffalo wrote to Burhoe in 1960 after attending a conference: "Nearly every reference was either gloating in the victory of science over religion, or a description of religion in terms that religious people might find it hard to recognize as religion." Maybe this was what Unitarianism meant, he said, but he still disliked it. George W. Walker to Ralph Burhoe, 6 August 1960, box 12, file: 1960, IRAS MSS. The Star Island meetings were generally a week long. Each day began with a chapel service and, after lectures and discussions, ended with a candlelight service and then the "owl sessions." Breed, "Toward a Credible Faith," 70.

26. Edwin Booth to the Advisory Board, "Purposes of IRAS," 12 January 1958, pp. 1–2, box [?], file: 1956–62, IRAS MSS.

27. "Announcement of the Boston Monthly Meeting," 16 November 1958, box: PUBL—Rosen, file: Planning and Development, Miscellaneous Notes, IRAS MSS.

28. "Minutes of Luncheon Meeting," 25 January 1956 (Burhoe, Booth, H. B. Phillips, Shapley et al.), box 12, file: 1956; Ralph Burhoe to Harlow Shapley, 26 August 1957, box [?], file: Shapley; Burhoe to Shapley, 19 January 1956, box 13c: file, IRAS, 1956, Ralph Burhoe to Henry Margenau, 5 May 1957, p. 2, box: Meeting—O, file: Margenau, Henry, IRAS MSS.

29. Ralph Burhoe to Harlow Shapley, 11 November 1956, box [?], file: Shapley, IRAS MSS; "Call for the Conference," p. 4, box 13c, file: IRAS, 1956, Shapley MSS.

30. Robert Pollak and Robert Ashenhurst, "Time Will Tell," box 1, folder 15, Darwin Centennial Papers, Manuscripts Division, Joseph Regenstein Library, University of Chicago. Hereafter cited as Darwin MSS. Lyrics of the musical numbers in the show reveal its satiric purposes:

Bishop Wilberforce sings:

> Consider the flight of the bumble bee
> as it wanders from hither to yon
> We have in the case of the humble bee
> an example to ponder upon.
> Mister Darwin himself has related
> How some most miraculous power
> For each type of bee was created
> an appropriate species of flower.
> Though this is scarcely new
> it's useful information,
> But what has it to do
> with species variation.
> The argument is clever and the presentation strong,
> It's an excellent theory—but it happens to be wrong. (pp. 37–38).

See also announcement, box 1, folder 1, Darwin MSS. The film *Inherit the Wind* was also shown during the celebration.

31. Julian Huxley, "Draft," pp. 1ff., box 4, folder 10, Darwin MSS. "Hush Shrouds Huxley Talk," *Chicago American,* 30 November 1959. Burhoe believed the centennial was an occasion to reconsider the importance of evolutionary thinking. See David R. Breed, *Yoking Science and Religion: The Life and Thought of Ralph Wendell Burhoe* (Chicago: Zygon Books, 1992), 15. Burhoe cited the importance of *Evolution: The Modern Synthesis* (1942) as a seminal book in cosmological thinking. In the revised edition of 1963 Huxley placed himself, Teilhard de Chardin, and Burhoe within a tradition that defined evolution as biological, social, cultural, and spiritual. Julian Huxley, *Evolution: The Modern Synthesis* (London: George Allen and Unwin, 1963), passim. Burhoe wrote of Huxley's work: "I think Julian Huxley has made a contribution to the religion of the future that is worth a hundred times as much as what his so-called religious brother Aldous has done." Ralph Burhoe to Robert Maybury, 15 October 1957, p. 3, box: Meeting—O, file: Maybury, IRAS MSS.

32. Harlow Shapley, "On Evidences of Inorganic Evolution," p. 3, box [?], file: Shapley, IRAS MSS. Sol Tax, "Remarks, Final Panel," n.d., box 6, folder 14, Darwin MSS.

33. Some of the press reaction to Huxley's remarks and the Darwin celebration at Chicago was incredulous and even hostile.

34. "Call for the Conference," p. 4, box 13c, file: IRAS, 1956, Shapley MSS.

35. Ralph Burhoe to Harold Duling, 2 February 1960, box: Meeting—O, file: Lilly Foundation, 1958, IRAS MSS.

36. "Records of the Meetings of the Advisory Board," 3 August 1956, p. 1, box 13c, file: 1956–57, Shapley MSS. Those who met at the monthly Boston colloquium included Kirtley Mather and Paul Tillich; "Boston Meetings," box 15, file: Meeting, 1958, IRAS MSS; "Announcement," October 19, p. 3, box 5, file: Theological Seminary Colloquia, St. Lawrence University, IRAS MSS; Harlow Shapley to Ralph Burhoe, 6 August 1958, box [], file: Shapley, IRAS MSS.

37. "Minutes of the Council Meeting," p. 1, box [?], file: Council, 1956–62, IRAS MSS.

38. John Harrison to Ralph Burhoe, 19 February 1958, box: PUBL—Rosen, file: Rockefeller Foundation, 1956–, IRAS MSS. The organization was keenly disappointed by this refusal and in fact considered turning down even the small grant in protest.

39. Ralph Burhoe to Sophia L. Fahs, 25 January 1957, box 13c, file: IRAS for 1959, Shapley MSS.

40. Ralph Burhoe to Sophia Fahs (copy to Kallen), 28 November 1960, box 5, file: IRAS Council Conferences, IRAS MSS; Joseph Royce to Ralph Burhoe, 17 January 1958, box 5, file: Royce, IRAS MSS.

41. Ralph Burhoe, "A Step toward a Scientific Theology: Notes on Certain Aspects of the 1957 Conference on Religion in an Age of Science," pp. 2–5, box 1, file: General Correspondence, January–June 1958, SSSR MSS.

42. Ralph Burhoe to Roy Hoskins, 14 July 1953, box: PUBL—Rosen, file: Publication Journal General 1953, IRAS MSS. Ralph Burhoe to Sophia L. Fahs, 23 July 1953, box: PUBL—Rosen, file: Records of the Meetings of the Advisory Board and Council, IRAS MSS.

43. Ralph Burhoe, "Memorandum on a Bulletin of the Institute on Religion in an Age of Science" 13 September 1957, box 14, loose memoranda, IRAS MSS; Ralph Burhoe, "Memo to the Officers and the Council of IRAS," box: Meeting—O, file: Publication Journal Committee, 1958, IRAS MSS; "Minutes," Committee on Publication, 19 October 1958, IRAS MSS. The proposed bulletin, later renamed "Memoirs," was designed to publish papers presented at the Institute's summer conferences.

44. Ralph Burhoe, "Report on Publications," 31 January 1959, p. 1, box [?], file: Council, 1956–62, IRAS MSS. Burhoe believed that IRAS declined at the end of the 1950s because new members came into the organization and because its direction was uncertain. Rusterholtz, "Burhoe Interview," Burhoe MSS. Despite Burhoe's feelings, the organization was quite active at the end of the 1950s, holding monthly meetings on questions inspired by advances in science and their implications for religion. See Institute on Religion in an Age of Science, *A Ten-Year View: 1953–1963* (Brookline, Mass.: IRAS, 1963), 8.

45. Shapley, *Science Ponders Religion*, vi–vii.

46. Hudson Hoagland, "Some Reflections on Science and Religion," and Henry Margenau, "Truth in Science and Religion," both in Shapley, *Science Ponders Religion*, 17–26, 101–14.

47. Gerard, "Comments on Religion in an Age of Science," 98.

48. Ralph W. Burhoe, "Salvation in the Twentieth Century," in Shapley, *Science Ponders Religion*, 65–86. In fact Burhoe was deeply influenced by Toynbee's theories, particularly his lectures on the decline of the West. See Breed, "Toward a Credible Faith," 201.

49. Edwin P. Booth, introduction to *Religion Ponders Science* (New York: Appleton-Century, 1964), vii–xii. Booth noted that no Catholic authors appeared in this modernist collection.

50. Walter Houston Clark, "Religion and the Consciousness Expanding Substances," in Booth, *Religion Ponders Science*, 14–16. Clark was also active in the SSSR.

51. Francis Gerald Ensley, "When Scientific Success Makes Religion Necessary," in Booth, *Religion Ponders Science*, 32.

52. Lyman Rutledge, "Changing Cultural Climate," and Sophia Lyon Fahs, "A Possible Partnership between Science and Religion," both in Booth, *Religion Ponders Science*, 198, 39.

53. [Ralph Burhoe?], "The Sources of the Institute," October 1972, p. 9, box 10, file: IRAS COD, IRAS MSS; Breed, "Toward a Credible Faith," 140.

54. [Burhoe?], "The Sources of the Institute," p. 10; Breed, *Ralph Burhoe*, 178, 196; Ralph Burhoe to Samuel Z. Klausner, 2 October 1964, box 4, file: General Correspondence, 1963–68, SSSR MSS.

55. Ralph Burhoe, "Confidential Memorandum," box 1, file: Confidential Memoranda, JTS Conference MSS. "In Memorium, Harlow Shapley," *Zygon* 8 (June 1973): 172. Eventually faculty opposition to the publication convinced the University of Chicago Press to terminate its agreement to publish the journal. See Breed, "Toward a Credible Faith," 130. Harlow Shapley, postcard, Christmas 1973, box S, file: Shapley, IRAS MSS.

56. Burhoe argues that after 1960 IRAS became more of a Unitarian organization and that more religious people joined after this date. Rusterholtz, "Burhoe Interview,"

Burhoe MSS. Quotation is from the "Prospectus" of *Zygon;* Breed, "Toward a Credible Faith," 292. Burhoe answers Shapley's query about the failure of Unitarianism in Ralph Burhoe to Harlow Shapley, 17 April 1965, box [?], file: Shapley, IRAS MSS.

57. Julian Huxley wrote the introduction to Teilhard de Chardin's *The Phenomenon of Man.* See Philip Hefner, *The Promise of Teilhard: The Meaning of the Twentieth Century in Christian Perspective* (Philadelphia: J. B. Lippincott, 1970), for the enormous influence and currency of Teilhard's theories in the 1970s and 1980s. See Errol E. Harris, *Cosmos and Theos: Ethical and Theological Implications of the Anthropic Cosmological Principle* (Atlantic Highlands, N.J.: Humanities Press, 1992); John D. Barrow and Frank J. Tipler, *The Anthropic Cosmological Principle* (Oxford: Clarendon Press, 1986); Paul C. W. Davies, *About Time: Einstein's Unfinished Revolution* (New York: Simon and Schuster, 1995); and Paul C. W. Davies, *The Mind of God: The Scientific Basis for a Rational World* (New York: Simon and Schuster, 1992). See also Hugh Ross, *The Creator and the Cosmos; How the Greatest Scientific Discoveries of the Century Reveal God* (Colorado Springs, Colo.: NavPress, 1993); Michael A. Corey, *God and the New Cosmology: The Anthropic Design Argument* (Lanham, Md.: Rowman and Littlefield, 1993).

CHAPTER THIRTEEN

1. Robert Campbell Jr. to Donald Menzel, 22 December 1958, Records of International Conferences, Commissions, and Expositions, U.S. Commission for the U.S. Science Exhibit, box: Century 21, file 1, 1958, RG 43, U.S. Archives Repository, Seattle, Washington. Hereafter cited as Exposition MSS. Robert Heinlein to Donald Menzel, 8 February 1959, p. 5, box: Century 21 Exposition, Correspondence, 1958–62, file: 1959, 2, HUG 4567.18, Harvard University Archives, Cambridge, Massachusetts. Hereafter cited as Menzel Century 21 MSS. Menzel wrote back to Campbell that he agreed with the editor's assessment. Menzel to Campbell, 13 January 1959, ibid.

2. In a history of the science exhibit written for the U.S. Department of Commerce, two groups are credited with promoting the Fair: Seattle boosters and "a small group of scientists . . . disturbed at the lack of U.S. popular understanding of science." U.S. Department of Commerce, *United States Science Exhibit, Seattle World's Fair, Final Report* (Washington, D.C.: Government Printing Office, 1963), 3.

3. For an excellent account of the origins and nature of the Seattle Fair see John M. Findlay, *Magic Lands: Western Cityscapes and American Culture after 1940* (Berkeley: University of California Press, 1992), 215ff. "Century 21 Exposition Report," Washington State Legislature, 37th Regular Session (Olympia: State Printing Plant, 1961), 4–8. The science motif appears to have been added somewhat later in the planning. See also "Eddie Carlson Dies," *Seattle Times,* 4 April 1990; Harold Mansfield, *Space Needle USA* (Seattle: Craftsman Press, 1962), 3–13; "Challenge and Change: More Than Fair Enough," *Seattle Times,* 13 August 1989, 9ff.

4. Testimony of Francis D. Miller, Committee on Science and Astronautics, U.S. House of Representatives, *Century 21 Exposition,* 86th Cong., 1st sess., 8, 9, 23 July (Washington, D.C.: Government Printing Office, 1959), 28. Miller had been deputy coordinator of the United States exhibit at the Brussels World's Fair. The Cold War implications of the fair were rarely mentioned, nor was defense spending an overt part of the federal display. This was not, of course, the first fair at which science was an important display or where scientists squabbled with administrators over how to present science.

See Peter Kuznick, "Losing the World of Tomorrow," unpublished paper in author's possession, 8–46. Including the Brussels International Science Exhibit in 1958, there were other science expositions at which science was prominent: the Oklahoma Semicentennial Exposition, 1957, and Berlin's "Space Unlimited" show of 1956.

5. U.S. Department of Commerce, *United States Science Exhibit*, 3.

6. Jim Faber to Ewen Dingwall et al., "Interoffice Memo," 20 May 1959, p. 1, box 5, file: ECD Personal, C-21, Ewen Dingwall Papers, Manuscripts and University Archives, University of Washington, Seattle. Hereafter cited as Dingwall MSS. "From Phil Evans, Confidential," 13 February 1959, box 15, file: Chronological File, January–April 1959, Exhibition MSS. C. T. Lloyd, "Reasons for Federal Agency Participation," 26 February 1959, pp. 1–2, Dingwall MSS.

7. Lloyd, "Reasons for Federal Agency Participation," Exposition MSS; Philip Evans, "Final Report," box 32, file: Federal: National Science Planning Board, 1960, 1961, and 1962, Exposition MSS. Killian was appointed in November 1957, shortly after the successful Soviet launch of *Sputnik*.

8. Minutes of the meeting of the National Science Planning Board, 5–6 October 1958, p. 1, box 14, file: National Science Planning Board Meetings, Minutes, Dingwall MSS.

9. Froelich Rainey to Donald Menzel et al., n.d., pp. 1–2, box: Century 21 Exposition, Correspondence, 1958–62, file: 1959, 2, Menzel Century 21 MSS.

10. "Report of the Stanford Research Institute on Prospects for the Fair," 14 November 1957, p. 2, and April 1958, p. 41, box 9, file: ECD Personal, Project Development, Dingwall MSS. Findlay concludes that the fair was aimed at middle-class patrons; Findlay, *Magic Lands*, passim. The report suggests that this might be a valid conclusion. George Whitney, who had worked with Disneyland and with the United States exhibit for the Brussels World's Fair, was appointed head of the division of concessions and amusement.

11. The Bureau of International Expositions formally approved Century 21 in 1961 and allowed it to change its name to the Seattle World's Fair.

12. Craig Colgate to Robert Adams, 24 October 1961, p. 1, box 41, file: Science Advisory Committee, Establishment, Exposition MSS. Dael Wolfle to Philip Evans, [April?] 1960, pp. 1–2; "Minutes of Meeting of the National Science Planning Board, 6 April 1960, p. 1, box 32, file: National Science Planning Board, 1960, 1961, 1962, Exposition MSS. Commissioner Evans wrote a frank and self-justifying historical note on his work with the commission in which he criticized the disagreements among scientists and justified his firm hand in guiding the process. Philip Evans, "USSE Relations with Century 21 and the Science Community," 1 February 1961, in "Report of the U.S. Commission on the U.S. Science Exhibit," pp. 22–24, box 32, file: National Science Planning Board, 1960, 1961, and 1962 (General Files), Exposition MSS.

13. Donald Menzel, "Exhibit Proposal," 15 November 1958, box 15, file: Exhibit Proposal by Menzel, Exposition MSS.

14. Donald H. Menzel, "Proposal," 15 November 1958, submitted and approved, pp. 1–4, box 9, file: Century 21 Proposals, Dingwall MSS.

15. "Minutes of Meeting of the Science Advisory Committee," 27 April 1960, p. 3, and 4 May 1960, p. 3, box 41, file: Science Advisory Committee, Meetings, Exposition MSS. Francis Miller of the Commerce Department obviously opposed Soviet coopera-

tion from the beginning. In December 1959 he wrote to the commissioner of Century 21 that he had been present when Menzel announced his first trip to the USSR. He had been, he confessed, "helpless to head it off." Francis D. Miller to Philip Evans, 4 December 1959, p. 1, box 31, file: National Science Planning Board, 1958–59, Exhibition MSS. Miller wrote to Ewen Dingwall to discourage him from sponsoring Menzel's plan. Francis D. Miller to Ewen Dingwall, 3 May 1960, box 39, file: Reports—Status, Annual, etc., Exposition MSS. Dingwall replied testily that Miller was "worrying over things where you have no administrative jurisdiction." But the State Department prevailed in its veto of Menzel's project. Ewen Dingwall to Francis Miller, 5 May 1960, box 46, file: Union of Soviet Socialist Republics, Exposition MSS.

16. Donald Menzel, "Remarks," "Minutes of the National Science Planning Board," 6 April 1960, p. 2, box 32, file: National Science Planning Board, 1960, 1961, 1962, Exhibition MSS, and Donald Menzel, "Remarks," "Minutes of the National Planning Board," 8 April 1960, p. 2, box 14, file: Minutes of the National Science Planning Board, Dingwall MSS.

17. Philip Evans to Boeing Corporation, 16 November 1960, box 5, file: Boeing Company, Exposition MSS. In this letter Evans explains that since the idea was his, as an employee of the federal government, this would not prejudice the "residual use or the extent of industrial participation." In effect, he was telling Boeing that officially the United States government claimed no ownership of the idea. Commerce Department, "Release," 19 October 1960, box 35, file: Public Relations, 1959 and 1960, Exposition MSS.

18. In late February 1960 Menzel sent Francis Miller an outline of a possible forty-minute planetarium–space platform show. Donald Menzel to Francis Miller, 23 February 1960, pp. 1ff., box 61, file: Exhibit Information, "Area III, Spacearium," Exposition MSS. Memo of a telephone call from Charles Barnes (U.S. Commerce Department) to Carl Conrad, 16 June 1960, p. 1, box 44, file: Teague Associates, 1959 and 1960, Exposition MSS. Menzel and Asimov wrote the script and submitted it to Boeing and the Hollywood group. In mid-1961 Menzel was still pushing for his original work. Donald Menzel to Athelstan Spilhaus, 11 May 1961, box: Century 21 Exposition, file: 1961, 2, Menzel Century 21 MSS.

19. Box 14, file: Chronological File, 1960, January–April, Exposition MSS.

20. Donald Menzel to Ewen Dingwall, 2 May 1961, box: Century 21 Exposition, Correspondence, 1958–62, file: 1960, 2, Donald Menzel to Athelstan Spilhaus, 11 May 1961, box: Century 21 Exposition; file: 1961, 2, Menzel Century 21 MSS. Menzel was furious about attributing gender to the sun and the planets in the script and suggested a rewrite. Of course in working with Capra he had agreed to personification and cartoon representations of the sun. "Comments on Journey to the Stars," 9 September 1961, box 44, file: Teague Associates, 1959 and 1960, Exposition MSS. Menzel believe that Dr. Leroy Augenstine had been forced out as science coordinator of the United States science exhibit in April 1961 for arguing strongly for an uncorrupted presentation of science.

21. Memo of a meeting with Menzel, Boeing, Fine Arts, and United States representatives, May 1960, pp. 2–3, box 19, file: Fine Arts Production, Inc., Exposition MSS. Athelstan Spilhaus, "Thoughts on Science and the U.S. Science Pavilion, n.d., p. 3, box 9, file: Spilhaus, Dr. Athelstan, Exposition MSS.

22. This crossover moment disclosed something of a crisis. When Evans resigned in January, the *Seattle Times* quoted a Defense Department spokesman who said, "the entire scientific set-up of Century 21 will flop if someone with scientific knowledge and contacts does not take control immediately." *Seattle Times*, 30 January 1961.

23. Craig Colgate Jr. to Orr Reynolds et al., 1 May 1961, box 41, file: Science Advisory Committee, Exposition MSS; Donald Menzel to Craig Colgate Jr., 2 October 1962, box, Century 21 Exposition, Correspondence, 1958–62, file: 1962, Exposition MSS. Even after the mid-May meeting with Fine Arts Productions, Colgate wrote to Wilson that "gimmicks like the rocket ship are unnecessary to induce a sense of audience participation." The Boeing Corporation did not, however, support Colgate or the Science Advisory Committee on this issue. Craig Colgate to John Wilson, 23 May 1961, box 19, file: Fine Arts Production, Inc., Exposition MSS.

24. "Final Report of Commissioner Evans," 1 February 1961, p. 26, Subject Files, 1959–63, box 32, file: National Science Planning Board, 1960, 1961, and 1962 (General Files), Exposition MSS.

25. *Seattle Times*, 25 March 1962. See also passim, box 16, file: International Science Writers Service, Dingwall MSS.

26. "Narrative of Area III," p. 7, box 46, file: Text—United States Science Exhibit, Exposition MSS; Alfred Stern et al., "Final Script: The Threat and the Threshold," p. 3, box 1, no file, Dingwall MSS. Paul J. Beeman, "The Gospel and Century 21," *Christian Century* 79 (21 November 1962): 1417–18. Beeman noted, however, that though the exhibits were intended to be religious, several "offered important reminders of ways the communication of the gospel can be endangered and ultimately lost" (1419). See also U.S. Department of Commerce, *U.S. Science Exhibit: World's Fair in Seattle, 1962* (Seattle: Craftsman Press, 1962), 2. This is a quotation from the exhibit.

27. Romaine Nicholson to Ewen C. Dingwall, 23 August 1957, box 9, file: Century 21 Exposition, Exhibits, Christian Witness, Dingwall MSS, and memo of a conversation between Rt. Rev. Stephen F. Bayne Jr., Edward Carlson, and Harold Shefelman, April 1958, Dingwall MSS. Edward E. Carlson to Rev. Stephen F. Bayne Jr., 18 April 1958, box 9, file: Century 21 Exposition, Exhibits, Christian Witness, Dingwall MSS.

28. Robert L. Durham to Ralph Turnidge and Lemuel Petersen, 23 September 1959, box 11, file: Incoming Letters, 1959–65, no. 31, Manuscripts of the Seattle Council of Churches, Manuscripts and University Archives, University of Washington, Seattle, Washington. Hereafter cited as Churches MSS.

29. Georgia Gellert to Perry Johanson, 26 August 1960, box 9, file: Century 21 Exposition, Exhibits, Christian Witness, Dingwall MSS. The Society of Friends and the YWCA supported the proposal, whereas the Seattle Evangelical Ministers' Association rejected it. Apparently Catholic and Orthodox groups were equally opposed to the temple. Beeman, "Gospel and Century 21," 1416. The commission sent one of its employees to visit a variety of different churches and groups to find out if they would support a temple of religion. See box 9, file: Century 21, Exposition, Exhibits, Christian Witness, passim, Dingwall MSS.

30. Barry Upson to Ewen C. Dingwall, 29 July 1960, box 9, file: Century 21, Exposition, Exhibits, Christian Witness, Dingwall MSS. Upson was secretary to the board of directors of the fair.

31. "Prospectus for a Christian Witness in the Century 21 Exposition," pp. 1, 7, box

11, file: Writings, no. 37, Churches MSS. Most of the initial plans of Christian Witness had to be abandoned because of lack of money and interest.

32. Minoru Yamasaki, *A Life in Architecture* (New York: Weatherhill, 1979), 33, 70. Yamasaki had been raised in the Japanese Baptist Church.

33. "Memo to the File regarding Conference on Great Religion Issues," 9 October 1961, box 9, file: Century 21 Exposition Exhibits, Christian Witness, Dingwall MSS. The commission staff worried about the Christian Witness group and whether its pavilion would meet the standards of other displays. "Whatever is done," said Georgia Gellert to representatives of the Witness group, "should have vitality and drama— something new to tell the old story." "Minutes of the Christian Witness Corporation Meeting," 19 September 1960, p. 3, box 11, file: Minutes, no. 36, Churches MSS.

34. "Christian Witness in Century 21, Inc.," box 11, file: Organizational Features, 1961–63, no. 30, Papers of the Seattle Council of Churches, Manuscripts and University Archives, University of Washington, Seattle, Washington. Hereafter cited as Witness MSS.

35. News Release, April 1962, box 12, file 2, Witness MSS.

36. "Articles of Incorporation of the Committee: Christian Witness in Century 21," box 9, file: Century 21, Exposition, Exhibits, Christian Witness, Dingwall MSS. The Christian Witness united all "non-Roman forces." Rev. Lemuel Petersen to Donald Johnson (of the Performing Arts Division), 16 January 1962, box 9, file: Century 21, Exposition Exhibits, Christian Witness, Dingwall MSS.

37. Robert L. Durham to Ralph Turnidge and Lemuel Petersen, 23 September 1959, box 11, file: Incoming Letters, 1959–65, no. 31, Churches MSS.

38. Mrs. Elwood V. Graves to Ewen Dingwall, 15 November 1961, box 9, file: Century 21, Exposition Exhibits, Christian Witness, Dingwall MSS.

39. "Handbook of the Christian Pavilion, Contents of the Building," p. 12, box 11, file: Writings, no. 37, Churches MSS.

40. *Seattle Times*, 2 December 1961, p. 3. "Handbook of the Christian Pavilion, Contents of the Building," p. 13, Churches MSS. See also "Hard to Get," *Newsweek*, 59 (11 June 1962): 89, and Beeman, "Gospel and Century 21," 1416, recounting some of the controversy surrounding the Witness film.

41. Lemuel Petersen, "The Churches at the Seattle World's Fair," material to accompany the gift of his papers to the University of Washington, p. 2, Churches MSS. R. T., "Reflections," *University Christian Church Visitor* 8 (7 June 1962): 2. Although Petersen and the Witness defended the film in public, their relations with Keller deteriorated. By midsummer there was a serious dispute about unpaid expenses. Keller finally wrote to say he was "sorry that you could not work with us again and/or suggest others to do so. That's your privilege." Relations ended there. Paul F. Keller to Lemuel Petersen, 16 July 1962, box 12, file: Sound and Light, no. 23, Churches MSS.

42. Handwritten memo, no author, [January 1962?], box 9, file: Century 21, Exposition Exhibits, Christian Witness, Dingwall MSS. When Episcopal priest and nuclear scientist William Pollard visited the fair he also attracted considerable crowds. When Graham came in early July he openly criticized science and progress: "As the sands of our age are falling," he warned, "our confidence and hope should be in God, not space exploration." Findlay, *Magic Lands*, 234. The Christian Witness group presented Graham with its Ichthus plaque on 7 July 1962.

43. Rt. Rev. Stephen F. Bayne Jr., *Space Age Christianity* (New York: Morehouse-Barlow, 1963).

44. To a considerable degree, the science demonstrations at Moody were similar to demonstrations in the United States pavilion, with the obvious exception of the larger Christian message. Mrs. Garnett K. Young to Lemuel Peterson, 22 June 1962, box 12, file: Sound and Light, no. 22, Churches MSS, and other letters in the same collection. "Sermons from Science" drew about 417,000 visits. Based on this success, the MIS planned a pavilion at the upcoming New York World's Fair.

45. Jay Rockey, "Final Report," 21 October 1962, box 78, file: ECD Personal, C-21, Public Relations—Final Report, Dingwall MSS. These admission figures need to be accepted with caution, for they report only entries and do not distinguish persons who may have come and gone several times from those who entered only once.

46. James B. Taylor et al., *Science on Display: A Study of the United States Science Exhibit, Seattle World's Fair, 1962* (Seattle: Institute for Sociological Research, 1963), part 63-5. Robert S. Weiss and Serge Boutourline Jr., *A Summary of Fairs, Pavilions, Exhibits, and Their Audiences* (n.p.: Robert S. Weiss, 1962), 19.

47. *New York Times*, 8 May 1962, 21, and "Stars May Guide Capsule to the Moon," *New York Times*, 1 March 1962, 15. Senator Robert Kerr of Oklahoma greeted Glenn at the meeting by congratulating him "on his spirit of reverence and his faith in God."

48. Scientists felt no compulsion to invite religion into their professional organizations or conferences. Nor, of course, did religious groups generally invite science into their deliberations. Still, there is a curious asymmetry revealed by Century 21: religion was seen as a necessary corrective to science—but certainly not the other way round.

CHAPTER FOURTEEN

1. Lee Butcher, *Accidental Millionaire: The Rise and Fall of Steve Jobs at Apple Computer* (New York: Paragon, 1988), 63, 72.

INDEX

Page numbers in italics refer to illustrations.